NEW ORLEANS ARCHITECTURE

VOLUME II

The American Sector

NEW ORLEANS ARCHITECTURE

VOLUME II

The American Sector (Faubourg St. Mary)

Howard Avenue to Iberville Street
Mississippi River to Claiborne Avenue

Authors and Editors:
MARY LOUISE CHRISTOVICH
ROULHAC TOLEDANO
BETSY SWANSON
PAT HOLDEN

Essays by
SAMUEL WILSON, JR.
BERNARD LEMANN

Photographs by
BETSY SWANSON

PELICAN PUBLISHING COMPANY
GRETNA 1984

CONTENTS

400 Magazine. Succession of granite pillars and cast-iron brackets.

FOREWORD

This, the second volume of *New Orleans Architecture*, reflects the wisdom of the Friends of the Cabildo to go outside the narrow realm of the Museum to the much broader field of preserving our culture, not merely our history. The instantaneous success of the first volume of this series, *The Lower Garden District*, has spurred the co-authors to greater heights in this work which has for its subject the buildings of old Faubourg St. Mary, an area now known as the Central Business District.

Architecturally, by the middle of the 19th century New Orleans was a most attractive city. Contemporary visitors and many people who lived in the city left glowing accounts of its buildings. A traveller arriving by steamer would first have seen the majestic white dome of the St. Charles Hotel rising high above the surrounding buildings. The St. Charles undoubtedly was New Orleans' most elegant building, and if a visitor had climbed to the colonnade under its dome and looked to the north across Canal Street, he could have seen the narrow streets and the closely built houses of the Vieux Carre. Conspicuous would have been the St. Louis Hotel with its dome, the newly rebuilt St. Louis Cathedral and the recently erected Pontalba Buildings with the dome of the Merchants Exchange in the foreground. Nearer, he would have seen the beautiful crescent of the Mississippi River that gave the city its nickname and the busy levee with its steamboats, sailing vessels and other shipping.

Around the base of the hotel the business blocks, with their simple, well-proportioned facades, might have struck the viewer as perhaps the finest examples of commercial architecture anywhere in America. Several church spires would have been visible, especially the Gothic tower of St. Patrick's; and to the south one could have viewed the gleaming white marble Ionic portico of the new City Hall. Further to the south one would have seen, in the distance, the columned residences and gardens of suburban Lafayette and the spires of still more outstanding churches. To the west toward Lake Pontchartrain stretched open country with wooded areas, canals and suburban roads.

Gone are the St. Charles Hotel, the Merchants Exchange and the St. Louis Hotel; gone, too, are the steamboats and sailing craft. But two of the most interesting great landmarks in the old Faubourg St. Mary — Gallier Hall and St. Patrick's Church — as well as the fine open space, Lafayette Square, have survived. Most of the buildings in the business blocks have survived, too, although time, fire and the wrecker's bar have been the fate of a great many of them.

There have been noteworthy buildings erected in the Central Business District since the palmy days of the 1850s, and these have been included in this study. Volume II encompasses buildings constructed during the period from 1803, when the Americans came, until the Crash of 1929. Also included is a section on "Banking and Commerce," an interesting historical study of banks and other businesses located in the business district.

We who have lived in New Orleans all our lives are quite familiar with this section of the city. We have passed the buildings for years, paying little attention to them and probably knowing little of their origins, their architecture, architects or builders. It is only when a building is taken out of context and photographed and its antecedents studied that we can begin to realize how interesting it can be. A tale by Harold Sinclair at the end of his book, *The Port of New Orleans*, some thirty years ago illustrates this point:

> Not long ago a porter at one of the Pontalba Buildings said to an acquaintance of the writer:
> "Mister Blank, it's a funny thing—but how come people are always writin' an' sayin' about N'Awlins is a very interesting city? Now I ask you, do you see anything interesting about it?"
> "Why, yes," Blank said, with a certain degree of natural surprise. "In some ways very much so."
> "Well," said the porter, "I've lived here all my life and *I* don't see anything interesting about it!"

Like the Lower Garden District, the Central Business District of New Orleans has had no one to champion it or ensure the preservation of some of its best buildings. Many of them have been mutilated almost beyond recognition; some of the very best have been destroyed to make parking lots. It is the hope of the Friends of the Cabildo that this volume will arouse new interest among the owners or purchasers of old buildings in this section, so that they can be restored to something of their former grace and their interiors remodeled to become useful once more.

This book, like its predecessor, represents the work of many of the Friends who volunteered to do tedious research; of the two architectural historians, Samuel Wilson, Jr., and Bernard Lemann, who contributed text; and of the tireless compilers and writers—Mary Louise Christovich, Pat Holden, Roulhac Toledano and Betsy Swanson, the latter of whom also did the excellent photography. To them, the Friends owe a great debt, but a still larger debt is owed by the community which we sincerely hope will read and heed the message: preserve before it is too late, before New Orleans becomes another characterless American city.

LEONARD V. HUBER
President, The Friends of the Cabildo, Inc.

ACKNOWLEDGMENTS

VOLUNTEER STAFF
Mrs. Harry C. Stahel, volunteer chairman
Mrs. Hugh M. Evans, Jr., title research chairman
Mrs. Arthur J. Axelrod, mortgage office
Mrs. W. Stanley Black, architects inventory
Miss Kathryn Chapotan, mortgage office
Miss Debbie Chattry, research assistant
Mrs. John Clark, title research
Miss Mary H. Cocchiara, public library research
Mr. Boyd Cruise, history consultant
Mr. William R. Cullison, research consultant
Mrs. John Dart, Jr., archives research
Mrs. Gerard M. Dillon, mortgage office
Mrs. David Eustis, title research
Mr. Stanton Frazer, research
Mrs. Edward J. Gay, III, archives
Mr. John Geiser, Jr., architectural consultant
Mr. John Geiser, III, architectural consultant
Mrs. Harvey G. Gleason, archives assistant
Mrs. Connie Griffith, Tulane University Library
Mr. Collin Hamer, Louisiana Room, New Orleans Public Library
Miss Ann Harris, clerical
Mrs. James F. Holmes, title research
Mr. Leonard Huber, illustrations
Mr. William Y. Kirby, public library research
Mr. Henry Krotzer, architectural advisor
Mrs. Octavie Livaudais Loria, Louisiana State Museum Library research
Mrs. Guy Lyman, mortgage office
Miss Preston Lyon, mortgage office
Mrs. Thomas J. McMahon, title research
Miss Margaret Mallory, mortgage office
Mrs. Edward F. Martin, title research
Mr. Andrew Martinez, research assistant
Mrs. Leland Montgomery, mortgage office
Mrs. Aline H. Morris, Louisiana State Museum Library research

x   ACKNOWLEDGMENTS

Mrs. August Mysing, research assistant
Mrs. R. L. Offut, title research
Dr. Jessie Poesch, architectural consultant
Mrs. James Ryan II, title research
Mr. Ray Samuel, production
Mr. D. F. Schultz, research
Mrs. William Jay Smith, mortgage office
Miss Charlotte Spencer, map
Mrs. Frank Duncan Strachan, III, title research
Mr. Joseph L. Swanson, III, color map
Mr. Joseph Vonau, public library research
Miss Melissa West, mortgage office
Miss Jeanne Wilcum, research assistant
Mrs. Harold York, clerical

INTRODUCTION

To put "Ignorance in Chains," as the stone carving from the old Howard Library represents, is one of the many objectives of the Friends of the Cabildo in this volume.

Regarding the older sections of our city as architectural museums, we have provided a verbal and visual tour through the 19th century American Sector, Faubourg St. Mary. Similar to a catalog, the inventory is a handbook for visitors and natives alike, and particularly for city agencies involved with city planning and those whose work relates in any way to the ultimate disposition of New Orleans properties.

The Housing Authority of New Orleans, for example, might respect the guidelines presented in this volume. The fire marshall should carefully consider the results of any action he may take on properties listed here. Building inspectors and taxing authorities could utilize the historic values information to take effective action against slum landlords and those deliberately involved in demolition by neglect. The Streets Department, Highway Department and Mississippi Bridge Authority should become well-acquainted with the importance of buildings illustrated here. To assist in quick evaluations, a dual-purpose map, noting the individual structures, along with a color-coded values-feasibility study, is included.

The material in this volume includes those structures remaining in old Faubourg St. Mary, bound by Common Street, to a diagonal running from just above Julia and Camp streets, and back to halfway between Dryades and Rampart streets. The area once known as the Commons, between Common and Canal, is included, as is the area between Canal and Iberville, part of the original Vieux Carre that has been deleted from legislation for preservation in the Vieux Carre. Between Julia Street and Howard Avenue continues a residential area that developed on remnants of the Gravier Plantation not included in Faubourg St. Mary and on parts of the Delord Sarpy holdings.

The Friends of the Cabildo envision this as a handbook for renovation and restoration. Details from building contracts quoted describe facade proportions, materials used, color combinations and decoration. This information can be used to re-create the character of a specific building.

Since motivation for preservation goes beyond education and aesthetic considerations, property owners and investors inevitably must consider financial benefits. This volume shows the creative and economic opportunities offered by rehabilitation, a goal toward which New Orleans banks and homesteads have not yet taken the initiative. Too often, progress has been equated with tearing down. Preservation of the Central Business District architecture can be an economic tool to regenerate the area and create a new industry. Once convinced that renovation is as strong an impetus for economic improvement as a new building, banking institutions and industrial leaders will surely encourage and direct the city on this course. This already has happened in Pittsburgh, Philadelphia, Savannah and Charleston.

The authors of this volume are members of the Board of Directors of the Friends of the Cabildo, which has borne the expense of compiling the material for this project and has participated in every phase of its production. There are, of course, many people and institutions outside the organization, without whom there could be no publication of a book of this scope.

Boyd Cruise, Director of the Historic New Orleans Collection, under the authorization of the Board of Trustees graciously opened its vast resources of prints and paintings for photographing and its extensive files for research. Collin Hamer and the staff of the Louisiana Room of the New Orleans Public Library were cooperative throughout two years of research. The Library's photograph file, original drawings by architects Charles and James Dakin, manuscripts, diaries and surveyors' books were major sources of material for this work.

The foundation of this volume, however, is information gathered from the New Orleans Notarial Archives. Two thousand notarial drawings were photographed and documented. The staff supplied a work area and hundreds of huge notary and plan books. The Mortgage Office and the Conveyance Office in the Civil Courts Building supplied manuscript records and work space for the many volunteer workers.

Working closely to provide essential source material were the staff of the Special Collections Division of the Tulane University Library. The staff trained volunteers for the specialized work required of them, and the director, Mrs. Connie Griffith, made available illustrations. The Louisiana State Museum library staff, under the direction of Mrs. Aline H. Morris, gave endless hours of research assistance and information from the Museum's collection of old newspapers. As in Volume I of this series, Lawyer's Title gave generously from its private collection of notarial notebooks.

Essential also was the financial participation of the Standard Fruit Company through a grant to the Friends of the Cabildo. The interest of members of that organization has aided the authors in their effort to gain community participation in this project.

It is as dangerous to idealize and romanticize the past as it is to overemphasize and glorify the present. Nevertheless, "skyscrapers and empty lots do not a city make." New Orleans' architecture is one of its greatest assets and, indeed, is a communal art form. As in few other American cities, New Orleans has entire blocks of 19th century buildings remaining intact, giving testimony to the excellence of well-modulated architectural rows. New buildings continue the patchwork of taste and design and reflect the historic development of the city. The architects, whose biographies are included in this volume, created buildings to satisfy civic pride; their work expressed distinctive regional adaptations of world-famous styles.

By comparing the present with the past, the reader may discover that he has been deprived of pleasure he never knew or suspected. Hopefully, he will discover applicable values that enrich his personal experience, improve his city and broaden the horizons of both. Art and historic artifacts can stand alone in museums, but architecture has a responsibility to the environment, today, tomorrow and throughout history.

MARY LOUISE CHRISTOVICH
ROULHAC TOLEDANO

NEW ORLEANS ARCHITECTURE

VOLUME II

The American Sector

Early History of Faubourg St. Mary

SAMUEL WILSON, JR.

I. Origins of a City

THE COLONIAL PERIOD

The area of the modern city of New Orleans included in this study, from Iberville Street to Howard Avenue and from the Mississippi River to Claiborne Avenue, was, in the French colonial period, occupied largely by the plantation of the city's founder, Jean Baptiste Le Moyne de Bienville. He had secured this land and much more by a grant from the Superior Council of Louisiana on March 27, 1719.

The lower boundary of Bienville's plantation, "above and at the limits of New Orleans," appears to have been, at first, somewhat indefinite, for the first known plans of the city show only four blocks facing the river on either side of the central square (now Jackson Square), the upper limit of the city then being present-day Bienville Street. On what is perhaps the earliest city plan, entitled "Plan of the City of New Orleans projected in March, 1721" (fig. 1), a proposed canal is shown less than a block above the last square, parallel to Bienville Street with locks at the river. This proposed canal had been contemplated as early as 1718 when the Company of the Indies issued its instructions to the Sieur Perrier, appointed engineer-in-chief of Louisiana, in which such a canal was ordered.

Perrier died before reaching Louisiana and his successor, Pierre Le Blond de la Tour, designed the plan of New Orleans soon after his arrival at Biloxi in December, 1720. On March 29, 1721, his assistant, Adrien de Pauger, arrived on the site and began to lay out the streets and, presumably, the proposed canal. The plan referred to above, on which the canal first appears, was sent to Paris with Pauger's letter of August 9, 1721. On this plan the proposed canal is indicated as the lower limit of Bienville's plantation, the area above it being designated as "Part of the Plantation of M. de Bienville." A more finished and formal plan of the city, drawn at Biloxi, signed by Le Blond de la Tour and dated April 23, 1722 (fig. 2), shows the same number of blocks facing the river, but includes a line of fortifications with four corner bastions in the Vauban manner. The upper line of these fortifications was placed between the last row of squares and the proposed canal, which was relocated farther upriver about where Iberville Street is today. A formal row of trees is indicated along the upper side of the canal forming the new lower boundary of Bienville's plantation.

This boundary was soon again to be moved further upstream, for in a letter to the Company dated January 15, 1723, de la Tour informed it that he had increased the size of the town by adding an extra row of blocks at both the upper and lower ends,

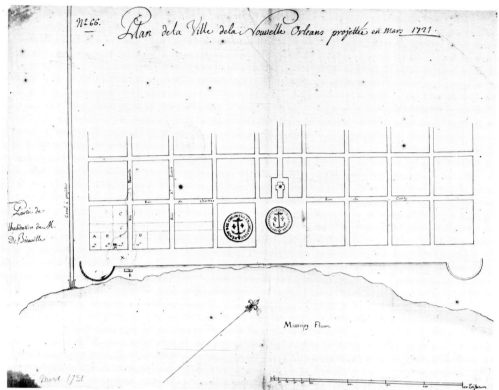

Fig. 1. Plan of New Orleans, 1721. (Courtesy *Archives Nationales,* Paris.)

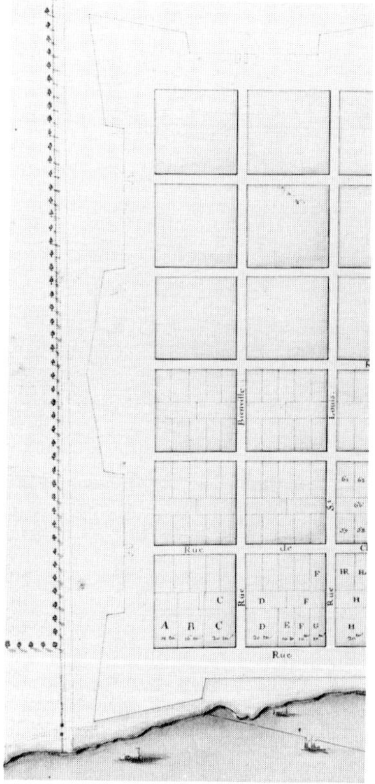

Fig. 2. New Orleans, April 23, 1722, by Le Blond de la Tour. (Courtesy *Archives Nationales,* Paris.)

thus making what is now Iberville Street the upper limit of the town and relocating the fortifications and canal correspondingly further up. Had the canal been built then, it would have been along present day Canal Street. This then became the new lower limit of Bienville's plantation, although he asked that he retain the ownership of an entire new square within the city, marked "T" on a copy of the plan now in Chicago's Newberry Library (fig. 3).

A similar plan now in the Yale University Library (fig. 4), undated and unsigned but probably dating from September, 1723, shows for the first time the buildings on Bienville's plantation. A principal house with symmetrical detached rear wings is set about 300 feet above the proposed canal, with formal gardens in front and alleys of trees in the manner of Versailles in the rear. This was probably the arrangement first proposed for the residence of the Commandant General, but it was somewhat modified in execution as shown on a later plan of the city dated May 30, 1725 (fig. 5). The principal house still contains three units, but in an asymmetrical arrangement, and there are formal gardens in the rear and an avenue of trees leading from the canal to the house. The axis of the composition, which in the earlier plan was a continuation of the line of present Decatur Street, has been shifted to parallel the river bank, which even then was probably beginning to build up. Thus, from his house Bienville had a fine view up and down the river and could look across the entire riverfront of his new city, watching its growth and activity. On the 1725 plan the property is marked "Land and House of M. de Bienville," making it fairly certain that these first buildings erected in this area had been constructed in 1723 or 1724 (fig. 5).

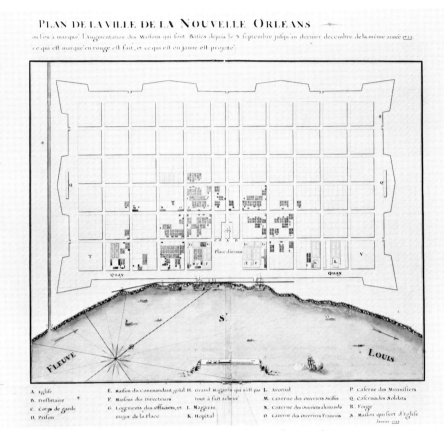

PLAN DE LA VILLE DE LA NOUVELLE ORLEANS

Fig. 3. Plan of New Orleans, 1722. (Courtesy Newberry Library, Chicago.)

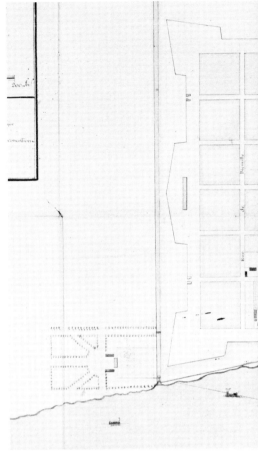

Fig. 4. Plan of New Orleans, circa 1723, un-dated and unsigned. (Courtesy Yale University Library.)

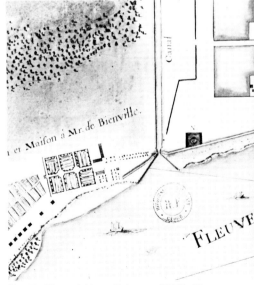

Fig. 5. Plan of New Orleans, 1725. (Courtesy *Bibliotheque Nationale*, Paris.)

By a notarial act passed at his temporary residence in Paris on April 1, 1726, Bienville sold to the Jesuit fathers a twenty-arpent tract which formed the lower part of his plantation. Included in the sale were the plantation buildings, described as "a house of fifty two feet in length, of wood colombage, built and constructed on part of the said twenty arpents, pigeon cote, a *corps de logis,* garden planted with fruit trees adjacent to the said house" (fig. 5A). The sale was made for 12,000 livres, payable in an annual and perpetual rent of 600 livres. The approximate site of these first buildings in what is now the city's Central Business District is indicated by a bronze plaque placed by the Founders Chapter of the Louisiana Colonials in 1962 on the Jaubert Brothers building at the corner of Common and Magazine streets.

Bienville's plantation buildings probably served the Jesuits for a few years, but being built only of colombage, a heavy timber frame covered on the outside with wide boards, they soon rotted. This was the fate of all the earliest New Orleans buildings that had been built in this impermanent manner. New buildings were erected soon after, estimates and specifications being sent to France in a letter dated March 30, 1728, for "The buildings to be built for lodging the Rev. Jesuit Fathers at New Orleans." These documents unfortunately have not yet been found, and no other accurate drawings of the new Jesuit buildings are known to exist. A crude sketch of the "convent of the Jesuits" by Dumont de Montigny appears on his "Plan of New Orleans, capital city of Louisiana, and its environs" (fig. 6), probably drawn in the 1730s and now in the Paris Archives. The main building, of three stories, is similar to the first Ursuline convent shown on the same map. It is much smaller,

Fig. 5A. Detail from drawing of New Orleans by Jean Pierre Lassus. (Courtesy *Archives Nationales,* Paris.)

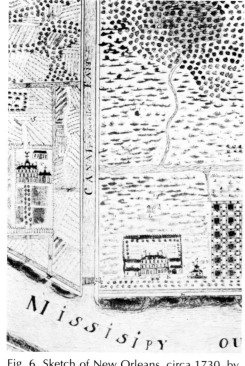

Fig. 6. Sketch of New Orleans, circa 1730, by Dumont de Montigny. (Courtesy *Musee de l'Armee,* Vincennes.)

however, being indicated as having five windows across the front, whereas the convent is shown with thirteen, the number it actually had according to the detailed architectural drawings that exist for that building.

Both the Jesuits and Ursuline convents are shown with a belfry cupola surmounted by a weather vane in the form of a rooster. Attached to the right or lower end of the Jesuits convent is a smaller one-story structure with a small belfry and cross, evidently the chapel. Behind these buildings which faced the river is another one-story structure, probably the kitchen. In the front an alley of trees leads to the entrance across a formal garden, the buildings and gardens being enclosed by a picket or palisade fence with front and rear gates. Beyond the rear gate are "lands under cultivation," with about fifteen cabins indicated as "habitation of their negroes." A canal labeled "Canal, newly built" leading from the river to Bayou St. John also appears on this map. This was probably the moat begun by engineer Pierre Baron in an attempt to fortify the city after the Natchez massacre of November, 1729, but never completed. In his published *Memoires de la Louisiane,* Dumont mentions that "at some distance from the town is a very fine plantation where the Jesuit Fathers reside. It formerly belonged to M. de Bienville, Commandant General in the country, who sold it to them." In a memoir of 1728 it was recorded that "there is nothing to exclaim so strongly about the grandeur and beauty of the plantation of the Jesuits at New Orleans; such magnificent things are not done in two years time. It is in truth beautiful for a country like New Orleans [and]...serves as an ornament to the town and a model to the inhabitants..."

The Jesuit plantation, which eventually extended nearly to present-day Felicity Street, served as headquarters for the missionary activities of this religious order throughout the Louisiana province until the suppression of the Jesuits, when their New Orleans plantation was confiscated and sold by a decree of the Superior Council of Louisiana on July 9, 1763. The inventory of their property made at this time lists the following buildings:

A principal house in bricks, with two upper stories.
Another house and cellar below, in bricks, gallery all around.
A building in brick containing four apartments (rooms).
Two dove cotes in brick and colombage, a brewery in brick, a stable for oxen with brick piers, surrounded with stakes, a large store house for the hay.
Item, a store house containing two apartments (rooms), in brick, a sheepfold containing two apartments (rooms) with brick piers, surrounded with stakes. A second sheepfold of posts in the ground, roofed and surrounded with stakes. Another building in brick containing carpentry shop, the forge and a small chamber, a coach house with brick piers and a shop in brick for the wheelwrights, a barn in wood, a storehouse of brick.

Besides these buildings were a five-room brick house galleried all around serving as a hospital, several hen houses, an indigo manufactory, forty-five Negro cabins and other farm buildings. Father Francis Watrin, one of the Jesuits at the plantation at the time of the expulsion, describes how the colonial officials and functionaries moved in to make the inventory and to sell the properties and "those who were employed therein took their meals in the house....They found themselves well feasted and they were sure that their employment was a lucrative one....The Superior of the Jesuits was obliged to be present at the great feasts which were given at his house during the depredation....After the sale of the real and personal property

...the chapel was razed to the ground and the sepulchres of the bodies buried for thirty years in this place and in the neighboring cemetery remained exposed to profanation." Some years later, in 1802, Dr. John Sibley wrote of having walked "by where the Jesuits used to live before their societies were abolished; the remainder of their buildings, their orange groves and garden are now existing though it is 40 years since they were abolished."

At the sale of the plantation, the first tract of seven arpents adjacent to the city was purchased by Charles de Pradel, who then bought the next five arpents from Larivee (fig. 7). Pradel died soon after and the plantation was inherited by his mother, Alexandrine de la Chaise, widow of the Chevalier Jean de Pradel, after a compromise with her widowed daughter-in-law. In June, 1766, Madame Pradel, as tutrix of her minor daughters, asked the Superior Council for authority to establish a sugar house on the plantation where the Jesuits had first attempted to grow sugarcane in Louisiana as early as 1744. At the same time, builders Francois Langlois and Francois Lioteau submitted estimates and appraisals for "the work and repairs to be done at the old buildings of the plantation of the Jesuits, as well as those of the new buildings to be built on the said plantation in order to render it proper to the cultivation and fabrication of sugar." Among the projected new buildings were a sugar house, two furnaces, a drying house, a distillery, two mills, cylinders and boilers. Thus, the area that was to become the Central Business District of New Orleans was probably the first extensive sugar plantation in Louisiana.

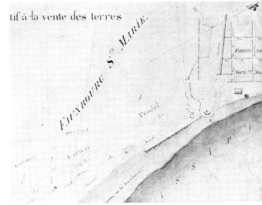

Fig. 7. Portion of plan of Faubourg St. Mary, 1763. (Courtesy New Orleans City Engineers Office.)

Meanwhile, former Governor Bienville, living his declining years in Paris, heard of the sale of his former property and protested the termination of payment of a 1,000 livre annuity which he had received from the Jesuits and which he had transferred to his nephew, Payen de Noyan. The senior de Noyan then petitioned the Superior Council to recover the annuity and arrears, which amounted to 7,700 livres, and a Negro gardener. The matter was then referred to the King for payment.

THE SPANISH COLONIAL PERIOD AND FAUBOURG ST. MARY

On January 11, 1773, before the notary Andres Almonester, Madame Pradel sold to Andres Reynard for 14,000 pesos the plantation, "a rural residence which I own and possess outside the walls of this city, close to the Capitular Gate, comprising twelve arpents front, with a depth extending up to the proper Bayou St. John...with a main structure, warehouses, kitchen, workshop, brick factory, huts and other lodgings...." When Reynard died on August 6, 1785, he left the plantation to his widow, Dona Maria Josefa Deslondes, a native of the German Coast, who later married Don Beltran (Bertrand) Gravier.

After the great fire of Good Friday, March 21, 1788, had devastated a large part of the city, Madame Gravier and her husband decided to subdivide their plantation and allow the city to expand upriver beyond the fortifications that had been built around it by the French in 1760. A plan was drawn up at the plantation on April 1, 1788, by Carlos Laveau Trudeau on which the Spanish Royal Surveyor explained that his plans showed "the front part of this plantation divided into lots, cut by three cross streets with four perpendicular streets and one oblique." These cross streets probably were Magazine, Camp and St. Charles, the perpendicular streets being

Poydras, Girod, Julia and Foucher, the oblique being given the name Gravier after the plantation's owners. On April 24, 1788, Trudeau drew up a second plan (fig. 8) adding Carondelet, Baronne and St. Philip (Dryades) streets. Along the levee in front ran the Royal Highway, *el Camino Real*.

Near the center of the plan was an entire square marked "Plaza," a public square surrounded by a double row of trees. This square was first known as the Place Gravier and, after Lafayette's visit to New Orleans in 1825, became Lafayette Square. The new suburb was first called Ville Gravier, but after the death of Madame Gravier her husband changed the name to Faubourg Ste. Marie (St. Mary) in her memory. A short street running from Girod to the Plaza had been given the name of "Calle Ste. Maria" on Trudeau's early plans, while the similar street across the square was called "Calle San Francisco."

In 1792, under the Spanish Governor Carondelet, the old French fortifications were demolished, and new ones designed by architect-engineer Gilberto Guillemard were erected in their place. Fort San Luis was constructed on the bank of the river between the city (fig. 8A) and the new Faubourg, with glacis and curtain walls of palisades running back to Fort Burgundy near the present intersection of Canal and Rampart streets. Inside Fort San Luis was the old French powder magazine with its handsome brick wall designed by Ignace Francois Broutin in 1730 (fig. 9). In front of the magazine on the site now occupied by the Custom House was the large Royal tobacco warehouse that had been built in 1783 by New Jersey builder Jacob Cowperthwait. When the second great fire (fig. 10) occurred on December 8, 1794, the powder magazine blew up, destroying the warehouse and much of the fort. It was probably from this warehouse *(magasin)* and the powder magazine that Magazine Street received its name, being the continuation of Decatur Street on which both were located.

Building activity in the new Faubourg St. Mary was slow at first. A few houses were built, including one for Nicolas Gravier on Magazine Street, designed by Carlos Trudeau and built by Francois Delery in 1796 (fig. 11). The house was of colombage

Fig. 8. Plan of the Villa Gravier, May 14, 1796, showing old lines of fortifications ruined in 1729. Drawing by Carlos Trudeau, notarized by Felix de Armas and signed by P. Pedesclaux, August 24, 1825, Plan Book 4, Folio 461, New Orleans Notarial Archives.

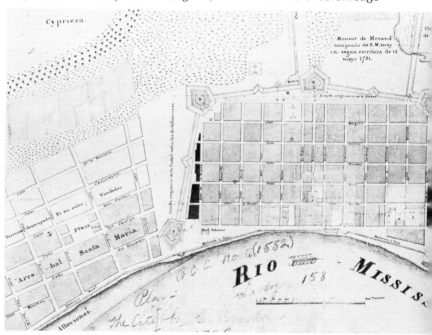

Fig. 8A. Drawing of New Orleans in 1798, by Carlos Trudeau. (Courtesy Louisiana State Museum.)

EARLY HISTORY 9

Fig. 9. Drawing of powder magazine, by Ignace Francois Broutin, dated 1733. (Courtesy *Archives Nationales,* Paris.)

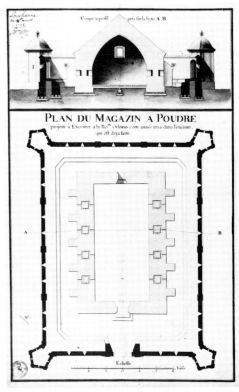

Fig. 9A. Drawing of powder magazine, by Ignace Francois Broutin, dated 1735. (Courtesy *Archives Nationales,* Paris.)

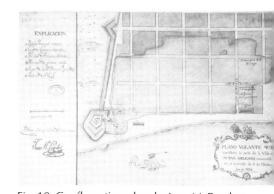

Fig. 10. Conflagration plan, by Juan M. Perchet, dated December 25, 1794. (Courtesy Spanish Archives, Simancas.)

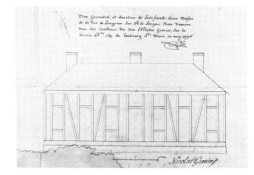

Fig. 11. House plan for Nicolas Gravier by Carlos Trudeau, Carlos Ximines, notary, 1801. (Courtesy New Orleans Notarial Archives.)

construction with three brick chimneys and six fireplaces, one for each of the rooms. The hipped roof was covered with shingles, and a gallery was added after the plans had been drawn and the contract signed. The house was located on lot 147 on the lakeside of Magazine Street, the third lot above Gravier. It was probably built on a raised basement of brick walls and piers, much in the manner of Madam John's Legacy, one of the first houses built in the Vieux Carre after the 1788 fire. Trudeau's drawings for this important early house are perhaps the most complete detailed plans extant for a colombage house in Spanish colonial New Orleans.

On June 6, 1807, the newspaper *Moniteur* carried in an advertisement for the sale of a house belonging to Nicholas Gravier what must have been a typical description of the first houses erected in the new Faubourg St. Mary:

A *House* now occupied by M. Forstall, situated in Magazine street, Faubourg Ste. Marie, on a lot adjoining on one side to Mr. Benjamin Morgan and on the other to Mr. MacDonogh, of 60 feet of front by the whole depth of the block. The said house in colombage, elevated nine feet on walls, consists of six chambers, four of which with fireplaces, three warehouses on the ground floor, a gallery of ten feet in width enclosed in jalousies in its entire length, a double staircase in brick and a large cellar in masonry.

On December 21, 1806, the Superior Court, Territory of Orleans, in a suit between Nicolas Gravier and Jean Gravier, had confirmed Nicolas' ownership of lots 147 and 152 on which this house stood, the two lots extending from Magazine to Camp Street. Nicolas Gravier then sold the two lots to Benjamin Morgan, one of the prominent developers in Faubourg St. Mary. On May 24, 1804, Morgan had purchased the adjacent property at the corner of Magazine and Gravier from Julien Poydras, executor of the estate of Felix Mathere. On this property was a house similar to, but larger than, the Gravier house. It was described in the act of sale by notary Pedro Pedesclaux as "a house constructed partly in walls of brick and partly in colombage, composed of a dining room, a company salon, a bed chamber, an office, two cabinets, a gallery, a kitchen, a warehouse, various chambers for the slaves and other buildings." After Morgan's death the properties were sold in 1827, a fine survey being drawn of them by the city surveyor, Joseph Pilie. This survey (fig. 12) shows both the Gravier and the Mathere houses, the latter facing on Gravier Street. Both are shown with impressive brick steps, a double flight leading up to a bowed platform in the rear center of the Gravier house and an off-center flight in the rear and a lesser one at one end of the Mathere house. Both houses are indicated with hipped roofs. Other buildings on the five lots shown on the survey probably were stores and warehouses built by Morgan after he acquired the properties.

In May, 1831, the corner lot at Magazine and Gravier on which the Mathere

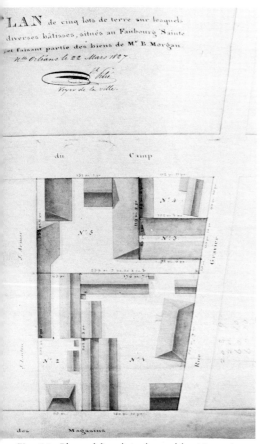

Fig. 12. Plan of five lots, bound by Magazine, Camp and Gravier streets, owned by Benjamin Morgan. Drawing by Pilie, Voyer de la Ville, dated March 27, 1827, J. M. Duncan, notary, June 5, 1827, Book 2, Folio 117, New Orleans Notarial Archives.

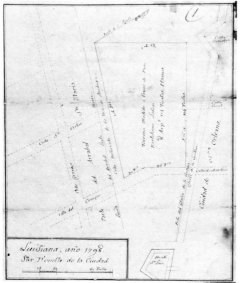

Fig. 13. Survey by Carlos Trudeau, 1798. (Courtesy James T. Hickey.)

house had stood in 1804 was sold to the New Orleans Canal and Banking Company, a bank organized to construct a canal to bring water-borne traffic from Lake Pontchartrain into Faubourg St. Mary. This became known as the New Basin Canal, its terminus and turning basin being at Rampart and Julia streets. The canal continued to function until the 1940s in competition with the old Basin or Canal Carondelet, which had been built from the headwaters of Bayou St. John to the rear of the old city in the 1790s by the Spanish Governor Carondelet.

THE COMMONS AND CANAL STREET

The original idea for Canal Street derives from the early French colonial project for a canal to connect the river with Lake Pontchartrain. It was in the Spanish colonial period that the commons originated. These were the lands outside the city limits which, when the fortifications were rebuilt by Governor Carondelet, could if necessary be cleared of any construction that would interfere with the fire from the forts and the defense of the city. Some of these lands outside the upper fortification line had already been sold and built upon. Mathias James O'Conway, an Irishman who came to New Orleans in 1788, had bought a house and lot in 1790 outside the old French fortifications from Gravier, but sold it in June, 1793, probably because of the building of the new fortifications that isolated him from the town.

A large tract of these public lands between the fortifications and Faubourg St. Mary was granted to Barthelemy Lafon, the noted architect-surveyor, by Carondelet in 1798 in accordance with a survey made at the time by Carlos Trudeau (fig. 13). Lafon "took possession of the land and enclosed with piquets a portion of it, and erected on it sheds to shelter his materials, etc. and commenced a foundry on a small scale by way of experiment and continued in the undisturbed possession of it until about a year thereafter, when by a report of the Engineer, he was forbidden by a military order to erect any buildings thereon which might interfere with the fire of the Fort St. Louis, the fortifications of which were about that time enlarged and improved in consequence of an apprehended invasion of the Province." Lafon tried unsuccessfully for years to reestablish his ownership of this large tract until his claim was finally confirmed by the Federal Land Office in 1818, two years before his death. When France under Napoleon regained possession of Louisiana from Spain in 1803, the French military engineer Vinache reported that the fortifications, scarcely ten years old, had already deteriorated and that Faubourg St. Mary had grown to such an extent that the fortifications "seem to be turned more against the place than to contribute to its exterior defence. The little advantage that can be drawn from these fortifications will without doubt bring about the decision to raze them entirely."

Soon after the United States took possession of Louisiana in 1803, the City Council petitioned the Federal government, stating that the land on which the fortifications were constructed belonged to the Council and asked "that the said forts be immediately demolished and the materials employed in filling up the ditches that surround them." By 1805 the poor citizens had practically demolished the old fortifications for firewood and "nearly every distinction of city and suburb was unnoticed. And between the old city and the upper suburbs a new street was opened, which filled up the fosse, [ditch] and infringed upon the tottering ramparts of an intervening fort." Decatur—Magazine (Old Levee) was the first street to connect the city and Faubourg St. Mary, to be followed by Chartres and Royal after the rope walk property, just within the walls, that had been granted in 1791 to Elisha Winters, a Kentuckian, could be removed (fig. 14).

By an Act of Congress passed March 3, 1807, the claims of the city to "the Commons adjacent to the said city and within 600 yards of fortifications of the same" were confirmed. The act also provided that the city "shall reserve for the purpose and convey gratuitously for the public benefit, to the company authorized by the Legislature of the Territory of Orleans, as much of the said Commons as shall be necessary to continue the Canal of Carondelet from the present Basin to the Mississippi, and shall not dispose of, for the purpose of building thereon, any lot within 60 feet of the space reserved for a Canal, which shall forever remain open as a public highway." Thus was Canal Street created by an Act of Congress.

In 1810 the city surveyor, Jacques Tanesse, prepared a "Plan of Division into Lots of a part of the Commons situated between the City and the reservation made by the Congress in favor of the Navigation Company." This map showed the division into lots of the lands between Elisha Winter's rope walk and Canal Street, from Levee Street (Decatur) back to Rampart, the site of old Fort Burgundy. Canal Street is shown with a double row of trees along the roadways on each side of the proposed canal, and although the canal was never completed, the broad tree-lined street became one of the widest and most attractive streets in the nation. The land reserved for the canal became known as neutral ground and separated the hostile French segment of the population in the Vieux Carre from the rapidly increasing American segment in Faubourg St. Mary.

Canal Street immediately began to develop until it became, and has remained, the principal business street of the city. In 1807 Benjamin Henry Latrobe, Surveyor of the Public Buildings of the United States, designed a new Custom House for the city (fig. 15) which was erected by Robert Alexander, a Washington builder who took up residence in New Orleans. The site was the same as that occupied by the present Custom House, Latrobe's building being one of the first in the city in which red brick, white columns and trim and green blinds were used, the materials and color that soon became the characteristics of American building in New Orleans.

By 1819 Latrobe's elegant little building was found to be too small and its foundations inadequate, and it was replaced by a new but undistinguished building designed by Benjamin Buisson, a Napoleonic French refugee military engineer and architect (fig. 16). Soon afterward, the Mariner's Church (see page 28) was begun adjacent to the Custom House, both buildings being demolished when the present, vast, granite building designed by Alexander T. Wood was begun in 1845. Various designs were proposed for the new Custom House, including Gothic and classic schemes designed by James H. Dakin (figs. 17A, B, C, D and 18). The Egyptianesque design by Wood was adopted, but he died in 1854 before its completion. His associate, T. K. Wharton, who sketched the building under construction, wrote that Wood was "a throughly practical architect...bold and daring in construction; abundant evidence remains in the grand edifice which he leaves incomplete but which will stand as an imperishable monument to his talents and architectural genius." Other architects, including Dakin and Lewis Reynolds,

Fig. 14. Survey by Carlos Trudeau, 1791. (Courtesy Samuel Wilson, Jr., Collection.)

Fig. 15. Detail of Latrobe's Custom House, from a French sheet music engraving. (Courtesy Historic New Orleans Collection.)

Fig. 16. Old Custom House, by Benjamin Buisson, 1819. (Courtesy Confederate Memorial Museum.)

succeeded Wood as architect of the Custom House, but the building was not completed until the 1880s. Its great Marble Hall is considered one of the finest Greek Revival interiors in America (see Inventory, page 133).

William Brand in 1810 built a fine house at Royal and Canal for Samuel B. Davis, the two street fronts faced with Baltimore brick. In 1823 Brand built a large three-story brick building for Phelps and Babcock on Canal, between Royal and Chartres, faced with Philadelphia bricks in Flemish bond and with a slate roof. Brand also built for himself five, three-story brick dwellings, across Canal at the corner of St. Charles, which were valued at $140,000 at the time of his wife's death in 1837 (see Inventory, page 138). It is interesting to note that when Brand had these buildings painted in 1831, he specified that "the brick work of the two fronts on Canal and

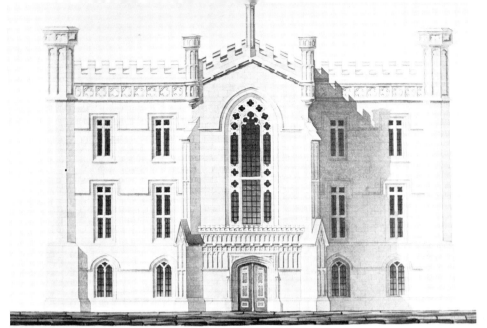

Fig. 17A. Plan for Custom House, by J. H. Dakin, January 1, 1846. (Courtesy New Orleans Public Library.)

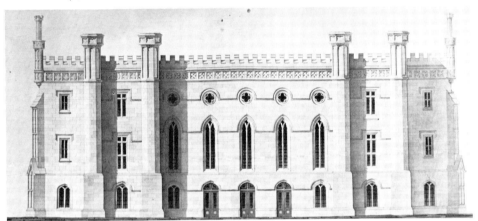

Fig. 17B. Flank elevation of Custom House, by J. H. Dakin, January 1, 1846. (Courtesy New Orleans Public Library.)

Fig. 17C. Longitudinal section of Custom House, by J. H. Dakin, January 1, 1846. (Courtesy New Orleans Public Library.)

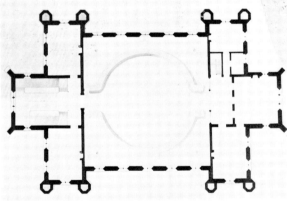

Fig. 17D. Plan of second floor of Custom House, by J. H. Dakin, January 1, 1846. (Courtesy New Orleans Public Library.)

Fig. 18. Plan for Custom House, by J. H. Dakin, 1847. (Courtesy New Orleans Public Library.)

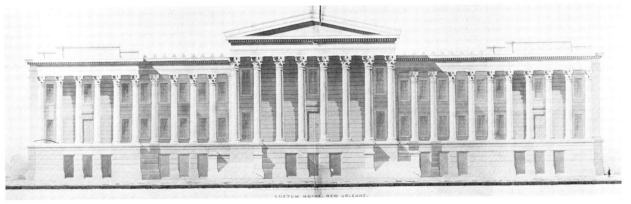

St. Charles, as far as the cornice, is to be painted with two good coats of red paint and the joints pencilled neatly with white lead; the cornices are to be in imitation of light stone colour... laid off in the same manner to imitate stone work."

In April, 1825, Maurice Piseta and Felix Pinson contracted with Germain Musson "for the construction of a house, stores and buildings on his lot forming one of the corners of Royal and Canal streets." When Musson's properties at the downtown river corner of Royal and Canal were appraised at $142,000 in 1839, they were described as "six stores in granite, of four stories." These splendid granite buildings, built by Musson, grandfather of the great French artist Edgar Degas, are still standing, their facades obscured by unsightly fire escapes and garish advertising signs. These are probably the oldest buildings still standing on Canal Street (see Inventory, page 137).

In 1815 young architect Henry S. Latrobe designed the octagonal Gothic Christ Church at Canal and Bourbon and the Charity Hospital, which occupied the entire block on the upper side of Canal between Baronne and what is now known as University Place. This building (fig. 19), with symmetrical wings forming a forecourt, became the Louisiana State House when the Charity Hospital moved to its present site in 1834 and to a large new building which had been begun on Common (now Tulane Avenue) in 1831 by H. Hemphill, architect and builder (figs. 20A, B). A new chamber for the House of Representatives, with sixteen 20-foot-high Corinthian columns, for which William Nichols was the architect and Owen Evans the builder, was constructed in the rear when the building was made the State Capitol. It was described in the 1838 *City Directory* as "handsome, but unfortunately speakers are heard with difficulty.... It is in contemplation to erect an edifice more worthy of the State, but when this will be done is uncertain." Nothing was done until the capital was moved to Baton Rouge, but James H. Dakin, who designed the Baton Rouge Capitol, did design a proposed State building for the Canal Street site (figs. 21A, B). In 1850 the State sold the old Canal Street State House site, which was subdivided into building lots. Some ideas were presented at the time for erecting an Italian opera house on the site, but these plans did not materialize and the square was soon filled with commercial buildings.

By the early 1830s Canal Street must have been a handsome thoroughfare. It was described by Joseph Holt Ingraham in his *The Southwest by a Yankee*, published in 1835, as

> the broadest in New Orleans and destined to be the most magnificent.... Through its center runs a double row of young trees, which, when they arrive at maturity, will form the finest mall in the United States.... Canal street... with its triple row of young sycamores extending throughout the whole length is one of the most spacious, and destined at no distant period, to be one of the first and handsomest streets in the city. Every building in the street is of modern construction, and some blocks of its brick edifices will vie in tasteful elegance with the boasted granite piles of Boston.

Ingraham was impressed by the State House and wrote:

> Its snow white front, though plain, is very imposing, and the whole structure, with its handsome, detached wings, and large green, thickly covered with shrubbery in front, luxuriant with orange and lemon trees, presents decidedly, one of the finest views to be met within the city. These two buildings [Christ Church and the State House], with the exception of some elegant private residences, are all that are worth remarking in this street, which, less than a mile from the river, terminates in the swampy commons, everywhere surrounding New Orleans, except on the river side.

Fig. 19. Louisiana State House on Canal Street; formerly the Latrobe Charity Hospital. (Courtesy Confederate Memorial Museum.)

Fig. 20A. Charity Hospital. (Courtesy Confederate Memorial Museum.)

Fig. 20B. Charity Hospital, from *Ballou's Pictorial*. (Courtesy Historic New Orleans Collection.)

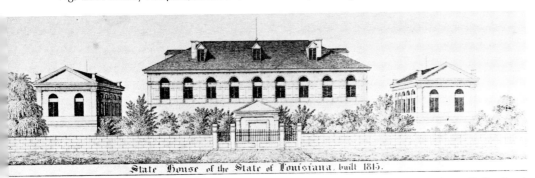

Fig. 21A. State House, from Zimpel map (1834). (Courtesy Historic New Orleans Collection.)

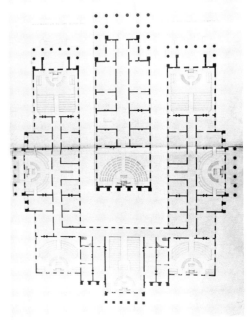

Fig. 21B. Plan for capitol buildings on State House Square. (Courtesy New Orleans Public Library.)

Fig. 22. View of Canal Street from a German magazine. (Courtesy Historic New Orleans Collection.)

Fig. 23. Christ Church on Canal Street, from a tintype. (Courtesy Historic New Orleans Collection.)

Fig. 23A. New Orleans in 1836, by G. W. Sully. (Courtesy Tulane University.)

Fig. 23B. An early view of Canal Street. (Courtesy Louisiana Collection, Special Collections Division, Tulane University Library.)

Fig. 24. "Sketch of a design for building on the centre of Canal St., N. O.," by Dakin and Dakin, dated January 3, 1837. (Courtesy New Orleans Public Library.)

Fig. 25. Residence on Canal Street, bound by Burgundy, Dauphine and Iberville, designed by Dakin. Drawing by George T. Dunbar, dated November 28, 1843, Plan Book 23A, Folio 57, New Orleans Notarial Archives.

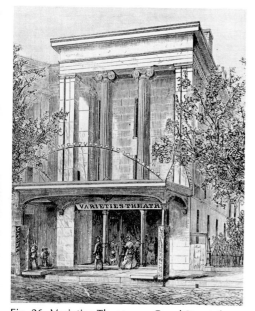

Fig. 26. Varieties Theatre on Canal Street, from Jewell's *Crescent City.*

Fig. 27. *Maison de Sante,* corner Canal and Claiborne, under the direction of the Sisters of Charity, from *Cohen's* (1853). (Courtesy New Orleans Public Library.)

With the development of Canal Street came inevitable changes. From originally a residential tree-lined street (figs. 22, 23, 23A), it gradually became the principal business street of the city. In the 1830s architects Dakin and Dakin proposed to build a block-long row of shops down the center of the Canal Street neutral ground beyond the Custom House. The shop building was to be surrounded by Corinthian columns, which, with Dakin's classic Custom House design, would have given that part of the city a truly Athenian character (fig. 24).

Dakin and Dakin, however, in 1836 and 1837 did construct a row of classic houses on Canal Street between Dauphine and Burgundy (fig. 25). These were four private residences for four prominent families, although they were designed to resemble a single monumental classical building with a curved central Ionic colonnade flanked by symmetrical wings, each with two great Ionic columns in antis. The row became known as Union Terrace and was described in the 1838 *City Directory* as "the elegant block of buildings...which is now raising its beautiful Ionic facade on the lower side of Canal street, opposite the State House...whose interior arrangements and architectural taste are in perfect keeping with their exterior chastity of design." Eventually, even these elegant residences were converted to commercial uses. One of them became Victor's Restaurant, and one became the entrance to the Varieties Theatre, which was erected behind it in 1871 (fig. 26). The latter, adjacent to Christ Church, was demolished when the Maison Blanche Building was erected in 1906.

On February 13, 1839, Dakin and Dakin signed a contract with Dr. Warren Stone and Dr. William Kennedy to erect an infirmary at the corner of Canal and Claiborne, where the Governor House Hotel now stands. This handsome *Maison de Sante* (fig. 27) had "a Grecian Doric Portico in front and two back galleries and a back building." In 1836 E. W. Sewell built a fine three-story brick residence for notary G. R. Stringer on Canal between Burgundy and Rampart, "the front to be painted and pencilled and there is to be a handsome iron gallery in front." In 1844 James Gallier designed the fine residence for Dr. W. Newton Mercer (see Inventory,

SHAKESPEARE CLUB.

Fig. 28. Tilton House, Canal at Dryades, from Jewell's *Crescent City.*

Fig. 29. Touro buildings, constructed in 1852, from *Crescent City Business Directory, 1858-59.*

Fig. 30. Cast-iron structure built to house the City Water Works, at the foot of Canal Street. The building apparently never was used for this purpose. The *Frank Pargoud* is docked in the background. (Courtesy Historic New Orleans Collection.)

page 142) that is now the Boston Club, the only one of these fine Canal Street buildings to survive.

The *Daily Crescent* for October 21, 1856, listed among the many city improvements a number of private residences, including that "of F. W. Tilton corner of Canal and Dryades street [University Place]—the finest residences in that part of the city—J. K. Collins & Co., architects and builders.—cost $30,000." This fine Italianate house (fig. 28) became the Shakespeare Club about 1870 and subsequently was demolished. The following year, in 1857, Gallier Turpin Co. built an even more elaborate residence further out Canal Street at Marais for Michael Heine at a cost of $34,000. In 1858 Crozier & Wing built a three-story brick residence for merchant Samuel N. Moody on Canal between Marais and Treme for which Howard and Diettel were the architects (see Inventory, page 146). Four years before, the same builders had erected a three-story residence with a two-story iron verandah for Francois V. Labarre across the street.

Most of the new buildings along Canal Street were for business purposes, such as the D. H. Holmes store built in 1849 and the Touro block (fig. 29) begun in 1852. These and many others employed iron verandahs or galleries, about which the *Daily Picayune* of July 7, 1852, reported: "One of the most admirable innovations upon the old system of building tall staring structures for business purposes is the plan...generally coming in use, of erecting galleries and verandahs of ornamental iron work. The contrast...shows every man of taste and judgment the superiority of...this improvement." Galleries of this sort were gradually extended over the sidewalks of Canal Street, providing an almost uninterrupted covered way where shoppers could walk along protected from sun and rain.

Unfortunately in the Canal Street renovations of the 1930s, these handsome amenities were ordered removed from all the Canal Street buildings that still had them. Other uses of iron on Canal Street were in the handsome lamp standards of the 1850s and later, the notable iron fountain (see end sheet) erected at Canal and Camp streets in 1871, "a very ornamental structure...embellished with fancy advertising cards painted on colored glass by Mr. J. T. Belknap." The iron building at the foot of Canal Street (fig. 30) erected for the City Water Works in 1859 was another unique structure, "a building of iron, brick and granite...27 feet high, 85 by 116, surmounted by an iron-plated reservoir about 7 by 82 by 42 and tastefully ornamented in moulded nereids, dolphins, etc., from designs by Mr. A. Defrasse, carver-sculptor." The castings were made in New Orleans by the foundry of Bennett & Lurges. During the Civil War this structure was used as a "free market for the poor of the city." In 1874 this unusual building, never used for its intended purpose, was sold by the city to be removed from the site.

The *Daily Crescent's* September 12, 1859, city improvements report remarked on the increased use of iron in building and listed three splendid iron-fronted buildings being constructed on the upper side of Canal Street: C. H. Slocomb's hardware store and Theodore Frois's store, both between Camp and Magazine, and the Merchants Insurance Company near St. Charles, all three designed by Wm. A. Freret, the Frois store being built by Peter Ross and the other two by Crozier and Wing. The report also listed, in addition to the Moody residence, two other large residences on Rampart just above Canal, one costing $20,000 for F. Williams by Gallier and Esterbrook, architects and builders, the other costing $18,000 for a Mr. Conners, for which T. B. Lee was the builder. The following year another major change in the appearance of Canal Street occurred with the dedication of the monument to Henry Clay at the intersection of Canal with Royal and St. Charles on April 12, 1860. Thomas K. Wharton describes in his diary having from the scaffolding of the Custom House "a superb view of the whole ceremony up the large densely crowded avenue of Canal street—the glittering costumes, and the unveiling of the statue.... [I] walked down...and examined the statue; it is colossal, over 12 feet high, finely designed and well cast. The granite pedestal, too, is beautiful but...is too scant in every dimension and at least 25 feet too low." In 1901, as traffic problems around the Clay monument increased, it was removed from Canal Street and re-erected on a taller pedestal in the center of Lafayette Square. Joel T. Hart of Kentucky was the sculptor of the bronze figure of Henry Clay.

Following the Civil War, building activities along Canal Street gradually resumed. By 1867 J. M. Howell was building a three-story brick building on the southeast corner of Canal and Rampart for Peter O'Donnell, for which Reid & Harrod were the architects. Iron work was used here extensively in the form of cast-iron columns and entablature on the ground floor, cast-iron lintels over the windows and cast-iron brackets to support the cornice. In 1874 Mrs. Anna Cartwright Jackson had a new building erected by Jos. H. Dorand, for which Benjamin Morgan Harrod was the architect, to replace one of the sections of the old Union Terrace on Canal between Dauphine and Burgundy. That part of the great classic row that had housed Victor's Restaurant shortly before had been destroyed by a fire. It must have narrowly missed destroying the adjacent new Varieties Theatre that had been built behind the row in 1871, a new theatre for which B. M. Harrod was also the architect.

One of the most impressive buildings built on the upper side of Canal Street in the post Civil War period must have been the new building for the Pickwick Club (fig. 31), for which Hinsdale and Marble were the architects and O'Neill and Garvey the builders in 1882. This building, at the corner of Canal and Carondelet, was later used as a department store and demolished, to be replaced by the present Gus Mayer store in recent years. Around the turn of the century the Pickwick Club built a handsome new clubhouse further out Canal Street near Rampart, for which

Fig. 31. Canal Street view from the Henry Clay statue in 1895, showing the Pickwick Club (left center) and the Boston Club (white structure immediately to its right). (Courtesy Louisiana State Museum.)

the noted Boston firm of Shepley, Rutan and Coolidge, successors to H. H. Richardson, were the architects (see Inventory, page 145). This building which, though mutilated, still stands, was sold by the club which, during the depression of the 1930s, moved to the Hibernia Bank Building Tower and later returned to Canal Street to occupy its present home in the old Crescent Billiard Hall at Canal and St. Charles.

Another prominent building of the late-nineteenth century on Canal Street was a five-story brick building between St. Charles and Carondelet designed by Wm. A. Freret and built by Wing and Muir for Mrs. Abigail L. Slark. On the lower side of Canal, at Claiborne, Diedrich Einseidel designed the great brewery buildings which later were used by the Coca Cola Company and demolished, to be replaced by the present modern automobile sales room.

A block closer to the river, on the same side of Canal, Tulane University in 1893

Fig. 32. Still-smouldering area of Canal Street razed by fire on February 17, 1892. (Courtesy Samuel Wilson, Jr., Collection.)

Fig. 33. Louisville and Nashville Railroad Station, near the foot of Canal, built in 1900. (Courtesy New Orleans Public Library.)

built a large building, designed by Thomas Sully and known as the Richardson Memorial, which occupied an entire square of ground to house the school's medical department. This building was demolished when the Medical School moved to the first unit of its present facilities adjacent to Charity Hospital on Tulane Avenue.

Fires also have taken their toll of old Canal Street structures. One of the most spectacular fires occurred on February 17, 1892, and destroyed a large part of the Touro block at Canal and Bourbon and some buildings on the other side of Bourbon. A photograph of the still smoldering ruins from this fire (fig. 32) also shows many interesting facets of the Canal Street story, the remaining Touro Building on the right, the ornate Mercier Building on the left, designed by William Freret and built in 1887, the old D. H. Holmes Building and other interesting structures. Horse-drawn vehicles crowd the upper lane of the street, the lower one being impassable because of the fire. The neutral ground is taken up by four tracks accommodating numerous mule-drawn streetcars. A maze of electric wires are strung from poles on each side of the neutral ground, and over all looms one of the open-work steel towers erected about that time to floodlight the street with the newly introduced electric lights. The idea was not a success, however, and the towers soon disappeared from the Canal Street-scene. Electric trolleycars replaced the mule cars and in turn were replaced by the present motor busses. The present ornamental light standards were installed during the extensive "improvement" program for Canal Street in the 1930s.

Larger and more modern buildings began replacing the older structures around the turn of the century. The old Godchaux Building was a multi-story structure at the corner of Canal and Chartres and was demolished in 1969 for the construction of the Marriot Hotel, now the tallest building on Canal Street. About 1900, Thomas Sully had designed the first modern skyscraper to be built on the street, the seven-story Morris Building at Canal and Camp, which, though shorn of its cornice and galleries, still stands.

The coming of the railroads also produced some changes in Canal Street. In 1900 the Louisville and Nashville Railroad built a new station near the foot of Canal Street, a red brick Richardsonian structure with an arched iron train shed adjacent to it (fig. 33). Soon after, the monumental Terminal Station, designed by noted Chicago architect Daniel H. Burnham, was constructed. Both of these structures have been demolished, the former to be replaced by an unsightly electric power installation and the latter by the Basin Street neutral ground with the monument to Simon Bolivar and other Latin American heroes.

Canal Street continues to go on with ever-increasing vitality. With the International Trade Mart and the Rivergate, the Spanish Plaza and the Place de France at the river end and new buildings appearing as far out as Claiborne and beyond, it is encouraging to see that some of the older structures are being restored and that Canal Street still retains many reminders of its distinguished past.

II. Churches of Faubourg St. Mary

CHRIST CHURCH

The first Protestant church in New Orleans was built in 1815 when Christ Church obtained from the city, at a price of $3,000, a lot at the corner of Canal and Bourbon streets, an area once occupied by the city fortifications and commons. At a meeting of the vestry on June 4, 1815, Benjamin Morgan and Richard Relf were appointed a committee "to obtain subscriptions for building a church...[and] to obtain an estimate of Mr. Latrobe for building said church." The building, of which no known drawings exist, was a small octagon structure in the Gothic style designed by Henry S. Latrobe, whose distinguished architect father, Benjamin Latrobe, had designed some of the first Gothic revival structures in America. The senior Latrobe was not, however, overly impressed with his son's design of Christ Church, for when he came to New Orleans after his son's death in 1817, he remarked: "It is a plain octagon without any architectural merit of design or execution, but at the same time it has no offensive features." Another critic described it as "an octagon edifice, with a cupola, in bad taste." Joseph Holt Ingraham, in *The Southwest by a Yankee* (1835), described a walk along Canal Street:

> The first object which struck me as worthy of notice was a small brick octagon church, enclosed by a white paling, on the corner of Bourbon street. The entrance was overgrown with long grass, and the footsteps of a worshipper seemed not to have pressed its threshold for many an unheeded Sunday. In its lonely and neglected appearance, there was a silent but forcible comment upon that censurable neglect of the Sabbath, which, it has been said, prevails too generally among the citizens of New Orleans. In front of this church, which is owned, I believe, by the Episcopalians, stands a white marble monument, surmounted by an urn, erected in memory of the late Governor Claiborne. With this solitary exception, there are no public monuments in this city.

On June 12, 1825, a committee was appointed by the vestry "to procure the necessary plans and make contracts for the erection of a suitable building to be used as a parsonage house." This new rectory was constructed on a lot facing Canal Street adjacent to the church and was built by Benjamin Fox and Peter Ogier. In May, 1828, the church mortgaged the new parsonage to the Reverend James Foster Hull, the rector, for $1,500 "for furnishing and completing the Parsonage House lately built," together with the lot, 45 feet on Canal Street by 100 feet in depth between the church and properties belonging to the builders Bickel and Hamblet, partners of Fox, "together with the three story brick dwelling house, the kitchens, stables and all other buildings and improvements." This handsome house with its fine wrought iron stairway and galleries is shown in a lithograph of this block of Canal Street as it was in 1840 (fig. 1).

In April, 1833, the vestry decided that the old building was "too small for the increased and increasing population of the city" and resolved that "the erection of a building on the present site on a more large and improved plan would be an ornament to our city, a credit to its founders and an invaluable legacy to our posterity." By December, 1833, the committee had "adopted a plan for the new church," but some controversy arose over the location and the vestry resolved "that the growing business character of the neighborhood of the present location of Christ Church renders it expedient, in erecting a new church, to retire to a more retired part of the city." Sites at Canal and Burgundy and on Lafayette Square were considered, but the majority of the pew holders decided to remain at the original site at Canal and Bourbon. New plans (fig. 1) for the church were procured in 1835 from architects Gallier and Dakin who had only recently arrived in New Orleans from New York. The new building was in the form of a Greek Ionic temple, and in December, 1835, one of the church officers wrote that "our church walls are up to the roof—it will be a magnificent building, altho' I am, myself, wedded to the Gothic order of architecture for church edifices." The contractor for the new church was D. H. Twogood, who completed it in the summer of 1837 at a cost of about $48,000.

In 1844 the congregation invited Dr. Francis Lister Hawkes, an Episcopal clergyman who then conducted a school at Holly Springs, Mississippi, to become the rector of Christ Church. He accepted, but asked that he and his drawing master at the school be allowed to submit plans for a new church building. The old Greek

Fig. 1. Second Christ Church, from an 1840 lithograph by Jules Lion. Gallier and Dakin were the architects. The rectory later served as the home of Judah Touro. (Courtesy Historic New Orleans Collection.)

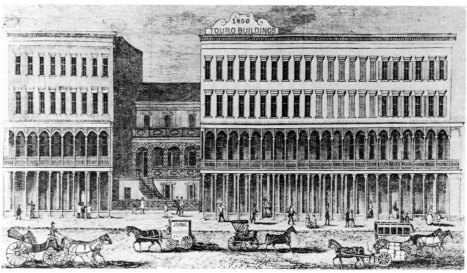

Fig. 1A. Judah Touro House. (Courtesy Leonard V. Huber Collection.)

temple church was sold to Judah Touro, along with its organ, reredos and all its fixtures, in exchange for six lots at Canal and Dauphine streets. The old church then became a synagogue, and the rectory served as Touro's residence until it was demolished in 1857, the last building in the block to be removed to make room for the great block-long Touro Building between Royal and Bourbon streets (fig. 1A).

On April 21, 1856, before notary William Christy, architect-builder James Gallier, signed a $56,000 contract with the vestry for a new Christ Church in accordance with " four plans and drawings furnished by Rev'd Francis L. Hawkes." The first of these drawings had been made by Dr. Hawkes' drawing master, Thomas K. Wharton, at Holly Springs in 1846. The new church was in the Gothic style with a central spire. Referring to Wharton's plans, Gallier recorded in his autobiography that they were "a sketch design for the new church, but I had to make so many alterations in the plan before it could be made practically fit to build from, as to make it amount to a new design" (fig. 2). A comparison of the Wharton drawings and photographs of the completed building, however, shows little major alteration, at least in the exterior design. The new church served the congregation until the present Christ Church Cathedral was built on St. Charles Avenue at Sixth Street in 1886.

THE PRESBYTERIAN CHURCH

The second Protestant church to be built in New Orleans was located in Faubourg St. Mary on St. Charles between Gravier and Union streets. In 1818 an eloquent young Presbyterian preacher, the Reverend Sylvester Larned, arrived in New Orleans and soon began collecting $40,000 to build a new church. He wrote:

> It is contemplated to make the church of brick from Philadelphia, dimensions about ninety feet by sixty, to comprise a bell, a clock, and perhaps an organ. ...The building is to contain two thousand one hundred to two thousand two hundred persons seated. Possibly the plan of Dr. Mason's will be the model, except that a church in this climate will need two additional doors in the side. They think of sending me to Philadelphia for an architect and to make the building an honor and an ornament to the city....A committee has been appointed to purchase a central lot in the city capable of containing a church, session house, and, if hereafter practicable, an academy.

The *City Directory* of 1822 stated that "the Presbyterian Church, a very handsome brick building, with a gothic front, situated in the suburb St. Mary, at the corner of St. Charles and Gravier streets has a belfry in which is a striking town clock, and is provided with an organ."

The new church was a simple rectangular structure with a square, squat tower in front and is shown in one of the notable St. Aulaire views of New Orleans (fig. 3). The 1838 *City Directory* described it as

> An edifice in brick in the plain Gothic style of architecture. Its cornerstone was laid January, 1819 and it was finished and consecrated during the same year, William Brand being the architect, at an expense, including the cost of land of $70,000. Rev. Sylvester Larned was the first pastor, but did not survive the epidemic of the year following [1820].

This was the same epidemic that claimed the life of Benjamin Latrobe. In a letter

Fig. 2. Second Christ Church. From Jewell's *Crescent City.*

to his wife on March 20, 1819, Latrobe wrote of Dr. Larned that "there is no Presbyterian church, but he preaches in the Episcopal church at 3 or ½ past.... They are building a large barn of a Presbyterian church for him, which will be finished this summer." The *Louisiana Gazette* announced on July 3, 1819, that "The Rev. Mr. Larned will preach in the new church on Sunday, 4th of July." While the new church was being erected, "the· Presbyterians were successful in obtaining a place of worship on Canal street, on the site of the building now occupied by Stauffer, Marcreadry & Co." This company, located at the corner of Canal and Dorsiere, later became Stauffer-Eshleman, Co., and the old building was demolished as part of the site of the new Marriott Hotel.

Dr. Larned died on August 31, 1820, and from his residence, "the little one story building on Camp street, nearly opposite the upper corner of Lafayette Square ...all that remained of Sylvester Larned was conveyed to the...cemetery."

After the death of Dr. Larned, the noted Reverend Theodore Clapp (fig. 4) became the minister of the church. He was a popular and brilliant preacher but eventually found himself in disagreement with basic Presbyterian doctrine. Ten years after he assumed the ministry of the church, several of the members decided to leave and form another church. They met in a warehouse on Lafayette Square belonging to Cornelius Paulding, from whom they ultimately purchased it. This is perhaps the curious "Presbyterian Church" that appears on Charles F. Zimpel's 1834 sketch of Lafayette Square (fig. 5), or it may be a design proposed by him for the new church on the site. In 1833 Dr. Clapp was deposed from the Presbyterian ministry and several more members left his church to join the others, meeting together in a room on Julia Street until March, 1835, when they occupied the basement of their new church on the site of Paulding's warehouse. This became the First Presbyterian Church.

The church on St. Charles Street had been purchased by Judah Touro for $20,000 to liquidate a church debt that existed when Dr. Clapp first arrived. When the Presbyterians withdrew, Touro allowed Dr. Clapp to retain the building and it became the Congregationalist Unitarian Church of the Messiah, better known as the Strangers Church. The building that had been constructed in 1819 by the local American builder, William Brand, was finally destroyed by the fire that burned the St. Charles Hotel in January, 1851. The Unitarian congregation then built a new church at the downtown-river corner of St. Charles and Julia streets. It was an interesting octagonal building in the Gothic style designed by architect John Barnett. Thomas K. Wharton mentioned in his diary that on April 16, 1855, he "went to Mr. Clapp's new church now near completion. The stained glass windows, as usual now, very strong and positive both in design and color (fig. 6)." The site of the former church was soon occupied by a row of six three-story brick stores built for Judah Touro by Little and Middlemiss, builders, in 1853 (see Inventory, page 203). These buildings still stand, but the church on Julia Street was later demolished and the congregation moved to a new church uptown.

The first church the Presbyterians built on Lafayette Square, in 1834 and 1835, was a handsome Greek Revival structure with a recessed entrance porch and a tall Wren-like spire. The architect was probably George Clarkson, to whom the church owed a small sum at the time of his death in 1835. It is referred to as the Second Presbyterian Church in the 1838 *City Directory* and described as

Fig. 3. First Presbyterian Church, from a lithograph by Felix-Achille Beaupoil de Saint-Aulaire. (Courtesy Leonard V. Huber Collection.)

an edifice of the Grecian Doric order and finely located, fronting as it does on Lafayette Square—the handsomest public place in the city. The basement story is of granite but the rest of the construction is brick plastered to imitate stone, and, on account of the humidity of the climate, this is already discoloured and needs repair.... In the court in front, a neat obelisk has been erected as a monument to the memory of Rev. Sylvester Larned.

This handsome church is shown in a sketch by an unidentified artist, made about 1840 (fig. 7), and appears prominently in the lower left corner of the well-known J. W. Hill and Smith view of "New Orleans from St. Patrick's Church, 1852" (see book jacket). In 1842 the noted Henry Ward Beecher taught in the basement of this old Presbyterian Church on Lafayette Square. On October 29, 1854, what was then the oldest Protestant church building standing in New Orleans was destroyed by fire. Thomas K. Wharton recorded in his diary that "nothing remained but a mere shell filled with smoking ruins."

The congregation immediately began planning to build a new church on the site. Henry Howard, the noted Irish-born New Orleans architect, was commissioned to

Fig. 5. Presbyterian Church, on Lafayette Square, from map by Charles Zimpel (1834). Paulding's building is at extreme right. From Plan Book 71, Folio 1, New Orleans Notarial Archives.

Fig. 4. The Reverend Theodore Clapp, dated February 24, 1844. (Courtesy New York Historical Society.)

design the new building. He used the then increasingly popular romantic style of the Gothic revival. The construction contract was awarded on August 21, 1855, to George Purves, a prominent architect-builder who had designed and built the nearby Odd Fellows Hall on Lafayette Square in 1849 and 1850 (fig. 7A). He also had designed and built a Gothic-style court house in St. Charles Parish and the Gothic Trinity Church on Jackson Avenue. On November 15, 1856, architect-diarist Wharton noted that he "examined the work on the new Church, Lafayette Square.... The spire is being constructed within the tower and then to be raised into position." He later described the excitement accompanying the raising of the spire. It was successfully accomplished and remained in place until its destruction by the furious hurricane of September, 1915. The church was repaired and continued in use until its demolition in 1938 for the construction of the Federal Building that still occupies the site. The church then built a new building on Claiborne Avenue in uptown New Orleans.

Fig. 6. Interior view of Second Unitarian Church of the Messiah. (Photograph by George F. Mugnier.) (Courtesy Samuel Wilson, Jr., Collection.)

THE METHODIST EPISCOPAL CHURCH

A map of a large part of Faubourg St. Mary drawn by Frederick Wilkinson on March 1, 1837, indicates the location of many of the churches and other prominent buildings in the area (fig. 8). On the lower side of Gravier Street between Carondelet and Baronne is shown the "Old Methodist Church." Little is known of this first Methodist Church on a lot purchased for it by Judge Edward McGehee in 1824, but Wilkinson's plan also shows the "New Methodist Church" then being completed at the uptown-river corner of Poydras and Carondelet streets. This lot also was

Fig. 7. First Presbyterian Church, on Lafayette Square. (Courtesy Samuel Wilson, Jr., Collection.)

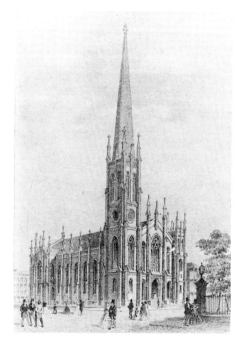

Fig. 7A. Second First Presbyterian Church, Henry Howard architect. (Courtesy Louisiana State Museum.)

purchased by Judge McGehee and other church members on March 6, 1835. On January 20, 1837, a contract was made with Charles B. Dakin, architect and former partner of James Gallier, and his brother James H. Dakin, who had come from New York the previous year. The facade of the church was similar to that of the Lafayette Square Presbyterian Church of the Greek Doric order, but the spire was an unusual Egyptian temple-like base surmounted by a tall octagonal obelisk, described in the 1838 *City Directory* as "a large octangular obelisk resting on a lofty pedestal of the Egyptian-order of architecture, combining a novel grandeur and beauty to be seen in no other similar structure in the Union" (fig. 9).

This unusual building unfortunately was destroyed by the same fire that destroyed Dr. Clapp's old church in 1851, sparks from the burning St. Charles Hotel evidently igniting both these churches.

The Methodists then sold the site of the old church, one of the lots being purchased by architect-builder George Purves on June 6, 1852. In the meantime, another lot had been acquired on Carondelet Street between Lafayette and Girod and a new church was soon erected, a fine late-Greek Revival building with an Ionic portico on a rusticated basement, surmounted by an octagonal domed belfry (see Inventory, page 152). A broad flight of steps led to a recessed entrance porch in the center of the portico. In 1905 this building was sold to the Scottish Rite Masons, and it is still standing as the Scottish Rite Cathedral. The church then moved to a new building on St. Charles Avenue above Lee Circle, a Romanesque-style brick building that was demolished when the Mississippi River bridge was built across the site in the 1950s. A new church was then built at Canal street at Jefferson Davis Parkway.

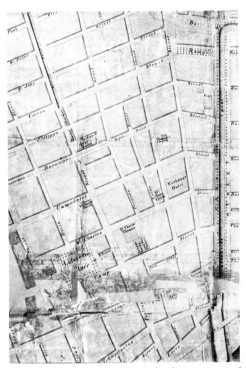

Fig. 8. Plan showing Methodist Episcopal Church and State House with rear wings. Drawing by Frederic Wilkinson, dated March 1, 1837, Plan Book 92, Folio 30, New Orleans Notarial Archives.

ST. PATRICK'S CHURCH

It was not until 1833 that the English-speaking Roman Catholics of New Orleans, most of whom were Irish immigrants living above Canal Street, organized a new parish separate from St. Louis Cathedral, which until then was the only Catholic parish in the city. Appropriately, the new church was dedicated to St. Patrick, patron of Ireland. A site was obtained on Camp Street between Girod and Julia and a small frame church constructed by the architect-builders Sidel and Stewart. Plans were underway for replacing this temporary building with a large, permanent structure (see Inventory, page 121).

St. Patrick's has suffered little change in its appearance, although the devout Irish who built it have long since moved from the area and the church is without a resident congregation. It is maintained by visitors and worshippers from other parishes who love the old church and contribute to its support. Although the exterior of the building has lost the upper pinnacles of its tower and the rich Gothic mouldings intended by Dakin have been replaced by a rough textured 20th century stucco, Dakin's church, with Gallier's great entrance doors, high altar and interior fittings, is the only one of the early churches of Faubourg St. Mary to survive until today. It is the oldest church building erected for a Catholic parish in New Orleans and served as the pro-cathedral when the St. Louis Cathedral was being rebuilt in 1850. It was in St. Patrick's that Antoine Blanc was installed as first archbishop of New Orleans.

Fig. 9. Methodist Episcopal Church, from *Norman's*. (Courtesy New Orleans Public Library.)

THE MARINERS CHURCH AND GRACE CHURCH

Among other churches that have stood in Faubourg St. Mary were the Mariners Church of 1827 on Canal Street, demolished when the Custom House was begun on the site in the 1840s; the First Baptist Church at St. Charles and Julia streets; Grace Episcopal Church on South Rampart near Canal; the Jesuit Church of the Immaculate Conception on Baronne near Canal; St. Katherine's Church on Tulane Avenue; and the Touro Synagogue on Carondelet.

The Mariners Church was organized by a group of New Orleanians interested in the welfare of the many seamen who visited the rapidly growing port of New Orleans. Plans for a handsome building with a raised basement, a pedimented portico and a handsome belfry were completed by architect-surveyor Joseph Pilie on September 13, 1827 (fig. 10). The use of a site adjacent to the old Custom House was obtained, and a contract for the construction of the building was awarded on March 23, 1828, to Philip Snow Hamblet, Jonathan Chase and James Gardiner, builders. Work on the building was begun, but financial and perhaps other difficulties prevented its completion in accordance with Pilie's beautiful plans. The unfinished structure was sketched in the 1830s by Charles Alexandre Le Sueur (fig. 11), and Joseph Holt Ingraham, in his *The Southwest by a Yankee* (1835), referred to it as "a huge, dark coloured, unshapely pile of brick, originally erected for a *Bethel church* for seamen, but never finished, and seldom occupied except by itinerant showmen with their wonders." When work on the new Custom House was begun in the 1840s, all that was left of what had been designed as a truly distinguished church building disappeared.

On January 18, 1846, the Reverend Charles Fay, an Episcopal minister, began to hold services at the corner of Carondelet and Perdido streets, and the following year a new parish was formed under the name of Grace Church. By 1851 a considerable sum had been subscribed for the erection of a church, but dissension arose over the proposed site for the building and in 1853 the project was abandoned. In 1872 the name of Grace Church was dropped from the roll of the Episcopal Church.

When Christ Church decided to move to its present location at St. Charles Avenue and Sixth Street, some of the members felt the church should not move because there was work still to be done in the downtown area. They then formed a new church called the Church in the Upper Room, meeting on Baronne Street near Canal. The new church soon took the abandoned name of Grace Church and erected a small, rather crude Gothic church on Rampart near Canal (fig. 12), using the roof slates and many of the windows of the old Christ Church building when it was demolished in 1886 to be replaced by the ornate, Victorian Mercier Building. This large commercial building was in time demolished for the construction of the present Maison Blanche Building in 1906.

THE JESUIT CHURCH OF THE IMMACULATE CONCEPTION

In 1814 the Jesuit Order was restored by papal decree, but it was not until 1847 that the Jesuit Fathers returned to New Orleans where their plantation had been seized in 1763 when the Order was suppressed. On June 8, 1848, the Jesuits purchased the first part of the large property at the corner of Baronne and Common streets where their church and school later were to be erected. This was part of the land that had once been theirs, part of the plantation they had bought from Bienville in 1726. It was later part of the city commons and had been bought at the city's auction of the commons in 1818 by the First Presbyterian Church. The Presbyterians, however, decided to build their church on St. Charles between Gravier and Union, and it was from Alfred Hennen that the Jesuits purchased the two lots at the corner of Baronne and Common in 1848. In 1849 and 1850 additional lots facing Baronne Street were bought and work was soon begun on the great Hispano-Moresque church, which, although rebuilt in 1929, still looks much the same as it did when first built (see Inventory, page 106.

FIRST BAPTIST CHURCH

The First Baptist Church also had its origins in Faubourg St. Mary. Although Baptist missionaries were sent to New Orleans as early as 1816 and held intermittent services in the home of Cornelius Paulding and in a building he erected in 1833 (see fig. 5), it was not until 1843 that the First Baptist Church was organized. The church was chartered in 1845, and the following year members erected a $4,000 church on three lots of ground that had been purchased on St. Charles between Julia and St. Joseph streets. No pictures or descriptions of this modest building are known, but financial difficulties intervened and brought about the sale of the property in 1851. Thus ended the Baptist Church in Faubourg St. Mary. From 1854 until it was reorganized in 1860, the congregation met with the Coliseum Place Church, which built the well-known red brick church on Coliseum Square in 1856.

Fig. 10. Mariners Church

Fig. 11. Mariners Church, drawn by Charles Alexandre Le Sueur. (Courtesy Leonard V. Huber Collection.)

Fig. 12. Grace Church, circa 1905. (Photograph by Nina King.)

TOURO SYNAGOGUE

When Christ Church moved from its original location at Canal and Bourbon streets in 1847, the old Ionic Temple-type church that had been designed by Gallier and Dakin in 1835 was purchased by Judah Touro and converted into a Jewish synagogue for the Congregation Dispersed of Judah (see fig. 1). Touro in 1840 had purchased the adjacent rectory and occupied it as his own residence. The reredos of the Christ Church altar, with its beautifully carved Greek Corinthian columns copied from the monument of Lysicrates at Athens, was converted into the synagogue's ark, and other interior alterations were made. Even the roof had to be rebuilt, and it was the spring of 1850 before the work was completed and the building dedicated as a synagogue. The following year, Touro built a Hebrew school next to the synagogue, probably facing Bourbon Street. However, soon after Touro's death in 1854 the congregation sold the old Christ Church properties that he had given them, purchased a new site on Carondelet between Julia and St. Joseph streets and erected a new synagogue (fig. 13).

The new building, like the old one on Canal Street, was in the form of a Greek Ionic temple and was designed by W. A. Freret, Jr., architect, and erected by Little and Middlemiss. The consecration took place on April 1, 1857, and architect-diarist T. K. Wharton who attended remarked that "the arrangements of the interior [are] similar to that of the great and ancient synagogue at Amsterdam."

Wharton evidently had submitted designs for the building and mentioned on February 8, 1856, that he had been to see "Mr. Kursheedt about the plan of New Jewish Synagogue." As early as March 14, 1855, he "commenced a sketch for a new synagogue at the request of Mr. William Florance" and a week later recorded that "by working every night this week until quite late, have finished a general design for a new synagogue on St. Charles Street (with buildings accessory thereto) which if approved, will furnish the basis of a complete set of plans for said proposed structure." As Wharton and Freret were good friends, it is possible that they may have collaborated in some way on the design.

Fig. 13. Touro Synagogue (later Knights of Columbus Hall and Carpenters Hall). (Courtesy Leonard V. Huber Collection.)

The new synagogue was a handsome building and many believed that it was actually the old Christ Church moved to a new location. It is possible that the Ionic capitals may have been reused, as well as the ark and the former reredos of Christ Church.

In 1907 the congregation built a new synagogue in which the old ark, extensively restored, was again used. The Carondelet Street building was sold to the Knights of Columbus, who added flanking wings near the rear. In the 1930s the old synagogue again changed hands and was occupied for a few years by the Carpenter's Union and then demolished, to be replaced by an automobile show room.

ST. JOSEPH'S CHURCH

The *Daily Picayune* of September 18, 1852, carried an article on "Building Improvements: New Churches," which noted: "There are several very handsome churches now in process of erection or completion in this city.... The Church of St. Joseph on Common street (Tulane Avenue), opposite the Charity Hospital, is a very fine edifice and built of brick. This building was commenced in 1847. In 1849 it was put in charge of its present architect, Mr. T. E. Giraud, who has already been mentioned by us as the architect of the Jesuit Church and the Pelican Club House, and under whose supervision it is now being finished. This church is conceived in the style of the middle of the fifteenth century" (figs. 14A, B).

The parish of St. Joseph's was established in 1844, one of several established by Bishop Antoine Blanc in the 1840s and 1850s to care for the rapidly expanding population of the city. The building was a simple but elegant Gothic revival structure with a square tower and tall spire. The beautifully detailed interior was divided into nave and side aisles by clustered columns supporting side galleries. The nave vaulting was of the fan type with unusual pendant vaulting in the center.

In 1869 ground was broken for a new and larger St. Joseph's further out across Tulane Avenue at Derbigny. On March 31, 1871, before notary W. J. Castell, the Reverend Thomas J. Smith, C. M., contracted with James Reynolds, a builder, for the stonework for St. Joseph's new church, according to a plan by Thomas O'Neill, the stone to come from St. Genevieve, Missouri. (Thomas O'Neill was the builder of the still-existing hall at the corner of Lafayette and O'Keefe, a large three-story brick building for the Turner Society of New Orleans, for which William Thiel was the architect in 1861.) In 1875 work on the church was discontinued and did not resume for more than ten years. New plans apparently were prepared for this massive Romanesque church by P. C. Keely, an architect of Brooklyn, New York. It was 1892 before the building was ready for use. The new church was the largest ever built in the city, although it has never been completed, the projected towers, apse and transepts never having been built.

The old church opposite the Charity Hospital was then renovated by the Vincentian Fathers who had administered St. Joseph's since 1858. When these renovations were completed in 1895, the old church was established as a separate parish for Negroes and dedicated to St. Katherine of Sienna in honor of Mother Katherine Drexel, who devoted her life and private fortune to Negro education through the Order of the Blessed Sacrament which she had founded. Xavier University in New Orleans is one result of her philanthropies.

Fig. 14B. St. Joseph's Church. Interior detail of fan vaulting. (Photograph by Arthur Kastler, 1966.)

Fig. 14A. St. Joseph's Church. (Photograph by Arthur Kastler, 1966.) (Courtesy Special Collections Division, Tulane University Library.)

The old church served its Negro parishioners for many years, but in the 1930s a noticeable sinkage of the building was observed and the tower leaned to such an extent that in 1952 the upper part of it was removed. In 1965 the property, in a badly deteriorated condition, was sold to Loyola University as a site for a proposed dental school and the "Splendid Catholic Church of St. Joseph," as it had been referred to in 1850, was demolished.

FOURTH PRESBYTERIAN CHURCH

The beginnings of what was to become the Fourth Presbyterian Church came about largely through the efforts of Herman Parkard, who came to New Orleans in 1838, distributing religious tracts among the boatmen and raftsmen on the Mississippi. He began the work of organizing and planning a new church but died in 1858 before the new church could be built. At first, a brick church to cost $9,000 was to be built at the corner of Canal and Franklin, but financial problems caused that site to be sold at a considerable profit, and a less expensive site at the corner of South Liberty and Cleveland (Gasquet) streets was purchased (fig. 15). A contract was then made with architect-builders Jamison and McIntosh to erect a handsome plastered-brick church on the new site for $29,000.

The building was a raised structure on a rusticated basement, in which the first services were held on May 6, 1860, and on November 4 that year, the church was dedicated. Entrance was gained through three basement doors in front, above which were three tall circular-headed windows between Ionic pilasters. These six pilasters supported a triangular pediment above which rose a handsome spire, an octagon with Ionic columns supported on a square base. The sides of the building each had six windows similar to the center front one, separated by Doric pilasters.

On May 12, 1872, the church building was sold and the congregation moved to a new location. The name was changed to the Canal Street Presbyterian Church. A new frame church by P. R. Middlemiss, builder, was erected at Canal and Derbigny and later replaced by a brick building. The old church on South Liberty became the Central Congregational Church and was demolished in 1935. A complete set of measured drawings was made by the Historic American Buildings Survey, many of the measurements being made as the demolishers were engaged in its destruction.

MASONIC TEMPLES

In 1812 city surveyor Jacques Tanesse prepared a plan of the city showing the original town and the newer surrounding faubourgs. This was in accordance with a decree of the City Council of June 20, 1812, for the subdivision into lots of the newly acquired Treme plantation in the rear of the city and the lands that reverted to the city through the demolition of the fortifications and the absorption of the city commons. On this map, at the corner of Camp and Gravier streets where the Chamber of Commerce Building now stands, Tanesse shows a single, hipped-roof building, the only building he indicates in Faubourg St. Mary. This structure is marked in French, *PARFAIT UNION*. This was the first Masonic structure in New Orleans and, surprisingly, had been established on this site during the Spanish regime. The disfavor with which the Masonic orders were then regarded by the Catholic King of Spain probably accounts for this first Masonic Temple being constructed outside the city walls.

The site was acquired for the lodge by Thomas Poree from Jean Baptiste Sarpy in 1797 and was "fenced with planks, with the buildings." This was lot 162 of Faubourg St. Mary, adjoining lot 163 that he had previously acquired. The lots were acquired secretly for the Perfect Union Lodge, organized in 1793. No drawings or descriptions of this first Masonic Temple are known but it was probably a simple and unobtrusive structure. When the first Catholic bishop of New Orleans, Luis Penalver y Cardenas, arrived in the city in 1795, he was shocked to find a Masonic lodge, blaming it on the emigration from the western part of the new United States. He reported: "A lodge of free masons has been formed in one of the suburbs of the city and counts among its members officers of the garrison and of the civil administration, merchants, natives and foreigners."

After the Louisiana Purchase, Thomas Poree could transfer title to the property at Camp and Gravier to the lodge. On June 1, 1810, he appeared before the notary Pedesclaux and declared the two lots that he had purchased in 1797, or before,

Fig. 15. Fourth Presbyterian Church (later Congregational Church). Steeple of St. Katherine's Church can be seen in the background. (Photograph by Richard Koch.)

"were acquired...for the Masonic Society under the distinctive title of the Perfect Union No. 29, in session in this Orient of New Orleans and that it was with the funds of this respectable Lodge that he made the payment." This lodge initiated the movement to form a Grand Lodge for the state after Louisiana was admitted to the Union in 1812. Each of the lodges in the state sent three delegates to a meeting held in the Perfect Union Lodge Hall at the corner of Camp and Gravier streets on April 18, 1812, and on June 20 of that year the Grand Lodge of Louisiana was formed.

On October 30, 1817, surveyor Tanesse made a survey of the "Property of the Perfect Union Lodge No. 1, Faubourg St. Mary" on which a large hipped-roof structure is shown with two smaller outbuildings in opposite corners of the lot, one facing Camp Street, the other on Gravier. At its meeting on December 11, 1824, the lodge decided to dispose of its property in the Faubourg and authorized a committee of its officers composed of J. B. Plauche, Manuel Cruzat and Victor St. Victor to arrange for its sale and to seek a new location for the lodge. On June 22, 1825, before notary H. K. Gordon, the first Masonic Temple in Louisiana was sold for $30,000 to Vincent Nolte & Co. to establish a cotton press on the site, probably incorporating the Camp Street outbuilding into the new complex of buildings built around a large yard opening on Camp. Nolte also purchased other property in the adjacent square across Gravier Street, and later a lot in the rear of the lodge property extending to St. Charles Street was added to the cotton press.

In 1826 Nolte, who was associated with the noted banking house of Baring in London, found himself in financial difficulties, and his properties were sold by his creditors, as Nolte bitterly relates in his book *Fifty Years in Both Hemispheres*. The creditors, William Nott, W. W. Montgomery and Laurent Millaudon, became the purchasers. They apparently enlarged and operated the cotton press until 1833 when they sold the property to John Richardson, whose hotel on Conti Street was one of the most prominent in the city. Richardson apparently demolished the old cotton press and erected a series of four-story red brick buildings, typical of the commercial structures of the time. The ground floor stores had the characteristic granite pilasters with brick fronts with well-proportioned windows above. The roofs, hipped at the corner, were covered with slate. Some of the stores of this type and period still survive in the old Faubourg St. Mary, but this row of Richardson's was demolished when the present Chamber of Commerce Building was erected in 1968.

By 1834 the Perfect Union Lodge was holding its sessions on Rampart Street, between Dumaine and St. Philip, and it was not until after 1845 that a Masonic Temple again was located in Faubourg St. Mary. In that year, according to James Gallier's autobiography,

Fig. 16. Commercial Exchange (later second Masonic Temple, now demolished).

> a company was formed to build a Commercial Exchange to front on St. Charles Street. I made the design for it and entered into a contract to erect the building. It consisted of one large room on the lower story intended for the Exchange; another large and lofty room on the second story intended for lectures and public exhibitions and two stories of rooms on each side for offices;...It was found necessary in a short time to alter the arrangements of the building so that the lower story was converted into stores and offices, while the large room above was used as a Masonic lodge; and since that time the whole building has become the property of the Masonic society of New Orleans.

This handsome building at the corner of St. Charles and Perdido was built at a cost of $52,000 and was sold to the Grand Lodge of Louisiana on February 4, 1853 (fig. 16).

In 1860 extensive alterations were made to the building and on December 10, 1860, the *Daily Crescent* reported: "The lofty public hall has been shorn of its loftiness by a flooring some sixteen feet below the former ceiling. On this flooring has been constructed a suite of elegant and capacious lodge rooms.... The new ceiling of the grand salon... and the walls have been decorated in fresco in the most beautiful manner by Mr. Boulet, the scenic artist...."

In 1869 the Masons decided to erect a new temple and purchased a large site on St. Charles Avenue at Tivoli (Lee) Circle. According to Jewell's *Crescent City,* the cornerstone for the new temple was ceremoniously laid on February 15, 1872. "The New Temple will be built according to the design and plans of S. B. Haggart, Esq., the architect selected to supervise its construction," *Jewell's* reported. After the foundations had been constructed, this elaborate project was abandoned and the site was later occupied by the Public Library. In 1891 the old Commercial Exchange building at St. Charles and Perdido was demolished and a new Masonic Temple in the Gothic style with a high peaked roof surmounted by a statue of Solomon replaced it (fig. 17). This new building was designed by architect James Freret, who twenty years before had made a Gothic design for a new Masonic Temple in 1871. In 1926 the present Masonic Temple, in a modified modern Gothic style designed by Sam Stone, replaced it, the third Masonic Temple to occupy the site (fig. 18).

Fig. 17. Old Masonic Temple, corner Perdido and St. Charles, circa 1920. (Photograph by Charles L. Franck; courtesy New Orleans Public Library.)

Fig. 18. Masonic Building on St. Charles Avenue.

III: Houses

With the exception of the Nicolas Gravier house, little is recorded regarding the early houses of Faubourg St. Mary. The sketch map of the city by Mathias James O'Conway in 1793 (fig. 1) shows, along the upper line of the commons, a house near the river marked EVIS'S and behind it "Mr. Gravier's house and garden." These may have been houses remaining from the Jesuit-Pradel period. Beyond these is "Mons'r Percy's garden," followed by "O'Conway's house and lot" and a lot marked "Jean Louis," with "Mons'r Gravier's fields" extending from that point back to the "cypress swamp."

One of the most interesting of the early houses of the new faubourg appears on a drawing by surveyor Mansury Pelletier and architect Hyacinthe Laclotte in 1807 to show the buildup of the levee and batture of the faubourg, indicating the old levee and a new "levee built by the city in 1805 and 1806" (fig. 2). At the corner of Poydras Street and the "Chemin Royal" along the levee is a handsome two-story house. The ground floor has a series of segmental-headed doors and windows, each surrounded by a stucco band and with a key block in each arched head, like those of the Spanish colonial period in the Vieux Carre. The upper story has a gallery along the sides toward Poydras Street and the river and a broad, double-pitched, overhanging roof supported by masonry columns like those of the slightly later Delord-Sarpy house just above the faubourg. Dormer windows and a chimney pierce the roof at the rear and side. At the rear is a small two-story wing with a terrace roof surrounded by a balustrade. Only this drawing from the City Engineer's Office is known of this important colonial structure. Laclotte's drawing also shows a simple little hipped roof, one-story house marked "P. Bailly" at Gravier Street and a two-story hipped roof building with a large American flag at the edge of the commons (fig. 3). These buildings were no doubt among the first in Faubourg St. Mary.

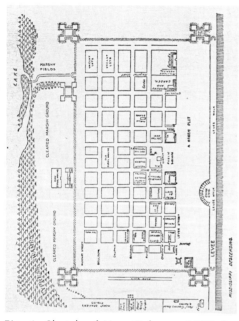

Fig. 1. Sketch of New Orleans, 1793, by Mathias James O'Conway. (Courtesy American Catholic Historic Society of Philadelphia.)

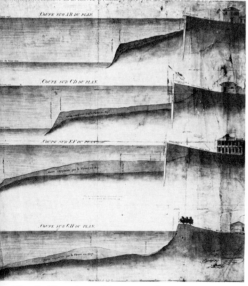

Fig. 3. Drawing of levee at Common, Gravier and Poydras, 1807, by Hyacinthe Laclotte and Mansury Pelletier. (Courtesy Samuel Wilson, Jr., Collection.)

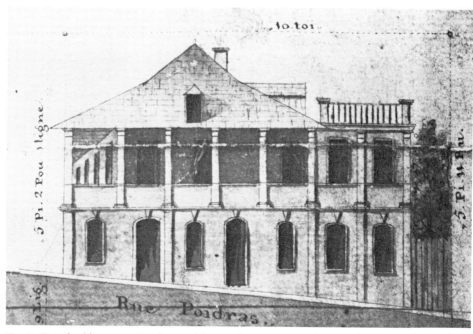

Fig. 2. Detail of house at Poydras and Levee, from an 1807 drawing by Hyacinthe Laclotte and Mansury Pelletier. (Courtesy Samuel Wilson, Jr., Collection.)

Fig. 4. House on Julia, corner Baronne, by J. N. de Pouilly, Plan Book 37, Folio 47, dated December 4, 1847, New Orleans Notarial Archives.

Fig. 5. Elevation of house on Julia, bound by Magazine, Camp and St. Joseph, by Charles Arthur de Armas, Book 12, Folio 38, dated May 8, 1849, New Orleans Notarial Archives.

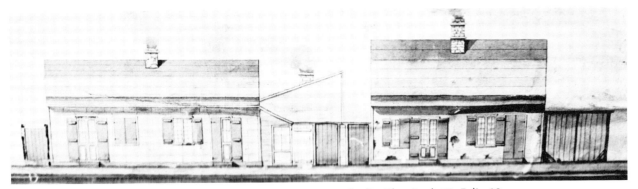

Fig. 6. Houses on Girod, bound by Carondelet, Baronne and Julia, Plan Book 71, Folio 19, New Orleans Notarial Archives.

During the post-Colonial period (1803-1830) the development of the upper faubourg continued slowly. The houses generally followed the form of the small cottages being built at the same time in the outer limits of the Vieux Carre, toward Rampart Street and Esplanade (figs. 4,5,6). Almost none of these simple houses have survived, although the little hipped roof, frame, one-story structure at the corner of Magazine and St. Joesph may be an interesting exception (see page 53).

As more Americans moved into the new suburb, its character soon changed. Benjamin Latrobe remarked in 1819 that

> Americans are pouring in daily, not in families but in large bodies. In a few years therefore, this will be an American town. What is good and bad in the French manners and opinions must give way and the American notions of right and wrong, of convenience and inconvenience will take their place....After a longer residence I shall be better qualified to speak of the private houses. But this much I may say, that altho' the sort of house built here by the French is not the best specimen of French arrangement, yet it is infinitely, in my opinion, superior to that arrangement which we have inherited from the English. But so inveterate is habit that the merchants from the old United States, who are daily gaining ground on the manners, the habits, the opinions, & the domestic arrangements of the French, have already begun to introduce the detestable, lopsided, London house, in which a common passage & stairs acts as a common sewer to all the necessities of the dwelling & renders it impossible to preserve a temperature within the house materially different from that of the atmosphere, as the coughs, colds, & consumptions of our Eastern cities amply testify. With the English arrangement, the red brick fronts are also gaining ground, & the suburb St. Mary, the American suburb, already exhibits the flat, dull, dingy character of Market Street, in Philadelphia, or Baltimore street, instead of the motley & picturesque effect of the stuccoed French buildings of the city. We shall introduce many grand & profitable improvements, but they will take the place of much elegance, ease, & some convenience.

Deploring the increasing use of red brick, Latrobe continued:

> In the Faubourg St. Mary & wherever the Americans build, they exhibit their flat brick fronts with a sufficient number of holes for light & entrance. The only French circumstance which they retain is the balcony in the upper story. The French stucco the fronts of their buildings and often color them; the Americans exhibit their red staring brickwork, imbibing heat thro' the whole unshaded substance of the wall. The old English side-passage house with the stairs at the end is also gaining ground & is taking place of the French porte-cochere....I have no doubt but that the American style will ultimately be that of the whole city, especially as carpenters from the eastern border of the union are the architects, &, of course, work on in their old habits, for men accustomed to these very sort of houses. But altho' room may be thereby gained, the convenience of the houses will by no means be promoted—nor the health of the city improved.

Latrobe's friend, architect-builder-bricklayer William Brand, built a house for himself on Magazine Street between Poydras and Natchez. It was probably to Brand that Latrobe referred when he wrote: "An American bricklayer, a very worthy man, consulted me as to a house he has built for himself on the London plan. I objected to many parts of his design as contrary to every principle of good architecture. He could not well answer my objections, and at last cut the argument short by exclaiming: 'I have been at war with architecture all my life and will continue so to the end, *having all New York in my favor*.'"

W. H. Sparks, in his *Memories of Fifty Years* published in 1872, wrote that in the 1820s "commerce was chiefly conducted by Americans and most of these were of recent establishment in the city. That portion of the city above Canal street, and then known as the Faubourg St. Mary, was little better than a marsh in its greater portion. Along the river and Canal street there was something of a city appearance in the improvements and business where there were buildings. In every other part there were shanties and these were filled with a most miserable population."

By the 1830s, red brick, American style, early Greek Revival houses had sprung up in all parts of Faubourg St. Mary, as well as in the Vieux Carre. Row houses similar to those in New York, Philadelphia and Baltimore appeared, and several companies were organized to build such rows. In 1832 the New Orleans Building Company purchased the entire block on the upper side of Julia Street between Camp and St. Charles and erected a row of three-story and attic row houses that has come to be known as the "Thirteen Sisters" (see Inventory, page 175).

Samuel Livermore, president of the New Orleans Building Company, also built

Fig. 7. Building on Carondelet, bound by Lafayette, Girod and St. Charles, by Charles F. Zimpel, Plan Book 71, Folio 8, dated November 15, 1834, New Orleans Notarial Archives.

Fig. 7A. One of four identical row houses, two of which were the residences of Theodore Clapp and Samuel J. Peters, on Carondelet, bound by Lafayette, Baronne and Poydras. Drawing by Pecquet and Crampon, dated April 20, 1865, Plan Book 77, Folio 21, New Orleans Notarial Archives.

other rows of houses on opposite corners of Carondelet and Lafayette streets. Most of the fine row of three-story houses on the river side of Carondelet Street was demolished when the Barnett Furniture Store was erected on the site in the 1920s. The contract between the New Orleans Building Company and D. H. Twogood was signed before notary Jules Mossy on May 7, 1833, for "the erection of eight three story brick dwelling houses...(fig. 7) in conformity with the plan thereof drawn by A. T. Wood." On May 22, 1833, before the same notary, Livermore contracted with Twogood for two more three-story brick houses on the opposite side of Carondelet between Lafayette and Poydras, also according to the plans of architect A. T. Wood. Livermore was just completing two similar houses adjacent to these, one of which he sold on May 11, 1833, to the noted Unitarian minister, the Reverend Theodore Clapp. The other was sold to Samuel J. Peters, the man so largely responsible for the development of Faubourg St. Mary. Here (fig. 7A) Peters lived until his death in 1854. Dr. Clapp lived in the former until he sold it in 1855. These houses, of such great historical and architectural importance, were pulled down a few years ago and replaced by a parking lot. Some of the fine marble mantels and carved woodwork details were salvaged and incorporated into a restored Vieux Carre residence.

The row house, consisting of two or more identical houses, continued to be built by private investors in this area, and many of them were houses of distinction. Some still stand, but many have disappeared. In 1836 James Gallier built a row of four, two-story houses for Samuel Moore at St. Charles and Girod (see Inventory, page 208) and two years later built six, three-story ones for Charles Diamond on Tchoupi-toulas between St. Joseph and Delord (Howard Avenue) (demolished). In September, 1840, the heirs of John Leslie, an Englishman who died in New Orleans in December, 1839, contracted with William Saunders to build three, two-story houses at the corner of Camp and St. Joseph, according to plans by architect W. L. Atkinson, another Englishman (see Inventory; page 129). Seven months later they were compelled to make a new contract with the well-known builders, Sidle and Stewart, to complete the houses, which were to have "an iron gallery rail like Mr. McCall's house on Camp street." The front and side walls were to be painted red and pencilled, and the blinds were to be painted green. The fine Greek Revival interior details of these houses evidently were adopted from Menard Lafever's *The Beauties of Modern Architecture,* published shortly before that time. The fine plaster centerpiece (fig. 8), door and window trim and cornice details were removed from one of these houses several years ago. They were donated by the owner to the Anglo-American Art Museum at Louisiana State University in Baton Rouge where they have been installed to form a Greek Revival gallery.

In 1844 James H. Dakin made plans for a row of six houses (demolished) at Lafayette and St. John (Basin), built by Jacob Ott for A. M. Holbrook. These were simple frame houses, built in part of flatboat timbers "covered with thin clapboards laid six inches to the weather." Flatboat timbers were salvaged from the flatboats that had come down the Mississippi River and, being unable to re-ascend the river, were broken up for cheap building material.

Gallier Turpin & Co. were the architect-builders for five, three-story stores and dwellings on Poydras and Baronne in 1850 for Samuel J. Peters and his son, and in 1852 John K. Collins built five splendid three-story brick houses with cast-iron balconies (fig. 9) for Thomas Hale. These fine houses, demolished in 1952 for the construction of a YMCA gymnasium, were designed by architect Henry Howard,

Fig. 8. Centerpiece from 865 Camp by architect William Atkinson; now housed in the Louisiana State University Anglo-American Art Museum. (Courtesy Samuel Wilson, Jr., Collection.)

who in 1860 designed two brick dwellings on Baronne between Julia and St. Joseph for Abraham Haber (see Inventory, page 111). These few of the many row houses built in the antebellum period illustrate the changing styles and tastes of the times and the continuity of the basic form.

Individual houses in Faubourg St. Mary generally were built on narrow, deep lots, often between party walls, but sometimes with an open carriageway or garden at one side and a long, narrow courtyard in the rear. Two such houses were built in 1839 by James H. Dakin, architect, for Henry W. Palfrey, one on Carondelet between Julia and Girod and one on Gravier between Baronne and Philippa (Dryades) (demolished). Each house was of two stories, with a gallery having "square antae," or columns, rails and balusters, and, like earlier houses, the front and end walls painted red and pencilled. In 1844 Dakin drew plans for a somewhat similar house on Julia between St. Charles and Carondelet for Benedict Baggett, with Rand and Spooner the builders. Architect Lewis Reynolds, then coming into prominence, in 1848 designed a house (demolished) for notary Hilary B. Cenas on Circus (S. Rampart) between Canal and Common, like the adjoining house of Theodore Rion. Jamison and McIntosh were the builders.

Fig. 9. Five dwellings in the 900 block of Camp designed by architect Henry Howard. (Courtesy Alexander Allison Collection, New Orleans Public Library.)

The building of St. Patrick's Church on Camp Street in the late 1830s was soon followed by an increasing number of fine city houses, many of which still remain. In 1840 architect Francis D. Gott built a house, referred to in the contract as a tenement (rental property), for Colles, Morgan and Glendy Burke on Camp between Poydras and North and extending back to St. Mary (St. Francis). In 1841 Maunsel White had two houses built on Julia near Philippa (Dryades) (demolished). It is interesting to note that the same year two houses of brick-between-posts construction were being built on Circus (S. Rampart) Street between Gravier and Perdido by and for free people of color.

The 1850s witnessed a resurgence of the building of fine residences, mostly in the fringe areas of old Faubourg St. Mary. These were often built on larger lots with gardens around them, houses of the type that were at the same time being built in other suburban areas such as the Garden District. Among the most notable of these was the great Italianate residence of Dr. George W. Campbell at St. Charles and Julia (fig. 10).

During the Civil War occupation of the city, this notable house was seized and used as headquarters for the Federal forces. In a city improvements report in 1859, the *Daily Crescent* listed among new residences "the dwelling of Dr. Campbell---approaching completion; one of the finest in the city; L. E. Reynolds, architect and builder---$40,000." This splendid mansion, built on a site leased from the Poydras Orphan Asylum, had a cast-iron fence of the cornstalk pattern, probably brought from the Philadelphia foundry of Wood and Perot through their New Orleans agents, Wood and Miltenberger. The spiral staircase and elaborately carved interior trim were salvaged when the much-mutilated mansion was demolished in 1965 and replaced by a used car lot. Only the carriage house remains.

Fig. 10. Campbell Mansion, corner St. Charles and Julia, Lewis Reynolds, architect. (Courtesy Samuel Wilson, Jr., Collection.)

Nearby, on St. Charles between Julia and St. Joseph, Joseph H. Murdy in 1856 had built a fine three-story brick house for John P. Cady similar to the Behan residence on Rampart, with a four-foot-wide iron verandah at the second floor. This latter house had been built the previous year by Cook and Moorehouse, builders, for James B. Behan on Rampart next to the residence of E. J. McCall, between Canal and Common. The McCall house, adjacent to that of H. B. Cenas, had also been built by Cook and

Fig. 11. Spiral staircase in Kock house on Rampart Street. (Courtesy Samuel Wilson, Jr., Collection.)

Moorehouse in 1853 for Evan Jones McCall. Henry Howard was the architect for this three-story brick house that included among its more modern features a tub, shower and water closet. The specifications called for "the verandah to be finished …with ornamental and fancy pattern iron railings, pilasters, brackets and cornice in the best and richest style." Perhaps the most elegant of these new residences being built on this fashionable street was the home of Charles Kock, built for him by Little and Middlemiss at an initial cost of $36,875 and additions of $12,500. The spiral staircase, with its skylighted dome above and its elaborate enframing Corinthian columns and cornices, must have been one of the finest in the city (fig. 11). This great house later became a fashionable dress designer's establishment and was demolished in the 1930s. The California Building now occupies part of the site.

Lafayette Square was also a fashionable residential center. One of the earliest of the great Lafayette Square houses was the one built by Samuel B. Slocomb adjacent to the site later occupied by the City Hall (fig. 12). This house was built shortly before Slocomb's death in 1834, and his widow, Cora Ann Cox Slocomb, lived there until some years after the Civil War. It was bought by the Howard family, who later sold it to the city as an annex to the City Hall, known as the Howard Annex. In 1839 Dakin and Dakin added a back building to the residence of Dr. Levi S. Parmley on North Street fronting the square. Across the park, at South and Camp, A. T. Wood contracted to build in 1834 a three-story house for Jacob Levy Florance. This was later enlarged or replaced by a larger one that became a hotel known as the Florance House. In 1854 Baumiller and Goodwin, builders, erected around this building a fine cast-iron gallery 131 feet, 6 inches in length on cast-iron columns extending through two stories above. The patterns for the castings were selected from the catalog of Horton and Macy of Cincinnati, Ohio. It was in this interesting old building that the Christian Women's Exchange had its first home (fig. 13).

Near this house in 1856 Little and Middlemiss built another fine brick three-story

Fig. 12. New Orleans City Hall, with Slocomb House at right, from an etching by Louis Schwarz. (Courtesy Historic New Orleans Collection.)

house for Alfred Penn, with William A. Freret the architect. This house, too, had the convenience of indoor plumbing, the specifications stating that "the bathroom shall have a neat moulded wood panelled bathing tub with shower bath, neatly lined with lead and supplied with all necessary pipes and cocks for hot and cold water." These interesting South Street houses were demolished along with the neighboring First Presbyterian Church in the 1930s when the present Federal Building was constructed.

In 1855 Wm. Drews and Co. built a fine three-story brick residence for Carl Kohn on St. Charles opposite Lafayette Square, dismantling most of his former residence on the site. Plans were drawn by Drews and Charles Hillger.

Other elegant residences were built in the area of Tivoli Circle (Lee Circle) in the 1850s and early 1860s, but with the coming of the Civil War, the building of residences in old Faubourg St. Mary ended and the area gradually lost its residential character. Among the few post-Civil War residences built there was the rectory for St. Patrick's Church, in 1874, with Henry Howard the architect and Thomas Mulligan the builder. This house, with some alterations, is still in use as the church rectory.

Fig. 13. Christian Woman's Exchange, South Street and Camp, from the *Picayune's Guide to New Orleans* (1900).

IV: Markets and Theatres

Faubourg St. Mary and the adjacent Common and Canal street area in the 19th century contained many of the city's most important and impressive public and private buildings. Besides its residences, banks, churches, Masonic temples and commercial structures discussed elsewhere in this volume, the new faubourg contained great public markets, theatres, hotels, exchanges, hospitals, schools, municipal buildings (figs. 1,2) and other monumental structures, few of which remain.

Among the earliest of these was the St. Mary Market (see Inventory, page 219), built on a site reserved for it in the upper part of the faubourg between North and South Market streets, now known as Diamond Street. The first section of the market, designed by city surveyor Joseph Pilie, followed closely the design of the older *Halles des Boucheries* of the French Market, designed by city surveyor Jacques Tanesse in 1813. The first unit of the St. Mary Market, 165 feet long, was built by Mitchell and Lemoine at a cost of $22,000 in 1822, a year before the vegetable market was erected in the Vieux Carre. Additions by J. D. Baldwin in 1830 and 1836 more than doubled the size of this handsome arcaded structure that for years was an important center of activity in the American section of New Orleans. It was described in 1838 as "plainly but firmly built of brick, plastered to imitate granite, with a wooden frame roof and tile covering." No sign of this once important structure remains except the site on which it stood, the Diamond Street neutral ground.

In 1837 and 1838, another public market was built on the neutral ground of Poydras Street. Its original plans were drawn by Frederick Wilkinson, surveyor of the Second Municipality and architect of Jackson Barracks and Cypress Grove Cemetery. Wilkinson specified that the pillars and roof frame should be entirely of iron, with a zinc roof and flagstone floor to insure incombustability. Because of a delay in procuring the iron, the roof design was changed to wood covered with slate. The

Fig. 1. Design for the Louisiana Hose House, by Dakin, June 28, 1841. (Courtesy New Orleans Public Library.)

picturesque old market that extended from near Baronne Street to Rampart continued in operation through the 1920s when it was demolished. A third market to serve the area was erected in 1871 (fig. 3) on the Claiborne Avenue neutral ground and was also demolished in the late 1920s or early 1930s.

Theatres were another interesting and important element in the development of Faubourg St. Mary. James Caldwell who introduced gas for lighting and was influential in obtaining the paving of streets in the new faubourg, built the first American Theatre on Camp Street (fig. 4). The cornerstone of the theatre, on Camp Street (opposite Natchez Alley), was laid on May 29, 1822, and the theatre opened a year later. *Gibson's Guide* (1838) said that "for the earliest building of its kind [it] is a handsome and spacious structure." *Gibson's* added that "at the time of laying the

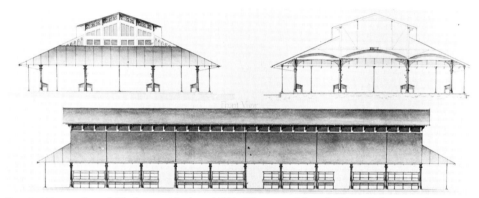

Fig. 3. Watercolor of Claiborne Market, 1871. (Courtesy Historic New Orleans Collection.)

Fig. 4. American Theatre, built in 1823, from the Zimpel map (1834). (Courtesy Historic New Orleans Collection.)

Fig. 2. Louisiana Hose Co. building, from *History of the Fire Department of New Orleans* (1895). (Courtesy Samuel Wilson, Jr., Collection.)

Fig. 5. American Theatre and Arcade Baths. (Courtesy Historic New Orleans Collection.)

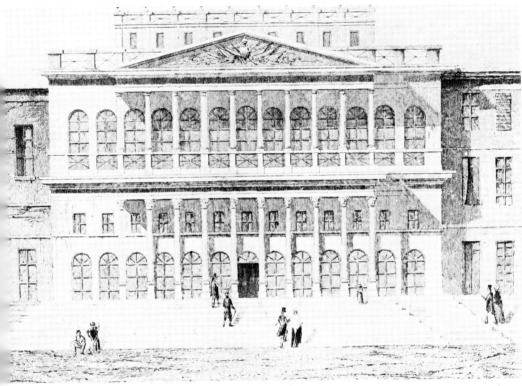

Fig. 6. Drawing of the St. Charles Theatre, by Lemaitre. (Courtesy Historic New Orleans Collection.)

foundation of the Camp Theatre there were no houses nearer to it than at the corner of Common street, and it was with great difficulty it could be reached in wet weather." The building of this theatre was a great stimulus to the area, and in 1835 Caldwell began adjacent to it construction of the handsome Corinthian porticoed Arcade Baths (fig. 5), with James Gacher the builder. The portico and glazed roof arcade were dispensed with, however, and the contract price reduced from $50,000 to $40,000.

In 1835 Caldwell also began the construction of a new and longer theatre behind the one on Camp Street, facing on St. Charles, from which it took its name of the St. Charles Theatre (fig. 6). Its cornerstone was laid on May 9, 1835, and the theatre opened on November 30 of the same year. The St. Charles, designed by Anthony Mondelli, was said to be the largest and finest theatre in the United States, exceeded in size only by one in Russia and two in Italy. It is said to have cost $350,000 and *Gibson's Guide* (1838) says that "this magnificent temple of the Drama was...built entirely by James H. Caldwell, to whose enterprise and energy the upper section of our city owes so much...the proudest monument of zeal and industry ever raised to the honor of an individual citizen in his life time." Unfortunately, this splendid building was destroyed by fire on March 12, 1842, a fire that also damaged Caldwell's Arcade Baths in the rear. The theatre was immediately rebuilt by others, but on a much smaller and less imposing style. A third St. Charles Theatre was built on the same site in 1902, Favrot and Livaudais being the architects. It was demolished about 1967 after having been unused for a number of years. The site is now a parking lot.

On November 10, 1840, a new American Theatre was opened by Mark Ludlow and Solomon Smith, theatre pioneers in the South. According to a study of this theatre by Jane Vaughters in the Tulane University Library, the building on the upper side of Poydras between Camp and St. Francis and running through to Lafayette Square had been begun as a livery stable, but the plans were altered by F. D. Gott and A. Mondelli. Not as large as the St. Charles, it nevertheless had an impressive interior, and like the St. Charles, was destroyed by fire in 1842. It was poorly rebuilt and again destroyed by fire. T. K. Wharton referred to it as "that abomination" and on April 20, 1854, recorded in his diary: "Last night that *ancient nuisance* and perpetual eye sore that American Theatre, was effectively annihilated. ...When I reached Lafayette Square the Theatre and the entire block on which it stands were wrapt in sheets of fire." The great cast-iron Moresque Building was erected on the site a few years later (see Inventory, page 102).

Other theatres built around the turn of the century were the Tulane and the Crescent on Baronne, on the site of the old buildings of the University of Louisiana. Numerous motion picture theatres arose on Canal, Baronne and St. Charles, climaxed by the building of the Saenger and Loew's State theatres in the 1920s.

The University buildings (fig. 7) were built in the rear part of what had been the State House Square, facing Common Street, and it is possible that parts of the old State House were incorporated into the new buildings. The first of these was the Medical College, designed by Dakin and built in 1842-1843 near the corner of Common and Philippa (Dryades). By 1848 this first building had become a preparatory or grammar school, and a new and larger building had been built for the medical school. A third building, near the corner of Common and Baronne, was contemplated to complete the symmetrical trio. On February 27, 1848, the *Daily Delta* presented a front page illustrated account of the progress being made and remarked that the new central building "is 100 feet in front by 109 feet deep, fronted by a very beautiful *facade* which is supported by six Corinthian pillars. ...The cost of the building when completed will be about $40,000. ...As soon as the buildings are completed the grounds will be enclosed and handsomely laid off."

Behind the University a building was erected facing Dryades Street in 1851 for the Mechanics Institute. R. P. Rice was the architect. This structure burned on December 26, 1854, and new plans by James Gallier were adopted the following

Fig. 7. University of Louisiana on State House Square. (Courtesy Historic New Orleans Collection.)

Fig. 8. The Mechanic's Institute, from Jewell's *Crescent City*.

Fig. 9. City Hotel, built in 1831, from the Zimpel map (1834). (Courtesy Historic New Orleans Collection.)

Fig. 9A. City Hotel after remodeling, 187: from Jewell's *Crescent City*.

December. Progress was slow, and in March, 1857, it was described as "still in the rough brick and mortar stage." The building was used as a State Capitol during the Civil War occupation and Reconstruction period and eventually became part of the University. Behind it, facing Baronne Street was Grunewald Hall which, with the old Mechanics Institute (fig. 8), was demolished and replaced by the Grunewald Hotel.

Hotels were an important element in Faubourg St. Mary. Bishop's City Hotel, designed by Charles F. Zimpel in 1831 (figs. 9,9A), stood at the corner of Camp and Common, just above Canal, and was a popular stopping place for American travellers. The St. Charles, designed by Gallier and Dakin, was built in 1835. The same year, on May 15, 1835, a smaller Canal Street establishment, the Planters Hotel which had been built before 1827, collapsed with several casualties (fig. 10). Overton Seawell advertised in the 1830 *Paxton's Directory* that he had "taken the above named well known [Planters] Hotel on Canal street, formerly kept by Thomas Beale and recently by Mr. Harvey Elkins. The building is spacious, situated near the levee and contiguous to the shipping and steam boat landings." In July, 1835, plans for rebuilding it as a four-story hotel were drawn by Thomas Irwin, and the building was erected by Jonathan Chase.

The Verandah (fig. 11), diagonally opposite the St. Charles, was designed by

Fig. 10. Destruction of Planters Hotel, by Currier. (Courtesy Historic New Orleans Collection.)

Dakin and Dakin for Richard O. Pritchard, taking its name from the iron galleries along its St. Charles and Common street facades. The Verandah burned on July 19, 1855, and a new building, now the John Mitchell Hotel, was erected on the site (see Inventory, page 199). Another important hotel built in the 1850s was the St. James, which was used as a Union hospital during the Civil War. In badly deteriorated condition, it was demolished in 1966 and replaced by the Board of Trade Plaza.

Fig. 11. Verandah Hotel. (Courtesy Historic New Orleans Collection.)

City Timescape
—The Shifting Scene

BERNARD LEMANN

The City of New Orleans, and in particular its vital commercial center, has shared a pattern of development with nearly every major American city—a promising 18th century colonial background, a 19th century of energetic Americanization and a 20th century with the threats or, indeed, the crisis, of megalopolis (fig. 1).

New Orleans has shared the American destiny, yes—but with a difference. More than a century ago the impersonal eye of many a transient noted the causes that

Fig. 1. Camp Street perspective, divided by St. Charles, from the 1840s to the 1970s (see Inventory).

made the difference: the relaxed ways of a subtropical atmosphere; the tolerance and easy moral code; the colorful scenes, including the rapid mellowing effects of climate on buildings and the rather lackadaisical sanitation; and the extraordinary ethnic mix.

Note, for example, an 1842 description by one of New Orleans' international visitors, a Monsieur Isidore Löwenstern, a geographer from Paris and member of the Order of Knights Hospitalers. In his first paragraph on New Orleans he noted the picturesque mixture of French and Spanish flavor, the long, unhealthy summers that forced everyone who could to escape, the numerous spectacles and balls and the lively character of the inhabitants. A visit here is like life itself, since one must make the most of his time, he said, with one of those typically Gallic negatives, "l'on n'est pas dans le pays des puritains."

Or, as seen by a self-styled "Yankee," author of a series of letters entitled *The South West* (1835), it was

> the city of Frenchmen and garlic soups, steamboats and yellow fever, negroes and quadroons, hells and convents, soldiers and slaves, and things, and people of every language and kindred, nation and tribe upon the face of the earth.

Observers today reiterate this theme. New Orleans has its business-like goals, but always modified by long-entrenched local traditions. In his plea for revitalization of the Central Business District, the Mayor has declared that "the future of our city... cannot be foretold by looking to other places. It is to be found by looking at what we've been and what we are." He also said: "I know politicians are not supposed to wonder about these things. I'm a politician, but I'm also a New Orleanian, and that means I'm different" (*Times-Picayune*, May 5, 1972). A leading entrepreneur and controlling influence in the district's expansion has offered a similar comment: "New Orleans has never been... the boom type [but a] kind of stable, slow town that never goes in any one direction.... You know there are other things besides business climate in a city.... The social climate in a city is important" (*Dixie*, June 11, 1972).

Somewhat along the same line, nationally syndicated newspaper columnist Russell Kirk reported: "Of the twenty biggest cities in this land, perhaps New Orleans still retains the fairest prospect for reinvigoration short of bulldozing and starting over again afresh.... Though New Orleans has real difficulties today, still that city keeps a civic character, a vigor in neighborhoods, and an architectural patrimony that have vanished, perhaps forever, in most other old American cities" (*State-Times*, Baton Rouge, October 14, 1971).

All these statements do indeed bring up to date the long-time recognition of a unique set of circumstances, qualities and visual aspects in New Orleans that have set it apart from the cities of the world in spite of its relatively lesser size or wealth. One noteworthy historic circumstance that makes the central core atypical as compared with normal urban patterns is the manner in which the development shifted its site. The earliest of the city's three expansions, the Faubourg St. Mary, rapidly ceased to be a suburb and became the major source of growth. It was as though New Orleans had made a complete flip and stepped out of its past into a new geographic and chronological area that was to be the foundation of what it is today. Beginning in 1836 for a stretch of seventeen years, it was like twin cities, adjacent but distinct and separate, and not very compatible twins at that. Alexander MacKay, an Englishman who passed through New Orleans in 1847 remarked on this contrast...between the old town and the American quarter. The dividing line between them is Canal-street, a broad and spacious thoroughfare, lined throughout with trees dividing the two quarters from each other....But still the contrast is very great, as not only exhibiting a marked difference in architecture, but also a difference of race. You not only, in crossing Canal-street, seem to bound from one century into another, but you might also fancy that you had crossed the boundary line between two coterminous nations.

Already well established was the continuous local tradition of internal dissension, of a town that never goes in any one direction. All the descriptions and accounts never fail to mention the predominance of the French language, in speech and street signs, during the first half of the century, especially in the lower portion of the city, which did not immediately give up its dominance. Norman's descriptive guide of 1845 tells of an old Frenchman who had never ventured above Canal Street and his amused incredulity when told it was not just an old water bog up there, but the busy streets of a rising city.

But the ultimate source of misapprehensions in this latter-day Babel was, as today, monetary motivation, much more than life-styles or languages. In several passages of his *Memories of Fifty Years,* W. H. Sparks describes the situation vividly:

The Gallic or French-American is less enterprising, yet sufficiently so for the necessary uses of life; he is more honest and less speculative...more open and less designing...more refined and less presumptuous, and altogether a man of more chivalrous spirit and purer aspirations. The Anglo-American commences to succeed and will not scruple at the means...and this is called enterprise combined with energy. Moral considerations may cause him to hesitate but never restrain his action. The maxim is ever present in his mind: it is honorable and respectable to succeed—dishonest and disreputable to fail; it is only folly to yield a bold enterprise to nice considerations of moral right. If he can avoid the penalties of the civil law, success obviates those of the moral law.

Like most striking generalizations, this offers a clear-cut guideline toward the approximate region of Truth, rather than the pure, unadulterated product itself. It sets our time in perspective, this American century, against its preparatory background during which all that we are was already in the works. Yet, in its simplified form, it fails to explain, for example, how after all it was a Frenchman, Louis-Philippe, the Bourgeois King from 1830 to 1848 (previously, while in exile in New Orleans, a house guest of Bernard Marigny), who proclaimed the keynote, *enrichissez–vous,* the motto, guiding principle and ultimate virtue of 19th century laissez faire mercantilism, the foundation of the more expansionist free enterprise of today.

In greater particularity, Sparks recounts the local situation, in which it is revealed that the original French segment of the city, while it still held the preponderant influence, was not above a certain reactionary ignominiousness.

There was not, forty years ago, or in 1828, a paving stone above Canal Street, nor could any necessity induce the government of the city to pave a single street. Where now stands the great St. Charles Hotel, there was an unsightly and disgusting pond of fetid water, and the locations now occupied by the City Hotel and the St. James were cattle-pens. There was not a wharf in the entire length of the city, and the consequence was an enormous tax levied upon produces, in the shape of drayage and repairs of injuries to packages....
    The navigation of the Bayou St. John commanded, for the lower portion of the city, the commerce crossing the lake, and to monopolize the profits of travel,

a railroad was proposed from the lake to the river, and speedily completed [Ponchartrain Railroad, 1831]. The people of the Faubourg, to counteract as much as possible these advantages, constructed a canal from the city to the lake [New Basin, 1832-38], which was to enter the city, or Faubourg St. Mary, at the foot of Julia Street, one of the broadest and best streets in that quarter of the city. This was of sufficient capacity for schooners and steamboats of two hundred tons burden. When it was completed, with great difficulty the authorities were prevailed upon to pave Julia Street; still the greatly increasing demands of commerce were neglected, and while by these refusals the population of the city proper was doing all it could to force down to the city [i.e. below Canal Street] this increasing trade, they neglected to do anything there for its accommodation. The streets were very narrow; the warehouses small and inconvenient; the merchants close and unenterprising, seemingly unconscious of the great revolution going on in their midst.

These and other conditions led to a legislative amendment establishing the separate municipalities, each with its own system of taxation. Meanwhile, the Faubourg St. Mary, fed by the rich midland of the entire continent, continued to forge ahead. Through history, the long-term memory, we come to recognize this inescapable Anglo-Franco background as it perseveres in the business and social climate now.

After a look at the general state of affairs that prevailed during virtually the entire century, it might be useful to scan the successive stages of development, very rapidly, in order to view the historic panorama and still keep in sight the unchanging qualities of the locale.

Well past the mid-century of the Faubourg, a lingering sense of the drenched land in its primeval state remained. Indeed, its visual reminders hovered with forceful emphasis in a tight proximity of girdling wasteland that seemed to seep into the muddy roadways of the hopeful little new town.

In one of his stories from *Old Creole Days,* George Washington Cable included a description, too graphic to be entirely fictional, that could have reflected the memories of older persons still living in 1879. Here the disintegration of colonial settlement in the area is pictured in retrospect from the viewpoint of rising modern times:

> In the first decade of the nineteenth century, when the newly established American Government was the most hateful thing in Louisiana — when the Creoles were still kicking at such vile innovations as trial by jury, American dances, anti-smuggling laws and the printing of the Governor's proclamation in English...there stood, a short distance above what is now Canal Street, and considerably back from the line of villas that fringed the river-bank on Tchoupitoulas Road, an old colonial plantation-house half in ruin.
>
> It stood aloof from civilization, the tracts that had once been its indigo fields given over to their first noxious wildness....Its dark, weatherbeaten roof and sides were hoisted above the jungly plain in a distracted way...Two lone forest-trees, dead cypresses, stood in the center of the marsh, dotted with roosting vultures. The shallow strips of water were hid by myriads of aquatic plants, under whose coarse and spiritless flowers, could one have seen it, was a harbor of reptiles, great and small.

As one tramps amid the dramatic concrete canyons in the vicinity, say, of today's Civic Center, the pavement hardly yields to the spongy remains of rotted jungle, still there just barely beneath our footsteps. As late as the 1830s, Sparks recollected, this same part of the city above Canal Street "was little better than a marsh in its greater portion. Along the river and Canal Street, there was something of a city appearance....In every other part there were shanties, and these were filled with a most miserable population.''

The very earliest convincing documentary of New Orleans' cityscape is a series of rare lithographs by Felix Achille Beaupoil de Saint-Aulaire, generally dated about 1821. One of these represents the Faubourg St. Mary, where the character of a city street begins to emerge. The galleried cottages (one in the far distance with a characteristically French colonial hipped roof), the gardens and the split rail fences have a distinctly suburban look. The use of brick seems to anticipate later developments. There are also walkways for pedestrians—earthen *banquettes* held in place by stout wooden curbs. Later drawings from the Notarial Archives seem to represent houses that could be survivors from such an earlier scene. One lone specimen of the characteristic French roof shape still stands at the corner of Magazine and St. Joseph streets.

Fig. 2. Faubourg St. Mary. Lithograph by Saint-Aulaire (see page 78).

Fig. 5. Girod Street at Magazine, bound by Tchoupitoulas, Notre Dame, from a watercolor, dated February 1, 1859, by C. A. de Armas in the New Orleans Notarial Archives.

Fig. 3. St. Charles Street, bound by Julia, Girod, from an 1840 drawing in the New Orleans Notarial Archives.

Fig. 4. Julia Street at Carondelet, from an 1860 watercolor in the New Orleans Notarial Archives.

Fig. 6. An early type, at 900 Magazine Street at St. Joseph, and adjacent brick structures of the mid-nineteenth century.

In one of the drawings a structure appears remarkably similar to one that stands nearby, at Magazine and St. Joseph streets. In both views, photograph and drawing, there are hints of the next phase, the rising American city (figs. 2, 3, 4, 5 and 6).

In the next Faubourg street scene, based on a drawing of Camp Street, presumably about 1830, the proportion of old style versus new is now in reverse. After a lapse of barely a decade, cottage types with quaint roofs are crowded out by a predominance of brick houses in groupings of identical fronts. One single public building, the American Theatre of James H. Caldwell, with its deliberately architectural facade treatment, is a conspicuous mutation. It is a forerunner of the metropolitan scale that will continue to take over in this quarter (fig. 7).

Fig. 7. Camp Street. Lithograph (1880) from an 1830 drawing by H. Reinagle. (Courtesy Special Collections Division, Tulane University Library.)

Another significant feature of the architectural setting is street lighting, from whale-oil lanterns with reflectors hung from chains stretched across the street. These are mentioned in a *City Directory* of 1822, with the observation that "perhaps no city in the Union can boast of being better lighted than New Orleans." The light standards at the curb may be fixtures for gas introduced by Caldwell for his theatre in 1822-24. Its success led him to organize in 1835 the New Orleans Gas Light and Banking Company. Soon the oil lamp with its chain and hoist arrangement was to be replaced in the streets—and eventually in the homes of the city.

Noticeably absent in the St. Aulaire print, the little dray that appears near the theatre is an ominous harbinger of transportation problems as the city expands from pedestrian scale to a scale of vehicular operations. Only one decade later than this prophetic little scene, the practice of using the public thoroughfare for parking drays, storing building materials or depositing refuse was to become a burden on the municipal budget.

Although the contrast of "two worlds" was often mentioned in a comparison of the street aspect in the First and Second Municipalities, in actuality the twin cities inevitably did partake of each other in appearance and mode of living. The Vieux Carre had its own program of building, necessitated by two devastating fires almost contemporaneous with the first establishment of Faubourg St. Mary, and much of this building followed the new, more economically geared procedures. Already the 18th century, especially in Georgian London, had settled upon the row house, a simple, tasteful outgrowth of an urbane society that increasingly drew its strength from trade rather than land, whether for shops, storage, residence or a combination of these. The unexceptional brick front with stone or wood trim, efficiently multiplied down the length of the street, became the norm for every American city during the early growth of the republic. The most noticeable local variation, as compared with Philadelphia, New York, Boston, Cincinnati or anywhere in Yankee-land, is the invariable use of shutter blinds, usually louvered.

The more American type was generally brick, whereas plastered surfaces tended to prevail in the lower city, in keeping with earlier facades. In both cases the cornice line was emphatic and the roof de-emphasized, but the American predisposition, perpetuating a Georgian scheme, was for roofs gabled at the sides and punctuated with a pair of chimneys. This was used in the fine row built in 1831 at Carondelet' and Lafayette streets, recently destroyed. However, in the give-and-take across the cultural frontier, the exception that proves the rule may be seen in the Miltenberger Building at Royal and Dumaine streets, among other similar examples in the French Quarter. Conversely, the Banks Arcade (see page 183), as more commonly in the French examples, has a hipped roof at the corner of the row, rather than the chimneyed gable end. After 1850, when wide cast-iron galleries were habitually added to these earlier facades, the difference between the French and English types becomes barely noticeable.

During this increasingly American period in the French sector, carriage passageways through the buildings became relatively less common, whereas they were not even introduced above Canal Street. Below Canal, patios with plantings tended to be larger and more frequent, although this amenity, like black coffee or gumbo, often was carried over across the line. Compare the Julia Row (page 175) and its series of narrow courts, created by a sequence of galleried service ells, with the similar arrangement that the Ursulines built as rental property behind the convent on Decatur Street.

During the peak years of New Orleans, from the 1830s to the 1860s, the pattern of change spread across the Faubourg, as here and there in an accelerated tempo the details of the shifting scene popped into view like an animated cinema. The older commercial district of Chartres Street shifted first along Canal, then across and into the American territory. The limit of the business activity and the beginning of residential land use was about at Girod Street. In the 1840s the famous Julia Row and its vicinity, as described by Eliza Ripley's memoirs, was considered the *ne plus ultra* of elegance, occupied by the power elite of the new regime (see page 175). The St. Mary Market (on Diamond Street) was at first thought to be far uptown, but by 1879, according to Waldo's *Illustrated Visitor's Guide to New Orleans*, it was already bypassed by population movement.

Lloyds of London was said to have prophesied in 1821 that New Orleans would become the greatest port in the world. By 1845, Norman's *New Orleans and Environs* forecast that by the end of the century a metropolis would extend up to Carrollton and back to Lake Pontchartrain, where the swamps "that now only echo the hoarse bellowing of the alligator [would be] rendered cheerful by the gay voices of ...a million human beings." Numerous reports were embellished with statistics of

Fig. 9. Row houses (demolished in 1968) as they appeared in 1831, Carondelet Street at Lafayette.

Fig. 10. Small courtyards and two-story privies. Factors Building (1858), Perdido Street at Carondelet.

Fig. 11. Suburban type Anglo-American, with survival of French Colonial gallery, on Camp Street, bound by St. Joseph, Julia, Magazine. From a drawing by John Schneider, dated May 21, 1836, in the New Orleans Notarial Archives.

population, shipping or cotton and sugar production arranged in staggering mul-
tiples. These optimistic views failed to see the forewarning signs, such as the Erie
and Pennsylvania canals, or Henry Cabot Lowell's manufacturing company at the
falls of the Merrimac river.

Even after railroading shared with river and sea traffic some of the passenger ap-
proaches to the city, the relationship of New Orleans to the Mississippi was an ever-
present image before every observer. Today's tourists can hardly recover the excitement expressed in so many travel accounts, the gripping anticipation of an entry for
the first time into a port of world-wide trade. One lady tourist, a young governess
from Mississippi whose anonymous letters were printed under the title *The Sunny
South* (1860), apparently was at a loss for words (an unusual condition for her) and
resorted to what must have been sheer poetic license when she proclaimed:

> Tyre or Carthage, Alexandria nor Genoa, those aforetime imperial metropoles
> of merchant princes, boasted no Quay like the Levee of New Orleans.
> Picture to your mind's eye an esplanade or open front, a quarter of a mile
> broad...built up on one side by blocks of lofty brick or stone-stores, ware-
> houses, steampresses, hotels and sugar magazines....Opposite this league-
> front of stores lie the various vessels which are the winged servants of the
> princely merchants who occupy these commercial palaces.
> First are the cotton ships, which extend three in a tier for a mile and a half...
> their intermingled masts presenting the aspect of a wintry forest stripped of its
> leaves....I wondered at the sublime spectacle.

The skyline, dominated by the noble domed contour of the St. Charles Hotel (see
page 81) and the riverfront scene, a stimulating intermix of people, ships and piled-
up cargoes, were impressive to others besides susceptible young ladies. Innumerable

Fig. 12. "Am Kai"—levee in New Orleans, from a German engraving. (Courtesy Historic
New Orleans Collection.)

writers and artists have left their record of what, in its day, must have been a mem-
orable phenomenon. The Yankee author of *The South West* conveyed his feelings
and impressions in a way that hauntingly reaches to us from that moment back in
1835:

> The shades of night had long fallen over the town, when...an interminable
> line of lights gradually opened in quick succession upon our view; and a low
> hum, like the far off roaring of the sea with the heavy and irregular tolling of a
> deep mouthed bell, was borne over the waves upon the evening breeze, min-
> gling at intervals with loud calls far away on the shore...and anon, the wild,

clear, startling notes of a bugle, waking the slumbering echoes on the opposite shore, succeeded by the solitary voice of some lonely singer, blended with the thrumming notes of a guitar, falling with melancholy cadence upon the ear....

In a few minutes, as we still shot onward, we could trace a thousand masts, penciled distinctly with all their network rigging upon the clear evening sky. We moved swiftly in among them; and gradually checking her speed, the tow-boat soon came nearly to a full stop, and casting off the ship astern, rounded to and left us along side of a Salem ship, which lay outside of a tier "six deep...." So after much trouble in laying planks for the surer footing of the ladies, from gangway to gangway, we safely reached, after crossing half a dozen ships, the firm immovable Levee.

After a pause from the scurry of arrival, most travel diarists went on to investigate the characters, sights and sounds of the streets. Generally, they found the old Quarter more novel and worthy of comment, except for the splendid accommodations and spirited public activity at the St. Charles.

By the 1830s there was public transportation. For one bit (half a quarter) one could ride "in omnibus" with about a dozen passengers drawn by two or four horses. The driver, perched high in front, blew a bugle as a signal to start. Shortly before the outbreak of the Civil War, a roadbed of tracks was laid for vehicles drawn by horses or mules.

Street paving came slowly, and Captain Thomas Hamilton, in his *Men and Manners in America* (1833), wrote of the annoying conditions, especially for pedestrains:

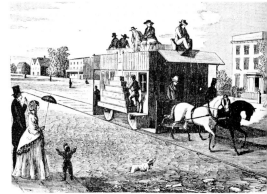

Fig. 13. "Street Railroad Car, New Orleans," from a wood engraving in *Ballou's Pictorial Drawing Room Companion* (September 8, 1855). (Courtesy Special Collections Division, Tulane University Library.)

There are brick *trottoirs,* but the carriage-way is left in a state of nature. The consequence is, that after rain...foot passengers...must either wade up to their knees, or set off on a wild goose chase after stepping stones...to get over dry shod.

The opening of the American Theatre in 1824 was considered foolhardy, since access through the mud along Camp Street had to be provided by the laying of flat-boat gunwales. Paving experiments began about this time. According to *Paxton's Directory* of 1822, Benjamin Morgan's "pebble stones" along one block of Gravier Street, at first ridiculed as extravagant folly, was so successful that it precipitated a program of paving, beginning on the city's main thoroughfare, Chartres Street, and financed by the predominantly French city administration. A price of $3.50 per ton for paving stones was announced in a public resolution as an inducement to ships' owners to carry them as ballast from Eastern ports. *Paxton's* reported that even un-paved streets had brick sidewalks and "gutters formed of wood, which are kept clean by the black prisoners of the city, who are generally run-aways, carrying heavy chains." They can be seen in St. Aulaire's drawing (see page 78).

Fig. 14. Carondelet Street. Sidewalk of Factors Row.

By the 1850s, there were fine sidewalks of broad slabs of slate, like the one still *in situ* at Factors Row on Perdido and Carondelet streets.

The dust or mud of unpaved streets were among the least troublesome threats to cleanliness during these years. A strong sensory experience of environmental conditions is offered in a few choice entries in the notebook of Simon Green, Commissary of the Fourth Ward, one of the more scrupulous of such public servants. He begins in April, 1847:

My attention being called to the manure lying on the Rail Road forming the conjunction of Bacchus St. [now Baronne] and Triton Walk [now Howard Avenue]. Notified Mr. L. L. Ferrier of this and to have it removed *forthwith* and also that I should seize all carts that I caught carrying the same to said place.

Notified Mr. Flood to clean your Privies within three days from date. Situated on the South side of St. Joseph St. between Baronne and Carondelet.

Had a dead horse removed from a lot on Triton Walk. Notified the chain gang to bury dead horse at the foot of Melpomene Canal.

Notified contractor of the First District to stop reporting work done when it is not so.

Bad holes in the road to be filled. Drays left on the streets. Dead dogs in the gutters. A stray horse with a broken leg. [It was not uncommon to abandon crippled dray animals. For a while they were kept within the fragmentary walls and unfinished basement rooms of the delayed construction of Municipality Hall]. Heedless lawbreakers or lethargic municipal functionaries.

Mr. Green's frustrations are endless. It is now July and his neat penmanship has become an exasperated scrawl:

In making my rounds this morning I have observed a very gross violation of the ordinance such as depositing dung in the streets by some persons unknown. Of late it has happened very frequently. I have tried every way to find out who the persons are but all to no purpose for I certainly believe that it is done after dark.

In addition to the debonair attitudes of the people, there were the open canals and the foul accumulations that collected in them. Many writers, including architect Thomas Wharton, referred to this repellent condition. The Englishman Charles Mac-Kay explained the drainage problems of a land partly below sea level with very little slope toward the lake:

What drainage there is is upon the surface, and even at this early season of the year the smell affects painfully the olfactory nerves of all who prefer the odors of the rose to those of the cesspool (*Life and Liberty in America,* 1859).

Benjamin F. Butler, in command of the Federal occupation, was appalled at the apathy of a population decimated by a tragic epidemic not long before and moved to protect his troops. He found that at the French Market, where the fever usually originated,

the stall women were accustomed to drop…all the refuse made in cleaning their birds, meats and fish. Here it was trodden on and into the earth floor. This had been going on for a century, more or less.

He inspected the New Basin Canal and found that "the air seemed filled with the most noxious and offensive stenches possible—so noxious as almost to take away the power of breathing." Butler peremptorily discharged the superintendent of streets and canals, who had said the "enormous stink" was no more than usual. He dispatched a party of men to the market "with an order, accompanied by a few bayonets." The poor man proudly reported his military exploits, and probably never realized he had failed, for all time, to conquer the traditional spirit of this city.

Antebellum New Orleans, impervious to an occasional bad odor, continued building handsome marble porticos and temple fronts and more classic monuments than Athens, Pergamon or Baalbec in their finest days. Besides the obvious examples, such as the St. Charles Hotel or City Hall, there once were temple churches (such as Gallier and Dakin's Christ Church on Canal Street); temple banks (the Union, on Royal Street at Iberville, and the Commercial, on Magazine at Natchez Street); Judah Touro's Greek Revival synagogue on Carondelet Street; temple row houses (Gallier's "Three Sisters" on Rampart Street); a Greek temple university, on

Common Street at University Place; temple theatre fronts; and a Doric Maison de Sante, administered by the Sisters of Charity, on Canal Street at the corner of Claiborne Avenue. Finally, there was the 107-foot-high chimney of the gas works, "constructed to resemble Trajan's pillar...a chaste specimen of classical architecture," according to Norman's descriptive guide. After all, those civilized Greeks and Romans were also slave-holding societies, virtual proof that a city could hardly have a civilized existence without a few black slaves and a garnishing of white temples.

To judge by the quantity of building in the late 1860s and the following decade, recovery must have followed the war years with appreciable speed. The general appearance of the business district was changed gradually but not radically, mainly through the styling of facades, rather than by any innovation in essential building type or scale. Beginning shortly before the Civil War and increasing thereafter, a new feeling crept in that could also be witnessed throughout the nation in entire streets of cities large and small, East and West, in Philadelphia or St. Louis, Natchez or Madison, Indiana.

No particular designation has been applied to this recognizable development of the mid-century, the American commercial building front. Though there were French Second Empire or British Victorian kinships, the resemblance from city to city was unmistakably American. It was as though the proud, sensible and restrained urbanity of the early Republic had been replaced by a stalwart, substantial presence, expressive of a generation that was exploiting and building the material riches of a continent.

The most representative examples of this American style are the Factors Row of 1858 and the adjacent structure, built in 1869, that completes the block on Perdido Street (see page 190). The entire business center of New Orleans is still liberally interspersed with similar examples that give it a personality reminiscent of its years of

Fig. 15. Common Street, bound by Baronne, Carondelet, Gravier. From a watercolor by P. Gualdi, dated April 14, 1855, in the New Orleans Notarial Archives.

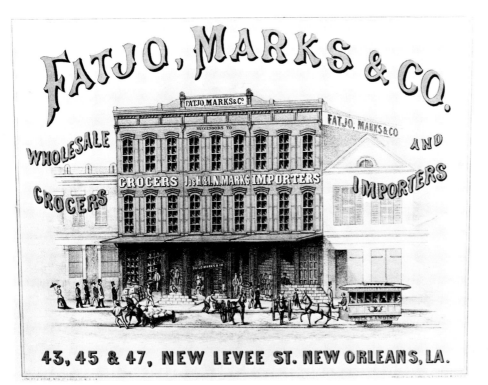

Fig. 16. Chromolithograph by B. Simon (1871).

struggle and growth. Until recently, they were disdained as tasteless, overexuberant or fusty. Now they begin to take on the dignity that comes with age, and their sturdy, self-confident character is occasionally recognized as a positive attribute.

Nearly all the commercial fronts that appear in the color lithographs of Benedict Simon, dating from 1871, are in this same style. This series of prints offers the best possible means of summarizing the new urban scenery of the expansive business activity in New 'Orleans. The facades are an appropriate background for the multiplied sidewalk activity, the busy transport of goods and public transportation. Above all, their visual staccato is reflected in, and almost engulfed by, the syncopation of signs and placards. In a modest way, these lively competitive distractions anticipate the gigantic jungle of billboards that devours the downtown district of today, a triumphant achievement of the influential advertising industry.

Beginning about the middle of the 1880s, as seen in the New Orleans National Bank of Thomas Sully (see page 113), the definitely enlarged "big city" scale began to emerge. It continued to accelerate in the subsequent decades, along with Sully's own very active career. His Hennen (now Maritime) Building of 1895 rose ten stories, to a height of 150 feet, and towered over the entire downtown area. In its own way, New Orleans attained the metropolitan character of major American centers. Eight years after the Hennen Building was erected, it was surpassed—to a height of 180 feet—by a new structure for the Hibernia Bank at Carondelet and Gravier streets (1903, presently the Carondelet Building), at a million-dollar cost that more than tripled the Hennen Building figure. In 1921, when the Hibernia Bank moved into its newest premises diagonally across the street, it was believed that the tower surmounting its twenty-three floors was the ultimate height that the soft clay bottom could ever support. So it stood, unchallenged, for about two generations.

Once again, a new thread becomes woven into the old frayed fabric of the city—until it becomes the conspicuous new pattern overlaid so as to obscure the faded, worn shreds which still show through in the overall.

In the meantime, the street aspect was being modified in other ways. The Southwestern Brush Electric Illuminating Company, named for Charles Brush, was established in 1882. Almost half a century earlier the company had been created, primarily for street gaslighting, which became a reality the following year. A report in *Harper's Weekly* for March 3, 1883, accompanied by a dramatic wood engraving, stated that "Even by night the levees present scenes of bustling activity. New Orleans is far ahead of most Northern cities in the use of electric light." The romance of the river front had not worn thin. The writer reported that the levees were "crowded day and night by picturesque motley throngs of people, representing every phase of sea-faring and river life." The lights were "suspended in rows from high poles" and provided sufficient light for nighttime loading and unloading. "Some of the globes are variously colored, to designate different localities."

The first electric street car was inaugurated with much excitement and ceremony on February 1, 1893. For the first time, it was possible to travel directly all the way from Carrollton to the downtown area. Previously, the trip had been made by a mule-drawn car on rails to Napoleon Avenue, then by steam railway. Finally, in 1902, the various electric lines under different ownership were united into the New Orleans Railway and Light Company, the first consolidated firm for all utilities and antecedent to the present Public Service. The centralized transportation system, along with mechanical drainage and land development, contributed to the spread of the city and consequent growth of the central area.

Fig. 17. Levee at night, from a sketch by J. O. Davidson. (Courtesy Tulane University Library.)

In the years just prior to and after the turn of the century, a growing spirit of progressivism and community consciousness was evidenced by building, street improvements, parks and various public works. This spirit was reflected in a number of guide books, testimonials and picture albums, publications of the Chamber of Commerce and Industry, the Young Men's Business League, the *Picayune* and the works of local architects.

A new movement in city planning and architectural design, sometimes called the "City Beautiful," was stimulated by Daniel Burnham's activity in the refurbishment of Washington, D. C. in 1901, his plans for San Francisco in 1905 and in Chicago in 1909. It accounts for building, in the classical idiom, executed in marble or white glazed terra cotta, such as the New Orleans Stock Exchange Building on Gravier Street, the Tulane-Newcomb Building (see page 113), Maison Blanche and the Southern Railway Station, by Burnham himself, which once stood as a gateway to Canal Street, on the site of the present Bolivar Fountain. Except for one or two noteworthy office buildings, such as the Pere Marquette on Baronne Street (see page 107), this was the familiar inner city until the recent upsurge.

Fig. 18. Southern Railway Station. The terminal, designed by architect Daniel Burnham, was built in 1907 and demolished in 1956. (Courtesy Special Collections Division, Tulane University Library.)

No summary of the area as an architectural experience, however, would be valid without mention of the impressive public rooms that have accommodated crowded gatherings and significant business activities. The list would include the rotonda of the St. Charles Hotel and the near-contemporary Merchants Exchange by Gallier and Dakin, which until recent years retained remnants of its "grand exchange rooms," with Corinthian capitals, on Royal Street just below Canal. Municipality Hall (the present Gallier Hall) once had a spacious Lyceum, a public lecture hall, on its upper floor. The grandest and most widely known of impressive spaces in the Greek Revival style is the marble hall of the Custom House (see page 133). After the Cotton Exchange acquired in 1883 its new building at Carondelet and Gravier streets (subsequently replaced at the same site), the *Picayune's Tourist Guide* described its trading space as "one grand apartment surmounted with a splendid dome supported on Corinthian columns and beautifully decorated with paintings." Futures were sold at a fountain in the rear of the room. Of the large banking floors still in use, that of the Hibernia Bank, a work of the office of Favrot and Livaudais, completed in 1921, remains an impressive symbol of the ordered procedures of daily financial transactions, small or large.

We zoom in on a last fadeout glance over our Central Business District as we have known it in our time, and thus view cinematically a representative timescape of an American city approaching its final phase, the fadeout of Western culture. The Mayor seemed to glimpse this when recently he asked: "What makes a city live and what makes one die?...The problems of this city, like any other, are deep and profound. We speak of the urban crisis and the death of our cities so often that the real meaning of these terms sometimes gets lost....Is Newark dead? If Newark is a dead city, is Los Angeles a live city? When does a city die and how does it live? Is Phoenix alive or dead, or is it a city at all?"

The answers would require complete clairvoyance, but a glimmer of understanding may be contained in a simple truism often overlooked. If one is to consider a city as a living organism according to the current custom, then it would apply, as for all living things, that the processes of growth and of dying are forever intermingled. The old Western credos that latched onto the inflexible, court of law, either-or view of true and false, good and bad, right and wrong, life and death — these are fading away, along with Western culture itself, before the subtleties and complexities of the cyber-

Fig. 19. Hibernia National Bank, 313 Carondelet. (Photograph by V. Thoma Kersh.)

netic, space-age outlook of a later generation. These newer directions of thought are implicit in the combined ideas of the Mayor, the journalist and the entrepreneur.

Since growth and change are inevitable, our only concern should be to cultivate and control growth to avoid over-accelerated or cancerous growth.

The decay of a city can be a promise and a stimulus, rather than a calamity. How often have Jerusalem and Rome died and reawakened, within the single brief period of Western culture, the cities of Romulus and David, Herod and Caesar, Peter, Rienzi, Garibaldi and Golda Meir? The concept of resurrection (or revitalization) is a heritage of Jerusalem and Rome, an Oriental input lost in the welter of the West. It is the eternity theme in the life-stream of mortal man.

New Orleans, in spite of the interest in its old buildings, has not been a center for famed architectural accomplishments. Chicago (whose famous Stock Exchange has just been destroyed) was of crucial importance in the creation of a whole new age of building. In New Orleans, an appealing style came about not so much from significant architectural innovation or influential monuments, but more from a mode of being or a state of mind.

The immortality of New Orleans will not consist of steel and concrete, "more fire stations, more overpasses, more incinerators and more streets," but in an elusive ambience summarized in the phrase, "a quality of life that is distinctively human." This could be destroyed for all time if we continue to uproot people and activities by

Fig. 20. Quality of life. Factors Row (1858), 812 Perdido. Waguespack Pratt, Inc.

Fig. 21. 700 block of Camp. One of the most complete collections of outstanding landmarks.

tearing down their physical setting, the little sidelights and byways, individually inconspicuous but collectively effective. Surprisingly, a number of these remain in the innermost business center, and it would be regrettable if all of them were sacrificed in the name of growth and renewal.

It would be presumptuous to stand in judgment over the deteriorative forces. In a sense, the blame is pervasive and collective, and most frequently the agents of favorable or unfortunate results are embodied in one and the same individual or institution. For example, every enlightened citizen foresees and bemoans the suffocating stalemate of traffic, even while he drives alone to his business in his large vehicle; the

transportation officials see the increase of mass transit services as a form of economic suicide until the private individual will cooperate to save his city and become a passenger.

Naturally, a business center must respond to business demands, but these should not exclude the human equation. Financial acumen and entrepreneurship are necessary to keep an urban economy viable, reaching into the total community. The Central Business District, because of its people-appeal, fortunately has escaped the enfeebling drain-off that plagues other cities. But when the financier's gain-centered attitude excludes all other considerations, all sense of healthy balance is lost. Land speculation must not be permitted to become an overwhelmingly destructive force. A totally depersonalized, oversized downtown, attacked by hardening of the arteries, could become a soulless carcass. The inevitable changes and growth should be selective, reasoned and planned for the sake of cultivating the lively, attractive downtown character that farsighted Orleanians seek to retain.

A few negative influences stand out so obviously there is hardly need to point to them. A glance back over this brief perspective will show they have always been there: first of all, the external historic conditions that inescapably surround every organism; then, our habitual easy-going expediency of make-do devices; and finally the all-consuming, empire-building ethos that attributes a virtue and a moral right to all enterprise, even for the sake of exclusive advantage, and so wipes out the understanding of how all the small parts and elements of community belong to each other.

Fig. 23. Expediency. Iberville Street, between Bourbon and Dauphine.

Allegoric figures, representing Commerce and Industry, above pediment of old Stock Exchange Building, 740 Gravier.

Banking and Commerce

MARY LOUISE CHRISTOVICH
and ROULHAC TOLEDANO

New Orleans was founded as a banking project in the early 18th century when John Law, through the Royal Bank of France, financed a world-wide holding company with exclusive rights to the Louisiana Territory and all its trading rights. This initial scheme failed and the original colonists were left with semibarter exchange practices in which commodities were the standard of value. Bills of credit and exchange, along with the lack of stable currency, beleaguered these early French colonists. The situation was only temporarily relieved by the Spanish importation of silver and the introduction of the *liberanza,* a form of paper money.

Following the Louisiana Purchase, W. C. C. Claiborne, Louisiana's first American Governor, seized upon the necessity of circulating medium and in 1804 established the first bank, the Louisiana Bank. Evan Jones, an American, and Paul Lanusse, a Creole, were president and secretary, respectively. The two nationalities were joined in a common venture. Julien Poydras, Steven Zacharie, James Pitot, Daniel Clark, Michel Fortier, John Soule, Thomas Urquhart, Nicholas Girod and Francois Duplessis were among the early founders. While the Louisiana Bank attempted to unite the Creoles and Americans, another group, in 1805, established a branch of the United States Bank of Philadelphia as an exclusively American institution. William Kenner, John Palfrey, Benjamin Morgan and Beverly Chew, early developers of Faubourg St. Mary, were organizers of the new bank, which ignored the French population and its needs.

Claiborne preempted the open field in banking, and the merchants who filled the city gave proof to Thomas Jefferson's prediction that New Orleans would become one of the most important commercial centers of the world. These bankers came from the Northeast, England and Ireland and soon were an integral part of the South's financial system. The merchant became the planter, who likewise became the founder or director of a bank while carrying on a lucrative factor business and participating in brokerage activities. Their financial and social differences with the Creole, coupled with the necessity for expansion, pushed them into real estate development above Canal Street in Faubourg St. Mary.

In 1811, two other banks were chartered, the Bank of Orleans and the Louisiana Planters Bank. Benjamin Morgan, who as early as 1805 lived at old No. 14 Gravier, and Samuel Packwood were officers of the former. Prominent planters Bellechasse, Duplantier, De la Croix, Montgomery, Cox and Butler formed the directorate of the latter. Commerce and a population increase gave indication of more and more prosperity. In 1812 a devastating hurricane and the war with England impeded the development of Faubourg St. Mary. The cooperation of the planters with pirates further disturbed the financial scene, according to cotton factor Vincente Nolte in

Fifty Years in Both Hemispheres (1859). New Orleans was to experience several "runs" throughout the next hundred years. The one reported by Nolte was a mild one:

Barataria was visited by the sugar planters, chiefly of French origin, who bought up the stolen slaves at from 150 to 200 dollars per head, when they could not have procured as good stock in the city for less than 600 to 700 dollars. This clandestine traffic was one of the causes to which the scarcity of ready money was to be attributed. The planters, instead of taking bank notes with them, invariably provided themselves with coin to pay for their purchases. This money, however, did not leave the country, but was hoarded away in the private coffers of those who performed the part of secret agents for the pirates, and was thus withdrawn from general circulation. The French and Catalonian population of the city had never been able to persuade themselves that bank notes are just as good as cash in representing value when based upon the security of a well-managed banking capital, and just when the prejudice against them was passing away, the jealous maneuvering of two cashiers, one T. L. Harman, in the Planter's Bank, the other Joseph Saul, in the Bank of Orleans, both Englishmen by birth, again revived it. The latter cashier aimed at destroying the credit of the Planter's Bank, and attracting its customers to his own, as they were mostly planters who allowed their deposits to lie longer than the merchants were accustomed to do. The cashier had contracted its discounting operations and thus brought about a much smaller issue of paper than the Planter's Bank had made; he then carefully collected the notes of the rival bank as they were coming in, and after getting unfavorable reports into circulation concerning the Planter's Bank, he suddenly presented the accumulated mass of notes, requiring payment of the same in silver, on a day when he knew that his neighbors' supply of that metal was very much reduced. The amount demanded by the notes went far beyond the quantity of silver in the possession of the Planter's Bank, and the clerk of the Bank of Orleans who presented them instantly returned with word that they would have further consultation on the subject. This was enough. The whole population was thrown in excitement; there was an immediate run upon the Planter's Bank but there was no distinction drawn by the excited public between it and the Bank of Orleans, which like its rival and anticipated victim, was likewise brought to a standstill in the payment of its notes. The inhabitants hurried to the exchange, and named a committee of five members: Messrs. Nott, H. Landreaux, and P. F. Dubourg, merchants, Mr. Mazureau, a lawyer, and myself, for the purpose of examining into the actual condition of the banks, and reporting thereupon.

The Louisiana Bank, housed at the present site of Brennan's, failed in 1818. It was reorganized as the Louisiana State Bank, and in 1820 B. H. Latrobe designed the famous banking house in the old quarter at a site now occupied by Manheim's. By 1822 the Bank of Orleans, Louisiana Planters Bank, the United States Bank and the Louisiana State Bank were in business, all of them located in the Vieux Carre but nevertheless having a major interest in the development of the new faubourg. By this time the city was the commercial and financial center for the entire South and West and the great primary cotton market of the world and was striving to meet the New York port competition. After the arrival of the steamboat *New Orleans* in January, 1812, a quick succession of river boats joined the oceangoing vessels and keelboats lining the banks of the river. The *Comet, Vesuvius, Enterprise, Etna, Dispatch, Franklin, General Pike* and *United States,* the latter owned by New Orleans banker Edmond Forstall, were among the first.

By 1821 at least forty more steamboats created a fleet servicing New Orleans, making products available from 30,000 miles of inland waterways. Nine years were to pass before the first railroad, the Pontchartrain, was chartered, with Governor Claiborne and Samuel J. Peters among the first presidents. In addition to opening the lake area for resorts and summer homes, the railroad launched a produce transportation system, spurring the development of commercial public markets in Faubourg St. Mary. By 1836 the railroad had acquired banking privileges. The Carrollton Railroad, operating by 1835, was a speculative development of the Canal Bank and Samuel Kohn, Laurent Millaudon and John Slidell. The Poydras Market was built in 1837 on land donated by the Carrollton Railroad to sell produce transported by rail.

Throughout this golden financial era the middlemen, the factors and brokers, the merchants and bankers, provided the South's greatest scenario. The performers listed in the order of their appearance usually were factor, planter, broker, banker. The factor was the agent for either his own company or a representative partner linked to eastern or foreign firms. The planter turned over his crop to his factor, allowing sale and destination prices to be decided by the factor. The broker reported sales and prices and enforced regulations. The banks furnished capital on short terms to the factor, who advanced long-term arrangements to the planter. In a typical procedure in 1825, John Hagan & Co., New Orleans factors, offered to a client, Louisiana planter W. S. Hamilton, an advance utilizing a discount note with the bank. The bank loaned the money on the factor's endorsement. The factor further expanded his economic power by becoming purchasing agent for all aspects of plantation life. The factor was essential also to the development of New Orleans' transportation system, the warehouse district and the insurance companies, services related to the marketing of cotton.

By 1805 The New Orleans Insurance Company was reimbursing shipping losses to factors and shipping agents such as Jacob Hart. Insurance companies were vital to the speculative land and agrarian economy. Bankers, brokers and factors alike saw the opportunity and became the directors of many companies. Richard O. Pritchard, for example, was a wholesale grocer and director of the Bank of Louisiana and the Louisiana State Marine and Fire Insurance Company. The American sector bulged with insurance companies by the 1840s. The Commercial Insurance Company was at 46 Magazine, Eagle Insurance at 43 Canal, Western Marine and Fire Insurance at the southwest corner of Camp and Common, Union Insurance at 42 Canal and Atlantic Marine and Fire Insurance at 55 Canal.

Because of the extension of credit, the factoring and banking system has been blamed for the economic problems—chronic debt and lack of diversification—that plagued the antebellum South. J. B. De Bow of New Orleans published the major agricultural journal of the antebellum South, 1846–80 and in 1849 his journal warned: "Keep out of debt, and control your cotton" (*De Bow's Review*, VII [1849], p. 411). At an 1855 Commercial Convention in New Orleans it was proposed by Louisiana planters that the "Chambers of Commerce and Commission Merchants" in Southern cities agree not to give advances to planters.

While the factors and bankers were managing the agrarian economy, few were unaware of the values of city real estate. The early development of Faubourg St. Mary from 1810 plantations to a residential-commercial area gave testimony to the aggressive and versatile business acumen held by these men. Blocks of 19th century commercial buildings remain as sentinels to these speculators who, gambling for fortunes, built a city. A study of the political, financial and social registers reveals the

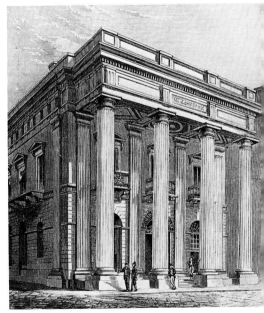

Fig. 1. Union Bank, later Citizens Bank, corner Royal and Customhouse. From *Jewell's* (1871). (Courtesy Historic New Orleans Collection.)

Fig. 2. Gas Light and Banking Company, corner Camp and Gravier, in 1858. From *Leslie's Popular Monthly* (1898). (Courtesy Special Collections Division, Tulane University.)

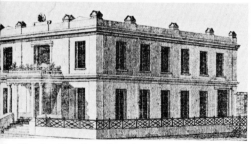

Fig. 3. Canal and Banking Company. From Zimpel's map (1834). (Courtesy Historic New Orleans Collection.)

same names repeatedly. Among those active in every phase of city life were John Slidell, Rezin D. Sheperd, Beverly Chew, Richard Relf, Samuel Kohn and Samuel J. Peters, all of whom maintained businesses and often residences in Faubourg St. Mary.

The giant of them all was John McDonogh, whose diversification of investment and financial activity typifies the period. McDonogh arrived in New Orleans in 1800, a former indentured apprentice and then commission merchant representing a Baltimore mercantile firm. By 1804 he was building warehouses to store the vast amount of manufactured goods passing through his hands. At first, capital and manufactured goods were furnished by William Taylor of Baltimore. Shepherd Brown and Company of New Orleans supplied the agricultural products. As a commission merchant, McDonogh supplied himself with funds to become Louisiana's foremost land speculator, real estate manager and landlord. Among his rental holdings in Faubourg St. Mary were the Citizens Bank, Union Bank, a ferry, Mansion House Hotel and even tables in the vegetable markets.

Another early participant in development of the faubourg was Julien Poydras, planter and merchant from Point Coupee Parish. Cognizant of the far-reaching devastation of the great fire in the Vieux Carre in 1788, he encouraged Jean Gravier to subdivide and purchased the first lot sold for development in Faubourg St. Mary. He paid Gravier $1,000 for a lot on the street Barthelemy Lafon named for him — at the corner of Poydras and Public Road (Tchoupitoulas).

As elsewhere in the South, the primary need was for capital to produce and market the most important crops, cotton and sugar. The answer was provided by the property bank, an ingenious new institution and the brainchild of New Orleans planter-merchant J. B. Moussier. The Union Bank (fig. 1), Martin Duralde, director, and the Citizens Bank, chartered in 1832 and 1833, were property banks that provided mortgages on moveable and immoveable property: slaves, plantations, and large tracts of city lots. The state, rather than the banks, usually sold bonds to raise capital. They were eagerly purchased by foreign enterprises when the full faith and credit of the state was placed behind them. Property banks enhanced the potential of the agrarian economy, but they also made possible the private speculation that gave rise to the building of New Orleans suburbs.

To raise money for city improvements, another form of bank came into existence in 1829 with James H. Caldwell's New Orleans Gas Light and Banking Company, the first of many improvement banks (fig. 2). It had the monopoly of supplying gas to the French Quarter and Faubourgs St. Mary, Marigny, and Treme for 25 years. Caldwell's bank was moved in 1839 from the Vieux Carre to new quarters on St. Charles, between Canal and Common. The new building was designed by James Gallier, Sr., and built by Sidle and Stewart for $25,000 on a lot costing $25,000 (see 211 St. Charles). Among the directors were Judah P. Benjamin, P. N. Wood, Henry Lonsdale and Cornelius Fellowes. After the panic of 1837, James Robb purchased controlling interest in this company and was elected president in 1842. Reorganized by Robb under a new name, it survives today as the New Orleans Public Service Company.

The Commercial Bank Waterworks, chartered in 1833, another improvement bank, was housed in a classic structure designed by George Clarkson and built for $75,000 at 70 Magazine (fig. 4). The building is now demolished but was long known as offices for the Morgan Line. By 1846 the Commercial Bank had moved into elegant offices on Common, across from the St. Charles Hotel in a building designed by

Fig. 4. Commercial Bank and Atchafalaya Bank, on Magazine. From *Gibson's* (1838). (Courtesy New Orleans Public Library.)

James Gallier, Sr. (demolished). The Exchange and Banking Company, 29 Camp, chartered as an improvement bank in 1835, with factors John Hagan, Maunsell White and James Dick as prime movers, was for the express purpose of building the St. Charles Hotel to compete with the St. Louis Hotel constructed by the Improvement Bank. Designed by James Gallier, Sr., the first St. Charles Hotel cost $750,000.

The Canal and Banking Company sponsored the New Basin Canal, which was begun in 1832 and completed in 1838 at the cost of $1 million and the lives of thousands of Irish and German immigrants who succumbed to yellow fever and cholera epidemics. The Canal and Banking Building, constructed in 1832, was designed by J. M. Zacharie and John Reynolds (fig. 3). Portions of this Greek Revival structure remain at 301–307 Magazine within an 1843 rebuilding by James Dakin. The firm of Gallier and Esterbrook in 1858 built a new facility (demolished) for $45,000 at the

Fig. 5. Bank of Orleans in 1832; later Bank of America. From Zimpel's map (1834). (Courtesy Historic New Orleans Collection.)

corner of Camp and Gravier, designed by Lewis Reynolds. The Citizens Bank was a combination property and improvement bank which stood first on Toulouse, between Royal and Chartres, then moved to the old Union Bank Building at Royal and Customhouse, nearer the American sector. Magazine Street continued as a banking row when the Atchafalaya Railroad and Banking Company located opposite Banks Arcade in 1838 in a building designed by W. L. Atkinson (fig. 4).

Faubourg St. Mary and its banks were in a boom period in the 1830s. The earlier banks with quarters in the Vieux Carre began to relocate in the American sector, and there were fine examples of banking house architecture, which lent emphasis to the classic characterization of the faubourg. As they were built, the bank buildings were either lauded or criticized in newspapers and city guides for their contributions to New Orleans architecture. The Bank of Orleans, chartered in 1811, moved to the American sector in 1832. C. F. Zimpel designed its building at the north corner of Canal and Exchange Place. Cost of the building (fig. 5) was $60,000. It later housed the Bank of America, illustrated in *Jewell's* (1871). The Bank of New Orleans moved from the corner of Royal and Conti to 312 St. Charles, at Union, in the 1830s. The exodus continued, with the Mechanics and Traders Bank, founded in 1836, locating at old 47 Canal and the City Bank spending $50,000 for their new home, designed by W. L. Atkinson and contracted by James Gallier, Sr., at 111 Camp (fig. 6). The Merchants Bank of New Orleans followed in 1839 to the east side of Camp, between Poydras and Lafayette, in a building designed by Gallier, Sr. All of these buildings have been demolished.

By 1836 the competition between the French Quarter and Faubourg St. Mary had reached a climax, and merchant-banker Samuel J. Peters led the effort to establish the Second Municipality as a governing body with the Charter of 1836. The new municipality corresponded to Faubourg St. Mary, extending upriver to encompass the present Lower Garden District to Felicity Street. With other merchant bankers, Peters directed the affairs of the sector as its newly elected officials and the first Council took office in 1836. Joshua Baldwin, director of the Union Insurance Company and the Orleans Steam Cotton Press, was recorder. James H. Caldwell, James P. Freret of Freret Brothers cotton yard, residence 117 Carondelet, and Dr. Thomas Meux, chairman of the Commercial Water Works, residence, 29 Magazine, represented the new First Ward. Samuel J. Peters, Thomas Sloo of the firm, Sloo & Byrne, commission merchants, 1503 Tchoupitoulas, and Edward Yorke, president of the Exchange and Banking Company, residence 125 Julia, represented the Second Ward. W. J. Hepp, director of the Orleans Steam Cotton Press, and Victor Burthe, an attorney, represented the Third Ward. Burthe was the only member who resided outside Faubourg St. Mary.

Peters was also a prime mover of the Merchants Exchange, financed by a joint stock company, 1835–36 (fig. 7). James Gallier, Sr., and C. B. Dakin designed the handsome domed building at Royal and Exchange. It was convenient to both the French and American sectors. Daniel Twogood was the builder and Dakin the superintendent for the $100,000 structure. It has now been replaced by the Holiday Inn Motel. Business was conducted beneath the great dome of the St. Charles Hotel, known officially as the St. Charles Exchange, and at the City Hotel, corner of Camp and Common. Banks Arcade, built in 1833, was envisioned by its promoter, Thomas Banks, as a commercial center on Magazine Street to compete with Maspero's Ex-

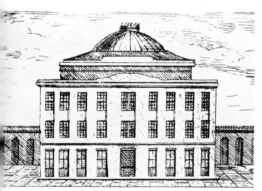

Fig. 6. City Bank, on Camp. From *Norman's* (1838). (Courtesy New Orleans Public Library).

Fig. 7. Merchant's Exchange, Royal and Customhouse. From *Gibson's* (1839). (Courtesy Louisiana State Museum.)

change in the French Quarter. Hewlett's Exchange was located at Banks Arcade and later moved to the corner of Camp and Common.

The 1830s also saw the commercial center of New Orleans move to Canal and the American sector. In 1839 rents were increased 15 percent for stores on Chartres Street by agents of owners living abroad. Merchants looked elsewhere. Among the first of the commission merchants to move to Canal was A. D. Crossman, a New Orleans resident from 1829 and future mayor for whom Crossman Street is named. John Minturn, a contractor and banker who received the contract for paving Faubourg St. Mary, followed, as did Samuel J. Peters, with his wholesale grocery firm, Peters and Millard, the largest in the South. Paul Tulane moved from Chartres to Gravier, between Magazine and Tchoupitoulas. These and other merchants in 1833 had formed a Chamber of Commerce, with Peters as chairman and H. C. Cammack as secretary.

This was also the period of the private, nonchartered banks, made possible by the free banking laws of Louisiana. Best known of these private bankers were Peter Conrey, Jr., and James Robb, New Orleans' leading international banking figure. In addition to his New Orleans banking house, Hoge and Robb, he founded banks in New York, St. Louis, San Francisco, London, and Liverpool.

All seemed secure in New Orleans' expansive financial system, but long-term loans, acquisitions of large amounts of foreign capital, easy credit and land specula-

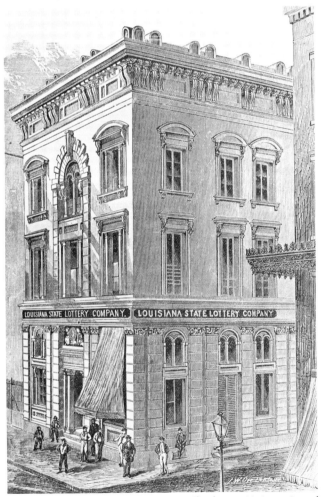

Fig. 8. Louisiana State Lottery, St. Charles at Union, site of present International City Bank. From *Jewell's* (1871). Designed and built for the Bank of New Orleans in 1856. (Courtesy Historic New Orleans Collection.)

Fig. 9. Bank of America, formerly Bank of Orleans. From *Jewell's* (1871). (Courtesy Historic New Orleans Collection.)

tions made New Orleans one of the most seriously affected sections of America in the Panic of 1837. The inevitable bank runs began. Most banks suspended payment. Foreclosures and note demands forced factors, merchants and planters into instant financial ruin. The deadly cycle had begun, and New Orleans remained in a financial quagmire until 1845. This slow recovery was aggravated by yellow fever epidemics in 1837 and·1839, unfavorable tariffs on sugar and cotton and finally by the 1840 flood, one of the worst ever. In spite of failures and bankruptcies, commerce continued throughout the crisis, but the city's competitive attempts often were thwarted by discount species, and business moved to New York, Charleston and Savannah.

The Louisiana Bank Act of 1842 required one-third of the public liabilities to be backed by specie, with the remainder in ninety-day paper. By 1845 eleven banks accepted this Act, and a new conservative sound banking system was the order of the day. Indeed, no failures or suspensions were reported until the capture of New Orleans during the Civil War.

In 1851 James Robb discussed the lack of external commerce in New Orleans in an address to the state legislature. Ships serving the city were owned by outsiders when they should be home-owned and operated, he said. He pleaded with the people to build up an import, as well as export, trade. New Orleans had need of industry manufactures. In 1851 she was a commercial city with only an export trade, which helped cause the depreciated credit of the city. Robb felt that free banking laws should be abolished as being dangerous to the healthy economic development of the city, although he had personally profited from them.

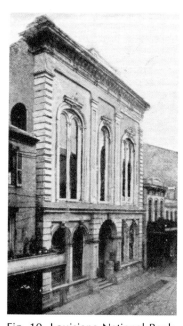

Fig. 10. Louisiana National Bank. From *Leslie's Popular Monthly* (1898).

Realizing the city was already late in providing railroads to augment the river trade, he sought to develop the New Orleans, Jackson and Great Northern Railroads. Joining him in this venture were Glendy Burke, H. S. Buckner and Maunsell White, all bank directors and commission merchants. Thus, James Robb, more so than any other man, deserves the credit for trying to awaken New Orleans to many of the problems she still has. Cognizant of the appalling inadequacies of wharves and facilities on the levee, he was unable to bring about sufficient improvement. Major imports continued to be few, principally bananas, sugar and coffee. Industry, such as Paul Tulane's manufacture of men's clothes, the cotton presses and the refineries were related to commercial interests, and today the city continues as a wholesale center.

In 1857 the Bank of New Orleans opened new offices on St. Charles, at Union, in a $35,000 building designed by Gallier, Turpin and Company. The building housed the Louisiana State Lottery after the Civil War (fig. 8). The Louisiana State Bank relocated at 37 Camp, at Gravier, in 1867, and the Bank of America, first established in the French Quarter, moved to Canal in 1868 (fig. 9). The Citizens Bank, founded in 1833 in the French Quarter, moved to Royal and Customhouse into a building once occupied by the Union Bank (fig. 1). By 1916 it had been moved to Gravier, to a structure remodeled by Torre, soon after it merged with the Canal Bank and Trust Co. By the end of the 1850s the faubourg was at the height of its commercial development. Directories show more than 300 firms in the commission business. Some 70 sugar factors were in business, but cotton factors headed all listings. The *Picayune* of August 23, 1859, reported on the general location of many of Faubourg St. Mary's businesses:

Carondelet Street was devoted entirely to cotton and shipping; Canal was nearly taken up with the dry goods trade; Chartres was expected to retain the variety trade; St. Charles, with its various places of amusement, could retain only certain classes of offices, besides coffee saloons and cigar stores; Magazine had a near monopoly of the wholesale boot and shoe and a goodly part of the wholesale dry goods trade; from Tchoupitoulas to the levee, Canal to Lafayette, Western produce reigned; Poydras claimed as a specialty bagging and rope.

After fifteen years of commercial expansion and banking security, the fall of New Orleans to Federal troops spelled ruin, which lasted more than a decade. The city's banks had been used for investments in the Confederate cause, and Generals Ben Butler and Nathaniel Banks imposed harsh military rule. Fines of 25 percent, equal to their investment in the Confederacy, were imposed on every Rebel bank. New Orleans banks all but closed because of forced gifts, the loss of $4 million in confiscated Confederate currency and constant harassment. The first post-war directories show fewer than 15 commission houses remaining in business. The wharves were empty; commerce of every kind stagnated. General Banks organized the Free Labor Bank in New Orleans in 1864 for Negroes only. It operated for four years before moving to Washington. The Freedmen's Bank, authorized by Congress in 1865, had a New Orleans branch of the Freedmen's Saving Bank throughout Reconstruction. The National Bank Act of 1863 caused seven banks to fail. During Reconstruction, however, local banks began to reorganize as national banks. The first was the Louisiana National Bank, which in 1865 commissioned James Gallier, Jr., to build a bank based on designs of Edward Burling and Company at 614 Common (fig. 10) (see 826 St. Charles). Joseph H. Oglesby, the founder and president, had come to New Orleans as a Western Produce commission merchant and in 1865 formed the Commercial Insurance Company.

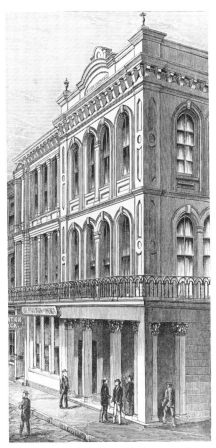

Fig. 11. First Cotton Exchange. From *Jewell's* (1873). (Courtesy Historic New Orleans Collection.)

The Louisiana State Lottery Company also was the result of Reconstruction government—and the poverty of the state, as well. Chartered in 1868 under the leadership of Charles T. Howard, the lottery included New Orleans banks as sponsors. Albert Baldwin, a leading merchant-banker associated with the New Orleans National Bank, was a major stockholder. The Louisiana National Bank, the State National Bank, the Union National Bank and the New Orleans National Bank also participated. Corruptive practices negated the value of the lottery, which survived 25 years before losing its state charter.

The overthrow of the extravagant, divisive Carpetbag rule brought instant improvements. Captain Eads's jetty plan in 1874 reopened New Orleans to deep-water transportation and gave a tremendous boost to the port position. With this increase in commerce, the railroads expanded and four new trunk lines provided new frontiers. When the Clearing House Association was organized in 1872, 13 of 20 banks were qualified to join. The Clearing House brought further stability by requiring cash reserves of its members.

Large-scale centralization of the commercial interests began as early as 1868 with the Real Estate Exchange on Perdido (old Spencer Business College). Between 1881 and 1883 the Cotton Exchange built offices (demolished) at Gravier and Carondelet (fig. 11). John Hawkins built the structure and rented it to the Exchange for $4,000 per annum. Soon afterward, the Cotton Exchange offices were built in the style of the Second Empire (fig. 12). The statues which once adorned this building stand in front of the Acme Marble Building on City Park Avenue. A $1,222,500 seven-story

Fig. 12. Second New Orleans Cotton Exchange. From Harper's, March 17, 1883. (Courtesy Historic New Orleans Collection.)

Fig. 14. Hibernia National Bank, Carondelet and Gravier.

Fig. 13. First National Bank of Commerce. (Photograph by Charles L. Franck.)

building designed by Favrot and Livaudais replaced this structure in 1920. Henry G. Hester edited the *Price Current* newspaper for the Exchange, disseminating information on cotton. One of the South's most innovative financial journalists and cotton experts, Hester retired after 62 years. The frantic importance of New Orleans' cotton economy is well described by Edward King in his book *The Great South* (1875):

> In the American Quarter during certain hours of the day cotton is the only subject spoken of; the pavements of all the principal avenues in the vicinity of the Exchange are crowded with smartly dressed gentlemen who eagerly discuss crops and values...whose mouths are filled with the slang of the Liverpool market; and with the skippers of steamers from all parts of the West and Southwest.
>
> From high noon until dark the planter, the factor, the speculator, flit feverishly to and from the portals of the Exchange, and nothing can be heard above the excited hum of their conversation except the sharp voice of the clerk reading the latest telegram.

Following the lead of cotton, the produce merchants opened their Exchange at 316 Magazine in 1880 (see Inventory). They soon formed a coalition with the Chamber of

Commerce and the Merchants and Manufacturers Association and established the Board of Trade in 1889. The Cotton Exchange and the Maritime Association joined the group in 1898 and stimulated the formation of the Dock Board in 1901. The latter immediately took control of the wharves, reduced fees and created the publicly owned cotton terminals and a public grain elevator. A bond issue provided the waterfront with the Public Belt Railroad by 1908. The Stock Exchange opened new headquarters in 1906 at 740 Gravier (see Inventory) in a structure by Andry and Bendernagel. Their original offices in 1877 were on Carondelet. Only the Sugar Exchange was located outside of the faubourg. Established in 1883 on North Front and Bienville, it was soon to reorganize and merged as the Louisiana Sugar and Rice Exchange in 1889.

The commercial renaissance of the 1880s lasted until the crash of 1929. First to resurge were life insurance companies, which built impressive new buildings such as those of the Teutonia Company and Crescent Company at 211 Camp and 405–407 Camp, respectively (see Inventory). The Southern Insurance Company moved to 314 Camp. Liverpool and London and Globe (L&L&G), a home-operated agency since 1853, left offices at 828 Gravier and moved to new quarters costing $135,000 at Carondelet and Gravier (demolished), site of the National American Bank. Peoples Insurance Company still stands at 132 Carondelet.

The Louisiana Homestead League, organized in 1891, was incorporated with 12 members. By 1896 twenty-four homesteads had begun and reached record sales in real estate transactions. Although there are fewer New Orleans banks and insurance companies in 1972 than in previous history, and even fewer which have main offices in the Central Business District, there remain five fine bank buildings, the result of the commercial expansion before the depression.

The First National Bank of Commerce at 210 Baronne is the 1971 name of a banking institution with a history stretching back to the 1830s. Ten financial institutions, including the Provident, Germania-American National, Commercial Trust and Savings and the Citizens banks, were merged into the New Orleans Canal and Banking Company in 1831. The Canal Bank, as it was known, was reorganized and absorbed into the National Bank of Commerce in 1933. The 19-story building, designed by Emile Weil and built in 1927, is presently part of the Richards Center. A photograph shows the building (fig. 13) as it appeared soon after its construction. Few have had the opportunity to observe the three female sculptures at the base of the flagpole or the pelican relief sculptures accentuating the tripartite scheme of the building at the thirteenth level. In the foreground of the photograph is the old Feibleman Building. To the left is the Pere Marquette Building.

Hibernia National Bank, chartered in 1870, occupied its first home at Camp; its second was the old City Bank (both demolished). In 1902 it merged with Southern Trust and Banking Company, occupying a 13-story building (Carondelet Building) at Carondelet and Gravier where it remained until 1921 when the present 23-story building was constructed. Built by George A. Fuller Company of New York and New Orleans, its architects were Favrot and Livaudais (fig. 14). The wings of the building facing Union and Gravier are 14 stories, and the tower is a landmark, officially considered a sailor's beacon. Completely framed in steel, which supports the Indiana limestone facade, the building incorporates neo-Renaissance decoration employed in the early 20th century.

Fig. 15. Whitney National Bank, 228 St. Charles.

Fig. 16. Formerly Commercial National Bank and Federal Reserve Bank, 147 Carondelet.

Fig. 17. National American Bank, 145 Carondelet.

Fig. 18. International City Bank and Trust, 321 St. Charles.

Whitney National Bank, 228 St. Charles, at Gravier, was chartered in 1883. The original building is a massive red granite structure (see Inventory) which now houses the safety deposit section at 613–17 Gravier. The 14-story main office was designed by New York architects Clinton and Russell, in association with Emile Weil of New Orleans. The $1.5 million structure (fig. 15) was built by George Glover in 1911 and is steel, granite and Bedford stone.

The New Orleans branch of the Federal Reserve Bank of Atlanta was first housed in 1915 in the Exchange Bank Building at Carondelet and Union (demolished). It then moved to the former Morris Plan Bank Building on Camp before a facility was built at 147 Carondelet in 1923 for $1,250,000 (fig. 16). Designed by architect Rathone De Buys, with J. Frank Coleman. as consulting engineer, it was built by George J. Glover in 1922. It is a steel-frame building with concrete floor joists and concrete floor slabs. The front facades are granite and limestone; the rear and side walls are brick.

The National American Bank, founded in 1917, was first known as the Bankers Trust Company, then the American Bank and Trust Company. In 1944 it became the National American Bank. The National American Bank Building, 145 Carondelet, was designed by architect Moise Goldstein, with Jens B. Jensen Consulting Engineer, and built in 1928–29 by George T. Glover, company contractor. Of steel skeleton construction with hollow tile and concrete, the building's facade is faced with granite and limestone, with rear and party walls of brick. The building replaced the Liverpool, London and Globe Insurance Company Building. The 23-story building and site cost $3.5 million dollars (fig. 17).

The International City Bank and Trust Company, 321 St. Charles, one of the newest banks in the Central Business District, was founded in 1966 (fig. 18). It occupies the former United Fruit Company offices, an 11-story brick building erected in 1920 from designs by General Allison Owen. The ornate entrance features fruit-filled cornucopia, symbolic of the banana empire established by the late Samuel Zemurray. A William Woodward painting which covered the oval ceiling of the entrance rotunda is being preserved by the International City Bank.

The banking and commercial history of New Orleans paralleled the development of Faubourg St. Mary, which has become the Central Business District. This chapter provides but a glimpse of 170 years of the history and physical appearance of the area. The economic vibrations, the complexity of the banking and commercial system and the influence of natural and political occurrences cannot be minimized. Motivated toward economic success, the banking and commercial interests activated the major building programs. But since the late 1920s the scene has shifted; commercial and financial interests, here as elsewhere, began the flight to satellite communities. The pull of the old American Sector was strong, however, and New Orleans Central Business District is intact. The challenge for a creative performance in the revitalization of the Central Business District is there; the major props—the Mississippi River and the visual history in architecture, its greatest assets—remain, to be used and incorporated into the future development of a city envisioned internationally for a century as potentially the greatest port in the world.

ALBUM

The earlier of two churches erected on the same site on Lafayette Square (South Street side) for the First Presbyterian congregation in 1835. Unsigned drawing dating from about 1840. (From the collection of Samuel Wilson, Jr.)

Faubourg St. Mary street scene of the 1820s showing the prevalence of small wooden struc-tures. Lithograph by Felix-Achille Beaupoil de Saint-Aulaire. (Courtesy Historic New Orleans Collection.)

A lithograph by Felix-Achille Beaupoil de Saint-Aulaire of Parson Clapp's Protestant church, formerly located on St. Charles, bound by Gravier and Union, shows the rural character of Faubourg St. Mary in the 1820s. (Courtesy Historic New Orleans Collection.)

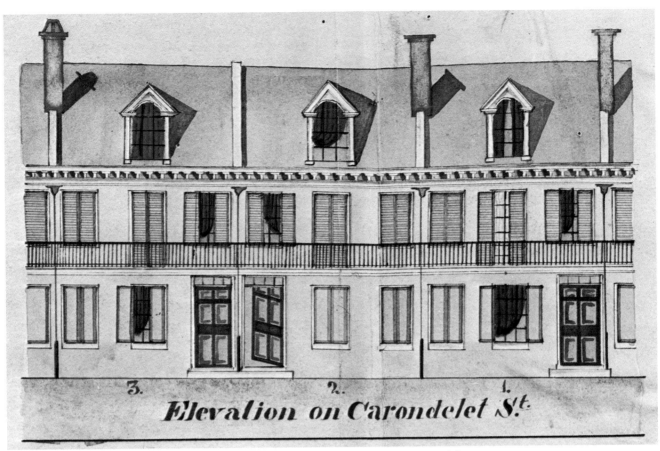

Dormered row houses erected in 1832 by John Fitz Miller, builder, at 630-34-40 Carondelet.
Drawing by Frederick Wilkinson, February 23, 1839. Plan Book 32, Folio 8, New Orleans
Notarial Archives.

Row houses and a small cottage (demolished) on Tulane Avenue, bound by S. Liberty, Loyola,
Gravier. Drawing by E. Surgi, December 15, 1840. Plan Book 61, Folio 52, New Orleans
Notarial Archives.

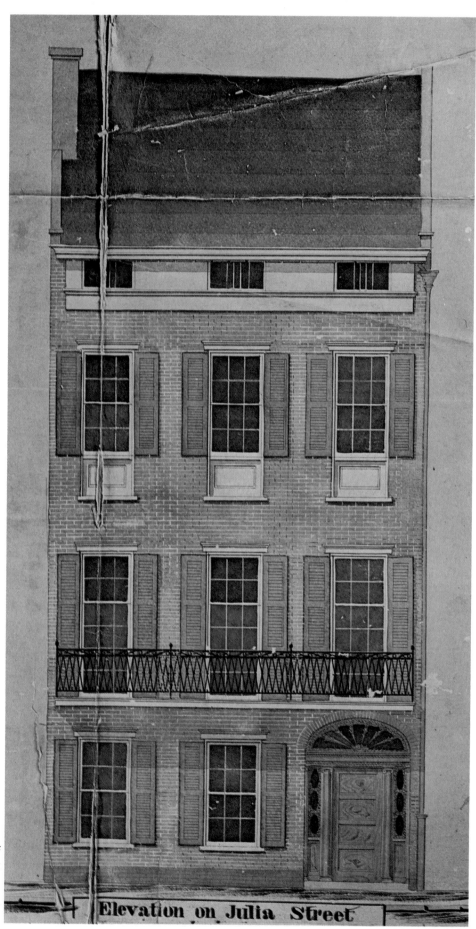

One of row houses in 600 block of Julia, with late Georgian style *faux bois* door, built in 1833. A. T. Wood, architect. Unsigned drawing, May 4, 1857. Plan Book 43, Folio 46, New Orleans Notarial Archives.

80

Greek Revival masonry row houses and a small frame galleried cottage, with dome of the St. Charles Hotel in background (all demolished). On Baronne, bound by Canal, Common, Carondelet. Drawing by L. Surgi, January 15, 1847. Plan Book 82, Folio 33, New Orleans Notarial Archives.

Greek Revival houses built about 1850 at 822 and 826 St. Charles (now greatly altered). Unsigned drawing, May 4, 1857. Plan Book 43, Folio 46, New Orleans Notarial Archives.

Greek Revival house having raised basement with carriage entrance and a gabled cottage (demolished). On Iberville, bound by Burgundy, Rampart, Canal. Drawing by Charles A. de Armas, March 28, 1853. Plan Book 62, Folio 8, New Orleans Notarial Archives.

Classical style house with cast-iron gallery, 827 St. Charles, erected in 1856, J. H. Murphy, builder. Drawing by Charles A. de Armas, August 1, 1866. Plan Book 43, Folio 68, New Orleans Notarial Archives.

Greek Revival row house with iron balconies, *faux bois* door with rosettes (demolished). On Dauphine, bound by Canal, Iberville, Bourbon. Drawing by J. N. B. de Pouilly, February 23, 1867. Plan Book 82, Folio 49, New Orleans Notarial Archives.

Typical corner scene in Faubourg St. Mary showing residential properties, masonry and wood cottages and a two-story brick house (all demolished). On Girod, corner Magazine, bound by Tchoupitoulas, Notre Dame. Drawing by Charles A. de Armas, February 7, 1859. Plan Book 43, Folio 58, New Orleans Notarial Archives.

Masonry gabled cottages (demolished), with St. Patrick's Church in background. On Girod, bound by Camp, Magazine, Julia. Drawing by Charles A. de Armas, April 9, 1860. Plan Book 42, Folio 47, New Orleans Notarial Archives.

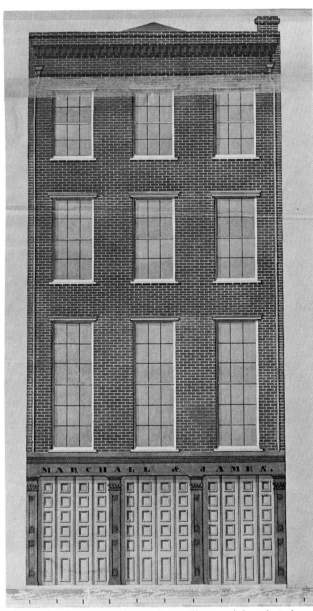

Classical style store with cast-iron pillars and *faux bois* four-fold doors at 317 Camp. Built in 1850 by Charles Pride for Charles Mason, attorney for Robert Heath of England. Drawing by C. A. Hedin, February 26, 1853. Plan Book 95, Folio 46, New Orleans Notarial Archives.

Classical style store with granite pillars and two fold doors at 512 Magazine. Erected 1838, Sidel and Stewart, builders. Drawing by C. A. Hedin, September 11, 1858. Plan Book 42, Folio 33, New Orleans Notarial Archives.

Row of three Classical style stores, painted contrasting colors, at 115-117-121 Chartres. Built about 1832. Drawing by Charles A. de Armas, May 8, 1859. Plan Book 58, Folio 22, New Orleans Notarial Archives.

Masonry stores with granite pillars and cast-iron gallery, built in 1851 for H. C. Cammack by Gallier and Turpin, architects (demolished). On Carondelet, corner Common, bound by Baronne, Gravier. Unsigned, undated drawing. Plan Book 95, Folio 47, New Orleans Notarial Archives.

Six stores with cast-iron pillars, balcony and canopy, built for Judah Touro by Thomas Murray in 1851, at 301-17 St. Charles. Drawing by Hedin and Schlarbaum, April 3, 1854. Plan Book 62, Folio 16, New Orleans Notarial Archives.

Store with segmental arched windows at second level and a pediment parapet (demolished). Tchoupitoulas, corner Common. Lithograph by B. Simon, 1871. (Courtesy Historic New Orleans Collection.)

Italianate store with bracketed cornice and cast-iron hood molds and pillars (demolished). Corner Magazine and Poydras. Lithograph by B. Simon, 1871. (Courtesy Historic New Orleans Collection.)

THEO FROIS & CO

THEO FROIS & CO

co81. THEO FROIS & CO. **8163**

FRONT ELEVATION.

Architect's drawing of the cast-iron facade of the Frois Building (demolished), on Canal, bound by Camp, Magazine, Common. Built in 1859. William A. Freret, architect, A. De Frasse, sculptor, cast by New Orleans foundry of Bennett and Lurges. (Courtesy Louisiana State Museum.)

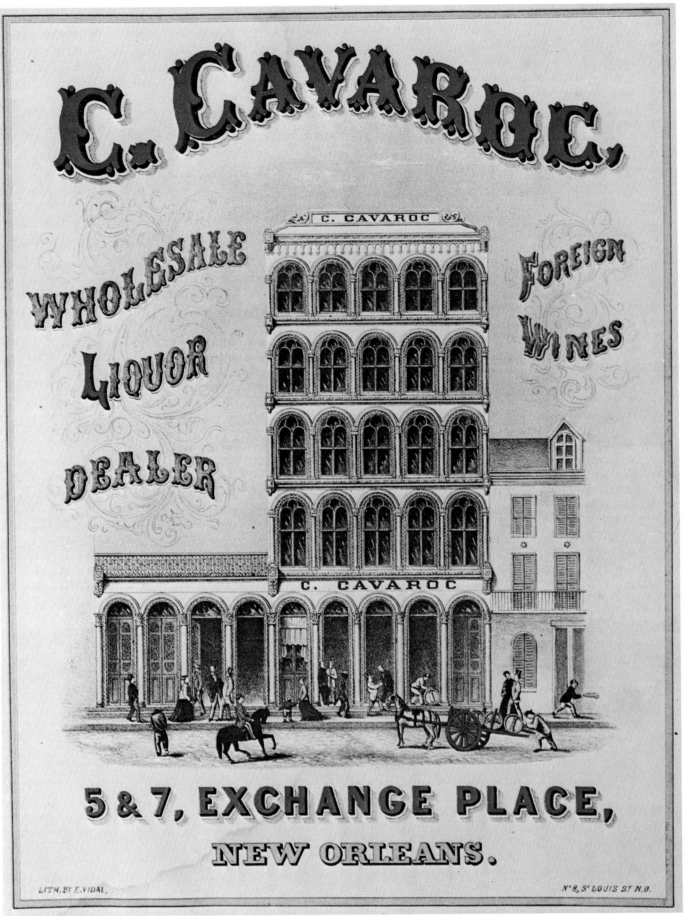

C. CAVAROC.

C. CAVAROC

WHOLESALE

LIQUOR

DEALER

FOREIGN

WINES

C. CAVAROC

5 & 7, EXCHANGE PLACE,

NEW ORLEANS.

LITH. BY E. VIDAL.

N° 8, S¹ LOUIS S¹ N.O.

One of New Orleans' two remaining cast-iron facades, at 111 Exchange. Built in 1866, designed by Gallier and Esterbrook in the Venetian Renaissance style. Lithograph by B. Simon, 1871. (Courtesy Historic New Orleans Collection.)

The American Sector

marks buildings, areas or streets which, because of architectural or historic importance or value to the street scene, should be preserved. No demolition should take place in these areas, and renovation should approach original appearance. Preservation of these blocks as units should be considered.

marks buildings and areas important to the presentation of the Central Business District. Although new development ultimately may surround these areas, they should remain intact. All are potentially adaptable to creative modern usage.

marks buildings that are interesting for their period, but are located in low-density historic areas.

marks areas most obviously suitable for redevelopment. Areas with few or no notable structures are logical areas for modern development.

marks granite and brick streets and unique New Orleans pedestrian alleys.

Map by Joseph L. Swanson, III

ARCHITECTURAL INVENTORY

Faubourg St. Mary, now the Central Business District for more than a million people, always has been the most mobile and fast-changing of New Orleans' various neighborhoods. Its development coincided with the most rapid population growth in the city's 250-year history.

Eighteenth century sugar plantations, from Common Street to Howard Avenue, and farms with modest frame houses surrendered to high density residential-commercial areas between the 1820s and 1860s. Building contracts indicate the building boom was equal to this period of peak economic growth, the richest years the city has known. The waterfront, including Water, Levee, Delta, Front, Tchoupitoulas and Magazine streets, was swiftly built with commercial buildings and warehouses for merchants and factories, importers and exporters. Residential areas sprang up on Lafayette, Girod, Julia, St. Joseph and Howard, then onto Camp, St. Charles, Carondelet and Baronne above Poydras.

Fortunes were made and lost quickly in the wheelings and dealings of real estate in the development of speculative property, and New Orleans architects and builders were among the speculators. William Brand, the Galliers and the Frerets invested extensively in land from Rampart to Carondelet, and Canal to Gravier. Jamison, a brick layer, and McVittie and Lee, builders, bought land and built row after row of residences on St. Joseph, Baronne and Poydras streets, selling some, renting others. These and other builders had but to look about them for models and follow standard formula plans. It was customary for an owner to specify that his building resemble another in the area, thus building by analogy. This custom of repeating the module gave unity and harmony to the street scene.

Mortgage office books reveal the speculators and developers to be well-known community leaders, among whom were John McDonogh, Carl Kohn, Samuel J. Peters, Benjamin Caldwell, Armand and Michel Heine, Duncan Kenner and Thomas Barrett. The Pritchard, Gasquet, Slocomb, Lanfear and Montgomery families were all heavy investors in this new section. These men employed James and Charles Dakin, Henry Howard and Louis Reynolds, to name but a few of the architects who were filling the squares with public edifices, mansions and commercial structures. Churches, synagogues, banks and buildings for fraternal orders erected in the grandiose, classical style have, with the exception of Gallier Hall, the Custom House and Turner's Hall, been demolished. The great mansions on large lots exemplified by the Sheppard house and the Heine, Kohn and Campbell mansions have all disappeared. The A. H. May house once stood on St. Charles Street; in its former garden now stands the YMCA building at Lee Circle (fig. 1).

Also gone is the greenery. Lists of trees appear in city surveyors' books, indicating

93

Fig. 1. Old 238 St. Charles (demolished), at Lee Circle. From *J. C. Waldo's Illustrated Visitor's Guide to New Orleans* (1879). (Courtesy New Orleans Public Library.)

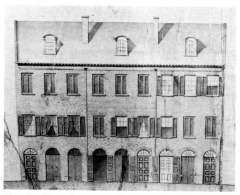

Fig. 2. Row houses (demolished) of the first quarter of the 19th century, N. Diamond, bound by S. Front, Tchoupitoulas, St. Joseph. Drawing by H. Moelhausen, July 12, 1841. Plan Book 63, Folio 12, New Orleans Notarial Archives.

that commercial and residential streets were lined with elms, water oaks, live oaks and pecans. Flagstone patios and side yards were planted with luxuriant tropical gardens. Gone, then, are the Creole dormered cottages, mansions and the majority of the 19th century public buildings, but the descriptions which follow pertain to the types and styles of 450 fine buildings remaining in the Central Business District.

A few remaining early buildings of the 1830s exhibit stylistic features traditional with early Vieux Carre styles, particularly the arched door and the dormer (fig. 2). Two of the earliest buildings in the area, at 703 Tchoupitoulas, corner Girod, have semicircular arches at ground level. A remnant of the arched openings can be seen on the Poydras Street facade of an 1830 commercial building at 501 Magazine. Row houses of the 600 block of Julia Street had arched doors with fanlights, a late Georgian characteristic. Dormers with arched openings flanked by fluted pilasters, as seen on the buildings at 630, 640 and 658 Carondelet and 834–36 Julia, usually date from the early 1830s. Later Greek Revival houses tended to have attic windows instead of dormers. Numbers 630, 640 and 658 Carondelet also illustrate the small-scale fenestration generally used in the early 1830s. The buildings themselves are of small scale, 2½ stories high, while later townhouses were generally of 3½ stories. Their modest floorplan derives from the 18th century Regency plan of two rooms deep sided by a stair hall. Later townhouse plans, although also based on the Regency, tended to be more extensive.

Architects James Gallier, Sr., the Dakin brothers and Henry Howard saw the Greek Revival style initiated in London, Dublin and New York in the 1820s and 1830s. In fact, Gallier and James H. Dakin were responsible for some of the plates in Minard Lafever's *The Modern Builder's Guide* (1833), one of the primary influences in the spread of the Greek Revival style of architecture in America. Therefore, it is not surprising that New Orleans Greek Revival architecture is comparable in quality to that found anywhere in the United States. The old Second Municipality Hall (Gallier Hall), designed by James Gallier, Sr., in 1845, with its handsome Ionic portico and Greek detailing, is equaled only by similar temple-type institutional buildings and churches in the Northeast. The spacious interior of the Custom House, with its colossal columns, has perhaps the finest Greek Revival interior in America.

Residences and commercial buildings, often built in rows with party walls, between 1830 and 1860, have Anglo-American features: plain wall surfaces, simple classical detailing, red brick, white trim, green shutters and double-hung windows.

Fig. 4. Anthemion scroll decoration, 838 Camp.

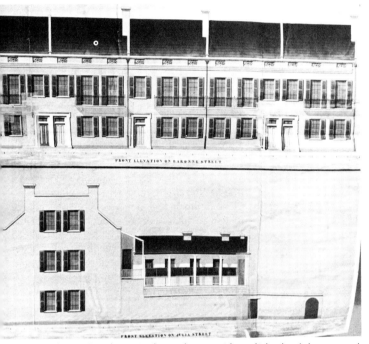

Fig. 3. Greek Revival row houses (demolished) of the second quarter of the 19th century, Baronne, corner Julia, Howard, O'Keefe. Unsigned, undated drawing. Plan Book 95, Folio 37, New Orleans Notarial Archives.

Fig. 5. Greek Key door, 929 Julia. Unsigned, undated drawing. Plan Book 42, Folio 59, New Orleans Notarial Archives.

Fig. 6. *Faux bois* door framed by pilasters as antae supporting entablature, 826 St. Charles. Unsigned drawing, May 4, 1857. Plan Book 43, Folio 46, New Orleans Notarial Archives.

There is essentially little variation in the basic appearance of the masonry structures, but the local individualistic variations of the international style create a charm special to each structure (fig. 3). The 600 block of Julia is the only block-long row extant. Double townhouses remain at 706–10 and 753–55 Carondelet, 723–27 Girod and 820–22 Baronne. Free-standing or individual houses survive at 822 Camp, 609 St. Charles and 468 St. Joseph. Generally 3½ stories in height, they occupied lots from 22 to 25 feet wide by 100 to 150 feet deep. The entrance, placed to one side, was embellished with Greek Revival casings, columns on pilasters and sometimes carved Greek mouldings and anthemions (fig. 4). The Greek Key moulding, or, as it is referred to in building contracts of the period, "a moulding with diminished architraves," was the simplest of door casings; its distinguishing feature is a crosset, or double-mitered "ear" at the top side architrave projection (fig. 5). Often pilasters as antae frame the door and support an entablature with decorated moulded cornice. Free-standing columns of Greek order were also used in place of pilasters (fig. 6). Entrances recessed several feet behind the casings often contained an exterior set of doors or shutters for privacy and protection (fig. 7).

Otherwise the facade was undecorated except for an entablature at the roofline,

Fig. 7. Recessed door framed by fluted Ionic columns supporting entablature, 706 Carondelet.

Fig. 8. Roofline entablature of house (demolished) on Rampart, bound by Canal, Iberville, Burgundy. Drawing by Judice and Frenaux, December 18, 1866. Plan Book 38, Folio 28, New Orleans Notarial Archives.

which usually contained a cornice with dentils, frieze with attic windows and an architrave (fig. 8). Windows had plain stone lintels or lintels with restrained cap or pedimented mouldings. They had louvered or paneled shutters, generally painted "Paris green," a bright yellow-green. In the 1830s and 1840s wrought iron balconies were placed at the second level; windows opening onto the balconies were floor length. Most townhouses of the 1850s and 60s had ornate cast-iron galleries, sometimes for every level of the facade. The presence of cast-iron galleries must be taken cautiously as a determinant in dating buildings, because they often were added to earlier structures. Cast iron also was employed for grills in attic windows and for gates and fences.

Townhouse facades usually were constructed of fine-quality brick, Baltimore pressed brick or the less desirable Lake brick, while the other walls usually were composed of inferior "country brick." These facades were often painted, usually red, with white penciled joints. Some exterior walls were plastered and scored to resemble stone and were then painted. Earth colors—light yellow, pale orange, and terra cotta—were popular. The New Orleans *Weekly Delta* of October 29, 1849, lamented the custom of painting brick buildings an intense red:

> The painting of houses is the subject to which too little attention is devoted. We are glad to observe that the light colors, such as straw, stone, cream, chocolate and yellow are becoming fashionable. The custom of painting brick houses a flaming red, particularly in a sultry climate like ours, ought to be "reformed altogether." Red is the color of savages, and as all admit...seems to add to the heated atmosphere of our long summers. Besides the pencilling of the bricks produces a disagreeable effect upon the eyes owing to the smallness of the lines, which, at a little distance, seem to run into each other, and thus become indistinct. This is quite perceptible in our large three-story brick buildings. The size of the bricks, as indicated by lines of white paint, being out of all proportion to that of the edifice. No wonder that strangers, landing in our midst in mid-summer, and walking through streets lined on either side with glaring red buildings complain of the suffocating sensation produced by the air.

Marble or granite trim was popular around doors and windows. Door casings and attic friezes, however, were often of wood. Wood trim was generally either painted white or painted to resemble marble or granite. Feathers and rags were the instruments used by painters to simulate the veins of marble, and a light grey ground was spattered with a darker color to imitate granite. Entrance doors, usually cypress, were, almost without exception, painted in *faux bois* to imitate quartersawed oak which exposed the edge of the grain. Only the entrance door, and not the casing, was given *faux bois* treatment. A ground coat of tan oak-color was first laid, then a darker brown applied and manipulated with a metal comb to achieve the effect of wood grain. Cross grains were lifted out with a rag. Roofs were hipped or gabled and covered with Welsh slate and English ridge tiles usually hidden by cornices. Gutters were copper.

The townhouse was two or three rooms deep with a stair hall to one side and a two-story service wing with kitchen and servants' quarters extending lengthwise to one side at the rear (fig. 9). This arrangement of service wing, with a wooden gallery, extending at the rear and sided by a courtyard seems to derive from local building traditions originated in the Vieux Carre. The courtyard was either paved with brick or flagstone (North River or Yorkshire) and contained a privy and cistern. Interior bathrooms with hot and cold running water made their appearance in New Orleans in the 1840s.

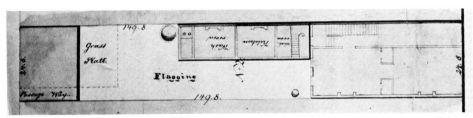

Fig. 9. Typical plan of house with service wing, dating from about 1830. House (demolished), South Street, bound by St. Charles, Camp, Girod. Drawing by Charles F. Zimpel, January 6, 1834. Plan Book 71, Folio 1, New Orleans Notarial Archives.

The ground floor contained a double parlor, often divided by sliding doors encased in an architectonic screen framed by Greek columns and surmounted by an entablature often adorned with carvings. In the center of the high ceilings were large plaster floral medallions. Mantels were carved marble. The dining room was either behind the parlor or on the ground floor of the service wing. Doorknobs and escutcheons on this first level often were silver plated. The millwork, usually cypress, was either in *faux bois* or painted white. Mahogany, curled maple, walnut and oak were the most popular woods for painters to imitate, and millwork throughout the house often was grained with a variety of them. Even when the millwork was painted white, doors inevitably were grained and baseboards often marbleized to match the genuine marble mantels.

Doyle and May, "house, sign and ornamental painters" located on Carondelet Street near Canal, published an advertisement in Gibson's 1838 *City Directory* offering:

"Imitations of the following Woods and Marbles, executed in a masterly manner"

Woods:	Marbles:
Mahogany,	Egyptian, black and gold,
Oak,	Cialla and Antico,
Pollard Oak,	Oriental or Verd Antique,
Curled Oak,	Jasper,
Curled Maple,	Blood Stone,
Bird's Eye Maple,	Darby Granite,
Satin Wood,	Potomac,
Hair Wood,	Dove, or Burdello,
Yew Tree,	Italian White,
Coromandel or Black Rose Wood,	Sienna and Broctella,
Ash White Oak,	American Grey,
Curled Elm.	&c. &c. &c.

The main staircase, authentic mahogany or walnut, usually had a fancy newell post and turned balusters. The bedrooms and nursery of the upper floors were sparsely decorated. Mouldings around doors and windows were plainer, and the fireplace mantels were usually of wood painted to resemble marble. The servants' quarters were devoid of decoration and their mantels were of wood.

This form of house continued in use into the 1870s, but examples of late date are seen with an overlay of Italianate decoration, with facades receiving the addition of high parapets and heavy ornamentation. As at 842 Camp, fronts often were rusticated and windows and door were segmentally arched. Interior decoration was correspondingly more elaborate.

The classical style of commercial and industrial buildings of 1830 to the 1860s is best described by Talbot Hamlin in *Greek Revival Architecture in America:*

Fig. 10. Brick classical style store on Tchoupitoulas, bound by St. Joseph, Julia, Commerce. Drawing by Charles A. de Armas, May 22, 1861. Plan Book 42, Folio 49, New Orleans Notarial Archives.

Its essentials were: a ground floor supported on monolithic granite piers, often with Greek anta capitals and carrying a simply molded granite architrave; above this three or four stories of brick or granite wall, pierced with well-proportioned windows, regularly spaced and often furnished with iron shutters; then, as a crown to the whole, a restrained, simple cornice of moderate projection, with moldings of Greek profile...the uniformity of their cornice lines, the monumental repetition of their granite piers, and the rhythmical regularity of their openings give a pleasant harmony and unity to the streets they border. The best of these buildings are simple, useful, unostentatious, human in scale, and restrained and delicate in detail.

Built in rows, joined by party walls, and lining whole blocks, the stores front directly on the street. Most prevalent were the three-bay stores, with three windows across and three openings at the ground level (fig. 10). These usually occupied lots about

Fig. 12. Ovolo capital on granite pillar.

Fig. 13. Beak capital on granite pillar.

Fig. 11. Granite pillars and lintel course on store at 512 Magazine. Drawing by C. A. Hedin, February 26, 1853. Plan Book 95, Folio 28, New Orleans Notarial Archives.

Fig. 15. Cast-iron lintel course and pillars on store, 317 Camp. Drawing by C. A. Hedin, February 26, 1853. Plan Book 95, Folio 46, New Orleans Notarial Archives.

Fig. 14. Acanthus leaf capital and palmette relief on cast-iron pillar.

20 to 25 feet wide by depths of from 50 to 100 feet. Not uncommon were two-bay and four-bay stores. Facades usually were constructed of Baltimore brick or Lake brick and the other walls and foundations of "country brick," with brick denticulated cornices at the roofline. Side walls were extended up above the roofline in an attempt to contain fires and, as such, are called fire walls.

Granite was employed for window lintels and sills, for ground-floor pillars and the lintel course (fig. 11). Two types of capitals are found on the granite pillars. The earlier ovolo capital has a simple, rounded profile similar to Greek moulding and dates from the 1830s (fig. 12). After 1840 a beak capital, with a deep undercut beneath the rounded profile, was used (fig. 13). Cast-iron pillars were also used, beginning in the late 1840s, some with ornate Corinthian or Acanthus leaf capitals, and examples of brick pillars remain (figs. 14–15). A variety of pillar types were often employed on the same building, as with cast-iron pillars on the front and granite pillars on the side.

Doors, either two-fold or four-fold, were installed between the pillars and when open they folded back behind the jambs, entirely exposing the interior to the street. They contained recessed panels, and the upper portions of some were glazed. These were fitted with portable shutters which could be placed over the glass and secured by interior thumbscrews. A number of such doors remain on buildings today. They originally were either grained in *faux bois* to resemble oak or painted green. Two-tone green doors were popular, with the recessed panels painted a lighter green than the rest of the door. Depending on the use of the building, display windows, some with bays and large panes of glass, filled openings between the pillars.

In these buildings, the height of each successive story diminishes in size. Windows on the second story originally had 18 lights, and those on the third and fourth story

Fig. 16. Cast-iron trim, labels, tracery and coupled columns of commercial building at 923 Tchoupitoulas.

Fig. 17. Cast-iron Italianate hood moulds and bracketed cornice, Factors Row, 802-22 Perdido.

Fig. 18. Commercial use of cast-iron balcony and canopy. Drawing by Hedin and Schlarbaum, April 3, 1854. Plan Book 62, Folio 16, New Orleans Notarial Archives.

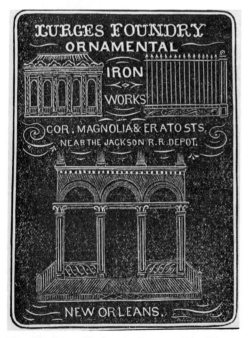

Fig. 19. From *Graham's Crescent City Directory* (1870). (Courtesy New Orleans Public Library.)

12, but the fourth-story windows were smaller. Windows were double-hung, and could have exterior green shutters, either metal or wooden. More often, interior louvered shutters of four folds were provided. The facades of stores, like residences, often were painted red with white penciled mortar joints, or they were plastered, scored and painted to resemble stone. Window trim was painted white. A few stores were constructed entirely of granite, and at least one row was composed of marble. Granite stores (which have been painted) remain at 325–43 Carondelet, and marble stores still stand at 400 Magazine. Stone was not readily available in New Orleans and was not used as frequently as in the Northeast.

A departure from the standardized commercial form began to appear in the 1850s and 1860s when Gothic labels or Italianate hood moulds and parapets enlivened some facades (figs. 16–17). Number 325–43 Carondelet is detailed with simple Gothic labels, and 923 Tchoupitoulas is a splendid example of the commercial Gothic, with cast-iron Gothic ornament. Commercial structures in the Gothic mode were not uncommon in New Orleans, but few have survived.

In Italianate stores, segmental arched windows are a standard feature, capped with cast-iron hood moulds embellished with derivatives of classical floral motifs, at the ends of which are decorative brackets. Rooflines, usually with parapets, have enlarged, projecting cornices supported by scroll brackets. Numbers 130–38 and 304–14 St. Charles and 802–22 Perdido are fine examples of the Italianate style. Another classical variation in commercial buildings of the 1850s can be seen in the use of Roman, or Tuscan, decoration on the stores at 407 Camp, with restrained use of large, pedimented projecting lintels. These commercial building types originally had ornate cast-iron galleries at the second level and all utilized cast-iron pillars, usually with Corinthian or foliated capitals at the ground level (fig. 18).

Just before the Civil War larger and more grandiose stores began to replace the simple classical style brick ones. This was the beginning of the era of the "dry-goods palace," the large department store and the "merchant aristocracy." As retail trading expanded, the commercial edifice assumed new importance and emerged as a major building type. Concurrent with the new architectural demands of commercialism were technical and structural advances which contributed to innovations in design. Primary among these was the use of cast-iron for structural as well as decorative purposes.

James Bogardus and Daniel D. Badger, two New York innovators in the field, expanded the use of iron in architecture beyond simple decorative and supportive devices to methods used for constructing whole fronts and entire buildings of iron. Bogardus' 1856 publication, *Cast Iron Buildings: Their Construction and Advantages*, explains his development of a system of bolts and tie rods to join standardized prefabricated parts into a stable whole. Badger's 1865 iron foundry catalogue, *Illustrations of Iron Architecture*, shows specific designs of entire facades and a rich variety of lintels, arches, cornices, brackets, columns, stairways, grills, fences, and galleries.

The advantages of cast-iron as a building material were many. Slender structural members resisted heavy loads, allowing increased building height and large window openings. Mass produced and easily assembled, cast iron could be fashioned into any variety of forms to imitate stone, brick or wood. Its versatility was further enhanced by its durability and fire-resistant qualities. Cast-iron buildings were a significant step in the American development of the steel-framed skyscraper and were an

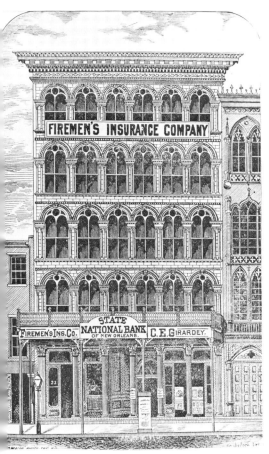

Fig. 20. Tulane Building. From *J. C. Waldo's Illustrated Visitor's Guide to New Orleans* (1879). (Courtesy New Orleans Public Library.)

Fig. 21. Levois and Jamison Building. From *Jewell's Crescent City* (1873). (Courtesy Historic New Orleans Collection.)

Fig. 22. Story Building. From *Jewell's Crescent City* (1873). (Courtesy New Orleans Public Library.)

advance toward the modern use of prefabrication. By 1850 cast-iron was being extensively used in New Orleans' business district. Many main thoroughfares were transformed by the erection of ornate iron facades. Two excellent examples survive, one at 622 Canal, designed by William A. Freret in 1859, another at 111 Exchange Place, designed in 1866 by Gallier and Esterbrook.

Local iron foundries such as Leeds, Armstrong, Holmes and Bennett Baumiller, and the Julia Street Foundry were manufacturing a wide variety of architectural elements for application to masonry buildings (fig. 19). Iron columns, railings, verandahs, shutters, cornices, lintels, brackets, pilasters, pillars and hood moulds were readily available. An 1852 newspaper article criticized the fact that iron casting work was being sent from New York when local foundries could supply them.

By 1859 the *Daily Crescent* reported: "The chief feature of building this year is an increased degree of ornamentation, and increased use of iron. Granite was the rage a few years since for store doors and window cornices, but now it is altogether iron. Not only iron basements, but whole iron fronts are becoming fashionable."

A wide variety of historic styles, such as Gothic, Renaissance, Baroque, and Moorish, and combinations of styles were executed in iron facades. An important example of New York cast-iron was the Tulane Building, formerly on Camp, between Common and Gravier, occupied by the Fireman's Insurance Company and the State National Bank (fig. 20). Daniel Badger's catalogue states that Paul Tulane ordered this facade, plate No. VII, from his foundry some time before 1865. The Levois and Jamison Building (old 126 Canal) also greatly resembled another of the illustrations in the Badger catalogue, plate No. III (fig. 21).

Fig. 23. Slocomb-Baldwin Building. From *Jewell's Crescent City* (1873). (Courtesy New Orleans Public Library.)

The Story Building, built for Mrs. Monroe Mackie in honor of her prominent father, Benjamin Story, formerly located at the corner of Camp and Common, bound by Magazine and Gravier, was one of the most important iron buildings constructed in the business district (fig. 22). It was similar in appearance to one of Badger's illustrations, plate XVII, No. 4. Louis E. Reynolds was the local architect, although the designers were Tiffany and Bottom of Philadelphia. Cast in Trenton, New Jersey, and erected in 1859, it was Corinthian in style, with iron columns painted bright red and both fronts surmounted by magnificent relief representations of an allegory of commerce: Neptune in his chariot drawn by dolphins or seahorses, surrounded by Tritons, plus emblems of ships under full sail.

The demolished iron front hardware store of Slocomb Baldwin & Company on Canal, between Camp and Magazine, was the model for the extant building at 111 Exchange Place (fig. 23). The Slocomb Baldwin store was erected in 1859 at a cost of $50,000. William A. Freret was the architect and Crozier and Wing the builders. The repetition of standardized units was highly effective in this building. The fact that it was copied in the foundry of Bennett & Lurges for the 111 Exchange Place building seven years later is a rare example of building by analogy in the 1860s. Whereas one of the advantages of cast-iron prefabrication was that identical structures could be easily erected, this was not often the case, as distinctive facades were preferred.

A significant example of a cast-iron facade of distinctly original design was the Frois Building (fig. 24), once located on Canal between Camp and Magazine. Both the iron front and the brick building behind it were designed by architect William A. Freret. Carvings and modeling of patterns were done by A. De Frasse, sculptor and wood-carver. Ironwork was cast in the New Orleans foundry of Bennett and Lurges. Peter Ross was the builder. Building contract information on this store shows that the brick building was first constructed, then the front of cast-iron sections bolted together was secured with tie rods to the masonry. An article in the *Picayune* of Sep-

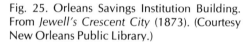

Fig. 24. Cast-iron caryatids of Frois Building. (Courtesy Historic New Orleans Collection.)

Fig. 25. Orleans Savings Institution Building. From *Jewell's Crescent City* (1873). (Courtesy New Orleans Public Library.)

Fig. 26. Moresque Building. From *Jewell's Crescent City* (1873). (Courtesy New Orleans Public Library.)

tember 27, 1859, describes Theodore Frois and Company's four-story dry goods store: "W. A. Freret, architect, adopted a slightly mixed style for the pillars of the lower three stories in disposition of ornaments; beneath the third story cornice was a very pretty relievo of little children playing, holding up a wreath; the fourth story displayed four females supporting a very elaborate architrave; an eagle in relievo held the centre of the blocking course." The Merchants Mutual Building, still standing at 622 Canal, is another notable example of an original design in an iron front building. It was a matter of local pride that both the designs and castings were of New Orleans origin and comparable to iron buildings anywhere.

Another excellent later example of the cast-iron facade, formerly standing at old 156 Canal, between Baronne and Carondelet, was the New Orleans Savings Institution designed by W. A. Freret and built by L. N. Olivier in 1873 (fig. 25). The front was cast by the New Orleans foundry of Leeds and Company and was considered, at that time, the best work ever put together. *Jewell's Crescent City* gives a description of the building: "The style of the new bank is...a faithful copy of the Renaissance of Louis Quatorze. The front of iron is florid and ornate...the aesthetic eye of the connoisseur can appreciate the graceful curves of the blocking course over the cornice of the front. The cornice proper has the pleasing effect of the Grecian....Immediately over the door, shaded by the heavy *fronton* of the frame, is a handsomely-finished window in the French style." The largest and perhaps most important cast-iron building erected in New Orleans was the Moresque Building, constructed entirely of cast-iron (fig. 26). Located in the square bound by Camp, Poydras, North and St. Mary streets, it was begun in 1859 but not completed until after the Civil War. The ironwork was cast at the foundry of Jones, McElvain and Company in Holly Springs, Mississippi. Built for J. O. Barelli, it was to house rental stores and a hall and rooms for concerts and balls. The structure, purchased in 1865 by John Gauche who ran a large crockery business, was destroyed in a spectacular fire April 15, 1897.

A city waterworks, formerly located on the neutral ground of Canal near the river, was another massive structure composed entirely of iron (fig. 27). Erected in 1861, the iron superstructure, 84 by 42 feet, was built by the New Orleans foundry of Bennett and Lurges. Panels of the doors represented a fountain, with water falling on growing stalks of corn, sugar and cotton. On panels of the arched windows were representations of water nymphs riding on seahorses, and the space between the windows contained mermaids, the sea god Neptune, and dolphins. The reservoir was to hold 175,000 gallons of water and was supported by 36 cast-iron columns. Painted to represent brownstone, it was much acclaimed. Later converted to use as the Free Market, where needy families received food from the surplus of upriver plantations, it was demolished sometime after 1874.

The Southern foundries were reorganized to produce war materials during the Civil War, and many were never reopened during the years of Reconstruction. After a flourishing beginning, cast-iron fronts were seldom used after the war, and most of the fine examples have been demolished.

In high Victorian Italianate structures, masonry with iron detail was the popular building material. Elongated openings, sometimes ascending through two stories, are characteristically framed by engaged pilasters or columns bearing stilted arches, which rise vertically from the impost block before arching over the opening. Variations of the stilted arch form are flat-topped or square-headed, segmental and round. Also characteristic are heavy rustication, quoins, enlarged cornices, parapets and

Fig. 27. City waterworks on Canal Street in an 1861 lithograph by Jules Lion. (Courtesy Historic New Orleans Collection.)

Fig. 28. Italianate style stilted arches of the High Victorian period, 218-20 Camp.

Fig. 29. Eclectic Victorian decoration, 201 Camp.

Fig. 30. The Richardson Romanesque style Howard Library, 601 Howard.

Fig. 31. Terra cotta relief decoration, 211 Camp.

boldly modelled brackets and decorative devices. In masonry buildings as in cast-iron structures, windows are large, occupying much of the surface of the facade (fig. 28). Fine applications of this style can be seen at 218–20 Camp, 115 St. Charles, and 826–30 Perdido.

New styles were attempted from a variety of borrowed elements in the late Victorian period. At 201 Camp and 217 Camp are buildings with combinations of forms drawn vaguely and indiscriminately from Baroque, Renaissance, medieval, and classical prototypes, foliage and animal forms, as indefinable as the specific sources of their decoration. Ornaments and varied surface texture are used as picturesque devices in these buildings which are typical of the free expressionism of Victorian eclecticism (fig. 29).

In the Howard Library at 601 Howard Avenue, Louisiana is fortunate to have a posthumous design by a native son, Henry Hobson Richardson, whose style achieved international fame (fig. 30). The building's rugged masonry textures, massive walls pierced with groups of arched or rectangular apertures, restrained ornamentation, towers and wall dormers all recall the Romanesque architecture of medieval Europe. The structure, one of New Orleans' finest of the late 19th century, is a typical example of Richardson's personal interpretation of a historic style.

In the early 20th century, architects turned with renewed interest to the revival forms of early Victorian architecture, rejecting the confusion of historically inappropriate stylistic associations appreciated by the preceding generation. There ensued a "Revival of Revivals," and one excellent example of this trend may be seen on Lafayette Square in the old Post Office, designed in the mode of the Italian Renaissance palazzo. Typically, individual elements of the building are literal historic translations, but the structure is also typically overscaled with a large rusticated base and columns of colossal order.

One must look up to see some of the most attractive decorative devices on commercial buildings of the late 19th and early 20th centuries. Above street level, some buildings exhibit interesting relief sculpture and some fine sculpture in the round, such as the two splendid allegorical figures above the entrance of 740 Gravier. Rich displays of terra cotta decoration can be seen; some facades were faced entirely with tile, either glazed or flat in finish and sometimes polychromed and modeled in a variety of relief decoration (fig. 31). The virtues of terra cotta were pointed out in *Architectural Art and Its Allies*, (September, 1910): "It must be remembered that terra cotta is not, although so often considered, an imitation stone. Terra cotta is a distinct material, individual in its make-up, that not only is, in many respects, more economical than stone, but results can be gained by its use through its coloring possibilities and other finishing effects, utterly impossible in stone."

The Gravier Building at 224–28 Camp is strikingly "modern" for its date, 1888. Its architectural qualities are purely abstract, free of historical reminiscence, an early visual expression anticipating the 20th century skyscraper design. Many tall steel-frame buildings, using brick not to support loads but to form curtain walls and to fireproof the metal, were erected in New Orleans just after the turn of the century. By that time, the structural advantages of steel and reinforced concrete and the passenger elevator, telephone and electric light bulb had stimulated the development of the skyscraper. Among the notable early "skyscrapers" in New Orleans are the Hennen–Maritime Building, 201–11 Carondelet, and the Roosevelt and Le Pavillon hotels.

In keeping with the current national trend, early New Orleans skyscrapers were expressions of classic-Renaissance design, their facades articulated to resemble the load-bearing, masonry buildings of historic styles rather than the true function of their metal-cage construction. The buildings were conceived in three parts, as in a classical column, with a base or podium having rustication, string courses and other decorative features, a relatively clean midsection with extruded bay windows emphasizing the vertical, as does the fluting in a column shaft, and terminating in a projecting, ornamented cornice, comparable to the capital of a column. This tripartite scheme was repeated in tall buildings of the early 20th century. The bay window, a most notable feature, afforded an additional facade dimension (fig. 32).

Fig. 32. Le Pavillon Hotel, on Baronne.

New Orleans does not possess a complete range of late 19th and early 20th century commercial styles, since the rate of expansion did not compare with that of Chicago, Detroit and New York. However, the intermittent examples here are important ingredients of the local architectural ensemble. Contrasting with the long years of Reconstruction, there was a significant acceleration of growth in New Orleans beginning in the 1890s and lasting until the Crash of 1929. The architects of the turn of the century whose works are an important contribution to the New Orleans Central Business District include Thomas Sully, Andry and Bendernagel, Samuel Stone, Wogan and Todelano, and Diboll, Owen and Goldstein. Major works by them already have been demolished, and the fine examples remaining should be retained.

It is remarkable that numerous examples of buildings of various periods and diverse uses, some dating from the early days of Faubourg St. Mary, remain in the midst of the ever vital, still changing central commercial area of New Orleans. Along its streets small classical-style stores stand beside modern skyscrapers, making the continuity of development visually apparent. It is to be hoped that while progress and change continue in the Central Business District, the remaining structures, remnants of a fascinating architectural chronology, will be preserved as a legacy for future generations.

On the following pages those entries not illustrated will be designated by ruled lines top and bottom.

The inventory that follows is presented alphabetically by street names. Each address has block boundaries indicated. Streets and areas of prominence are introduced with special illustrations.

BETSY SWANSON
MARY LOUISE CHRISTOVICH
ROULHAC TOLEDANO
PAT HOLDEN

132 Baronne. Church of the Immaculate Conception. The church standing today is a replica of this church originally built between 1851 and 1857 on this site. It was designed by the Reverend John Cambiaso, S. J., working with architect T. E. Giraud. Much of the old material was reused in the construction of the present church, notably the cast-iron pews and columns of the interior, when it was erected in 1929-30 by architects Wogan, Bernard and Toledano. The church was designed in the Moorish style, or, as newspapers of the 1850s described it: "Saracenic or Arabian style, somewhat more ancient than the Mauresque or Moorish."

Horseshoe arches, characteristic of the Moorish style, are repeated on the exterior and interior. The front was to be flanked by minaret-type towers of open cast-iron work 186 feet high. These were never completed, but similar towers with onion domes were erected when the church was rebuilt. The original church was 138 feet in length by 60 feet in width. The sanctuary, or chancel, was a half-octagon vaulted by a dome 32 feet in diameter and 130 feet from floor to ceiling; the ceiling in the interior of the nave was 76 feet long and 32 feet wide. The aisle was 25 feet wide. Over the aisle is a triforium gallery. The floors were to be of mosaic imitation marble and the original interior colors white, pearl and gold.

The original church was constructed of lake brick and wrought and cast-iron. An iron cupola rose over the rear of the building 35 feet above the roof. More than 200 tons of iron work, cast in Baltimore, were used in construction. The altar of gilt bronze, designed for the 1851 structure by architect James Freret and made in Lyons, France, was awarded first prize at the Paris Exposition of 1867-68. The marble statue of the Virgin Mary was ordered by Marie Amelie, Queen of France, for the Royal Chapel in the Tuilleries, but the Revolution of 1848 drove the Queen from France and the statue was offered for sale. It was brought to New Orleans and purchased for $5,000 with funds obtained by ladies of the congregation.

In the chapel on the right is the altar of St. Joseph, and on the left is the altar dedicated to the Sacred Heart of Jesus. The bronze statue of St. Peter, near the main entrance, is a replica of the famous figure in St. Peter's in Rome. This was one of the first churches in the world to be dedicated to the Immaculate Conception, following shortly upon the promulgation of the doctrine by Pope Pius IX in 1854.

According to Roger Baudier in *The Catholic Church in Louisiana* (1939), the Jesuit Church was established in 1847 as a church and school for boys. The school exists today as Loyola University and Jesuit High School. The land at the corner of Baronne and Common was purchased in 1848 for $22,000. On February 1, 1849, the College of Immaculate Conception was opened. Despite elaborate plans to lighten the weight of the structure on the soft alluvial soil, substantial changes had to be made as the third story was reached. The upper story had to be built of wood strengthened with wrought iron, with the roof and side elevations covered with copper laid on steel rods.

The foundations Father Cambiaso built were solid when the church was demolished in 1926. In 1881 the large building for classrooms on the Common side of the church was demolished and replaced with a larger three-story building. This building cost $30,000 and was designed by James Freret. This class building was leveled in 1901 and replaced by even larger and more modern college buildings designed by the architects Diboll and Owen. The Pere Marquette Building replaced this 1901 structure in 1925. (Photograph courtesy Historic New Orleans Collection.)

132 Baronne. Church of the Immaculate Conception. Cast-iron pews.

132 Baronne. Church of the Immaculate Conception. (Photograph from the Charles L. Franck Collection, New Orleans Public Library.)

132 Baronne. Church of the Immaculate Conception. Altar.

150 Baronne, corner Common, bound by Canal, Carondelet. Pere Marquette Building. One of New Orleans' early skyscrapers, designed in 1925 by architects Scott Joy and William E. Spink. It is an example of Gothic forms used to decorate and articulate a modern skyscraper. Here the two-tone effect popularized in the 1880s is continued. Like many commercial-style buildings of Lewis Sullivan, this building has a tripartite scheme in which the lower three stories are emphasized by light-colored tile and Gothic decoration, corresponding to the base of a column. The other twelve stories are equivalent to the shaft of a column, and the top three stories are emphasized by a light-colored string course, vertical members and deep, pierced cornice to the capital.

132 Baronne. Church of the Immaculate Conception. Cast-iron capital.

132 Baronne. Church of the Immaculate Conception. Nave.

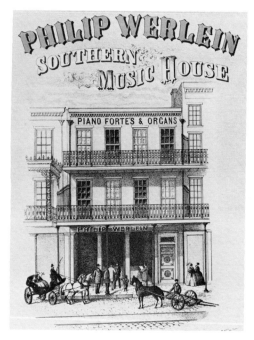

329-335 Baronne, corner Union, bound by Perdido, Dryades (above right). A four-story, four-bay, brick commercial building with granite window lintels and sills, brick denticulated cornice, with plastered and scored facade. Altered at first level. At the left is a three-story four-bay, brick commercial building with plastered facade pictured in *Simon* (above) as Werlein Music House. The original store had granite pillars and lintel course and cast-iron balconies at second and third levels. Original sash window light arrangement remains, although inside paneled shutters are no longer evident. The lithograph shows a three-panel door with carved medallions. The facade was not scored, although the present scoring is correct for the period. The lower facade, now mutilated, could easily be restored. The corner building was valued at $12,000 in 1862 when owned by T. B. See. The building on the left, owned by H. H. Hansley in 1862, was valued at $8,000. In 1871 the buildings were painted a warm peach tone with light-green balconies. Although the three adjacent buildings uptown in the block are not included in this survey, the scale and proportion of these later buildings, if maintained and painted, could be attractive parts of the street scene.

Other buildings built in this block during the 1850s included seven, two-story stores by Jamison and McIntosh, in 1856, for B. Saulay, at a cost of $15,000, and a store and house built by James Gallier, Jr., for John Cocks, on Baronne near Union, before 1855. They have been demolished. (B. Simon lithograph, 1871. Courtesy Historic New Orleans Collection.)

330, 332, 334 Baronne, corner Union, bound by Perdido, Carondelet. Three-story masonry commercial building with fifteen bays divided symmetrically into sections of two, three and five openings on its Baronne Street elevation. Semi-circular arches at the first and second level contrast with segmental arched openings on the third level. Cornice brackets grouped in different progressions serve to add interest to the wide expanse of facade. Although the store was probably built in the 1880s, the designer maintained the scale and classic forms of earlier buildings, such as the Lemann-Abraham Building, corner Baronne and Gravier, designed by C. L. Hillyer and demolished for construction of the Richardson Building.

The illustration in *Englehardt's* (1904) shows modification by removal of brackets on second floor cornice and quoins. Curved pediments over bays on Union have been removed, as has chimneyed gable on Baronne. In 1904 the Interstate Electric Co., Ltd., one of the most extensive electrical supply and contracting houses in the South, was located in this building. According to J. B. Walton, surveyor, the owners of these lots in 1866 were Octave Saulay, Merchants Mutual Insurance Co., George Clapp and Rotchford Brown.

401-403-405-407-409 Baronne, bound by Perdido, Market, Penn. Masonry facades of various periods from the 1840s and 1870s to World War I. If renovated, these would be valid portions of the old street scenes. The Baronne Hotel has iron pillars and lintel course. Second level windows have brick voussoirs. The third story has segmental arches with keystones in relief. The variation in fenestration is pleasing in this block.

431 Baronne, bound by Perdido, Market, Penn. This is a three-story, three-bay store which could date from the 1840s, with moulded cornice and recessed sash windows with no lintels or sills. Ground floor has been mutilated, but could be easily restored to original tasteful appearance.

400 block Baronne, bound by Perdido, Poydras, Carroll. Le Pavillon Hotel. This nine-story structure was built as the Denechaud Hotel in 1906 and known for many years as the DeSoto Hotel. Toledano and Wogan, architects, assisted by Rathbone DuBuys. Cost was $450,000. The luxurious hotel was described in *Architectural Art and its Allies* (Vol. 1, October, 1905): ''The style of architecture adopted is modern Renaissance, the two lower floors to be faced with terra cotta and the others of pressed brick . . . with a granite and limestone base. Exterior trim to be dark in tone.''

The structure, built of steel and reinforced concrete except for wood doors and windows, was considered fireproof. The horizontal emphasis of the rusticated base balancing the vertical lines of the bay windows and the repetition of the horizontal in the cornice utilize the formula for turn-of-the-century skyscrapers. The interior has marble floors with massive Sienna marble columns and pilasters and bronze and mahogany railings. Unfortunately, the original ornate crowning cornice was removed in a previous renovation, giving the roofline a severe character (see accompanying drawing). The recent remodeling by the owners is commendable, since it retains most of the original decorative elements. Remodeling by Seiferth and Gibert in 1971.

400 block Baronne. Denechaud Hotel. *Architectural Art and Its Allies* (1905). (Courtesy New Orleans Public Library.)

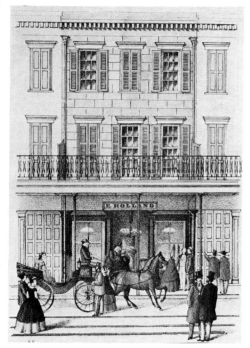

631 Baronne (demolished). B. Simon lithograph (1870). E. Rolland's Lady's Hair Store. (Courtesy Historic New Orleans Collection.)

621, 623, 625 Baronne, bound by Girod, Lafayette, O'Keefe. Three of a former row of six, three-story, three-bay, brick commercial buildings probably built in the 1850s. Plastered facades, cap-moulded lintels at third level and flat block lintels on second level, with iron pillars below the lintel course. The iron pillars have been removed or plastered over and the dentils of the cornice removed in the building on right. The building at left has been obscured by a modern louvered front. The Simon lithograph of the 1870s of the recently demolished Rolland Building shows that it had glass display windows between the pillars, but all originally had four-fold paneled doors as appear on the buildings on either side of the lithographs. It also shows that the buildings had cast-iron balconies at the second level, a scored plaster facade and louvered or paneled shutters.

606, 608 Baronne, bound by Girod, Lafayette, Carondelet. Two, two-and-one-half story brick row houses with altered facades, of the type built from the late 1840s.

624, 628, 630 Baronne, bound by Girod, Lafayette, Carondelet. Three, three-bay, three-story, brick commercial buildings. No. 624 has altered facade throughout. First floors of all buildings are altered. Mid-nineteenth century cornice with modillions and dentils. Simple stone sills and lintels. Pillars at first levels have been removed.

549 Baronne, corner Lafayette, bound by Dryades, Poydras. Five-story, three-bay, brick commercial building built for the Merganthaler Linotype Co. in 1911. Diboll, Owen and Goldstein, architects; Murphy and Mitchell, general contractors; Turner Construction Company, builder. The vertical articulation anticipates that of the modern skyscraper. Except for a Greek cresting of anthemion antefixae now removed from the building, the absence of any period decoration is a modern characteristic. The bronze medallions and the carved stone relief at the entrance are of abstract geometric designs, slightly reminiscent of Sullivanesque decoration. The building is said to be the first flat slab construction in New Orleans.

618 Baronne, bound by Girod, Lafayette, Carondelet. Glass art nouveau-style building built in the early part of the century for an automobile company. Unusual not only in style, which is said by present owner Max M. Dreyfus to have been designed after a Parisian prototype, but also because automobile dealers in the first quarter of the 20th century did not usually have buildings with show rooms designed for them. A hand-operated automobile elevator is still in operation. The Zilbermann brothers opened a Stern Knight Agency at this location in 1915. Heavy scroll brackets enframe the two-level, semi-oval glass front. A minimum of restoration is needed to rejuvenate this facade.

803 Baronne, corner Julia, bound by St. Joseph, O'Keefe. Two-and-one-half story masonry classic-style building with unusual stepped, rounded gable. Few architectural characteristics remain on altered facade. Yet the indications of a fine mid-nineteenth century commercial structure remain.

814 Baronne, bound by Julia, St. Joseph, Carondelet. An altered facade obscures a mid-nineteenth century three-story house-store, which retains the rear elevation of the main building, showing wood lintels and the original configuration of the complex.

815 Baronne, bound by Julia, St. Joseph, Dryades. Two-and-one-half story brick house with iron balcony at second level. Altered facade obscures the fact that this was one of a row of houses built in the late 1840s.

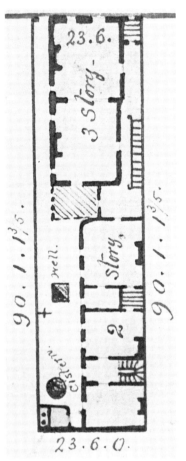

820 Baronne. Drawing and floor plan by D. E. Seghers, 1879, Plan Book 80, Folio 11, New Orleans Notarial Archives.

820, 822 Baronne, bound by Julia, St. Joseph, Carondelet. Two once-identical Greek Revival houses with party walls. Designed by Henry Howard in 1860 for Abraham Haber; Elijah Cox, builder; cost, $13,500. Recessed doorways are framed by pilasters, with egg and dart decorated capitals surmounted by cornice with paired brackets. A drawing from the Notarial Archives (1879) of 820 Baronne when it was sold for $4,100 in a sheriff's sale in Pierre V. McCarty's succession shows that this building has been greatly altered. It no longer has the crested cast-iron verandah or louvered blinds at each window and front door. The high-pitched roof above the parapet still exists, although it is not visible in this photograph.

According to the building contract specifications recorded by E. Barnett, notary, January 11, 1860, earlier buildings on the property were demolished and salvageable materials were reused: "There are to be fourteen cast-iron ventilators, Quincy granite steps...front and flank windows of main building to have Brown Stone sills and lintels, those lintels at the front to be moulded...ground floor of basement story occupied by wash room, stairways, wood and coal rooms shall be flagged with good Northern flagstones laid in good sharp sand mortar...yellow pine interior floors...mahogany ballusters and seven inch diameter newells (interior)...exterior rails of cypress...each parlor and dining room with marble mantels, ornamental iron grate valued at $50.00... bedrooms for two and three stories have wood mantels, slate hearths, iron grates ($10.00). Servants' room mantels with brick hearths...several windows throughout shall be trimmed and finished to correspond with doorways...side and front windows except those on the verandah,

shall have moulded paneled backs...the windows in the dining rooms shall have paneled backs...The whole of the windows shall have 1½" glazed sashes double hung in proper cased and boxed frames with patent axle pullies, metal weights and best sash cord: each window shall have a pair of 1¾" outside blind shutters well hung with best loose *Parliment* butts and secured with *Mackerall's* shutter fastenings and with 8" crop shutter bolts. The blinds to have rolling or stationary slats at option of owner...store rooms and kitchen and passageway from dining rooms properly fitted with four rows of shelves...plastering should be three coats, Thomaston lime, coarse sharp gritted sand mixed with plenty plastering hair: three coats paint inside, four coats outside... each bathroom shall have one plunge and shower bath completely furnished with hot and cold water pipes, brass cocks, plugs, etc... finished with paneled woodwork, water carried up from hydrants in yard ...bells shall have copper wire in tubes to be installed prior to plastering in walls, hall doorways, dining rooms...necessary gas pipes with mitre and wood box introduced from the street into each hall...verandah, pilasters, brackets, cornice and railing appropriate ornamental pattern $10.00 a lineal foot...roof to be sheathed in zinc..."

A. A. Prado owned both lots in 1849. Title research indicates that the 820 Baronne building was owned by O. Drouet in 1872 and decreased in value to $4,150 in 1892 under owners Miss P. C. Frank of New York and Isadore Hernsheim. The latter held the property until 1920 when he sold it for $13,650 to Mrs. A. S. Dyar. The value of these properties returned to original prices ($5,000) in 1939.

833 Baronne, bound by St. Joseph, Julia, Dryades. (Old No. 242.) One of a former row of three-story brick Greek Revival houses, each measuring 24 feet by 147 feet. The remaining building, with mutilated first story, is one of a group of similar residences with party walls once owned by Samuel Jamison, the builder. Jamison owned many lots in this square from the 1840s, apparently building row houses as his own investment on some lots and selling other lots to speculators for whom he built houses similar to his own. Jamison lived and had his offices with his partner, McIntosh, in the now-demolished house two houses to the left of the one here (old No. 248).

In the *Picayune* of October 5, 1924, John P. Coleman describes the houses. Each had a classic entrance, a plastered brick front and a two-level cast-iron gallery. Coleman described the interior of one of the rows: "The main hall, with its lovely cornice and centerpiece extended to the dining room in the rear. On the left were the handsome double parlors, separated by folding doors. Elaborate cornices and centerpieces of a feather design, touched in gold, from which hung handsome chandeliers of bronze with chains and medallion and cut glass globes, were also a feature of these apartments. Mantels were of black marble, veined in whitish gray, over which hung lovely gilt mirrors that reached the ceiling....The hall, parlours and dining room were beautifully embellished by the Seibrechts, the famous decorators of that day, who imported almost exclusively from Paris."

The building was built for Mrs. L. T. Elliot (Lavinia Johnson), who bought the property from J. W. Coeler on February 9, 1859. The act of H. B. Cenas specifies that "said purchaser shall erect dwelling houses on the said lots of ground equal to the adjoining ones." Mrs. Elliot paid $6,500 for this lot and an adjacent one. The house sold at a sheriff's sale on April 14, 1874, to the Bank of America in a bankruptcy sale for $6,400 in the succession of Charles Kreher, Sr.

108, 110 Camp, bound by Canal, Common, Magazine. Two brick, four-story, three-bay stores with splayed brick lintels. Note the extreme shallowness of these structures to accommodate the buildings which face Canal. The gallery now on the building on the right probably is not original. No. 110 is painted a 20th century "shocking pink."

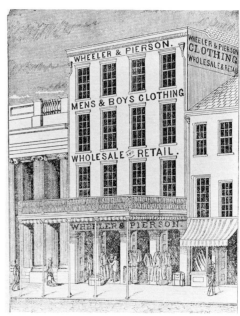

113 Camp. J. C. Waldo's *Visitors Guide to New Orleans* (1879). (Courtesy New Orleans Public Library.)

113-117 Camp, bound by Canal, Common, St. Charles. A four-bay, four-story, brick commercial building having cap-moulded lintels and cornice with brick dentils and frieze. As illustrated in *Waldo's* (1879), the building had a second-level balcony projecting over a sidewalk and supported by iron posts. All windows were double-hung with multi-lights, none of which remain. Originally there were granite pillars, three of which remain, supporting a granite lintel course at the first level. In 1879 the store was occupied by Wheeler and Pierson. The fire escapes and tasteless signs disfigure the structure, and the dual paint shades make the building appear smaller.

127 Camp, bound by Canal, Common, St. Charles. Four-story, three-bay, brick commercial building. Cornice is decorated with brick sawtooth course, creating deep shadows above the string course and brick dentils. An identical cornice is found in the 1838 buildings at 834-836 Julia and is a prevalent French Quarter type. Splayed brick lintels and brick sills are obscured beneath layers of paint. Original 6/6 light windows unfortunately have been replaced by modern metal ones. The iron or granite pillars and paneled doors and the display windows with muntins have been removed at the first level.

129-133 Camp, corner Common, bound by Carondelet, Canal. Three-story, masonry commercial building with wrought iron balcony at second level, probably built in the 1840s. Shown in *Jewell's* (1873) as Gonzales Brothers, importers of Havana cigars (Partagas, Upmann, La Carona). The ground floor once had cast-iron pillars with Corinthian capitals and was spanned by low arches on the Camp side. Sebastien Pizarro Martinez, architect and builder, made alterations and repairs to this store in 1865 (A. Barnett, notary, Vol. 17, No. 139) for Hope Insurance Company for $1,828. This building occupies three lots which in 1828 belonged to Daniel Warburg. A succession of owners during the past 145 years includes: Matthew Morgan, Walter R. Potts, C. W. Henderson, Grey Hopkins, St. Denis Villere, H. Latter, D. W. Dietrich, H. Grimma, H. Manassas, D. B. Cohen, and Pan American Life. Illustration (on right) from Jewell's *Crescent City* (1873). (Courtesy New Orleans Public Library.)

201 Camp, corner Common, bound by Gravier, St. Charles. Red brick and rock-faced stone, four-story commercial building designed by Thomas Sully, built between 1884 and 1888 as the New Orleans National Bank. Stone-sculptured spandrels below third-story windows, as well as carved heads on columns and pilaster capitals, depict allegoric figures. A heavy rock-faced first story has arched openings; brick pilasters extend the length of the second and third stories. This verticality is enhanced by the high pitch of the original roof, now altered, as illustrated in *Soards* (1888). A deep entablature has foliated reliefs and brackets which appear on the Camp and Common elevations.

Dormers of this type were popular in commercial, religious and residential architecture throughout the country during this period. This free eclecticism was a typical rejection of classical proportions. Designers felt free to incorporate English Renaissance, French Baroque or Romanesque forms, combining them rampantly to an effect of solidity and massiveness appropriate to the American commercial spirit of the 1880s. A previous building which occupied this site was owned by Edward Chapman and later purchased by the Reverend William Leacock in 1871 for $22,690. In 1862 this property was owned by H. W. Montgomery, Edward J. Jay and H. Sauvoy. Illustration (upper center) from Soards's *New Orleans City Directory* (1888). (Courtesy New Orleans Public Library.)

211 Camp, bound by Gravier, Common, St. Charles. Norman Mayer Memorial Building (Tulane-Newcomb Building). Six-story, brick, tile and terra cotta commercial building with bay windows in center of the facade. Designed in 1900 by Andry and Bendernagel, architects. Cost was $172,000. This property, on which the Louisiana State National Bank stood in 1882, was given to the Tulane Educational Fund by the Paul Tulane Estate in 1882. Paul Tulane had owned the property for many years.

The building on this site before erection of this building was a Venetian Renaissance-style cast-iron building occupied by the Fireman's Insurance Co. and also known as the Tulane Building. Tulane University continued to lease this five-story store to the Louisiana State National Bank for $12,000 a year until the erection of the present building. Designed of steel and considered fire-proof, the building has a combination of texture, tones and spatial relationships effecting an animated facade. The craftsmanship of the moulded, glazed terra cotta detail is of outstanding quality.

217 Camp, bound by Common, Gravier, St. Charles. Commercial building, reminiscent of the French Baroque style, built for the Teutonia Insurance Company in the late 1880s. Teutonia was one of the most substantial companies insuring fire and marine risks. It occupied an earlier structure on this site in 1875.

The *New Orleans Republican* newspaper of September 9, 1871, reported: "The building, Number 35 Camp Street, until lately occupied as a clothing store, will be converted into a banking house for the Cosmopolitan Bank, in which E. A. Tyler, B. T. Walshe and other gentlemen are interested. It will be reshaped under the direction of Mr. S. B. Haggart, architect."

The Teutonia occupied the above building before constructing the present structure. An early illustration of the present building shows that the pavillion roof was removed, causing a loss of the vertical effect. The recessed entrance has been filled in; the Corinthian capitals remain in view, while the two smaller center columns are incorporated into the present window treatment. Stone finials and torches once flanked the columns of the shell niche at the roofline in which an allegorical diaphanous-draped female holds a lion's head. The facade pilasters are also capped with allegorial female heads of Teutonia. The fire escape disrupts the unity of the facade. Illustration from George W. Engelhardt, *The City of New Orleans* (1894). (Courtesy New Orleans Public Library.)

220 Camp, bound by Gravier, Common, Magazine. This rare example of a Victorian, late Italianate commercial structure with stilted arches was designed by architect Henry Howard for a Mr. Gardes to be occupied by the firm Katz and Barnett, which was first listed at this address in the *City Directory* of 1881. A hallmark of the late Italianate, stilted arches, which rise vertically from the pilasters and columns before arching horizontally, are seen on the first three stories.

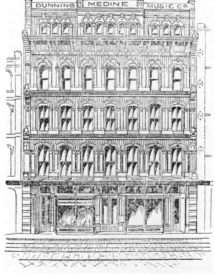

Between the columns on the ground floor are moulded, stilted lintels. The windows of the second and third floors have segmental arches, and the fenestration of the two upper floors has round arches. All the windows have large keystones. A projecting, bracketed cornice above the fourth-story level supports an arcaded attic or fifth story.

According to an illustration in the *Picayune Guide* (1896), the building was occupied by the Dunning Medine Music House. The 1903 *Englehardt* publication lists the Phoenix Furniture Store, with W. G. Thibault, manager, as occupying the building, presently known as the Junior Achievement Building. Free-standing Corinthian columns on plinths decorate the first-floor facade supporting flat arches. The Victorian elements of this late Italianate building include the grouping of pilasters, free combination of Baroque, classic and other decorative forms. A good example of adaptive use for this vivacious building, which catches the attention and contributes much to the character of the street. Illustration from *Picayune Guide to New Orleans* (1896). (Courtesy New Orleans Public Library.)

224-228 Camp, corner Gravier, bound by Magazine, Common. Eight-story I. L. Lyons Building, built in 1888 of pressed brick and granite. Lyons and Company was one of the largest drug houses in the United States, having outlets throughout the South, Mexico and Central and South America. The building is devoid of eclectic ornamental motifs so characteristic of buildings of the 1880s. The sparsely decorated geometric articulation of the structure, the optimum wall surface devoted to windows and the vertical emphasis of the structural members all relate this building to the early style of the Chicago School of Design.

An interesting rhythmic progression of fenestration can be seen in the Gravier elevation. Vertical members divide two single windows, then two double windows, followed by eight triple windows, such as appear on the Camp facade. The ground floor has been altered and a fire escape added to the side of the structure, which has stone rustication on the lower level. Cast-iron anchors in the form of wheels and geometric designs appear at each level. Brickwork with alternating headers provides a woven effect. The brick courses are increased in number below each window segment, reaching a fine pattern below partially segmented section and embattled parapet.

The conservative mode of framing did not adopt the innovative steel cage of the American skyscraper type being developed in Chicago at the time. Illustration from 1926 Letterhead.

In 1862 this corner and the lots on which the Junior Achievement Building stand were owned by the widow of Hart M. Shiff and were valued at $140,000. Presently owned by Hyman-Barton Realty Company, the building is now known as the Gravier Building. (Courtesy New Orleans Public Library.)

300 Camp, corner Gravier, bound by Natchez, Magazine. A four-story, four-bay, brick commercial building with granite trim, built at a cost of $7,400 in 1841 by James Williamson, builder for Western Marine and Fire Insurance Company, represented by Charles A. Jacobs. It replaces and probably reproduces a burned structure that had been built in a group of ten by David Sidle and Samuel Stewart in 1832. Flat stone lintels and sills adorned all windows. Ten stores were built for Charles A. Jacobs and Samuel Elkins at this corner in 1833. Some of them probably remain around the corner on Gravier (see 500 block Gravier), and others recently were demolished. Walton's surveyor's plan values this property site in 1850 at $27,860 and records that Jean J. Jandot purchased it in 1862 for $25,000.

326-28, 330, 332, 336, 338 Camp, bound by Gravier, Natchez, Magazine. This row of substantial four-story stores once was part of Newspaper Row. Alternating granite and cast-iron pillars and varying treatments of window lintels, cornices and parapets give this row a pleasant multi-facade appearance. Although several of the ground level fronts have been altered, upper levels retain the mid-nineteenth century design. Several of these buildings were used by the *Picayune* for its newspaper offices before it moved to facilities on Lafayette Square and subsequently to its present location at 3800 Howard.

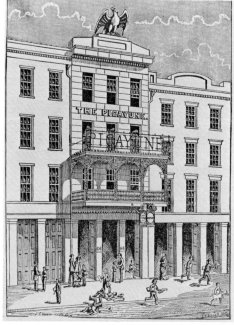

326-28 Camp, bound by Gravier, Magazine. The Picayune Building (at left) was erected in 1850 by Jamison and McIntosh. The granite front was designed and built by Newton Richards, and the carpentry work executed by Robert Crozier and Frederick Wing. The *Daily Picayune* was one of the first newspapers to erect its own plant. It replaced a building, constructed in 1847, which burned in the February 16, 1850, Camp Street fire. This fire also destroyed some 20 other buildings on both sides of Camp.

A lengthy article in the *Picayune* of November 3, 1850, describes the newly completed building. It was built with large granite pillars at the ground level, with square blocks of smoothly dressed Quincy granite completing the facade. The verandah of scroll-worked cast-iron at the second level was made by the local foundry of Holmes and Bennett. The building extended through the block and fronted at old No. 17 Bank Place. Because of this great depth, it was necessary to introduce light from the center of the building by a large lantern in the roof. All the interior wood was painted white.

In the editorial room was a white Italian marble mantel, and in the

counting room stood an Egyptian black marble mantel, slightly mixed with white. Carved into the granite between the third and fourth levels were the words THE PICAYUNE, which are still vaguely visible on the present structure. A copper eagle, hand-worked by Robert Weiss, once perched on the parapet but has been removed, as has the verandah. The building partially visible to the left of the Picayune Building in the Waldo (1879) illustration was also used in an expansion of *Picayune* facilities. This building, also built in 1850, was erected for Francis Dupuy by Duncan Sinclair for $9,500 to replace the two stores at old No. 62 and No. 15 Bank Place, which had burned in the 1850 fire. They were to be built in the same style as the fronts of the stores at old No. 28 and No. 30 Camp which also have been demolished.

The present building to the left of the Picayune Building is of a much later date. The brick building to the right is smaller in scale, with cap-moulded lintels, dentils in cornice and a well-proportioned parapet. It also was occupied by the *Picayune*. (Illustration from J. C. Waldo's *Visitors Guide to New Orleans* (1879); courtesy New Orleans Public Library.)

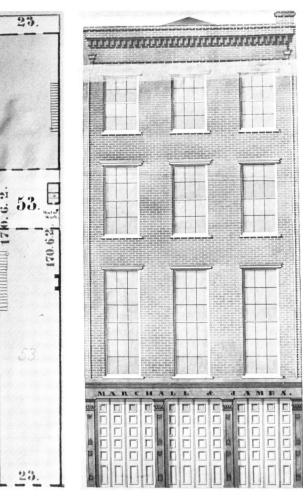

317-27 Camp. Drawing and floor plan (which demonstrates double entrance, Camp at St. Charles) by C. A. Hedin, 1853, Plan Book 95, Folio 46, New Orleans Notarial Archives.

317-327 Camp, bound by Gravier, Commercial Place, St. Charles. A row of three, three-story, brick commercial buildings with cast-iron pillars and foliated capitals at first level. Built in 1850 by Charles Pride for Charles Mason, attorney for Robert Heath of England, for $10,000. A notarial drawing shows one store of this row when it was sold at a sheriff's sale in 1853. The drawing indicates that four-fold paneled doors painted two shades of green were hung between pillars. Narrow cap-moulded lintels were early replaced by flat ones. The stores retain window muntins, which vary on each tier with the numbers of lights as the size of the windows diminishes from eighteen lights at the second level, twelve at the third level and twelve smaller ones at the fourth level. The floor plan indicates the simplicity of such stores in the interior: a large space with a stairway, small courtyard and privy, behind which is another large area with entrances on St. Charles (see 308-10 and 314 St. Charles). Each store had a 23-foot front, with 170.62-foot depth fronting both streets.

Many Orleanians remember when Camp Street was the Park Row of New Orleans. *Jewell's* (1873), a business directory of New Orleans, printed a lengthy list of New Orleans newspapers at that time. Among them were *The German Gazette,* J. Hassinger, publisher, 108 Camp; *New Orleans Republican,* 94 Camp; *New Orleans Times,* C. A. Weed, publisher, 70 Camp; and the *Picayune,* 66 Camp.

327 Camp, corner Commercial Place, bound by Gravier, St. Charles. Three-story plastered brick building with long elevation on Commercial Place, designed by Henry Howard in the 1850s. Howard's own architect office was located here at old No. 13 Commercial Place. The lower level has been ruined, but could be restored in keeping with the building's character.

401-05 Camp. George W. Engelhardt's *City of New Orleans* (1894). (Courtesy New Orleans Public Library.)

401-05 Camp. Jewell's *Crescent City, Illustrated* (1873). (Courtesy New Orleans Public Library.)

401-05, 407 Camp, corner Commercial Place, bound by Poydras, St. Charles. Noted architects Henry Howard and Lewis Reynolds are listed in *Jewell's* as having designed the five-story building at the corner of Commercial Place, running through to St. Charles, for the Crescent Mutual Insurance Company. They may have associated in the construction. Built in 1850, the structure appears in *Jewell's* (1871) as a four-story building with a cast-iron gallery on the second floor of the Camp facade. The gallery has been removed and a fifth floor, which conforms to the design of the rest of the building, has been added. Cast-iron pillars on the first level and heavy projecting lintels, some pedimented, remain over the windows, although slightly altered. Cast-iron balconies have been removed, with only vestiges left on the center windows. Since 1946 this structure has been part of the Balter Building, which also incorporates the other buildings along Commercial Place.   No. 407 Camp (at left) is one of the earliest remaining four-story commercial structures, dating from the mid-1830s. It has simple cap-moulded lintels and brick sills. A group of merchants, including James Colles, Harvard Henderson and George and Matthew Morgan, purchased the land in 1835 and constructed three identical buildings. Only this one remains. The improved properties were valued at $25,000 each.

500-504 Camp, corner Poydras, bound by Magazine, Lafayette. Two, four-story, three-bay, plastered brick stores, one with paired granite pillars on Poydras, the other with cast-iron paneled pillars on Camp. Building at right has denticulated brick cornice contrasting with the simple cornice of the corner building, from which similar dentils may have been removed. Cast-iron balcony at second level runs across the entire Camp facade. Windows are designed without lintels. Built in 1853 by Robert Huyghe, builder for J. D. Marsh and P. N. Wood, as two of three former stores. (One is replaced by the present 1880s building at 506 Camp). Cost for the three stores was $21,400. The building contract (H. B. Cenas, notary, May 14, 1853) specifies that the soft brick facades were to be plastered.

408 Camp, bound by Poydras, Natchez, Magazine. Four-story brick store with granite pillars having ovolo capitals in the style of the late 1830s. The cap-moulded dentils and a brick blocking course and cornice remain.

420-22 Camp, corner Poydras, bound by Natchez, Magazine. Four-story brick store in the style of the' mid-nineteenth century, with granite pillars and beak-type capitals. Original muntins, granite lintels and brick cornice and frieze remain. The ground floor alterations easily could be made more in character with the building.

Camp, bound by Lafayette, Capdevielle Place, Magazine. Former Post Office. The old Post Office, erected in 1914 at a cost of $2,500,000, was designed by architects Hale and Rogers in an eclectic style, reflecting Italian Renaissance origin. The three-story masonry structure has a rusticated base, with arched arcade at the lower level and a colonnade at the upper levels. On the roof at each corner are 25-foot-high copper sculptures, each showing a globe and female figures of history, industry, commerce and the arts. The site was formerly occupied by the Odd Fellows Hall, erected in 1852 by architect George Purvis. This large Greek Revival domed structure was the scene of many gatherings, balls and concerts. It burned in 1866 and St. Patrick's Hall was erected on the site. St. Patrick's Hall served briefly as the state government administration center in 1877. Governor F. T. Nicholls was inaugurated here.

LAFAYETTE SQUARE

Lafayette Square, originally named Place Gravier, was laid out by Carlos Trudeau in 1788. The city gained possession of the square in 1822, built streets on its north and south borders and in 1824 renamed it in honor of General Lafayette. The bronze statues of Benjamin Franklin, Henry Clay and John McDonogh, as well as a geodetic stone marking the longitude and latitude, are located in the center section between St. Charles and Camp. A stone marker paying tribute to Lafayette was added recently. The cast-iron fence which once surrounded the square is gone, as are most of the original buildings which once faced it. Federal buildings form three boundaries, shared with Gallier Hall on the east and the Lafayette Hotel on the south. The square is an important open space and green area of prime significance to 20th century planning.

Post Office from Lafayette Square. (Photograph by Charles L. Franck.)

644 Camp, corner Girod, bound by Magazine, Capdevielle. This three-story, scored-brick building in the 1890s replaced a typical early Greek Revival structure, part of which may remain in the two-story, flat-roofed rear section. The cast-iron hood moulds are surmounted by crowned Neptune heads in deep relief, with cast-iron dentils beneath. Cast-iron cartouches appear between each bay, with only one missing on the Camp elevation. The corner pavilion is roofed with silver layered tin. The simple iron bow rails at the second-floor balcony surround the entire building and are rare in the city. The distinctive character of this corner feature makes it a landmark along the street. The exterior condition is excellent and is enhanced by the choice of grey walls and black trim. The present owner, John Vicari, purchased it in 1964 from attorney Kurtz. Vicari's restaurant carried on the traditional use from the early 1900s. A professional employment agency presently occupies the first floor. Apartments are above.

700-04 Camp, corner Girod, bound by Julia, Magazine. Row of mid-nineteenth century stores of four stories, with denticulated cornice, cast-iron pedimented moulded lintels over the windows and cast-iron balcony at the second level. The ground floor on Camp contains cast-iron pillars with recessed panels and Corinthian capitals surmounted by a cast-iron lintel course, having a cornice with egg and dart mouldings. On the ground floor of the Girod facade are granite pillars and original double-hung paneled outside shutters. The protruding shop windows are an addition to the building. Some original four-fold paneled doors and hardware remain, however. The brick building is plastered and scored to imitate masonry blocks. The lot, 63 feet x 90 feet, was owned in 1862 by John Larkin Story and valued at $24,000, indicating that a building existed on the site.

ST. PATRICK'S CHURCH

724 Camp, bound by Girod, Julia, Magazine. In 1838, Irish Catholics of the Faubourg St. Mary under the Rev. James Ignatuis Mullon contracted with brothers Charles B. Dakin and James H. Dakin to design and erect St. Patrick's Church for $115,000. Gibson's *Guide to New Orleans* commented that it would "by far surpass every attempt at Gothic architecture on this side of the Atlantic, and may proudly challenge comparison with any parochial edifice in Europe." The building contract (H. B. Cenas, notary, June 6, 1838) describes the usual building specifications, as well as the architects' thoughts in developing the design. The specifications begin with the following:

"General Description. The style of architecture exhibited in the composition of the design for the exterior is that of the Pointed Style of the Second Period of Ecclesiastical Architecture and has been principally imitated from that unrivalled example of splendor and majesty, York Minster Cathedral.

"Windows. The windows are in the florid Gothic style of the third period, which display more elegance in their tracery than earlier examples.

"Ceiling. The ceiling of the interior is in imitation of the ceiling of Exeter Cathedral which is also another gorgeous example of the second period. The slips and galleries are in the richest florid style of the third period, and display the most chastened elegance of the art.

"Altar and Tabernacle. The Altar and Tabernacle are composed in the style of the second and third period, and in richness, elegance and variety, they possess all that the art is susceptible of."

A major problem facing the builders was the soft and unstable soil. Even though a wide pyramid base was used, one wall began to lean during construction. Perhaps following a disagreement over the solution of this problem, the Dakin brothers were relieved of their duties before the walls of the church reached the roof. On October 1, 1839, the trustees signed a new contract with James Gallier, Sr. He was to make all the necessary drawings for completing the church for a fee of $1,000 and to direct its construction for an additional fee of five percent of the cost. Gallier succeeded in establishing a firm foundation without destroying the completed construction. Some changes in the design of the church were made by

Gallier, as is shown by comparison of the original elevation drawing by the Dakins in the New Orleans Public Library and one by Gallier in the Louisiana State Museum.

Gallier retained the Dakins' design of the base of the tower, but simplified the overall appearance of the church by adding an undecorated stage in the tower (containing clocks), substituting a single window at the top of the tower for the Dakins' paired windows, and omitting the Dakins' foliated crockets over the openings and on the pinnacles (except for those at the top of the tower which have since been removed). He also simplified the crenelation of the parapet.

A drawing by Dakin and Dakin in the New Orleans Public Library shows the ground plan of the church as constructed. The tower in the center of the facade contains the vestibule. Buttresses support the side walls of the church and at the corners of the facade and tower are diagonal buttresses. Most of the interior is Gallier's work. The nave and aisles have fan vaulting, with the ribs terminating in floral bosses. Long, pointed, arched windows with Gothic tracery pierce the side walls. The nave piers are composed of engaged shafts, and the aisle galleries are decorated with quatrefoil paneling. The stained glass vaulting of the sanctuary is one of the most remarkable features of the interior. Stained glass skylights of various sorts had been used by Gallier and Dakin when they did work together, as in the Merchant's Exchange and in the old Capitol at Baton Rouge. The intricate woodwork supporting it, as well as the rest of the plaster vaulting, is extremely well done. The light filtering down from above, over the high altar, is one of the most dramatic features of this building.

Gallier's beautifully detailed altar elevation in the Louisiana State Museum shows it as it was finally executed. Originally, this altar probably was painted in imitation of marble, with the ornament highlighted in gold. In recent years the old paint was removed, and the altar is finished in its natural wood color, with some gold and color applied. Adorning the sanctuary are three enormous oil paintings, executed in 1840 by Leon Pomarede: a copy of Raphael's "Transfiguration," St. Peter walking on the waves and St. Patrick baptizing the Princess Ethnea and her sister, daughters of King Leogaire of Ireland.

St. Patrick's has experienced a number of major renovations. The interior was repainted several times. Excellent *faux bois* and *faux marble,* perhaps dating from an 1872 renovation supervised by builder Thomas Mulligan (specifications state that doors were to be oak grained and walls painted in imitation of veined Sienna marble), can be seen on the sanctuary walls. In 1889 the floor of the end bay of the gallery over each of the side altars was removed and the pulpit was renovated. Other minor changes concern the side tower entrances, which have been changed to windows, and the removal of Gallier's original wooden communion rail, which was replaced by one of cast-iron. The exterior has been covered with rough-cast weatherproofing cement. The exterior stucco probably was originally smooth, blocked off and painted in imitation of stone.

St. Patrick's Church and rectory. From *Waldo's* (1879). (Courtesy New Orleans Public Library.)

Interior of St. Patrick's Church.

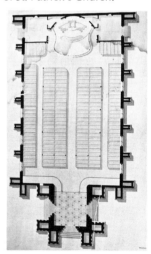

Plan of St. Patrick's Church, watercolor and ink, unsigned and undated drawing by James H. and Charles B. Dakin. (Courtesy New Orleans Public Library.)

724 Camp, bound by Girod, Julia, Magazine, St. Patrick's Rectory. The rectory of St. Patrick's, erected adjacent to the church in 1874 for the Reverend Patrick F. Allen, is a two-story masonry Italianate building with ornate entrance. Designed by architect Henry Howard and built by Thomas Mulligan for $22,000. Building contract specifications (Castell, notary, April 6, 1874, Vol. 42, p. 7731) show that expenses were curtailed in the construction of the building. The iron window caps as designed by Howard were to be omitted. (The windows were capped by cemented brick hood moulds.) The balcony was to have a wood floor and facias in place of marble tiles and granite, and a German flagstone pavement was to be dispensed with and Lake brick used instead. An illustration in *Waldo's* (1879) shows that the building was slightly altered after that date. The recessed portion of the facade was enclosed, destroying the original asymmetry of the structure so characteristic of the Italianate. Parapets and balconies were removed.

Vaulting, with stained glass over the sanctuary, St. Patrick's Church.

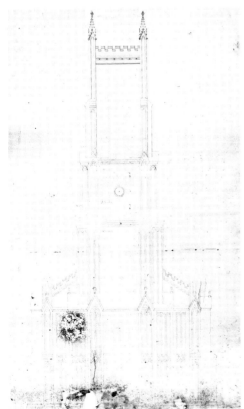

Elevation of St. Patrick's Church, pencil and ink, signed James Gallier. (Courtesy Louisiana State Museum.)

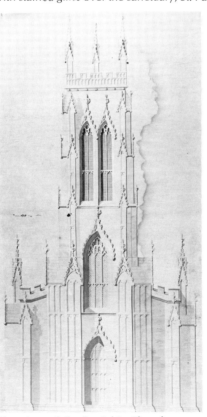

Elevation of St. Patrick's Church, watercolor and ink, signed and dated "Dakin and Dakin, June 6, 1838." (Courtesy New Orleans Public Library.)

Elevation of altar at St. Patrick's Church, ink and watercolor, signed by "James Gallier [Sr.]" (Courtesy Louisiana State Museum).

728 Camp, bound by Julia, Girod, Magazine. A three-story, plastered brick commercial structure with cast-iron gallery, iron pillars on the first floor, cap-moulded lintels over the windows and a parapet. The building was erected after 1871, as an illustration of this block of Camp in *Jewell's* of that date shows that the lot was occupied by a small dormered Creole cottage. The building is similar in appearance to structures of the mid-nineteenth century, however, and harmonizes with the other earlier buildings in the block. Since the entire block on both Lakeside and Riverside retains so many important buildings, this building should be preserved and utilized for a 20th century adaptive use.

740 Camp, bound by Julia, Girod, Magazine. A three-story, plastered brick commercial building with a parapet, corbeled cornice, recessed panels in the facade and granite lintels and sills on the windows. Cast-iron pillars on the first floor support a cast-iron lintel course with shouldered arches and a cornice having dentils and consoles. Charles Magill Conrad, who had purchased the property in 1853, had the building erected in 1861 for $8,935. Lewis E. Reynolds was the architect and builder. The ground floor has been modernized.

748 Camp, bound by Julia, Girod, Magazine. A three-story, plastered brick commercial building of the mid-nineteenth century, with a low parapet and dentil course at the roofline, cornices over the windows on the third floor and cast-iron lintels over the second-floor windows. The lintels have three decorative divisions with floral motifs, the center elements each containing a pineapple. Of buildings standing in the business district, such lintels have been observed only on the 1830 stores at 501 Magazine, corner Poydras, and the warehouses at 448 Julia. The ground story contains cast-iron pillars with recessed panels. The slightly asymmetrical arrangement of fenestration and openings is unusual in this building.

713-15 Camp, bound by Girod, Julia, St. Charles. Four-story, four-bay, red brick commercial building, mutilated first floor and facade windows, lintels removed from second- and third-floor windows, denticulated cornice and deep parapet. Built in 1852 by James Gallier for Dr. J. C. Weiderstrandt who bought the property in 1847 for $5,000. The property measures 27 feet x 149 feet. Dr. Weiderstrandt's offices were located here, according to *City Directory* of 1853.

705-07 Camp, bound by Girod, Julia, St. Charles. Four-story, four-bay, brick commercial building. Built soon after Alexander Brothers bought the property in 1851 for $4,825. Property measures 27 feet x 89 feet. Brick denticulated cornice and stone sills and lintels. Mutilated on first and second levels; cast-iron first story was probably at one time similar to the adjoining building at the left.

703 Camp, corner Girod, bound by Julia, St. Charles. Three-story brick store (partially shown right) with splayed brick segmental arched lintels. Cast-iron pillars support a cast-iron lintel with shouldered arches. Title research indicates it was built shortly after the Civil War. The widow of John Donovan owned the property in 1852 and Walton, auctioneer, valued it at $6,000. Property measures 27 feet x 74 feet.

709-711 Camp, bound by Girod, Julia, St. Charles (middle building in photograph). Four-story, four-bay, plastered brick commercial building, with cast-iron pillars at first level. Stone lintels and sills. Built between 1839 and 1841 for J. W. Stillwell. Stillwell bought the property in 1839 from A. H. Clayton, and by 1841 the building housed the office of J. W. Stillwell and Company. An 1869 archival drawing shows that the store formerly had granite pillars and may still have its granite lintel course. It had a cast-iron gallery at the second level supported by cast-iron columns. The facade had four-fold doors paneled below and glazed above. There were fixed louvered shutters in upper-story windows and the plaster was scored. In 1869 it housed Cafe Richelieu.

This building is pictured in *Englehardt's* (1903) as "Electra Water Co. Ltd. Works and Central Depot," where water was scientifically filtered and pumped by electric process. At one time it housed the Catholic Maritime Club. As illustrated in the archival drawing, the plan of the store had a stair hall and large open rooms. A detached service wing extended to the rear behind the large rooms. A cistern and privy also were in the yard. In 1852 the property was valued at $12,000 by Walton in the estate of Dr. John Farrell. The property measures 27 feet x 149 feet.

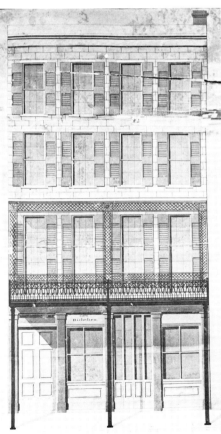

717 Camp, bound by Girod, Julia, St. Charles. (Old No. 157.) Three-story, three-bay, brick building with string course and heavy wooden entablature and parapet. Egg and dart motif and wooden architrave with three fasciae decorate the entablature. Marble flat moulded lintels are intact, as are paneled inside shutters. Mutilated at first-floor level so that it cannot be determined whether this was a residence or commercial building. Henry W. Palfrey had the building erected soon after he bought the property in June, 1838, from speculators Oakley, Lockhart and Green for $8,000. Palfrey sold the building in 1840 to I. S. Harman, who in 1843 sold it to Dr. J. C. Weiderstrandt, whose office was built next door. Strangely, the sale was for only $4,000. Property measures 27 feet x 149 feet.

719 Camp, bound by Julia, Girod, St. Charles. Three-story, three-bay, brick townhouse, with handsome Greek Key entrance based on the Erectheum door. This type door was first shown in an 1833 pattern book, Minard LaFever's *Modern Builders Guide.* Marble pedimented lintels are above the windows, with original twelve-part muntins. The wooden entablature was once embellished with six carved reliefs on frieze, probably triglyphs. Built in 1838 for Wm. E. Thompson for his residence and lost by him in a sheriff's sale in 1845. Purchased by Chas. Kock and leased, furnished, at $1,000 per annum to John Mountfort. Paintings by Sassoferroto and Secour, as well as Rosewood tables, bed

In the above photograph building numbers read right to left.

and armoires, are listed in lease inventory. This property measures 27 feet x 149 feet.

721-23 Camp, bound by Julia, Girod, St. Charles. This three-bay, three-story, brick residence is typical of red brick Eastern Seaboard-style residences, with louvered shutters at the original 18 muntined windows on second floor. Balcony with iron arrow pattern on second level. The first-floor double-hung windows have been slightly altered, yet the entrance appears intact. This property, as that of the entire square, was owned in 1818 by Pierre Bauclet St. Martin and purchased by Thomas Harman. His heirs sold it for $11,600 to Edward Chapman in 1836. The 1849 directory records Edward Chapman as having his residence here. The Chapman heirs sold the property in 1899 to E. and A. Beauregard. They held it until 1904 when it was sold to the G. H. A. Thomas family, who held the property until 1939. This property measures 27 feet x 150 feet. (727 Camp shown on opposite page.)

729 Camp, bound by Girod, Julia, St. Charles. (Old No. 213.) Three-story, three-bay, brick townhouse, with iron balcony at second level and denticulated cornice with flat brick frieze below. Marble caps and lintels remain intact, as do window lights on second and third levels. The cross and bow iron work, Greek Key recessed entrance and Quincy granite steps bear a great similarity to those at 721-23 Camp. They differ, however, in level heights.

700 block Camp, Lakeside. Aerial view.

727 Camp, bound by Julia, Girod, Carondelet, St. Charles. Bible House. Handsome three-story, three-bay building with paneled pilasters running from the denticulated lintel course at first level to the frieze below the cornice. These pilasters, each with a deep cement base and foliated capitals of cast-iron, give strong verticality to the facade. Decorative cast-iron hood moulds are supported by iron brackets. The first floor facade has been removed for modernization and is not in keeping with the character of the building. The structure was designed by John Barnett, architect, and built by Little and Middlemiss, builders for the Southwestern Bible Society, at a cost of $9,940. The facade was reworked by T. K. Wharton in 1858, according to his diary. By 1862 A. B. Walton had valued the property at $13,000 for the Southwestern Bible Society.

According to the building contract (H. B. Cenas, notary, April 19, 1854), the building had a "portico" with cast-iron columns supporting it. The contract continued: "The first story doors will be made in two folds, three inches thick moulded bottom panels 1½ inch, the upper part open work similar to front door of Odd Fellows Hall. To have cast iron sills and solid plain three inch casings inside the piers, the bottom of the doors to be dressed with copper. The doors to be hung with three pairs 6 x 6 loose butt hinges.... The back door to be three inches thick, hung with three inch butts and finished similar to the front doors, with a suitable lock and glazed. All the back openings to have iron doors or shutters of No. 15 iron with loose butt hinges and frames built in the walls.... The exterior of front will be cemented with hydraulic cement in the proportions of two thirds clean coarse sharp sand clear of salt to one third cement, the basement to be rusticated and channelled as per elevation.... All outside doors in the front to be finished in oak graining and all exterior iron painted the color of the stucco."

The interior included marbel mantels on second levels which were to cost not more than $35 each. The first level was designed as a store, to be fitted with a cast-iron railing "to be fixed at a height of nine feet from the store floor on both sides and rear of an ornamental pattern with one iron staircase. The gallery to be of the width of three feet to start on each side within about eight feet of the front wall."

cian architraves with large band mouldings and plinth block, the heads to have projecting cornices." Other doors were finished with the same architraves and mouldings. Openings on the second and third floors had plain eight-inch architraves with band mouldings. Marble mantels costing $100 each were in the parlor, drawing room and dining room. The second-floor rooms also had marble mantels. The bedrooms and nursery were to have "pilaster pattern wood mantels painted in imitation of marble," and the servant's quarters, plain wood mantels.

First-floor door knobs and escutcheons were silver-plated, while the upstairs door knobs were porcelain.

838-840 Camp, bound by St. Joseph, Julia, Magazine. Daniel Parish, who owned this property in 1842, subdivided it during the 1840s. During that period this once-elegant three-story brick townhouse was built. It was sold in 1867 at a sheriff's sale for $13,000. A handsome Greek Revival entrance with pilasters flanks a door and sidelights with octagon glass panes. Anthemion decorations crown the entrance cornice which also has garlands. Alteration of the first floor for use as a shop obscures an otherwise fine residence which had a balcony at the second level with French doors. The structure retains the cornice with dentils and windows with stone lintels. The interior of this house retains the wood mantels of Greek Key design at the second level, interior millwork and medallions. The service wing is intact.

822 Camp, bound by St. Joseph, Julia, Magazine. One of the finest houses remaining in the business district. Three stories, each with a cast-iron gallery, it was built for W. P. Converse in 1851 for $15,250, Henry Howard, architect, with Samuel Stewart, builder. Samuel Stewart and partner David Sidle owned the property, selling it to Converse and building the house for him.

According to building contract specifications (H. P. Caire, notary, April 14, 1851) the front wall was faced with Baltimore pressed brick. Plinths, steps and landing to the front door were white marble, as were the cap-moulded lintels of the facade. Side window lintels were Quincy granite. The underside of the verandah floors were moulded panels. The front door was to have square antaes and entablature and Venetian blinds. Front iron gates were "like Mr. Saul's on St. Charles Street" (see 826 St. Charles). Windows had rolling Venetian blind shutters painted Paris green, and the front door was grained in imitation of oak.

Double parlors were to have "sliding doorways to be finished with 14" diminished Gre-

842 Camp, bound by St. Joseph, Julia, Magazine. (Old No. "206" is etched in entrance transom.) Three-story masonry townhouse with rusticated first story and quoins at the ends of the upper levels. Entablature has paired brackets and deep-pierced parapet with central decorated crest. Cast-iron gallery at second level and projecting balcony with iron rail at first level. The underside of the verandah floor is decorated with carved bosses and panels. The original recessed paneled door has glass above and an applied cartouche below. As early as 1842 Henry Parish and W. A. Gasquet had bought most of the property in this block for speculative real estate ventures. A building existed on this property at that time. The present highly sophisticated facade, however, post-dates the Civil War, as evidenced by the parapet and entablature decorations and the front door. The interior has remnants of a ceiling cornice incorporating busts of female figures.

854-56, 858, 862, 866 Camp, corner St. Joseph, bound by Magazine, Julia. Four, three-story, formerly three-bay, brick townhouses. William A. Gasquet and Daniel Parish of New York had this row of four party wall townhouses built between 1842 and 1859 when they began selling their holdings at $10,000 for each house. The four properties are shallower than nearby residences in the middle of the block, and the facades unfortunately have been mutilated in the buildings to the right. All cornices have been removed and the structures refaced with rough plaster and trimmed with tile, a feature not in keeping with the character of the buildings. The two buildings at the left illustrate that there was a balcony across the second level, the original remnants of·which are now used throughout the facade. Classic pilasters and a heavy cornice framed recessed doors. These once-attractive houses graced what used to be one of the most attractive blocks in the Faubourg. The remaining buildings could be easily restored and used as offices and residences.

929 Camp, bound by Howard, St. Joseph, St. Charles. Confederate Memorial Hall. Erected in 1891 for Frank T. Howard. Howard presented the building to the Association of Confederate Veterans to be used as a museum for war relics and meeting place. It is still used for this purpose. Built of brown pressed brick, trimmed with terra cotta decoration, it was designed by architects Sully and Toledano to harmonize with the features of the adjacent Richardsonian Howard Memorial Library. In 1908 Stone Brothers architects added the portico and tower.

867 Camp, corner St. Joseph, bound by St. Charles, Julia. Two remaining of a former three, two-and-one-half story, three-bay, brick townhouses, with party wall step-gabled end, wood entablature and wood cap-moulded lintels. Homes designed by W. L. Atkinson in 1840 and begun by William Saunders, builder, for John Lesslie, Jr., at a projected cost of $23,000. By 1841 Lesslie had died and his heirs re-contracted the house, arranging for the firm of Sidle and Stewart to build it. Sidle and Stewart owned the adjoining properties and apparently built similar houses (now demolished) there, continuing this handsome row. The specifications of William Saunders were largely used in the building, except that Sidle and Stewart were instructed to include an ''iron rail in front and iron gallery like Mr. McCall's house on Camp Street.'' The front and side walls were to be painted red and penciled, and shutters were to be painted green. Saunders' specifications are but one version of the appearance of the hundreds of houses lining the streets of Faubourg St. Mary by 1850.

The description in the specifications could apply to many such houses with minimum variation (William Christy, notary, September 25, 1840): ''The front gable and wall on St. Joseph Street to be lake bricks, filled with country bricks; all rest of brickwork of country bricks laid in a sufficient proportion of the best quality of Thomaston lime and sharp sand. Walls to be 1½ bricks thick, except the front and gables of the main buildings which are to be two bricks up to the level of the second story. Front to have white marble base two feet high—corresponding base on gable to be of cement and painted. Steps and landings to front doors to be white marble—windows to have marble sills and moulded lintels—handsome moulded cornice to run round the entrance passage and parlours, with handsome center ornament with hook for lamp in passages and parlours—roofs slate, copper gutters—all parlours to have black marble mantels—bedrooms to have handsome wood mantels, floors to be cypress. Windows of first story twelve lights each, 12'' x 18'', second story 18 lights 12'' x 18'', double hung—lower story windows to be glazed with the best Boston or French crown glass, others of best American sheet glass. Venetian rolling blinds to be hung to all windows to correspond. Principal stairs to have a strong rounded mahogany rail and turned mahogany balusters—back stairs cypress; all timber exposed to the weather to be heart cypress. Attics to be divided into two rooms. Three cisterns with well to be dug in each yard 12 feet deep and three feet in diameter with a good pump to each. All woodwork and iron work inside and outside such as is usually painted to have three coats of good white lead and oil. The mantels of bedrooms to be imitation marble, venetian blinds to be installed.''

The interior mouldings and decorations of one of these formerly elegant homes were installed in the Anglo-American Art Museum at Baton Rouge. The design of the millwork evidently was based on Plate 14, ''Parlour Elevation,'' and the plaster ceiling center piece on Plate 21, ''Design for a Centre Flower,'' from Minard LaFever's *The Beauties of Modern Architecture,* published in New York in 1839 (third edition), one of the most important builders' handbooks of the Greek Revival period. The plaster centerpiece and the doorway, with its silverplated knobs, the casing and door band carving are from the Lesslie house. Three of the other doors and window band carvings also are original. The cornice is reproduced from moulds made from the original ornament.

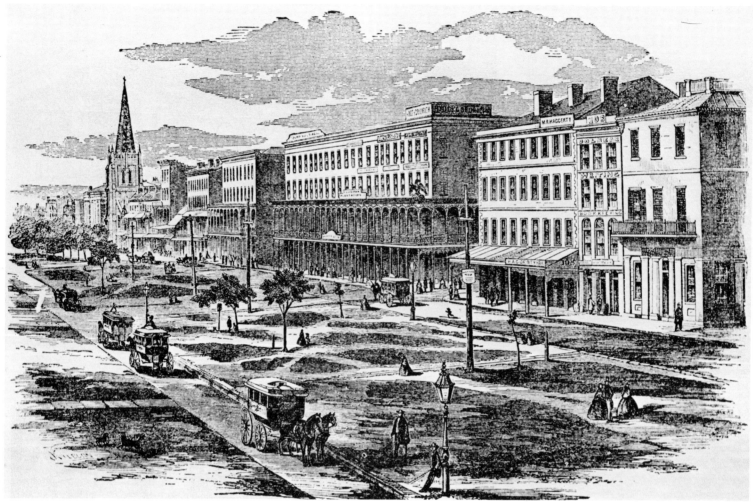

Canal Street in 1850. From Chambers' *History of Louisiana* (1925). (Courtesy Louisiana Collection, Special Collections Division, Tulane University Library.)

200 block Canal, bound by N. Peters, N. Front, Iberville. A block-long row of mid-nineteenth century stores, suggesting in style and scale the general appearance of Canal in that era. From across the width of Canal the row can be seen in perspective. Typically, the windows have gran-ite lintels, cornices decorate rooflines and one store retains granite pillars at ground level. The two buildings at the far left recently have been refaced with new yellow brick.

423 Canal, bound by Decatur, N. Peters, Iberville. U.S. Custom House. Architecturally and historically, the New Orleans Custom House is one of the most important Federal buildings in the South. It is the fourth customs structure to occupy the site. The first, an old Spanish customs house, was demolished in 1807 when the American government erected a new building designed by noted architect Benjamin H. Latrobe. Latrobe's building in turn was demolished in 1819 when a larger edifice designed by French architect Benjamin Buisson was constructed.

Work on the present building was begun in 1848, and the cornerstone was laid the following year by Henry Clay. The architect, Alexander Thompson Wood, had come to New Orleans in the early 1830s from New York. During 1850-51, Wood was superceded as architect of the building by James Harrison Dakin, who resigned the position in September, 1851. The work was executed under the direction of the great Confederate general, P. G. T. Beauregard, until 1861, when he was succeeded by Thomas K. Wharton, who had served for many years as an assistant to the architect. The first superintendent had been Col. Wm. Turnbull of the U.S. Engineers.

Wharton's diary, preserved in the New York Public Library, contains many details and sketches of the construction of the building, one of the largest Federal structures in the United States at the time. When architect A. T. Wood died on October 9, 1854, Wharton recorded that "he had no equal in this city in the profession—he was a thoroughly practical architect—confident and self reliant—bold and daring in construction—of which abundant evidence remains in the grand edifice which he leaves incomplete, but which will stand as an imperishable monument to his talents and architectural genius."

The building's business room, the "Marble Hall," is regarded as one of the finest Greek Revival interiors in America. It measures 125 feet by 95 feet and is 54 feet high. The ceiling is of ground glass, with a stained glass border, above which a skylight admits an abundance of illumination; the ceiling is supported by 14 marble columns, the capital of each of which is embellished with reliefs of Juno and Mercury. These columns cost $23,000 each. The modified Corinthian capitals were designed by Wood. Above the door at the N. Peters end of the hall are two panels containing life-size bas-reliefs of Bienville and General Andrew Jackson. Between them is a pelican feeding her young, the emblem of Louisiana, created by local sculptor A. Defrasse. The hall floor is of black and white marble, set with circular disks of heavy glass, through which light is admitted to the engine rooms beneath. The building is constructed of Quincy granite with a backing of brick and has a front of 340 feet on Canal Street.

A massive rusticated base with arched niches supports three additional levels. At the center of each facade are engaged portico-forms with fluted Egyptian-style columns supporting a pediment. Near the corner of each facade are slight projecting portico-forms with large pilasters, giving vertical emphasis to balance the horizontal scheme of the whole design. An 1856 drawing for the building shows that a cupola had been planned to rest over the marble hall in the center of the structure. By 1860 the walls had been carried up to the architrave line of the entablature. A temporary roof was put on, and work was abandoned at the outbreak of the Civil War. A portion of the building was used during the Civil War as a prison for Confederate officers taken at the siege of Port Hudson. Work on the structure resumed in 1871, but it was not completed until 1881.

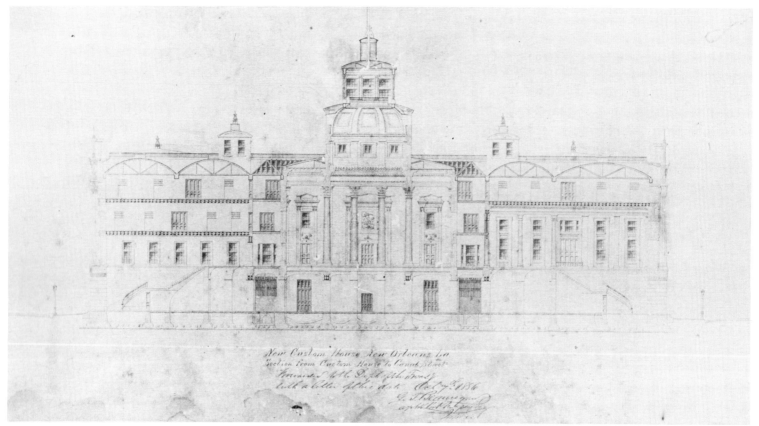

"New Custom House, Section from Custom House and Canal Street," dated October 7, 1856, accompanying a letter from P. G. T. Beauregard to the Department of the Treasury. (Courtesy Louisiana State Museum.)

423 Canal. U. S. Custom House. Exterior detail.

Custom House. Interior marble capital.

423 Canal. U. S. Custom House. Marble hall detail.

423 Canal. U. S. Custom House. Marble hall.

507-509 Canal, corner Decatur, bound by Dorsiere, Iberville. Beneath an 1899 remodeling of the facade is the oldest remaining structure on Canal Street. This five-bay, three-story storehouse was built in 1821 by Felix Pinson and Maurice Peseta, builders, for Joseph Mary at a cost of $11,500. It replaced a structure that had burned earlier in the year. Obscured by the pressed metal lintels, brick wall and heavy brick parapet dating from 1899 are five arched openings on each of three levels, a hip roof and dormers. There was a double-chimneyed gable at the Dorsiere side. This description is based on a Mugnier photograph of the Custom House which includes the Canal Street scene. The building contract (Marc Lafitte, notary, April 24, 1821) specifies that six rooms on the ground floor were to be used as separate stores, each of which had access to a central hallway. There were originally six chimneys. The present window placement is original and has four openings at each tier on the Dorsiere and Decatur sides.

500-514 Canal, corner Magazine, bound by Common, Camp. Corner building is a five-story, masonry commercial building with cast-iron hood moulds above segmental arched windows on three levels. Above a string course is a fifth level, added after 1889, which conforms in general style. The building originally had a heavy parapet with plain coupled brackets beneath the cornice. In 1883 it was occupied by A. Lehmann and Co. Dry Goods and later housed Kohn, Weil & Co., Manufacturers and Exporters. Adjacent at 512-514 Canal are two, three-bay, masonry commercial buildings with cast-iron lower floors, hood moulds and cornices above arched windows. The entablature includes a cornice with brackets, dentils and modillions, with a parapet surmounting the cornice. These buildings were occupied by Levy, Loeb, Scheuer and Co., wholesale dry goods. All three buildings were built by the Montgomery family, who owned the property from 1848 until 1918. The buildings replaced a row of four-story brick stores built in the 1830s.

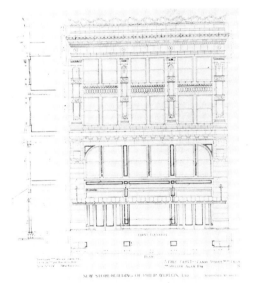

600 block Canal, bound by Exchange, Chartres, Iberville. Prior to 1810 the land here was part of the Commons, situated on the angular between the ruins of Fort St. Louis and Fort Bourgoyne. In 1810 the surveyor Jacques Tanesse divided the area into lots for the city to sell. The entire block facing Canal was built on the original land purchased from the city by Maunsell White & Co. in 1810.   **601 Canal,** corner Chartres, bound by Exchange Place, Iberville. This property was part of the purchase by Phelps and Babcock from Maunsell White in the 1820s. The first building here (at the right) was built between 1820 and 1831 when the property and brick building were sold to Charles Morgan, wholesale druggist. The present building is a remodeling of this earlier structure. It is remembered from the 1880s as Eugene May's drugstore, a landmark on Canal Street, famous for its $5,000 soda fountain. The May family sold the property at auction in 1905.   **605 Canal,** bound by Chartres, Exchange, Iberville. The design for this building by architects Toledano and Wogan for William Agar was pictured in *Architectural Art & Its Allies* (July, 1907). This is a typical building of the first decade of this century, with elaborate glazed terra cotta ornamentation. It was customary in this period to use two tones or polychrome terra cotta decoration as seen here. The parapet has cartouche cresting and deep dentils hang from the cornice. Ionic capitals on central pilasters utilize a classic motif and give central emphasis, while other decorations combine Italianate and Baroque interpretations. Second-story fenestration is enclosed by an elliptical arch, as seen in other Canal Street buildings of the period. (Photograph of 605 Canal courtesy New Orleans Public Library.)

"Vitascope Hall"
U.S. 1st movie theater
623 Canal

"vitascope hall" →

623 Canal

611 Canal, bound by Exchange, Chartres, Iberville. (Old Nos. 42 and 101.) This four-story brick store is similar to 615-17½ Canal, next door, with its arched windows and Italianate detailing. It does not appear in the *Jewell's* (1873) illustration of the building next door. It was therefore erected after that date. This lot is part of a parcel sold by Maunsell White in 1823 to Charles H. Phelps of Phelps and Babcock, which was established in a brick store here. In 1831 the firm sold out to Charles Morgan, a wholesale druggist, for $10,000. The building eventually was acquired by his brother, Matthew Morgan, in 1842 and was appraised at $12,500. The Morgan family kept the property until the 1920s when it was sold for $65,000. A relative of that owner, W. E. Anderson, inherited it in 1880 and improved the property. **613-17½ Canal** (center), bound by Exchange, Chartres, Iberville. A six-bay store with Italianate hood moulds and cornices over arched windows and a heavy decorative cornice. An illustration in *Jewell's* (1873) shows the store had a cast-iron balcony at the second level, supported by iron posts and overhanging the sidewalk. The building probably was erected in the late 1860s. A store was first built on this site in the early 1820s for Maunsell White, who resided there in 1823. His company was located on the ground floor. In 1824 White sold the complex to Thomas Barron for $11,000 and rented it to John T. Barnes, who operated a coffee house there until 1843. Barnes leased the property for $2,000 a year, according to the 1840 lease. The Barron family held the property until 1905 and undoubtly built the present building. Both 613 and 615-17½ are defaced by tasteless store fronts, fire escapes and ugly signs.
619-21 Canal (at left), corner Exchange, bound by Chartres, Iberville. This three-story, three-bay, plastered brick store was built for Mrs. Cora Ann Slocomb in 1837 in connection with family hardware business which joined it to the rear on Exchange Place. The bottom floor has been totally altered, but the upper floors retain pilasters that frame the windows and a deep dentilled cornice. Building contract specifications (H. B. Cenas, notary, March 22, 1837) show that the building was to have pillars and lintel course of blue Quincy granite on the first level. "Country bricks," sharp sand and Thomastown lime were to be used in construction. The exterior was to be plastered in imitation of granite or marble. Doors were to be painted in imitation of oak. Windows were to have inside shutters. There was to be a mahogany stair on the interior. The roof was to be covered with zinc.

615-17½ Canal. (Old No. 103.) Jewell's *Crescent City* (1873). (Courtesy New Orleans Public Library.)

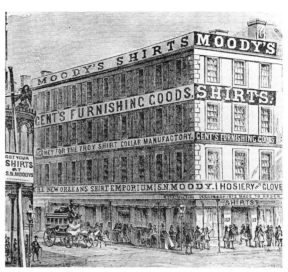

633-35-37 Canal. Jewell's *Crescent City* (1873). (Courtesy New Orleans Public Library.)

633-35-37 Canal, corner Royal, bound by Chartres, Iberville. Maurice Peseta and Felix Pinson, builders, had a private contract in 1825 with Germain Musson, grandfather of artist Edgar Degas, to build a house, stores and out-buildings at the corner of Canal and Royal for $11,500. The stores had increased in value to $25,000 by 1837 when Musson mortgaged them to Asher M. Nathan. The same stores were surveyed by M. Communy, civil engineer, and appraised at $142,000 in 1839. Musson then made an excellent investment, and his stores today remain among the oldest commercial buildings on Canal. The rough-cut Quincy granite was brought from Massachusetts in ships which later hauled away Musson's cotton. An illustration from *Jewell's* (1873) shows one of the four-story stores with granite pillars and lintel course at first level. The corners were quoined and, although the wood block print does not indicate it, the front facade and side were faced with rough-cut granite, the only example of such treatment in New Orleans until the latter part of the century when it became popular.

Plough's Museum was established in 1838 in the Musson Building. Twenty thousand dollars were subscribed to by the citizens to purchase articles for the museum, and a pledge was made by Dr. Plough to pay dividends semi-annually. Dr. Plough's office was at old No. 48 Canal, over Seates and Baggett's store. The interior picture is that of George E. Strong's establishment (old No. 115), a successor to E. A. Tyler, whose jewelry emporium was 30 years old in 1879. The Moody shirt emporium in 1873 occupied the corner store, as does the National Shirt Shop today. Moody's advertisements on every level of the building did nothing to enhance the architectural beauty. At the same time the Moody mansion, which still exists (1411 Canal), reflected a keen awareness of architectural values and tastes. The dreadful full-facade signs and lower level "wrap-around" baked enamel advertisement completely deface the three Canal fronts of these fine, early New Orleans business buildings.

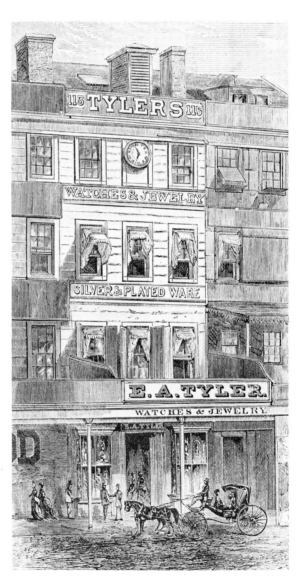

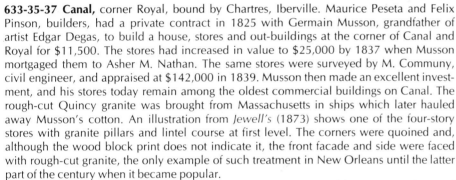

633, 635, 637 Canal. J. C. Waldo's *Visitors Guide to New Orleans* (1879). Interior view of Musson Building. (Courtesy New Orleans Public Library.)

635 Canal. (Old No. 115.) Jewell's *Crescent City* (1873). Musson Building. (Courtesy New Orleans Public Library.)

622, 624, 634, 636 Canal, and William Brand Building.

622 Canal, bound by St. Charles, Camp, Common. (Old No. 104.) One of New Orleans' finest surviving examples of a cast-iron facade on a commercial building. The Merchants Mutual Insurance Co. purchased this location in 1853. The firm utilized the extant building, formerly the banking house of the Merchants and Traders Bank of New Orleans and identical to the one at the corner of Canal and St. Charles. In 1859, the *Picayune* wrote that the cast-iron front of the three-and-one-half story Merchants Mutual Insurance Building was made by Bennett & Lurges' local foundry. The builder was C. Crozier, Esq., and the architect young W. A. Freret, Jr.

Iron pillars of each story differed in style, and the article reported critically that the second story's spiral, cream-colored, round columns with rope twisted around gave the profile an undulating, rather than a straight, appearance. Ornaments in the blocking course represented insurance company attributes. The parapet shows a fire plug, hose, pipe, anchor, cotton bales, barrels, prow of a vessel, spars, furled sails and the roof of a house, symbols of the concerns insured by the company. The third-level columns are an exotic adaptation of the Corinthian composite order. The bull's eye windows of the attic story are divided by brackets of the most decorative shape, and the low arches give to the entire facade an effect of high relief sculpture. The original cast-iron balustrade at the second level has been replaced with a modern one in wrought iron style entirely out of character.

An 1873 illustration in *Jewell's* shows that the first level, which unfortunately has been modernized, was supported by fluted iron Corinthian columns. Commendably, the upper facade has been painted recently the original cream-color mentioned in the 1859 newspaper article. The facade here is one of the most sophisticated in the city. It represents the fascination of the period with the plasticity of iron, which architects distorted into almost every conceivable form and shape. The building is architecturally rare and one of two remaining cast-iron structures in a city where cast-iron once predominated in popular design.

624 Canal, bound by St. Charles, Camp, Common. (Old No. 106.) Italian Renaissance Revival style masonry commercial building dating from before 1873 when it appears in *Jewell's*. The decorative elements in the center of the facade were removed after 1895, and windows were installed to create three stories where two had existed. *Jewell's* (1873) illustrates the original appearance of the store. Rusticated supports at the first level feature carved allegoric heads beneath volutes, and the decorative keystones of the segmental arched openings merge into the lintel course. The central element originally created an overall shouldered arch effect, a motif used in the remodeling to make three bays and a second level. The remodeling was well done, in keeping with the character of the structure. Present defacing of the first level is unfortunate. The Mutual National Bank was located at this address from 1873 until its liquidation in 1900. The company leased the building in 1873, when it must have been built for H. E. Dickey, whose family bought the property in 1857. Apparently the building was built for the bank and leased to them until 1887, when the bank bought it from the Dickey successors for $30,100 cash.

622 Canal. Jewell's *Crescent City* (1873). (Courtesy New Orleans Public Library.)

624 Canal. Soard's *New Orleans City Directory* (1886). (Courtesy New Orleans Public Library.)

632-34 Canal, bound by St. Charles, Camp. A late Victorian commercial building featuring free use of popular Italianate motifs in window surrounds, entablature and string course. The result is a highly decorative facade which adds interest to a block having structures of a variety of 19th century styles. William Brand sold the property on which this building stands to Joseph T. Janin, who retained the old three-story brick building until he sold it to Peter O'Donnel in February, 1867. An illustration in *Jewell's* shows that in 1873 this site was occupied by one of the row of three-story buildings built in the 1830s by William Brand identical to the one remaining next door on the corner of Canal and St. Charles. The present building probably was built shortly thereafter by O'Donnel. It remained in the O'Donnel family until 1899.

The Madison Shop at the left is a more restrained example of the commercial style of the late 1870s. Here the emphasis is toward the center, where double windows flanked by quoined supports on the second level and incised pilasters with Corinthian capitals on the third level are topped by a parapet with a pedimented segment emphasizing the center part of the facade. A string course with dentils and panels divides the second and third levels. A frieze with garlands and bracketed cornice articulates the roofline, and the cornices of the facade are contained by paneled pilasters and quoins.

Corner Canal and St. Charles, bound by Camp, Common. Rubenstein's. One remaining of five simple early two-bay, three-story stores built by architect William Brand for himself in 1833. An illustration in

Jewell's (1873) shows the appearance of the second store in the row (now demolished), which the present Mexic Brothers built on the site. The stores originally had a wrought iron balcony with diamond pattern at the second level. This type of store was typical of many to be found in the 19th century on Canal and is the only remaining example of this early type. Brand bought the Canal front of this square from the St. Charles corner to the Mechanics and Traders Bank and 156 feet on St. Charles in 1820, retaining the area until he began to develop it in 1833. In December, 1840, Brand sold the building at the corner of Canal and St. Charles (Rubenstein's), to Jacob Levy Florance for $21,500, along with the two buildings facing St. Charles (now demolished). He leased the other buildings on Canal for about $3,200 each per year in the 1830s. Brand had divested himself of all the Canal Street buildings by 1866.

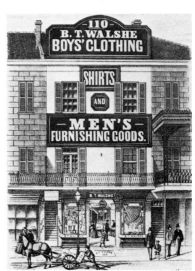

Corner Canal and St. Charles.

700 block Canal. Touro Buildings. Sheet Music, 1866. (Courtesy Historic New Orleans Collection.)

701, 705, 707 Canal, corner Royal, bound by Bourbon, Iberville. Touro Buildings. This block was among the many holdings of Judah Touro, who in 1840 built a series of stores, demolishing the existing buildings (see Wilson article, page 17) as the new stores went up. Here are pictured three remaining buildings of the Touro block. The four stores from the corner of Royal were built for Touro by Thomas Murray in 1852 for $31,000 (Thomas Layton, notary, February 23, 1852). The four-story stores have been altered, and fire escapes obscure the fine classic style facades, which have cornices with dentils. Among the tenants in 1873 were Gueble & Nippert; L. Grunewald; A. B. Griswold & Co.; J. Syme & Co.; Great Southern Dollar Store; August Koenig & Co.; B. Piffet; F. G. & C. W. Barriere; J. G. Bermel; Frederickson and Harte; and McGibbon, Allyn & Dubois. Beneath modern facades in the block may be other Touro buildings, with the exception of Woolworth's and Imperial Shoe Store. The latter is a fine glazed terra cotta building dating from the turn of the century.

739 Canal, corner Bourbon, bound by Royal, Iberville. Four-story, three-bay commercial building built at the turn of the century by Charles Edward Schmidt, grandfather of present owner Hugh de la Vergne. Under lease to Albert Wachenheim family since 1901, the building is decorated with quoins at the second and third levels, graceful bows and garlands of fruits on the fourth level. Classic window surrounds and decorative spandrels are employed along both facades.

710-714-718-20, 722, 728-30 Canal, bound by St. Charles, Carondelet, Common. The building at 710, barely visible at far left, is a four-story Italianate structure of the 1870s with cast-iron decoration on the facade. The projecting cornice is supported by floral scroll brackets. Pilasters between second- and third-level windows are ornamented cast-iron. Windows are partially obscured by awnings. First-floor level has been modernized. The building at 714 replaced an earlier one occupied by F. F. Hansell Co., Stationer, before the fire of 1908, which burned 714, 718-720 and 722 to the ground. Mayor Israel purchased 714 in 1910 for $140,000 and had the present structure erected. It has an excellent tile front.

On a second level is a blind eliptical arch; third, fourth and fifth levels have rhythmic arches with heavy keystones divided by Roman pilasters with Corinthian capitals. The spandrels also have Roman decorations. The cornice is supported by floral brackets and is surmounted by a parapet with balustrades. Nos. 718-20 and 722, presently occupied by Adler's Jewelry Store, were built in 1908 by Fromherz-Drennan for a group of French owners. Coleman E. Adler founded this jewelry store in 1897 when he moved to New Orleans from New York and established his business on this site.

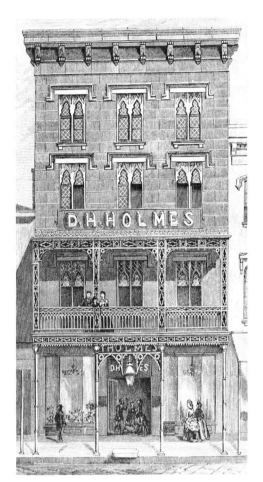

819 Canal, bound by Dauphine, Bourbon, Iberville. D. H. Holmes. First located at old No. 4 Magazine and old No. 22 Chartres, D. H. Holmes moved to its present location after its founder contracted in 1849 with architect Charles Pride to build a four-story store of Gothic design on Canal at Holmes' present location. Above the main floor were elaborately vaulted, buttressed interiors and a central rotunda. Three double windows with pointed arches, iron shutters and iron hood mouldings over lintels continued the Gothic theme. A two-story cast-iron verandah covered the banquette supports with thin iron columns and were painted dark green and bronze. Holmes continued to acquire property, having purchased lots on Bourbon and Iberville in 1853 and additional lots in the 1890s, as well as 76 feet on Dauphine, the Kell House.

After founder Holmes' death in 1906, a stockholding corporation was formed. By 1909 the corporation had demolished the Kell House and erected a three-story brick building designed by Muir and Fromherz. The Canal front was rebuilt in 1913 from designs of Favrot and Livaudais, with Glover and Company builders giving the store a neo-classic look with modernization in the multiple windows across the front between full-length pilasters with tower of the wind capitals. Surmounting the facade is a denticulated cornice and parapet. At street level was a wide marquee, beneath which appeared the famed Holmes clock ("Meet you under the clock at Holmes"). (*Jewell's* (1873) and *Englehardt's* (1894) illustrations courtesy New Orleans Public Library.)

801-805-807 Canal, bound by Bourbon, Dauphine, Iberville. Four-story brick building measuring 20 feet by 85 feet is attached to 109 Bourbon, an earlier building. Both were formerly three stories, the fourth floor having been added when Kreegers occupied No. 805 and remodeled it in 1946. In the fire of 1892 this corner was destroyed, but later was rebuilt. The double stores at 805-807, probably built in the late 1850s, were identical. Nos. 805 and 807 are four-story, three-bay brick buildings in Italianate style, with heavy window architrave lintels and console brackets. Windows on second and fourth floors are segmental, while third-floor windows have square heads. Both buildings have quoins. No. 807 has altered the first and second levels. The projecting cornice with brackets and dentils has been removed. A fire escape defaces the facade.

In 1857 Mills sold No. 801 to Hubert Rolling. It was a three-story brick store which later burned. Kamien and Goldman now handle this property. William Holmes and John Mills owned No. 805 in 1831, selling the property in 1860 to Dudley Atkens, whose heirs retain

ownership. Kreegers occupies three of these properties. The entire 800 block of Canal, both Lakeside and Riverside, retain buildings of good proportions which relate well. Only the fake fronts and exaggerated modernization change the scene from one familiar in the 1890s.

824 Canal, bound by Baronne, Carondelet, Common. Boston Club. This structure, the only residential building surviving intact in the business section of Canal, was erected in 1844 by Dr. Newton Mercer, who commissioned noted architect James Gallier, Sr., to design the house. Cost was $18,700. Dr. Mercer, a wealthy man and prominent citizen, was an Army surgeon who came to New Orleans after serving in the War of 1812. Building contract specifications (H. B. Cenas, notary, May 21, 1844) fully describe the house. It was constructed of "country brick" and the lower facade was faced with Missouri marble. The entrance antae pilasters and entablature, window sills and lintels and cornice of the Canal elevation are also marble. The brick walls are plastered and were originally scored and painted to imitate marble. Cornices along the side of the house were constructed of brick to match the design of the front cornice and were then cemented and painted to resemble marble. The entrance door is recessed and is framed by sidelights between engaged Ionic columns and pilasters.

At the second level is a wrought iron balcony with affixed cast-iron decoration. The front third-floor windows have individual iron balconies supported by marble consoles. Iron grills were placed in the attic windows. The windows of the second level have pedimented lintels. At the side of the house is a hexagonal bay and a granite and iron fence. At the rear was a courtyard and service wing. Interior decoration included moulded stucco ceiling cornices and large center ceiling medallions of floral design in "the three principal rooms and a small one in the hall." Fireplace mantels were of marble carved with cherubs and flute players. Windows and doors were trimmed in Greek mouldings of the Corinthian style. Stair railings were of Santo Domingo mahogany, "with scroll and wreaths complete and fancy turned mahogany balusters." The house was designed with interior waterclosets with cisterns above for flushing, and bathrooms were supplied with hot water piped from a boiler in the kitchen.

Since 1884 the Mercer house has been occupied by the Boston Club, founded in 1841 by a group of mercantile and professional men for privacy in playing Boston, a card game popular at that time. In the same year the club added a large wing at the rear of the building and renovated the interior in the Eastlake style of decoration, replacing the marble mantels with highly ornamental mantels of red cherry and adding a winding Old English staircase. Walters and Harrod were architects for the renovation.

828 Canal, bound by Carondelet, Baronne, Common. A seven-story, turn-of-the-century commercial building with two sets of bay-windows at the third through the sixth levels, giving a central emphasis to this large store. Godchaux's, as shown here, occupies the site of three former buildings, including the Grunewald Building. About 1901 the Macheca Real Estate and Improvement Co. demolished the old structures and built the present one.

In 1844 Leon Godchaux moved to New Orleans and opened a small store opposite the old French Meat Market. By 1865 Godchaux owned Nos. 81, 83, and 85 Canal, near the corner of Chartres, where he began a wholesale establishment designed to accommodate the orders of country storekeepers and to manufacture clothing. By 1870 Godchaux closed his store on Decatur to operate wholesale, retail and manufacturing at his Canal location. In 1899 the store expanded to the corner of Canal and Chartres, and Leon Godchaux finalized plans for a six-story structure at the site. The new store was being built in May of that year when he died at the age of 75. His death left the Leon Godchaux Co. with his seven sons as directors, in control of combined enterprises employing over 3,000 persons. In 1924 the store moved from here to 828 Canal.

810 Canal, bound by Carondelet, Baronne, Common. Leon Fellman Building. Handsome example of a tile-front building dating from 1910. Paired engaged columns at each side running three tiers frame a large area of plate glass enclosed above by a decorative tile entablature with Moorish motifs. Emphasis is given to the upper level by the trefoil arches in relief above upper windows. Cast-iron balconies, duplicating those at the Pontalba Buildings at Jackson Square, were added later, and the ground floor facade has been remodeled.

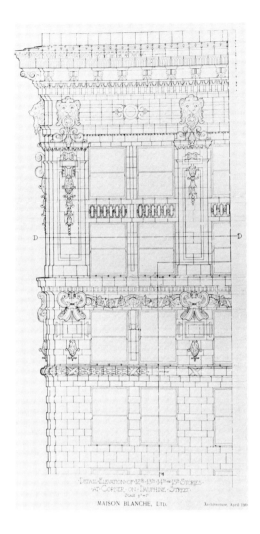

DETAIL ELEVATION OF 12ᵗʰ 13ᵗʰ 14ᵗʰ ᵃⁿᵈ 15ᵗʰ STORIES
AT CORNER ON DAUPHINE STREET
MAISON BLANCHE, LTD.   *Architecture, April 1908*

900 block Canal, bound by Burgundy, Dauphine, Iberville. "Progress" has altered this block, which in the 1840s presented a progression of Greek temple-like structures, including the elegant apartment complex designed by J. H. Dakin known as the Union Terrace, part of which housed the famous Varieties Theatre. Second Christ Church was a landmark on the block (see Wilson article, page 16). The late 1800s brought the complete disappearance of classic architecture here. In 1884 Christ Church was sold at auction for $95,000 to D. Mercier and Sons. The Mercier building was erected on the site about 1887. The present Maison Blanche Building was being built in 1908-09 with designs by Stone Brothers architects. It is a massive example of the glazed terra cotta, commercial style building with heavy fanciful decorations of baroque inspiration.

Engaged columns of tile give emphasis to the lower segment. Windows arranged in groups of threes and twos, divided by tiled piers giving a scored effect, articulate the middle seven tiers. The upper two levels, with projecting terminal cornice, culminate the tripartite scheme. Terra cotta for the building was supplied by Atlanta Terra Cotta Company. To the left of Maison Blanche is the Kress Building (not shown), with a fine terra cotta front erected in 1910 and completely defaced at present with baked enamel facade. Next to Kress is the Audubon Building (not shown), built by McWilliams and Company in 1910, with another glazed terra cotta front designed for the Audubon Hotel. A large metal canopy formerly hung over the wide sidewalk.

914, 916, 922, 924 Canal, bound by University Place, Baronne, Common. This square was occupied by the State House until 1850 when it was subdivided with 26 lots which sold for a total of $158,000. A *Picayune* article of May 21, 1850, states that following the demolition of the old State House, a "row of four beautiful buildings was planned by Mr. Burke." Other purchasers of the property in the block were Mr. Forshey (at University Place), Mrs. L. Harvey, Dr. Porter, Mr. Finch, Mr. Castell, Mr. Gernon (two lots), Mr. Grailhe (two), Mr. Labatut and S. B. Davis (at Baronne). Of the development in this square during the 1850s, only these four, three-story brick commercial buildings remain. Greatly altered, only portions of original facades with denticulated cornices may remain behind modern false fronts.

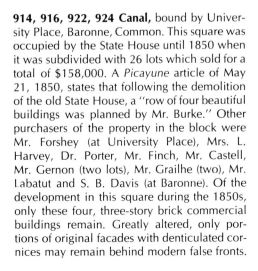

928 Canal, bound by Baronne, University Place, Common. A glazed brick facade with polychrome ornamentation of terra cotta frieze, string course and capitals. One of the best remaining examples in New Orleans of the polychrome style of the turn of the century, it is a typical example of the style introduced by Frank Lloyd Wright and Lewis Sullivan. It features large areas of plate glass contrasting with a solid brick curtain wall above and articulated by vertical members and a string course, with polychrome decoration above and below it.

930 Canal, bound by Baronne, University Place, Common. This masonry facade illustrates free use of decorative forms from various periods popular in commercial buildings of the 1870s. The ground floor front here has been replaced, and the neon sign obscures a handsome string course with consoles. The State of Louisiana sold this parcel of State House Square in 1850 to Royal Porter. This lot, with 28-foot front by 120-foot depth, sold for $9,000. Mrs. Benjamin H. Moss acquired the property in 1876, and the present structure was built for her. Moss' heirs retained the property until 1922.

940 Canal, corner University Place, bound by Baronne, Common. A late example of the classic-style commercial building popular in New Orleans since the 1830s. This three-bay, four-story store features cap-moulded cornices with egg and dart decorations at each window, and an architrave continues around the windows. A deep frieze area is surmounted by a cornice with deep dentils. While some New Orleans commercial facades after 1870 were Victorian or Italianate in decoration, one notes the continued popularity of simpler classic tradition.

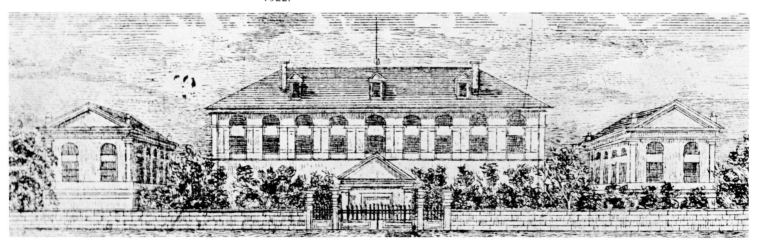

Buildings which formerly stood on State House Square, between University Place and Baronne. *Gibson's 1838.* (Courtesy New Orleans Public Library.)

1030 Canal, bound by Rampart, University Place, Common. Based on a Venetian Palazzo prototype, this elegant building was designed for the Pickwick Club by Shepley, Routan and Coolidge, successors of H. H. Richardson, in 1896. The structure follows the tradition of decoration and design popularized by the Columbian Exposition, Chicago, 1893. Incised polychrome rustication at the first level, which originally faced the ground floor, work well with the entablature where the balusters pierce the parapet to enclose the geometric articulation of carved stone against bricks. The banding around the windows and balconies, the cartouches and the railing of the cornice also show an awareness of the ornamental detailing used by Lewis Sullivan. The two-tone effect, an essential feature of the original design, is lost in the present painting, and the side entrance, once part of the palazzo design, has been filled with a second and third floor where the window decorations on the original facade have been continued. The ground floor front has been destroyed.

The *Times Democrat* of November 27, 1896, wrote that the building had a large lounging room of Turkish effect, billiard room and a cafe with a summer gallery, which extended the length of the building, with tall window openings. Leading to a roof garden was a stairway, as well as an Otis elevator, a radical innovation in the city. The second floor contained a main hall, reading room and cardroom. On the third floor the dining rooms were painted white and lighted from overhead. This once-handsome building could be a 19th century New Orleans landmark. For a history of the Pickwick Club, see 115 St. Charles. (Photograph by Charles L. Franck.)

1030 Canal. Shoe Town. Old Pickwick Club.

1201 Canal, bound by Crozat, Basin, Iberville. Krauss Department Store. This firm was founded by Leon Fellman and three Krauss brothers. The present building was built in 1903 and has four attached additions which were added in 1911, 1923, 1927 and 1952, respectively. The architectural treatment of the restrained arched openings offers a continuation of a valid 19th century style, while the modern additions display only a solution to a problem of space.

1411 Canal, bound by Treme, Marais, Iberville. This three-story masonry dwelling, with scored plaster and segmental arched windows capped by decorative cast-iron Italianate hood moulds, was built in 1858 for S. N. Moody by Crozier & Wing, builders, with Howard and Diettel as architects. It was hailed as one of the finest residences built in 1858, and when auctioned in 1883 it was advertised as an elegant "city house complete in every comfort for a large family. Throughout this most complete establishment, in thorough order of design, finish and repair, will be found all that is necessary for the most complete city home." It adjoined at that time the also elegant houses of Dr. Borde, W. B. Koontz, John Henderson, E. L. Carrier and E. E. Norton.

From an article in the *Daily Picayune* (March 24, 1883) and from the act of sale in August, 1884, a detailed description of the house is available. The entrance had Italian marble steps. There was a wide hall and spacious vestibule. Parlors had double-arched central openings. Dining room, pantry, storerooms, kitchen, wash and ironing room and stationary tub with hot and cold water completed the first floor. On the second floor was a hall, three bedrooms, dressing room, bathroom and English patent watercloset and two servants' rooms. The third story had three bedrooms, a large closet, linen storage and bathroom. The building had wide iron verandahs and broad galleries. Mantels were all of fine carved marble. In the rear was a two-story brick stable and coach house, with three stalls and billiard room above. There was a garden with an ornamental iron railing fronting on Canal. The house also had an observatory.

The building contract price was $15,500 and in 1884 the house was sold for $16,500. S. N. Moody, the original owner, became one of the leading merchants of New Orleans in the 1860s. His shirt manufacturing and sales business was located in the granite building at the corner of Canal and Royal, the Musson Building. The ground floor facade has been destroyed and the balconies removed. The cornice probably was Italianate with brackets. The house would make an excellent, colorful restaurant, offering tourists a treat in an area of Canal now in the process of developing.

thereon and erected new ones, which I rented out to various tenants, and received from them a handsome income.''

Gallier had built the first portion of what became known as Gallier Court on the Common side of the same square (demolished). The two buildings along Carondelet opened onto Gallier's building yard in the middle of the square. The *Daily Picayune* (September 19, 1850) describes the stores as having just "been finished, with stores underneath.…These houses each contain 25 rooms above, intended for boarding houses; they have galleries in front and are owned by Mr. Gallier, the architect. They have already been rented at $2,000 per annum each." In 1867 James Gallier, Jr., replanned the Court. The entire atmosphere changed; the carpenters' shops were converted into a bathing salon and bar room. The *Daily Picayune* (July 15, 1900) describes the junior Gallier's inner court where activities were "most cultured, most aristocratic," with "a beautiful courtyard, Spanish in nature with a splendid $2,500 fountain in its center of solid bronze.''

132, 134 Carondelet, bound by Canal, Common, St. Charles. No. 134 (at right) is a masonry building constructed in 1882 to house the People's Insurance Company. No. 132 probably was built about the same time. Both are similar in style, Italianate of the High Victorian period, with arched windows, heavy parapets and cornices and decorative console brackets. Both street levels have been modernized. No. 138 (not pictured), adjacent to the structure at right, is the earliest building remaining in the group. It is a three-story brick structure, with splayed brick lintels and brick entablature.

127, 131, 137, 139 Carondelet, bound by Canal, Common, Baronne. At the left is a six-bay, classical style, masonry commercial building, a remodeling of two stores which James Gallier, Sr., had built for himself in 1846. Parapet, window pediments and hood moulds have been added. The building formerly had scored plaster. To its right are two brick stores retaining the earlier features of the row. The present Orleans Shop is a four-story store, designed by Gallier, Sr., for Charles Mason. To its right is a store Gallier designed for E. D. Fenner in the 1840s. These stores, between the Federal Reserve Bank on the corner of Common and Gus Mayer on Canal, form a group of attractive mid-nineteenth century stores presently defaced by signs, fire escapes and ground floor fronts.

In the autobiography of James Gallier (pages 26 and 41) is a quote applicable to these properties: "Having by that time [1835] bought some lots of ground fronting on Common and Carondelet in New Orleans, I there established my office and workshops, and occupied them as such as long as I remained in business…In 1846 having some lots of ground adjoining my building yard, I pulled down the old edifices

122 Carondelet, bound by Canal, Common, St. Charles. A good example of the classisizing trend in the first two decades of this century, with fluted Corinthian columns of colossal order. Unfortunately modified by unnecessary attempts at modernizing. Built in 1905 for the City Bank and Trust on the site of a building used by the Boston Club in 1883.

140 Carondelet, bound by Canal, Common, St. Charles. A late-nineteenth century commercial building with a highly decorative facade having a variety of motifs, including putti, cartouches and garlands. The arched windows are vertically articulated by Ionic pilasters of classic order. The street-level front is a more modern replacement in the Neo-classic style, with Doric columns, entablature and cresting out of keeping with the original facade.

201-211 Carondelet. George W. Engelhardt's *City of New Orleans* (1894). (Courtesy New Orleans Public Library.)

312-320 Carondelet, corner Union, bound by Gravier, St. Charles. The Notarial Archives (Book 64, Folio 34, H. B. Cenas, 1853) records that Jamison and McIntosh, builders for Gilbert S. Hawkins, built a corner store in 1853 to match the adjoining buildings constructed earlier. This row of fine granite front buildings, of the type which were designed from the 1830s onward, reflect the New York influence on American New Orleans. This location was known for generations by New Orleanians as "Abadie's." It was demolished in 1971 by Louis Roussell and is presently a parking lot.

201-211 Carondelet, corner Common, bound by Gravier, Baronne. Maritime Building (Hennen Building). Thomas Sully was the architect of this structure, erected in 1893-95 by John A. Morris, contractor, for his brother-in-law, Judge Alfred Hennen. Erected on cypress pilings, it rose ten stories, with steel frame, yellow brick and terra cotta trim. The *Picayune Guide* (1900) estimates the cost at $300,000. The Canal Commercial Bank purchased it in 1922, adding an eleventh floor and changing the name from Hennen to Canal Commercial Bank Building and spending $1 million on renovation. In 1927 it was sold to the Maritime Building Corporation, and the name changed again to the one presently used, Maritime Building. The building was purchased in 1943 by Harry Latter and Jacques Mossler for $600,000 and remodeled. Purchased in 1959 by the Carondelet Realty Co., Thomas Favrot, Vice-President. A *States-Item* article (1960) states: "With the exception of the original door fixtures and stairwell railings, everything on the interior has been redesigned."

The exterior design includes medallion decorations, with various birds, eagles and pelicans and Roman profiles placed in first-level spandrels. Windows have Greek Key architraves with relief terra cotta carvings of garlands. The rows of bay-windows are in the mode of the influential Chicago School of Commercial Structures of the 1880s and 1890s. Cast-iron friezes were added with the eleventh floor. This building stands on the site of the Duncan F. Kenner Building. The Kenner family had owned the property since 1853. The Federal government confiscated the property during the Civil War, but it reverted to the Kenner heirs after Reconstruction.

300 Carondelet, corner Gravier, bound by Union, St. Charles. This four-story, multi-bay, plastered brick commercial building dates from before 1866. At that time the owner, Samuel Jamison, remodeled them himself, using plans by James Freret. Jamison made facilities for a "Bar Room, Pastry Store and Ladies Dining Room" costing $10,000. He then leased the property to D. G. Hitchcock for $4,000. The Cafe Imperial opened February 6, 1867, with facilities for "large balls, private rooms and excellent cooking." Since Jamison owned the property and, as a speculator-builder had built stores on his own properties throughout the Faubourg, it is logical to assume that he was builder for the original structure here. Jules de la Vergne, owner and architect, remodeled the stores in 1962 for the Hibernia Homestead Association. The renovation is a landmark in the vicinity, tastefully accomplished, reflecting mid-nineteenth century style, but with an addition of French Quarter style cast-iron balconies.

325-43 Carondelet. Drawing by C. A. Hedin, 1855 Plan Book 25, Folio 33, New Orleans Notarial Archives.

325-343 Carondelet, bound by Union, Perdido, Baronne. These six, four-story brick buildings, once a row of eight, were described in the *Daily Picayune* (September 19, 1850): "Eight large magnificent stores with granite fronts between Perdido and Union. They are facsimiles of the Washington stores in New York City. The windows have French molier casements and label lintels. The first one, on the corner of Perdido, is owned by Washington Jackson & Co.; the next, by Wright, Williams & Co.; the two following, by Dr. Mercer; the next, by Moon, Titus & Co.; the next, by Buckner, Stanton & Co.; the next, by J. Howell, and the last, by Fisk Sterver & Co. They are a great ornament to our city. The architect is Mr. George Purves and the builder Mr. Thomas Murray."

In 1886, the Union Street corner was occupied by Factors and Traders Insurance Co., as shown in the Soard's *Directory* (1886). A handsome, cast-iron gallery decorated the second level. The windows are headed with Gothic labels. One of the stores also appears in an auction drawing of 1855. The openings between the granite pillars were filled with four-fold paneled doors painted in *faux bois* to resemble oak. These are among the few granite stores of the mid-nineteenth century remaining in the city. The building is altered only on the first floor, by front modernization and an unimaginative fire escape and signs.

325-43 Carondelet. Soard's *New Orleans Directory* (1886). (Courtesy New Orleans Public Library.)

419-21-23-25-29-31 Carondelet, bound by Poydras, Perdido, Carroll. Three, four-story brick stores (from the right), identical when built in 1858 by Joshua Peebles for Francois Dupuy for $25,000. The specifications (Guyol, notary, Vol. 40, No. 212) called for an iron verandah and iron vault doors. The store doors were grained oak or bronzed and twice varnished. The ground floors of these buildings have been altered, but several cast-iron pillars remain. A parapet and cornice with paired brackets unify the three stores, but the contrasting color of the end store tends to obscure this unity. The cast-iron sill drops in the fourth level and the cast-iron hood moulds with dentils remain, as do some of the original window lights. Present owners are Edward Carrere, Jr., and Grace Warolin.

At the left are three particularly fine structures with Italianate decoration, built in 1859 by Little and Middlemiss for Dr. Wm. B. Wood. Designed by Howard and Diettel, these three, four-story brick stores rented as residences above. Cost was $27,000. The building contract supplies the following information (P. C. Cuvillier, notary, April 26, 1859): "Uniform cast-iron fronts with 10" x 15" story posts, imposts, segmental lintels, consoles, trusses and cornices of best quality cast-iron, moulded, enriched and formed....The doors finished as grained oak. Front windows shall have ornamental cast-iron caps, label moulding and corbels. The string or sill course under third story windows shall be of cast-iron handsomely moulded and finished to extend along the entire front of stores. Fourth story front windows shall have cast-iron sills. The twelve trusses under the main cornice and eight trusses under the brick and cement panels at each party wall shall be of cast-iron moulded and finished firmly anchored to the brick work. Interior wood mantels finished in imitation marble."

Two of these first-story iron fronts retain their "story posts and imposts" decorated with egg and dart motif. The "segmental lintels" have handsome cast-iron crests, all of which remain except one. Highly decorative hood moulds with brackets above the trefoil arched windows are identical in the first and third buildings. The middle segment of the row has contrasting hood mould details. The roofline originally had a cement cornice, pedimented above both end units, with paired brackets and dentils under the cornice. At the second level was a cast-iron balcony. Present owners are the University of Virginia, Tulane University and Trinity Church.

Corner Carondelet and Perdido. Factors Row (see 802-822 Perdido). This building, important historically and architecturally, sides on Carondelet and completes one of New Orleans' finest commercial squares.

500 Carondelet, corner Poydras, bound by St. Charles, Lafayette. Three-and-one-half story masonry building with fenestration on Carondelet in a one-four-four-one pattern, each window having granite sills and hood moulds. The attic windows below the denticulated cornice have wrought iron decorations in horizontal position, probably a later addition since they should be vertical. First-level alterations included garland decoration. A *Picayune* article (August 17, 1858) reports: "They planned the Poydras front in the Roper building style and the Carondelet front as an extension of ornamental, majestic Davidson's Row." According to the *Picayune*, the Davidson Row (now demolished) was built from brick and material from Dr. Clapp's church, which burned in the St. Charles Hotel fire. Davidson's Concert Hall, an L-shaped, two-story structure, enclosed the Roper Building. G. W. Roper owned this property in the 1850s and still retained ownership in 1862. In 1883 the Seiger Saloon occupied the building.

515, 517, 519 Carondelet, bound by Poydras, Lafayette, Baronne. Two, three-story, three-bay brick houses with party walls, refronted and altered at successive stages. The heavy decorative cornice with dentils remains at No. 515. The two formerly identical houses were those built in 1832 by Daniel Halsted Twogood, builder for the New Orleans Building Company, Samuel Livermore, President. The row could easily be restored, using any facade arrangement illustrated in this book and would make ideal apartments or offices.

546 Carondelet, corner Lafayette, bound by Poydras, St. Charles. Built as the City Hall Annex in 1908 and designed by Allison Owen. The city engineer was W. J. Hardee, with J. P. O'Leary contractor. When the City Hall was moved to the Civic Center, the New Orleans Public Belt Railroad Office was housed there. Now in private ownership, it houses offices. This commercial building exercises the classicizing element in vogue in the early 1900s. The tripartite scheme emphasizes both vertical and horizontal. Quoins between groups of three windows divide the facade vertically. A central entrance area employs classic motifs, including Doric columns and entablature of the classic order. The four central stories are enclosed above by a projecting cornice and deep parapet and below by a rusticated ground level with projecting lintel course. This building is a credit to the Central Business District. Elevations can be found in *Architectural Art and Its Allies* (1908). (Courtesy New Orleans Public Library.)

619 Carondelet, bound by Lafayette, Girod, Baronne. Built as the Edward McGehee Church of the Methodist Episcopal Church soon after 1851 when the former sanctuary, situated at the corner of Canal and Carondelet, burned. The congregation was the oldest Methodist group in the city. Between 1851 and May 14, 1853, while it was under construction, the walls spread and collapsed as the roof was being put on. The church was then rebuilt. Originally the plastered brick church had a Greek-form church tower in the center, modeled after the monument of Lysicrates. The Ionic portico and deep entablature remain, although the original entrance was replaced by a window when the Masons acquired the building and rededicated it as the Scottish Rite Cathedral in 1906. The basement-level doors are an unfortunate defacement to this temple-like structure, and the entrance steps have been reworked, spoiling the character of the structure as originally designed. The present entrance doors on either side of the window also were later additions.

630-634-640 Carondelet, corner Girod, bound by Lafayette, St. Charles. Three of the buildings in this row are remnants of a row of five built in 1832 and are among the earliest in the area. These are masonry houses with dormers, party walls and gabled ends and a simple wrought iron balcony extended across the entire row. The shutters on the main floor were battened for privacy, and those above were louvered for light and ventilation. The six paneled doors were wood grained natural color. Originally the cornice had dentils. The second building from the Girod corner retains its wrought iron balcony. The three remaining buildings retain the original fenestration configuration, a full-length center window flanked by smaller twelve-light windows.

In the Notarial Archives drawing by Fred Wilkinson in 1839, the plaster was yellow, the shutters light green and doors of two-tone brown possibly *faux bois*. A ground-floor plan of 1832 shows these structures as having two rooms, with side hall and service buildings separated along the back property line behind a courtyard. This early arrangement of service buildings differs from the later scheme of connecting the service wing to the rear of the structure. These buildings remain of five built in 1832 for John Prendergast, who lost them to his builder, John Fitz Miller, for $5,900. In 1834 Samuel Moore bought two of these for $7,500. One of the original 1832 buildings was destroyed before the Civil War, and the present building, third from the corner, was then built. This two-and-a-half story brick house has a cast-iron gallery at the second level and is a handsome part of the street scene.

Observe the 1839 notarial drawings of the eight brick rowhouses which stood on the site of Barnett's Furniture Store. This entire block was a typical New Orleans antebellum scene.

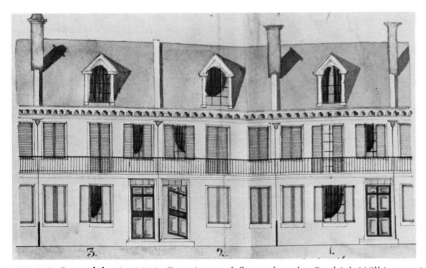

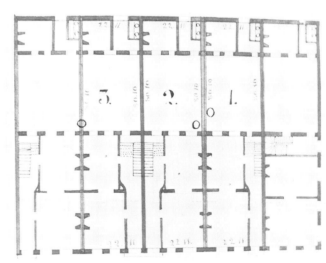

634-640 Carondelet in 1839. Drawing and floor plans by Fredrick Wilkinson, 1839. Plan Book 32, Folio 8, New Orleans Notarial Archives.

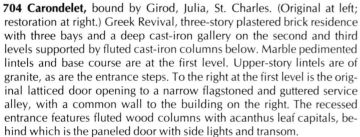

704 Carondelet, bound by Girod, Julia, St. Charles. (Original at left; restoration at right.) Greek Revival, three-story plastered brick residence with three bays and a deep cast-iron gallery on the second and third levels supported by fluted cast-iron columns below. Marble pedimented lintels and base course are at the first level. Upper-story lintels are of granite, as are the entrance steps. To the right at the first level is the original latticed door opening to a narrow flagstoned and guttered service alley, with a common wall to the building on the right. The recessed entrance features fluted wood columns with acanthus leaf capitals, behind which is the paneled door with side lights and transom.

The lot on which this building stands was purchased by James, John and William Freret in 1842 from the Louisiana Marine and Fire Insurance Company. The Freret brothers were listed in the *City Directory* of 1847 as residing in individual houses on Carondelet in the block between Girod and Lafayette. The family business was a cotton press on Baronne and Common. In 1847 the property here was sold to Edmond Freret, who probably had the present house built, selling it in 1858 to Thomas E. Lee, a builder residing next door at the corner of Carondelet and Girod. The sale was for $4,000. By 1862 Lee had sold the house to John Burnside, and it was valued at $8,500 by J. B. Walton, auctioneer. Restored in 1971 as law offices of Porteous, Toledano, Hainkel and Johnson, it is among the first adaptive use efforts in the area.

700 block Carondelet. This street scene shows a complex of different types of classic style buildings with common walls. Such groups should be preserved as part of New Orleans' Golden Era.

714-16 Carondelet, bound by Girod, Julia, St. Charles. Three-story, three-bay plastered brick dwelling built after 1865, as indicated by the records of J. B. Walton, auctioneer, who valued the lot at only $2,500 in 1865. Built for John Davidson, who had purchased the property from William Pinckard in 1860. The Italianate segmental-arched entrance with pilasters and denticulated cornice further indicates a late-1860 building date. Slender cast-iron fluted colonnettes support the ornate double cast-iron gallery. Behind the entrance way is a granite vestibule with paneled casing doors, which afforded privacy and protection. Although erected two decades after the three adjacent buildings at the left, the structure continues the classic pattern popularized in New Orleans in the 1840s.

706, 708, 710 Carondelet, bound by Girod, Julia, St. Charles. A double house of brick, with granite sills and lintels. A common alleyway runs through the center, leading to the flagstone court yard. The entrance to No. 706 retains its original features of classic design, Ionic capitals over fluted columns supported by a heavy cornice, with dentils and egg and dart motif. The recessed entrance has sidelights with double-paired pilasters and transom. The second-level iron balcony is delicate, in contrast with the opulent entrance. The brick, American bond, probably was painted and stenciled. The interior has medallions and cove mouldings, evidence that these two buildings were homes. The entrance for No. 710 has been altered, as has the entire first level. Duncan Sinclair purchased these two lots for $5,000 in 1847 from the Louisiana State Marine and Fire Insurance Company. Sinclair probably had the houses built, since his sister, Alexina Sinclair McBurney, inherited them, selling them 50 years later in 1909 for $16,000.

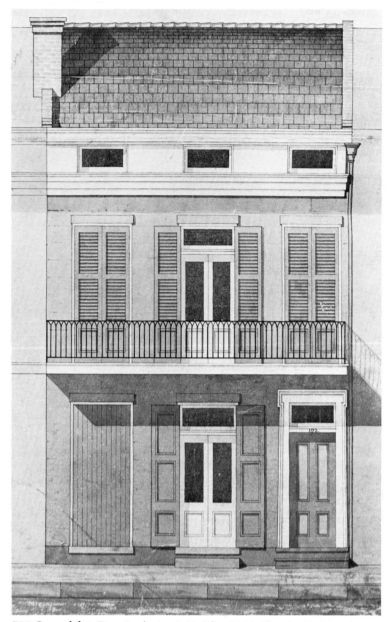

755 Carondelet. Drawing by Louis H. Pilie, 1880. Plan Book 100, Folio 17, New Orleans Notarial Archives.

753-755 Carondelet, bound by Julia, Girod, Baronne. Two, two-and-one-half story identical three-bay masonry houses, with party wall utilizing the traditional floor plan of side hallway and double parlor with stairs to second floor and attached service wing at rear. Wood entablature is applied to masonry facade. There is a strong indication that these two were once part of a row. The second-level windows of No. 755 have been shortened, and the bottom floors have been totally altered. A Notarial Archives drawing shows that the houses originally had Greek Key entrances. Julian Clovis bought this property from Norbert Vandry in 1838. Within the decade, he built the present structures and sold them in 1846 to Joseph Dumas, whose heirs owned the property until 1883.

At the time of the 1883 sale for $2,725, a *Times-Democrat* advertisement describes the house at the right: "A certain lot of ground... together with a handsome two-story and attic residence, No. 193, having on the ground floor hall, parlor and dining-room, with sliding door, four bedrooms above and balcony on the street; a two-story brick kitchen adjoining the house, of four rooms, cisterns, hydrant, privy, flagged yard, etc., rented for $27.50 per month."

801 Carondelet, bound by Julia, St. Joseph, Baronne. Two-story, four-bay brick commercial building with outstanding decorative brick architrave. Frieze articulated with sawtooth pattern bricks dividing it into four panels, a decorative abstraction of the classic metope. Segmental arch and splayed lintels with keystone. Brick segmental arched entrance on Julia.

821 Carondelet, bound by Julia, St. Joseph, Baronne. Three-level, three-bay masonry Greek Revival house with exterior finish and first level completely altered. Masonry frieze below cornice with dentils is typical of rows of residences which lined this street. An 1847 sale by John Lyeth to J. A. Blanc may indicate that the latter built the house at 211 Carondelet (old number). In 1860, the widow of Charles Oxley owned this property, valued at $15,000, and an adjacent one, both of which were sold in 1869 to August Reichard for $25,000.

852 Carondelet, bound by St. Joseph, Julia, St. Charles. Unusual commercial form featuring Italian villa square tower with deep overhanging cornice and roof. Other decorative elements derive from the 19th century Italian villa form. The yellow brick is one indication that the building dates from the early 20th century.

851, 853 Carondelet, bound by St. Joseph, Julia, Baronne. No. 853, three-and-one-half story house, has lost all its former character. Deteriorated cornice and frieze of wood, mutilated attic windows, added quoins and second-level delicate balcony bricked-in lower level complete the architectural ruination of this building and the adjoining three-level masonry structure (No. 851). Anthony Moybin owned lot No. 853 in 1852. In 1868 Theophile Nash sold No. 851 to Nathanial H. Bryants of Boston for $10,000. Each lot measures 25 feet x 153 feet.

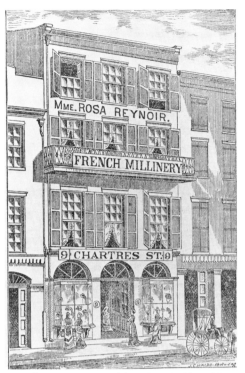

113 Chartres. J. C. Waldo's *City Guide to New Orleans* (1879). (Courtesy New Orleans Public Library.)

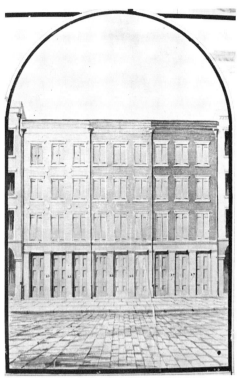

115-121 Chartres. Drawing by Charles de Armas, 1859. Plan Book 58, Folio 22, New Orleans Notarial Archives.

113 Chartres, bound by Canal, Iberville, Exchange Place. This four-story masonry building, with three arched opening with fanlight transoms below full-length windows at the upper levels, was built by Samuel B. Slocomb in 1832 for his hardware business. The business also fronted on Exchange Place. Both properties remained in the Slocomb family until 1937 (see 112 Exchange Place). An illustration in *Waldo's* (1879) shows the building with simple lintels. These subsequently have been decorated with projecting bracketed cornices. The third-floor balcony has been removed and a second-floor balcony added in a different railing pattern. The fire escape defaces the facade. In elevation, the style of the building is a continuation of types found throughout the Vieux Carre.

115-117-121 Chartres, bound by Canal, Iberville, Exchange Place. A row of three, four-story plastered brick stores with early Greek Revival granite pillars which originally had paneled bifold doors between them. Built about 1832 by Henry Babcock and Charles Gardiner, businessmen and partners, who had purchased the land from the heirs of William Kenner (see 600 block Canal). Babcock and Gardiner sold the three stores in 1834 to Manuel Lizardi at auction (Plan Book 58, Folio 22), where they were designated as Nos. 13, 15 and 17 Chartres, having "granite fronts and iron window shutters." They were leased at the time of the sale for $2,500 per year and sold for $28,000 each. The corresponding drawing from the Notarial Archives shows them as they appeared at the time of a sheriff's sale in 1859. Each was painted a different color: yellow, blue and brick red. The two-fold paneled doors were painted green and the shutters were solid cypress.

135-41 Chartres. J. C. Waldo's *Visitor's Guide to New Orleans* (1879). (Courtesy New Orleans Public Library.)

135-37-39-41 Chartres, corner Iberville, bound by Canal, Exchange Place. This excellent row of three-level, three-bay brick buildings was illustrated in *Waldo's* (1879). At No. 125-37 (old Nos. 27 and 29) was the establishment of F. R. Hardon, a prominent milliner and fancy goods merchant. It is quite possible that a building contract (recorded by D. L. McCoy, April 21, 1840) between James Gallier and John Hagan applies to at least two of these buildings. It reads: "For erection of two stores on Chartres and Customhouse...Lake bricks front painted and pencilled...all other wall country brick...Granite sills and lintels...Iron shutters front and rear...Store doors grained oak...First story 12', second story 11', third story 10', fourth 9'...Cypress stairs...Roof slate... copper gutters...Three doors and three windows...each store front to be finished September 1, 1840...." Only the lower level has been changed on the exterior of the building since 1879.

1565 Cleveland, corner S. Robertson. Late Greek Revival brick double house of the 1850s, with fine cast-iron balcony on two facades, with typical service wing with wood balcony. Hipped roof can be seen behind heavy brick parapet. One house has its entrance at the front facade facing Cleveland. The entrance to the other house is on the side of the building facing S. Robertson, an unusual arrangement. In 1840 James C. Wilson and Ed York sold the empty lot to Sumter Turner and Joshua Baldwin for $1,015, and they built the house which stayed in possession of the Turner and Baldwin heirs until 1900.

123, 125, 129 Chartres, bound by Canal, Iberville, Exchange Place. This row of four, four-story brick house-stores, with continuous arcade in the Vieux Carre tradition, was probably built in the 1830s. No. 123 Chartres (extreme left), formerly No. 21, was the property of Joseph McNeil from 1805-35. The building was erected in 1837 by Thomas Stackhouse for Gilbert Vance (building contract by H. K. Gordon, Vol. 59, December 29, 1837) as a three-story brick dwelling house, adjoining the house owned by McNeil. The front of the house, chimney tops, pillars and arches were to be of Philadelphia brick and the remainder of the manufacture of Delachaise. There was to be an iron gallery across the entire front of the second story. Vance resided in the house until 1832, and it remained in his estate until sold by his widow in 1882. No. 129 Chartres was extensively remodeled for A. R. Brousseau's Sons, a dry goods store, in 1882 when the partition wall between two stores (Nos. 23 and 25) was removed and the side walls extended back to Exchange Place.

418-422-426 Common, bound by Tchoupitoulas, Magazine, Gravier. Four, three-story brick commercial buildings with granite pillars, lintels and sills. No. 426 has cast-iron front, original doors and scroll brackets, added during 1880s, along with a first-level canopy.

429 Common, bound by Tchoupitoulas, Magazine, Canal. Four-story, four-bay brick commercial building, granite pillars, defaced at first level. Five-row brick string course between floors. Circle tie rod anchors appear on each level and down one side.

431-433 Common, bound by Tchoupitoulas, Magazine, Canal. Two, four-story, three-bay brick commercial buildings with granite pillars, sills and lintels. Proportions indicate an 1850 building date. Tin additions on the roof and a fire escape put the final touches to the building defacement.

600-636 Commercial Place, bound by Camp, St. Charles, Poydras. Three separate buildings, one of which is the side facade of the Crescent Mutual Insurance Company Building (see 401 Camp). Next is a row of offices and banking houses, and the third group is a row of stores extending to St. Charles. These comprise the present Balter Building complex. Henry Howard designed the Commercial Place facades in the middle of the block as banking houses and offices for Edward W. Sewell. Built in 1851, the Greek Revival row was designed as a single unit, with two slightly projecting entrance bays giving emphasis to a central element with double entrances and fluted columns in the Doric order *in antis* between granite pilasters. The upper floor features segmental arched windows, with a course of panels between the second and third level. The windows of the central segment are square-headed for contrast. The top story was added later in a well-designed remodeling in which the cornice designed by Howard was used as a string course. This is among the finest Greek Revival complexes in the city, of national merit, and should not be demolished.

611 Common, bound by Camp, St. Charles, Canal. Four-story, three-bay brick commercial building with cap-moulded lintels. Defaced with signs and "modern improvements."

600-636 Commercial Place. Balter Building. Greek Revival double entrance.

COMMERCIAL PLACE

Commercial Place is a walkery between St. Charles and Camp. Similar to Natchez Place, Picayune Place and the Board of Trade Place, it is a 19th century city planning device to afford quick access between busy thoroughfares. The 500 block of Constance, formed by the backs of five buildings facing Magazine and Tchoupitoulas, could be an attractive walkery with shops. The buildings fronting on Poydras have gray marble first levels on Constance. Only two blocks long, Constance formerly was named Foucher, in honor of Pierre Foucher, son-in-law of Etienne de Bore. This short street, along with Penn and Carroll, which are only one block long, between Perdido and Poydras, could be incorporated into a beautification scheme and recognized as another rare advantage available to New Orleans.

717-729 Common, bound by St. Charles, Carondelet, Canal. A row of four outstanding pedimented Greek Revival store-houses (defaced facade, second from left, hides one of the identical buildings). The pediments above the cornices are unusual, since New Orleans street scenes are ordinarily lacking in this style of facade. Two of the row were built by Samuel Stewart for H. C. Cammack and Leonard Spangenberg in 1846 for $10,000. The specifications (D. L. McCay, June 17, 1846) indicates the original appearance of the row. The fronts were to be "faced with Northern press bricks in running band and white mortar...Quincy granite front to first story with four iron columns and plain white sills and lintels to all front windows...granite in rear windows and door sills.

The yard was paved in Lake brick laid on edge in cement. Northern flags were on the banquette. There was an iron gallery at the second level with a "zinc roof and iron divisions." Windows were glazed with "good American or French cylinder glass." Interior marble mantels and grates cost $40 each. Tranchina's, at 729 Common, has a facade arcaded on three levels and if restored would be a handsome complement to the street scene. The modern facing erected by Continental Airlines not only defaces the building, but destroys the architectural unity of the entire row.

617 Common, bound by St. Charles, Camp, Canal. A three-story, Italianate style plastered brick commercial building having segmental arched windows and bracketed cornice with three-part parapet. Hood moulds at the second level follow the segmental arched openings, while the architrave of the third-story windows is post and lintel. Benjamin Story owned six lots in this block, and this structure was built by his heirs after the settlement of his estate in 1851. Stylistically, the structure may date from the late 1860s.

212, 214, 216, 220, 222, 226 Crossman, bound by N. Peters, N. Front, Canal. Most of these buildings are the backs of buildings facing the 200 block of Canal. The intrinsic architectural value of these double-faced structures lies in their harmonious groupings, brick and granite materials, denticulated cornices and variety of details, such as No. 214, with Doric fluted columns in antis with brick pilasters and No. 212, having beak granite pilasters.

632 Common, bound by St. Charles, Camp, Gravier. The elevation here is an Italianate remodeling of two stores designed by James Gallier, Sr., for R. O. Pritchard between 1835, when Pritchard acquired the lot from George Green, Ambrose Lanfear and C. L. Gravier, and 1839, when he sold the four-story brick store to H. C. Cammack for $15,100. The highly ornamental hood moulds now above the second-story windows are reminiscent of others in the city dating from the 1860s. The individual cast-iron balconies at the third level are not original, but probably are made up from a gallery which adjoined the buildings by the 1860s.

131-141 Decatur, bound by Canal, Iberville, Dorsiere. This row of stores and houses, ranging in date from 1814 to the 1860s, should be preserved and valued as an important contrast to the new Marriott Hotel on one side and the internationally important Custom House across the street. These five, four-story brick stores fronting on both Decatur and Dorsiere were built for James Hopkins after 1829. Hopkins collected the lots with John Hagan from about 1816, partly from the widow of Eugene Dorsiere, for whom the street in the rear was named. In 1840 the row was sold to Francois Xavier Martin for about $90,000.

111 Decatur, bound by Canal, Iberville, Dorsiere. At the extreme left in the photograph is a house (old No. 7) purchased in 1823 by La Selva de St. Avid, a Frenchman who owned property in New Orleans and France and son of the Baron of St. Avid and Marguerite Delfau Pontalba. According to St. Avid's will, he paid 8,000 francs for the house, which he reconstructed for 6,000 francs into a four-story brick store. The store was sold by his daughters in 1881 for $13,000 and immediately was resold to Hubert Rolling, who leased it for $1,700 per year. Alterations through the years have altered the character of this early 19th century building.

Second from left is 115 Decatur (old No. 9), a four-bay, three-story brick building with parapet which has had alterations, making a date for construction difficult to determine. The foundations and walls date from 1814 to 1819. Occupied in the 1880s by Hudson Brothers as a gun store, which was rented for $175 per month.

Second from right is 121-23 Decatur. This two-story plastered brick building with cast-iron pillars probably was built in the 1860s for Joseph Santini, who purchased the site in 1860 from the heirs of Dr. Lewis Heerman. Heerman had owned the property from 1818 and had erected a three-story building. At the right is 125-27 Decatur. A four-bay, two-story plastered brick house with Italianate features, it was built between 1859 and 1878 for Hugh McCloskey. It was known in 1878 as the Sumter Saloon and contained a "marble top counter, cigar stand, chandeliers, etc." The building was sold for $13,500 in 1882 when it was described as an elegant two-story building.

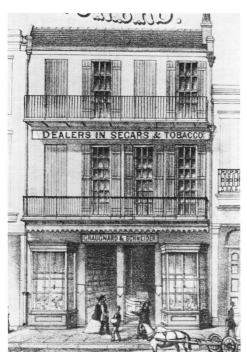

117-19 Decatur. B. Simon, lithograph (1871). (Courtesy New Orleans Public Library.)

117-119 Decatur, bound by Canal, Iberville, Dorsiere. (Formerly No. 11 Old Levee.) The three-story, brick-slated store (third from right), with simple square post and lintel openings

and plastered fronts on both Decatur and Dorsiere, is probably the oldest building in this volume. It was built soon after 1814 for Cornelius Paulding, who purchased the land in 1814 and sold it in 1819 to Jacob Brandegee for $18,000, at which time it was rented for $250 per month. The building was resold at auction by the heirs of Brandegee in 1854, and a notarial drawing shows its appearance at that time. The facade was painted pink. Plastered brick pillars and a plain lintel course framed solid two-fold doors with hinges on the inside. A plain wrought iron balcony is at the second and third levels, with shutters having panels on one side and tongue and groove on the other at the second level.

After passing through the ownership of the brothers Julien and Francois Lacroix, the building was used by Graugnard & Schneider, tobacco manufacturers, and was illustrated in a lithograph by B. Simon (1871), which shows projecting display casements had been added. In the 1880s the building was occupied by George Ellis Book and Stationery Store, and in 1946 it sold for $27,000.

111 Exchange Place. Detail.

111 Exchange Place, bound by Canal, Iberville, Royal. Constructed in 1866 by Gallier and Esterbrook as a commercial rental property for the Bank of America, which formerly was located on the corner of Canal and Exchange, this five-story building is an outstanding and rare example of an entirely cast-iron front building, a type significant in the development of American building technology. The impressive facade is handsomely detailed in the Venetian Renaissance style, with fluted Corinthian columns at the ground level and four ascendingly smaller rows of decorated arched windows separated at each level by a projecting cornice. Delicate foliated forms embellish the spandrels of all arches, and acanthus leaf brackets punctuate the ground level and fifth-story cornices. The Vidal lithograph of 1871 and an original drawing in the Labrot collection at Tulane University Library indicate the building once included an adjoining one-story, four-bay link matching in detail that of the remaining ground level facade. The interior originally was designed to function as one large space. C. Cavaroc and Co., wine merchants and importers, was a well known occupant of the building for many years. The building remains in good conditions, with its effective facade dominating the street scene.

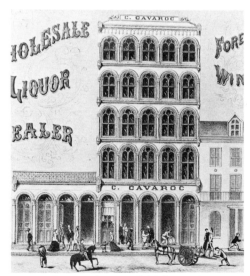

111 Exchange Place. Vidal lithograph. (Courtesy Historic New Orleans Collection.)

100 block Exchange Place, Riverside. Drawing by Charles A. de Armas, 1859. Plan Book 58, Folio 22, New Orleans Notarial Archives.

100 block Exchange Place, bound by Canal, Chartres, Iberville. Situated partly on a piece of land purchased in 1810 from the city by William Kenner and Steven Henderson, this row of four, three-story brick buildings was built about 1832 by several businessmen who had collected property in the square for several years for commercial purposes. In 1831 the group, which included Samuel B. Slocomb, Henry Babcock and Charles Watts, successfully petitioned the City Council to cut a new street through the square from Canal to Iberville on land ceded by them to the city. The commercial exchange planned by these businessmen was a bold project and noteworthy piece of urban design, related to the St. Louis Hotel project. The building at 112 Exchange Place (extreme right) was originally used by S. B. Slocomb in his business, Rogers and Slocomb Hardware, which also fronted on 113 Chartres (old Nos. 9-11, adjacent to the rear). These two buildings remained in the Slocomb family until 1933.

Nos. 114-116 and 120-22 Exchange Place (second and third from right) originally were owned by Babcock and Gardner Dry Goods, which sold them at auction in 1834 to Manuel Lizardi. The buildings were leased at the time of sale for $3,540 per year and valued at $25,000 together. The buildings were described by the auctioneer as a "three-story building 46' front x 50' deep with a 10' yard paved with best Yorkshire flagstones." A partition wall through the center of the building divided it into two distinct buildings with a total of 15 rooms.

In 1838 No. 12 was occupied by H. Sacerdotte Segar Store and H. A. Olival Hairdresser, while No. 14 was occupied by Fele and Percy Attornies. Nos. 124-132 Exchange Place (subsequent buildings extending to corner Iberville), originally were part of a 1792 Spanish land grant to the Francois Liotau family, one of whom subsequently willed a portion of the square to Eualie Mazange, a free woman of color. Her heirs sold the property in 1828 to Gilbert Vance, in whose estate all these buildings appear in 1847, with the exception of the small but well-detailed No. 128 Exchange Place (old No. 18), which Gilbert Vance sold in 1835 to his brother-in-law, Dr. Stephen D. McNeil.

This plastered brick building (fifth from right) has four pillars and wide paneled doors. Two stores in the row were sold at auction May 8, 1859, and the archival drawing illustrates their appearance at that time. The drawing corresponds to the two stores at the right in the photograph. In 1859 the brick was exposed and each opening had splayed brick lintels. Doors were paneled and louvered shutters were hung at the windows. Small dormers and the cornice with blocking course remained. The arched entrance doors have been increased in number in the building on the right and one has been removed in the building on the left. The present facade has been rusticated in an uncharacteristic manner. Cap-moulded lintels now head the windows. Few such buildings were built across Canal in Faubourg St. Mary, and none remain intact with arcades at the bottom level.

600 block S. Front, bound by Girod, Lafayette, Delta. A brick warehouse erected near the river front for Joseph Denegre in 1866 from designs by architect Benjamin Morgan Harrod; Joseph M. Howell and John Kirwin, builders; cost, $29,437. The brick pediment has denticulated string courses with intercepting panels and center medallion. The Romanesque arches have rounded brick edges, as do the building's corners. In the shadow of the International Trade Mart, this riverfront sugar and cotton warehouse should be preserved.

107, 113, 115 N. Front, bound by Canal, Crossman, N. Peters. No. 107 is a three-story, three-bay building with brick sills. Nos. 113-15 have cast-iron pillars with egg and dart decorations, while their Crossman elevation, much mutilated, has granite pillars. N. Front is one of the few granite and brick paved streets left in New Orleans.

500 block S. Front, bound by Lafayette, Poydras, Fulton. 519-521 S. Front are two, three-bay red brick stores, with granite lintels and brick sills. The granite pillars at ground level have capitals with egg and dart motif. No. 527 S. Front comprises four, three-bay, three-story brick stores, faced with scored plastered brick. Granite lintels and sills; first level entirely altered.

600 block S. Front, bound by Girod, Lafayette, Delta. Brick warehouses fronting on both Front and Delta. This harmonious street scene is a valuable and viable part of urban New Orleans.

800 block S. Front, bound by Delta, St. Joseph, Julia. Outstanding two-level brick warehouse with large arched openings; bricks laid in American bond. Such warehouses have sophisticated exterior architectural treatment and should be retained for future modern development along the riverfront.

500 block Fulton, both sides with fronts on S. Peters and S. Front. Row of brick warehouses with notable architectural features. Cast-iron pillars, between which are hung the original four-fold paneled doors. Granite lintels and sills and solid iron shutters at upper-level openings. Denticulated cornices. The Fulton Street facades, now used as warehouses and railroad depots, could make an attractive street scene. These buildings front on S. Peters and S. Front, respectively, and are still used to house import-export offices for which they had been designed in the early 19th century. According to an act of George Rareshide, November 9, 1853, Thomas Murray built in this square one brick building to be used as an ice house on Front, through to Fulton, for Stanton & Co., at a cost of $12,600. Murray also built the same year a three-story brick store on Front, adjoining Stanton warehouse, for George Rulef at a cost of $7,000.

600 block Fulton, Lakeside, bound by Lafayette, Girod, S. Peters. Now filled with box cars, railroad tracks and trash, this early cobblestoned street has some of the more attractive New Orleans commercial warehouse facades. The Lakeside buildings front on S. Peters. According to the act of George Rareshide, notary, December 9, 1853, the store at the corner of Girod fronting on Fulton and running through to Front was Murphy's Store, built sometime before 1853.

800 block Fulton, bound by Front, St. Joseph, Julia. Fine two-level, iron-shuttered brick warehouse, known as the Mississippi Warehouse in 1883. This full block would make excellent hotel rows and a shopping center with restaurants. Running through to S. Front, this building faces another fine warehouse with arched entrances. This group of warehouses and commercial buildings should be retained with the original granite block streets, which could be adapted as walkways between segments of the shopping center, an attractive complement to future waterfront development. In 1859 Louis Reynolds built a warehouse with a 418-foot front on Fulton and Front between Julia and St. Joseph for $50,000. The owner was Thomas Hale, who is reported to have lost another warehouse in 1859 on S. Peters, bound by Fulton, Julia and St. Joseph. This latter structure was replaced by Charles Pride and Samuel Stewart.

612, 614, 616, 618, 620 Girod, corner Church, bound by Camp, St. Charles. Three-story, nine-bay commercial building with brick pillars, wooden lintel course, granite window lintel and sills. Late 19th century example carrying on earlier traditions of house-store architecture. Charles Franck, commercial photographer, occupies No. 620.

Girod Street Warehouse, bound by S. Front, Fulton, Notre Dame. In this three-story brick warehouse, with fourth story added, a modern finish of course cement hides the building texture. Windows have granite lintels and sills. Cornice is denticulated. According to an act of George Rareshide, notary, June 23, 1855, this store was built in 1855 for Miss C. Rose Alvarez by Harrington and Armstrong, builders, for $7,750.

715 Girod, bound by Carondelet, St. Charles, Lafayette. (Old No. 169). Site of a two-story brick firehouse, dated from 1837, home of the famous horse-drawn Engine No. 13, with 40-foot front on Girod. Union troops were housed here during the Civil War. From 1836 until 1960 the property was occupied by fire companies. It was sold in 1960 to Francis J. Didier, who renovated the building for his business, Delta Visual, utilizing some parts of the Washington Artillery (see below, photograph courtesy Historic New Orleans Collection), which once stood in the lot adjacent toward Carondelet.

The first Washington Artillery Armory and Hall, now demolished, was built in 1859 by Joshua Peebles, builder, with W. A. Freret, architect. This Artillery was replaced by a new building designed by Albert Diettel in 1865 on Carondelet in the same block. The entire facade of the first armory was completely abandoned in 1880, and later the facade was reassembled and placed opposite Jackson Square. It was demolished in April, 1972.

A photograph in the *History of the Fire Department* (1895) shows that the structure was basically the same in 1895. The entrance, however, had been changed to a large rectangle. Curiously, the arch was added later. Photograph of 1895 shows the Washington Artillery still standing next door.

936 Girod, bound by Baronne, Julia, O'Keefe. Two-story brick stores, with high flat parapet, four bays, with unusual wood decoration framing windows and sunburst transoms. Three courses splayed brick and arch lintels with keystones.

731-733 Girod, bound by Carondelet, St. Charles Lafayette. Three-story brick house with denticulated cornice, gable ends and second-level iron balcony. Second floor covers three-foot alley on St. Charles side. Edward William Sewell, builder, purchased this property from Thomas L. Harmann in March, 1847, for $2,450, erecting the present combination commercial-residential building soon after. He sold it in 1859 for $6,000. At that time it was insured by the Crescent Mutual Insurance Co. for $4,500, with a note that the "gas pipes and fixtures now in the house belong to tenant," having been installed by the tenant, Mrs. Nelson. The present owner is Henry Barnett. With the adjacent structure, this would make excellent 20th century offices, with easy access to the expressway and parking space available. Two other restorations (704 Carondelet and Delta Visual at 715 Girod) give these buildings an increased value for restorative use.

723-27 Girod, bound by Carondelet, St. Charles, Lafayette. Girod Street Hotel. Three-and-one-half story brick double house in the Greek Revival style. Built for Andrew Hodge, president of the Bank of New Orleans and active real estate speculator, about 1838 or 1839. Unusual for the area is the raised basement story with carriage openings leading to a courtyard with two service buildings attached. Originally, double iron steps led to a balcony and the Greek Key entrances. A balcony of wrought iron in the diamond pattern at the third level indicates that a similar balcony was removed below. A wood entablature, typical of the 1830s, has an architrave with three facias, an attic frieze with windows and cornice with dentils. Formerly the facade was plastered.

Washington Artillery. (Courtesy Historic New Orleans Collection.)

400 block Gravier, bound by Tchoupitoulas and Magazine (both sides of the street). This street vista of flanking three- and four-story brick stores is another example of the aesthetically pleasing view of simple, unencumbered facades. This block has the distinction also of being one of the first roundstone paved streets in the city.   **416, 422, 424, 426, 430 Gravier,** bound by Tchoupitoulas, Board of Trade Place, Natchez. This row of well-maintained three-story brick and plastered brick commercial buildings illustrates the neat and cohesive appearance of mid-nineteenth century streets in this area. The repetition of sturdy granite pillars, slightly varying window lintel treatment and simple cornice handling provide a pleasant multi-facade view. Owners of the buildings during the period of 1850-1860 (from right to left in photograph) were: John Freeland, first two buildings valued at $23,000; Paul Tulane, third store, and J. P. Cazelar, fourth building, valued at $10,000 each; and Evan Rogers, fifth, sixth and seventh buildings.

500 block Gravier, bound by Camp, Magazine, Picayune Place. Street scene.

415, 417, 423, 425, 427 Gravier, bound by Tchoupitoulas, Magazine, Common. This was once a row of five, three-story brick and granite commercial buildings. The top floors of two stores, third from left, have been removed and replaced by one modern story. These two modernized stores are illustrated in an 1871 Simon lithograph as the cigar and tobacco warehouse of S. Hernsheim, whose cigar factory was later located at 755 Magazine. The lithograph shows the Gravier buildings' original appearance which closely resembles the present condition of the remaining buildings in the row.

Three of the stores, Nos. 415, 417 and 423, were built in 1845 by John Randolphe Pike for William Silliman at a cost of $8,800. The specifications for these buildings (Daniel I. Ricardo, notary, June 21, 1845) give a detailed description of the simple commercial building of this period. The stores were to front 60 feet on Gravier and be divided into three equal portions (old Nos. 26, 28, 30). The first floor was to be 13 feet in height; second, 12 feet; and third, 10 feet. Front was to be of the best Baltimore pressed brick.

The cornice was to be like that on a store erected by Pike on the corner of Lafayette and Tchoupitoulas (see 322-328 Lafayette). Sills, lintels and uprights of lower story in front were to be granite; "columns" to be 18 inches x 14 inches. The rear door and window heads were to be worked in brick arches. Second-story windows were to have fifteen lights; third story to have twelve lights. The rear windows were to be furnished with outside battened shutters to be covered with sheet iron. Front windows were to be furnished with four-fold paneled shutters. Front doors were to be grained in imitation oak. The second story inside was plastered, and other interior brickwork was whitewashed inside. The courtyard in the rear was surrounded by a ten-foot brick wall, and the banquette was blue flagstone.

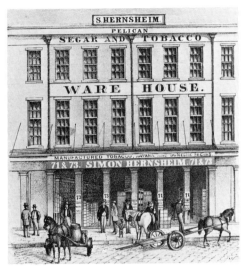

417, 423 Gravier. B. Simon lithograph. (Courtesy Historic New Orleans Collection.)

500 block Gravier, bound by Camp, and Magazine, both sides, and 300 block Picayune Place. In 1833 John Mitchell and Sidle and Stewart built 10 stores for Samuel Elkins and Charles A. Jacobs in the square bound by Gravier, Camp, Magazine and Natchez. Total cost was $47,000. Five were erected on the southeast corner of Camp and Gravier (see 300 Camp St), two on Gravier in the rear and three on Gravier on land acquired from New Orleans Canal and Banking Co. The row of three simple three-story masonry stores, with granite lintel course and pillars at ground level and plainly unified cornice and fenestration treatment (front right in photograph), are three of those built in 1833.

The four-story store across Gravier (front left in photograph), with its decorated iron ground-level pillars and Italianate window hood moulds, contrasts with the restrained building it faces. Presently 523 Gravier, it appears illustrated in 1879 in *Waldo's.* It housed S. L. Boyd and Company, a dry goods store, quite handsome with paneled shutters at the windows and paneled doors with glazing above covered with wire mesh. At that time there was a cornice with paired brackets and dentils and a deep multi-level parapet. The lintel course at the first level also had a denticulated cornice.

In 1852 Gallier and Turpin built a store for Elizabeth Clement, tutrix of Benjamin Story, at a cost of $12,500 on this block. The specifications (H. B. Canal, notary, May 7, 1852) describe the four-story building and suggest it may be at the left front of this photograph. The first story was to be 14 feet, the second, 13 feet, the third, 12 feet and the fourth, 10 feet. A quincy granite sill course, 8 inches by 18 inches, was to be finished and set to the front of the store, on which were set the iron columns and lintel course. Cornice above lintel was built of brick and cemented. Front outside was cemented with hydraulic cement and clean white sharp sand and colored to imitate stone work. Upper and lower cornices were to be run in cement and sanded and colored as above. Front windows were to have marble sills and lintels. Rear doors and windows were to have granite sills. Iron framed verandah was to be on front of the second story. Roof was of Dutchess or Countess slates. Door was grained oak or painted green. Interior was to have three marble mantels costing not more than $50 each.

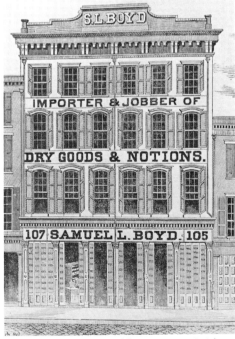

523 Gravier. J. C. Waldo's *Visitors Guide to New Orleans* (1879). (Courtesy New Orleans Public Library.)

512-514-516 Gravier, bound by Camp, Magazine, Natchez. This row of three-story granite-front stores was built by James Dakin in 1843 in conjunction with the building of the Canal Bank on the corner of Magazine and Gravier (see 301-07 Magazine). The 1855 Notarial Archives elevation clearly illustrates the nearly original appearance of the impressive row, which remains basically unchanged. The arrangement of four-fold paneled doors, painted in *faux bois* to resemble oak, is especially effective. One of these remains. The Simon lithograph of 1871 shows one section of the row and gives a comprehensive portrait of the structures, as well as their various uses. These particularly fine buildings are excellent examples of the human proportion and restrained uniformity of design in mid-nineteenth century commercial buildings.

512, 514, 516 Gravier. Drawing by C. A. Hedin, 1855, Book 27A, Folio 40, New Orleans Notarial Archives.

512, 514, 516 Gravier. B. Simon lithograph. (Courtesy Historic New Orleans Collection.)

607 Gravier, bound by Camp, St. Charles, Common. This New Orleans skyscraper of nine stories was designed by Diboll and Owen and built in 1906 for the Canal-Louisiana Bank and Trust Co. The foundation was to be of granite, the first and second stories of Bedford stone. The stories between the second and ninth levels are of red brick, with the top story of rich terra cotta, crowned with terra cotta frieze and bronze cresting.

The bank was established in 1832, and the cornerstone may confuse those who think the date applies to the International House (established in 1945) which now occupies the structure. In 1950 the International House was remodeled at a cost of $318,000, and the entrance was moved from Camp to Gravier, Illustration from *Architectural Art and Its Allies* (February, 1906). (Courtesy New Orleans Public Library.)

619 Gravier, bound by St. Charles, Camp, Common. Whitney National Bank (Safety Deposit Department). An impressive red stone structure, with polished granite columns, erected for this bank in 1888, with Sully and Toledano, architects. It is one of the best examples of the style, expressing solidity of the bank. One of the outstanding examples of work by the office of Thomas Sully, whose numerous productions of the 1890s later included many St. Charles Avenue mansions.

612, 614, 618 Gravier, bound by Camp, St. Charles, Commercial Place. These three, four-story brick stores with granite pillars, lintel courses and brick denticulated cornices were built after 1840 and are typical commercial buildings of the period.

620 Gravier, bound by Camp, St. Charles, Commercial Place. A representative example of the imaginative commercial facades of American cities in the 1890s or slightly before. The consistency of the design has been slightly disturbed by ground-level modifications and an additional floor above.

626-28-30-32 Gravier, bound by Camp, St. Charles, Commercial Place. This row of three, four-story, three-bay brick stores with granite pillars and denticulated cornice has a unified facade common to commercial buildings of the entire area. This simple Greek Revival row is flanked by Italianate structures and makes an attractive street scene. Little and Middlemiss in 1855 erected the stores, which were then occupied by Ward and Jones, according to a *Picayune* article of that date.

728, 738 Gravier, bound by Carondelet, St. Charles, Union. Two identical, four-story masonry Italianate commercial buildings and a three-story building in the same style. Cast-iron pillars below with foliated capitals. Cast-iron balcony at second level. Upper two stories have segmental arch openings with highly decorative hood moulds featuring brackets. The building on the left has deep paneled entablature. The larger building has a fourth story, flat headed windows with bracketed hood moulds and a simple entablature. The building at 300 St. Charles, built by Gallier and Turpin for Robert Heath in 1855, is nearly identical to these buildings. This indicates they were built about the same time, perhaps by the Gallier firm, for Dr. James Ritchie, who sold his new buildings for $35,000 in 1857. One of the fine rows of the city, these buildings were demolished in 1971 by Louis J. Roussel. The property is now being used as a parking lot.

740 Gravier, bound by Carondelet, St. Charles, Union. The New Orleans Stock Exchange built this structure in 1906 for its own occupancy. Plans by Andry and Bendernagel were selected from several in a competition. McNally & Mullaney were builders, at a cost of $25,000. The craftsmanship of all decorative details is of high quality.

An extensive article with measured drawing in Vol. 1 of *Architectural Art and Its Allies* gives a description of the building: "The front of the building will have massive walls of imported white Italian marble, in modern French Renaissance, with elegant but massive and strong details. Over the front entrance will be carved, in natural size, marble statues of Commerce and Industry. The interior of the building will be in the same style as the exterior, and the walls of the exchange room will be lined and paneled with different colors of imported Italian marble, which shall be richly carved and moulded, but panels will be left in the walls to permit decorative paintings. The cornices of the ceiling will be ornamented, and in one of the large panels of the ceiling will be a skylight in art glass, which shall be used for ventilation as well as for lighting."

The front portion, the exchange room proper, is one story, 31½ feet high. The rear portion is three stories high. The interior also was to have mahogany veneer work and highly carved mahogany wall cornices and mantels.

822-28 Gravier, bound by Baronne, Carondelet, Union. (Old Nos. 188-192.) A row of three-story Italianate masonry commercial buildings believed to have been designed by James Gallier, Jr., in the late 1860s, probably for a Mr. Thornhill who owned the property in 1862. This fine facade incorporates cast-iron details, pillars with capitals of Egyptian motif and low arches with paneled spandrels. A cast-iron balcony formerly crossed the entire facade at the second level, where segmental arched openings and heavy drip stones contrast with the third-story true-arch openings featuring moulded sills. The entablature has brackets, dentils and a multi-level parapet. An illustration from *Waldo's* (1879) shows these well-preserved buildings as they appeared with the other Italianate and Greek Revival stores on the block at that time. They were described as the "offices of influential cotton factors" John Phelps and Co. at No. 192 and Welshan and Woods, a marine fire and river insurance company at No. 188. Signs and air conditioning units deface this potentially superior mid-nineteenth century row.

740 Gravier. Entrance pediment detail.

822-28 Gravier. J. C. Waldo's *Visitors Guide to New Orleans* (1879). (Courtesy New Orleans Public Library.)

Howard, at Camp. Howard Library. A posthumous work of Henry Hobson Richardson, built as a reference library for public use. The material is rock-face Massachusetts sandstone. Built in 1888, two years after Richardson's death, for Mrs. Annie Howard Parrott as a memorial to her father, Charles T. Howard. Cost was $115,000. Richardson, a Louisiana native born in St. James Parish in 1838 and one-time resident of the Julia Street Row, is renowned internationally as the founder of the Romanesque Revival. This building is typical of his style, with its display of rugged textures in the rock-face stone, the cavernous arched opening of the entrance and the polygonal and round turrets. Supporting the entrance archivolt is a boss carved to represent "Ignorance in Chains," an appropriate theme. Straight-topped windows divided by engaged, coupled columns are employed, as well as the arched type in the front gable.

At the Lee Circle side of the building are steep-gabled wall dormers, often a prominent element in Richardson buildings. Piercing the facade are fortress-like slits. The resulting effect is one of massiveness and simplicity. The Camp Street fenestration is severe and impressive. Richardson died at 48 at the peak of a successful and influential career. It is appropriate that one of his designs, executed by Shepley, Rutan and Coolidge, his successors, should be used for a New Orleans building. The present building is covered with ficus vine which hides the sandstone, yet offers an attractive finish. The building is now owned by the U. S. Oil Co., formerly John Mecom Oil Co. of Houston. Photograph from *Art Work in New Orleans* (1895). (Courtesy New Orleans Public Library.)

Howard Library. Detail.

610 Iberville, bound by Exchange, Chartres, Canal. Built on land formerly owned by Eulalie Mazange, a free woman of color who inherited the property from the Liotau family (see 124-132 Exchange Place). This large five-bay brick house-store with cast-iron pillars below was sold in 1858 at auction, where it was described as a three-story, brick slate-roofed building with a large storeroom on the first floor; four rooms with fireplaces and two cabinets on the second floor; and three rooms on the third floor." There was an iron double gallery in front. In the rear were "double brick slate roofed privies, paved yard, water works, etc...." It was rented to "Nick L. Lafarque and Jas. Harrison" for $1,600 per year and was again sold in 1867 for $19,100.

524 Iberville, bound by Chartres, Decatur, Canal. Three-story townhouse with gallery on two levels. Formerly this was part of an arcaded storehouse, probably dating from the 1820s, in which Jules Labatut and J. B. Plauche were associated.

606-608 Iberville, bound by Exchange Place, Chartres, Canal. Two, three-story brick storehouses, with splayed brick lintels and granite pillars. These stand on part of a 1792 Spanish land grant to the Francois Liotau family. Henry Carleton purchased the property in 1821 and subdivided it into four lots, including these two and two others at the corner of Iberville and Chartres. He built these stores soon after. They were included in his succession of 1863 when the houses were known as Nos. 78 and 80 Customhouse Street and valued at $5,000 each.

614 Iberville, corner Exchange Place, bound by Canal, Chartres. This three-story plastered brick store with massive plastered brick pillars and gabled ends was probably built for Gilbert Vance between 1828 and 1835 on property he had purchased from the heirs of Eulalie Mazange (see 124-128 Exchange Place). It was purchased by his son, Hamilton McNeil Vance, from his succession in 1847 for $12,100. The cornice and the hip roof have been removed. Painting and exterior improvements have been made recently.

612-620 Iberville, bound by Royal, Chartres, Canal. These three-story, three- and five-bay brick buildings vary slightly in architectural details, yet form a fine 19th century street scene despite modern "abusements and improvements." No. 612, a three-story, five-bay store, has moulded lintel caps, marble sills and lintels at windows. Decorated cast-iron balcony at second and third levels, heavy denticulated cornice. First-level front is of cast-iron, with Corinthian pillar capitals. No. 620, of plastered brick, has been multilated at the second and third levels. This entire street could easily be improved and should follow Vieux Carre standards, even though the buildings are out of the Vieux Carre Commission jurisdiction.

724 Iberville, bound by Bourbon, Royal, Canal. Acme Oyster and Seafood House, a traditional New Orleans oyster bar for over a quarter of a century, occupies this four-story, three-bay, plastered brick commercial building, which has granite pillars, lintels and sills and decorative cast-iron balcony at the second level. Block cornice projects over flat frieze and is modern but not defacing. In excellent condition, this is an oasis between a 5 & 10 building and a parking garage.

Iberville Square, bound by Wells, N. Front, Crossman. Douglas Warehouse. Paired segmental arched fenestration articulates this massive brick facade. Windows with original muntins have triple course splayed lintels, and the brick is laid in American bond. Top floor probably was added, but retains the window pattern established below.

Iberville, corner N. Front, bound by Crossman, N. Peters. Maloney's Warehouse. Multi-level brick building, formerly having arched openings at ground level. Upper levels have segmental arched windows with iron shutters. This massive structure dates from the late 19th century. The brick streets here are among the few remaining in New Orleans.

841 Iberville and 140 Dauphine, bound by Royal, Canal. Three-story, three-bay brick residence-store, presently the La Famille Restaurant, with bar on Dauphine in former servants' quarters. Building of the 1830s has brick cornice with saw-toothed pattern, dentils beneath, scored plaster front, balcony at second level removed, segmental arch in three-bay servants' wing, stepped gable with arched opening and original window lights and mullions. Fire escape and first level alter original appearance.

537 Julia, corner Camp, bound by Girod, Magazine. (Old 141, 143 Julia; in prior years, 117, 118 Julia.) This group of three store-houses are among the earliest remaining in Faubourg St. Mary. In 1832, when Samuel Peters bought them from John Green, the act of sale stipulated: "Green will have completed at his own expense the building already commenced on or before January next, and Green has bound himself to pay Peters a daily rent of $8 for each day which will elapse between period aforesaid and full and final completion." The absence of Greek detail, the small fenestration, hipped roof and small cornice indicate the early date of the houses. The ground floor, now altered and refaced, may have had arched openings. The rear five-bay portion of the complex facing Camp was added after 1883, filling in the former yard beside the service wing. The addition conforms generally to the character of the 1832 structure, except for the cap-moulded lintels. The original iron balcony has been removed and the ground level completely changed. In 1854 Samuel Peters sold the houses to Charles Millard, whose heirs held it until 1884.

448 Julia, bound by Constance, Magazine, St. Joseph. A row of three, four-story brick stores with granite pillars and iron lintels above the windows. Brick cornice decorated with a row of dentils and a course in sawtooth pattern brick, similar to the buildings at 834-36 Julia, corner Baronne, and 127 Camp. The iron lintels with foliated decoration at ends and center are found in a downtown building dating from the 1830s (see 501 Magazine). The granite lintel course has a cornice with guttae. By 1852 these fine buildings were owned by Mrs. E. E. Parker. In 1853 T. L. Harmon was the owner. Each store measures 24 feet by 120 feet.

JULIA STREET'S THIRTEEN SISTERS

ALTHOUGH the red brick row house is a form generally associated with Philadelphia or Baltimore rather than New Orleans, the Creole City soon after the Louisiana Purchase began to see this type of building introduced by its new American residents. At first, such houses were built in groups of two or three only. But as time went by and the need for housing increased, more and more of these structures appeared, erected in all parts of the city as a source of revenue for their builders.

As early as 1828 a row of five houses was erected by Bernard Marigny on some of the land of his former plantation at Elysian Fields and Levee. The same year, Simon Cucullu built a row on Chartres at Dumaine. Even the Ursuline Nuns were attracted by this type of investment, and after they had moved from their old Chartres Street convent, they erected at the rear of their property facing Levee Street (Decatur) a row of twelve houses. These were begun in 1830, and the final payment was made early in 1832. Most of this interesting row still stands in a much-deteriorated condition, the houses having been sold to individual purchasers by the nuns some thirty or forty years ago.

Since this form was first introduced by Americans, it is not surprising to find that these enterprising newcomers also were attracted to this sort of investment, and numerous rows of interesting houses were erected by them in Faubourg St. Mary, as well as in other parts of the city. Of these, perhaps none is more interesting than the row of thirteen houses built on the upper side of Julia Street between Camp

and St. Charles. For the construction of these and several other similar rows, a corporation known as the New Orleans Building Company was formed. In April, 1832, this company purchased the several lots forming the west corner of Camp and Julia from Andrew Hodge, Jr., for $18,000. The remainder of the ground probably was purchased at about the same time, and. construction was soon begun. By April, 1833, the homes were near enough to completion to be offered for sale, and several were sold at an auction conducted by Isaac L. McCoy.

Incorporated in the acts of sale were several restrictions, including a servitude on a six-foot square corner of one lot for the placing of a cistern for the adjoining house. Another concerned the alley which was cut through at the rear of the new buildings from Camp to St. Charles. The third restriction stated that "the buildings on said lot shall be completely finished agreeably to the plan exhibited at the time of said public sale and conformably to their contract with Daniel H. Twogood, the builder." Daniel Halsted Twogood was one of the prominent builders of the day and did other work for the New Orleans Building Company and its president, Samuel Livermore. With the latter, in 1832, he contracted for two, three-story brick houses on Carondelet, between Hevia (Lafayette) and Poydras. He contracted with the company, also in 1833, for a row of eight, three-story brick houses on Carondelet, between Hevia (Lafayette) and Girod, (now demolished, site of Barnett Furniture).

For both these rows of houses, according to the building contracts, the architect was Alexander Thompson Wood, who later became noted as the architect of the Custom House on Canal. It is therefore almost certain that the Julia row also was designed by Wood, although the design often has been attributed to James Harrison Dakin, one-time partner of James Gallier. Dakin, however, did not arrive in New Orleans until 1835, so it would have been impossible for him to have designed these buildings completed nearly three years before. This confusion probably resulted from the fact that Dakin did design other houses in the neighborhood, including one on Julia (to be demolished) between St. Charles and Carondelet.

D. H. Twogood, builder of the Julia Street row, also constructed several important buildings designed by the firm of Gallier and Dakin (Charles B.) in 1835. Among these were the Merchant's Exchange on Royal (formerly Gluck's Restaurant; now Holiday Inn) and the old building for Christ's Church at the corner of Canal and Bourbon.

At the time of the sale of the Julia Street houses in 1833 the following advertisement appeared in the newspaper *Argus:*

On Tuesday, the 30th inst., at 12 o'clock, will be sold at the new Exchange, 13 new and beautiful Houses erected by the New Orleans Building Company on Julia between Camp and St. Charles streets, according to the plan which will be exhibited. Four or five of the houses will be finished and delivered immediately after the sale. The others will be finished in a corresponding style and delivered on or before the first day of August next.

At this auction, house number one at the corner of Camp and Julia was sold to G. W. Pritchard; the next, number two, to Isaac Ogden; the third, to Edward Yorke; the fourth, to Edward Ogden; and the fifth to Samuel Livermore, president of the company. The sixth, seventh and eighth houses evidently were not sold until some time later, and the ninth, tenth, eleventh and twelfth were bought by Edward Yorke on May 18. The thirteenth house, at the corner of St. Charles and Julia, was bought at the auction by Henry G. Schmidt. Prices ranged from $13,000 to $14,000.

According to the *City Directory* of 1838, Edward Yorke, of the firm of Yorke Bros., commission merchants, and alderman of the Second Ward of the Second Municipality, made his residence in house number three, then 125 Julia. His other houses, however, were sold by him in 1835, number nine to Judge Thomas Butler, number ten to a Mr. Florence and numbers eleven and twelve to George W. Pritchard and R. Brien.

For many years this neighborhood was the center of the best residential section of the newer American city. But before the turn of the century the character of the neighborhood had changed completely. Their interesting history, however, is vividly recalled by Eliza Ripley in her *Social Life in Old New Orleans* [D. Appleton & Co.: 1912]. Her father, Richard Henry Chinn, lived in one of these houses when she was a child.

"I wonder," wrote Mrs. Ripley, "if anyone under seventy-five years of age passes old 'Julia Street row' to-day and knows that those '13 Buildings' between Camp and St. Charles Streets have an aristocratic past, and were once occupied by the leading social element of the American colony residing in the early forties above Canal Street? '13 Buildings' it was called...and a decade later every one of them was tenanted by prominent citizens of New Orleans. There they lived and entertained a host of delightful guests, whose names were a power then, but whose descendants are perhaps little known to-day.

"There lived Mr. Lanfear with his two daughters...There lived Mrs. Slocomb and her three children...The Branders—Mr. Brander was a merchant of some note and social standing... The Smith family, a host of handsome girls, occupied the house next to the Camp Street corner, and in that the house the original J. P. Labouisse married beautiful Dora Smith... Charles Cammack married Sarah Smith in the same house, and Mary Smith married Morris, the son of Beverly Chew, who was a defendant in the noted Gaines case of that day.

"H. S. Buckner's home was midway of the

Julia Street Row.

Julia Street Row.

row, and there was born Ellen Buckner, who became the wife of James B. Eustis...United States ambassador to France.

"Leonard Mathews lived in one of the '13 Buildings'. He was agent of the Sun Insurance Company....There was also the family of Dr. William Kennedy. Mrs. Kennedy was sister of Mr. Levi Pierce and of Mrs. Hillary Cenas.

"My personal recollections," continues Mrs. Ripley, "of the guests who came to my father's House in '13 Buildings' are distinct. Henry Clay, a lifelong friend of father's...was a frequent visitor whenever he came to the Crescent City.

"General E. P. Gaines and his tiny, frisky wife, the noted Myra Clark Gaines...There also came Charles Gayarre, the Louisiana historian; John R. Grymes, the noted lawyer; Pierre Soule, diplomat; Alec Bullitt, Alec Walker and George W. Kendall—all three editors of the leading paper of the day, the Picayune....Even the well-known architect Henry Hobson Richardson lived on the Julia row with his family. Ironic that the world renown architect whose work was a total rejection of classicism should have had as a boy, the most classic environment available in America.

"In course of time, a Mme. Peuch took possession of the house on the St. Charles street corner, and horrors! opened a boarding house, whereupon the aristocratic element gradually fluttered away....The infection spread and in a short time the whole '13 Buildings' pimpled out into cheap boarding houses or rented rooms...."

This fine row still stands, but in a sadder state than even Mrs. Ripley could imagine. But there still remain a few architectural reminders of their vanished elegance. The great gable end facing Camp is an excellent composition, although, like most of the neighbors, its red brick has been painted and its courtyard built over. The third house is the only one which still possesses its original doorway and beautifully decorated fan light transom. The sixth one, except for the ground floor, has retained its facade, including the fine wrought iron balcony, the red brick and the wood cornice with its small attic windows.

From these few fragments it is not difficult to imagine the fine effect this row must have once presented before later owners, seeking to express their own individuality, destroyed the essential unity of the row by changing cornices, balconies, doors and windows and, more recently, adding a rash of signs and unsightly fire escapes. Restored to its original form, this row would be an architectural treasure comparable to the Pontalba Buildings, for which they might be considered the prototype.

SAMUEL WILSON, JR.

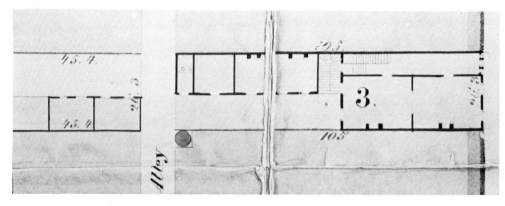

Julia Street Row. Detail.

632 Julia. Drawing and floor plan, 1857, Book 43, Folio 46, New Orleans Notarial Archives.

632 Julia. Door detail. Drawing. 1857, Book 43, Folio 46, New Orleans Notarial Archives.

610 Julia. Present doorway. Detail.

1885, with arched fenestrations and heavily rusticated facade. Designed by the architect and city surveyor, Benjamin Morgan Harrod, who designed similar firehouses in the city. Few of these firehouses remain in the Central Business District, and they should be preserved.

plastered brick building with dormers. Cornice with bricks laid in a row of dentils and sawtooth pattern above, as that at 127 Camp. Ground floor mutilated. Julia Street was being developed in the 1830s, and there are indications that this structure dates from the late 1830s. The downspouts have some of the oldest cast-iron boots, dating from the 1830s. The ground floor facade could be rebuilt according to notarial elevations of similar buildings. This is possibly one of the early buildings in Faubourg St. Mary.

Julia, corner Carondelet, bound by St. Joseph, St. Charles. This Greek Revival structure retains only the Greek Key entrance surrounded with anthemion cresting and a handsome cornice as a reminder of the dignity and importance of a once-sophisticated building.

830 Julia, bound by Carondelet, Baronne, St. Joseph. A masonry firehouse erected in

834-36 Julia, corner Baronne, bound by Carondelet, St. Joseph. Three-story, five-bay

933-35 Julia, bound by Baronne, O'Keefe, Girod. Two-and-one-half story plastered brick townhouse with common central alley leading to service wings with party walls. This once-handsome structure was built in the style popularized in the 1830s and may date from that early period of Faubourg St. Mary. There are building contracts for structures (now demolished) in this block dating from 1838. A notarial drawing with plan and elevation shows the house as it appeared at an 1852 sheriff's sale. The drawings show that the original cornice has been changed, attic frieze muntins altered and the architrave removed. Second-story, full-length sash windows have been shortened, although three lintels remain on the right.

The second-story balcony is intact, as is the Greek Key entrance at the right and the configuration of the alleyway entrance. At the right can be seen the granite steps and shutters like those in the drawing. Originally, the facade had scored plaster painted cream-color to resemble stone, with a contrasting foundation course. As seen from the plan, the stairway arrangement is somewhat unusual. One stairway on each side in a gallery to the rear of the double parlors offers access to the long entrance hall and to the two-story service wing. There was a common cistern for the two sides. The privies were to the rear of the lot.

The adjoining structure to the left in the photograph, 937 Julia, is a plastered brick, two-and-one-half story townhouse. It could once more be an example of New Orleans' Greek Revival style as exemplified in buildings dating from the 1838-1845 period. The attic windows have been enlarged, and other obvious defacements give little clue to the original appearance, but there is a wrought iron balcony at the second level and notarial drawings illustrated in this book show similar types.

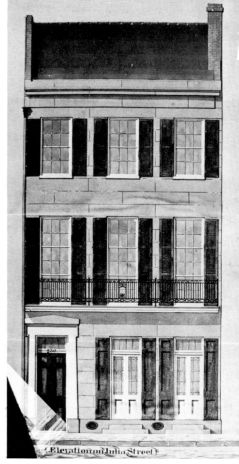

929 Julia, bound by Baronne, O'Keefe, Girod. This building remains of a former row of Greek Revival houses. A notarial drawing (Book 42, Folio 59) dated 1854 shows this house as it could be restored for modern usage. There was a wood Greek Key entrance with pediment above and an entrance door at banquette level. Two French windows paneled below, with transoms and glazing above, opened to a pair of granite steps leading to the banquette. These windows had paneled shutters, as opposed to the louvered shutters above.

The wrought iron balcony remains intact on the present building, although the sashed full-length windows with eighteen lights each have been enclosed. The original frieze and cornice remain, but chimneys have been removed. The facade was originally of scored plaster, painted brown. E. Grima, notary, accepted a contract dated June 17, 1837, for E. W. Sewell to build five houses for Evariste Blanc, starting at Julia and Baronne. There are plans at the Tulane University Library, Special Collections Division, Labrot Collection, of a row of houses designed by James Gallier, Sr., for Evariste Blanc. This may be one remaining of those five.

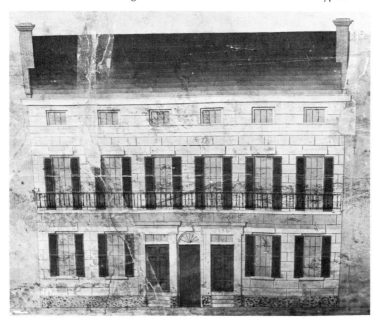

322-28 Lafayette, bound by Tchoupitoulas, Girod, Commerce. Row of five, three-story brick commercial buildings with granite pillars and lintel course. The two stores on the left in the photograph, old Nos. 9 and 10 Hevia (Lafayette) at the corner of Commerce, were built in 1844 by John Randall Pike for Francois Bizoton D'Aquin and Francis Adolphe D'Aquin. Cost of the two buildings was $6,750. Pike built the next two buildings for J. K. Wolff at the same time, and J. R. Pike owned the next two buildings, which were the first built of the row.

The specifications in the building contract for the D'Aquin stores (L. I. Caire, notary, June 25, 1844) reveal that the row largely retains its handsome original appearance, with only minor alterations. It was specified that Pike was to build the corner stores to match his own, already finished, at the other end: "Facade to be faced with Babbs pressed front bricks, wall on Commerce Street to be country bricks painted and penciled. Pressed brick on Lafayette Street front shall be laid in Flemish Bond with white mortar. Paneled doors to be grained oak and the other outside double lined doors shall be painted with the best Paris green." Each store has a front of 22½ feet by 63 feet, 7 inches.

922-924 Lafayette, bound by Baronne, O'Keefe, Girod. One-story, brick, double-shotgun house with segmental arched openings and fine original doors. Title information shows that property was owned by the city from 1848 to 1930, indicating the house was built by a lessee in the last third of the 19th century. Brick shotguns are rare in New Orleans. Research indicates that this is the only existing shotgun in the Central Business District. There are few of brick in the city.

832 Lafayette, bound by Baronne, Carondelet, Girod. Two-and-one-half story, Greek Revival, three-bay masonry house with 24-foot front. Building contracts of demolished houses indicate that the streets between Poydras and Howard were lined with three-bay houses similar to this. This simple variation features a wood pilastered entrance with deep entablature an iron balcony and deep wood architrave below attic windows.

A detached service wing runs across the back of the lot, suggesting it dates from the late 1830s.

916 Lafayette, bound by Baronne, O'Keefe, Girod. Three-story, three-bay house probably built about 1866 when, according to J. B. Walton, auctioneer, the value of this property rose from $3,000 to $15,000. The exterior has been altered through the years and the cornice and frieze have been removed. The interior plan of the main house, with stairhall and double rooms, and the extant service wing, however, show the traditional townhouse origins. The brick side evident here indicates that the house was detached, at least on one side, and that the segmental arched windows were part of the original design, another clue that the 1866 date for the structure is correct.

932 Lafayette, corner O'Keefe, Girod, Baronne. Turner's Hall, a handsome building of large proportions, built in 1868 for the Turner Society at a cost of $39,758; William Thiel, architect, Thomas O'Neill, builder. The Society of Turners was composed largely of Germans in New Orleans, a closely knit charitable group which fostered cultural enrichment through education. A newspaper article of the period called the hall an "Aladdin's palace, grand in character and design, and a worthy monument to the genius and patient labor of the population which called it into existence." The facades, which were originally painted a pale bluish shade, are enhanced by tall pilasters between the openings and a blocky parapet. Dentils and large console-forms decorate the cornice.

Building contract specifications (T. Cohn, notary, August 18, 1868) show that the building originally had iron "verandahs" at the upper level, supported by ornamental brackets. The arched windows which opened into the "salon" had ornamental bars and were glazed with colored glass. Exterior doors were grained in faux bois. The interior contained a hall and a gymnasium on the ground floor. A gallery overlooked the hall. The second floor had a library and was devoted to "conversation, reading and games of a social and elevating character." The third floor was "devoted exclusively to the arts, to dancing, music, and exercises of an intellectual character." One of the few remaining institutional buildings built by New Orleans' many charitable organizations, Turner's Hall is an imposing and important building, both by historic and architectural standards. Long ago abandoned by the Turner Society, it was used as a manual training school by Tulane University and later by a tinware manufacturer. It is now Labiche's warehouse.

115 Magazine, bound by Canal, Common, Camp. A four-story plastered brick store with granite pillars and lintel course on the ground floor and granite lintels and sills on the windows, dating from the mid-nineteenth century. The frieze of the entablature runs into the lintels of the third-story windows and creates a pattern with unusual proportions. A fire escape disfigures the facade.

225 Magazine, corner Gravier, bound by Camp, Common. Three-story brick store with granite pillars on first floor, granite sills and lintels on windows and cornice with dentils. The store was probably built in the 1830s since granite pillars are surmounted by ovolo capitals characteristic of that date. Portions of ground level side and two windows have been enclosed. At rear, fronting on Gravier, is a later store of similar design, but with cast-iron pillars on first floor.

208, 212, 214 Magazine, bound by Common, Gravier, Tchoupitoulas. Three, four-story stores erected for Miss Elinor McNeil in 1844 for $16,500 by James H. Dakin, important New Orleans architect, and John Mitchell, Howell and Coats, builders. Building contract specifications (Wm. Cristy, notary, June 20, 1844) show that facade was to be of Baltimore pressed brick laid in English bond, with white marble dust used in the mortar instead of sand. Remainder of the buildings was to be constructed of "brick of the best country make." Ground floor pillars, lintel course and window sills and lintels were to be of Quincy granite. Doors, painted in imitation of oak, were four-folds each, with paneled shutters, the upper panel of each to be fitted with plate glass. Front windows to have four-fold paneled interior shutters. Fire places to have wooden mantels painted "in imitation of Egyptian marble," and pendant gas lights hung from the ceilings. Awning at first level with ornate cast-iron brackets is a late 19th century addition.

200 Magazine, corner Common bound by Tchoupitoulas, Gravier. A four-story, brick commercial building with cemented exterior erected in 1881 for Aaron Wolf at a cost of $14,600, according to plans of A. F. Wrotnowski and Thomas W. Carter, architects. Ferdinand Reusch was the builder. The style is typical of the High Victorian period, as indicated by the keystone arches, the heavy cornices over the third-floor windows, segmental arch with keystone at fourth-floor windows and large brackets at the roofline. The rounded corner emphasized by quoins, engaged columns and a curved parapet lend interest to the elevation and are common features of the Italianate manner. Pillars of the first floor and cornice are cast-iron.

Specifications of the building contract (S. Cohn, notary, March 14, 1881) state that "band archivolts, architraves, cornice brackets and bed moulds are to be executed...in Jackson railroad bricks." Other parts of the building were to be of "Lake bricks." An awning, such as now exists on the building, was specified to be of iron, supported by cast-iron brackets of ornamental pattern. Cemented walls were to be "colored of light grey stone color." Store doors, grained in imitation of oak, were to be "double framed in three folds, moulded and paneled with hinges inside; window panels glazed with the best double strong American window glass." This design is particularly distinctive and noteworthy in the street scene, and the distracting third-story bridge is unfortunate. The building stands on the site of Bienville's plantation house.

300-06 Magazine. Cohen's *New Orleans Directory* (1855). (Courtesy New Orleans Public Library.)

301-07 Magazine. Drawing by J. M. Zacharie and John Reynolds, architects, J. Cuvillier, notary, Article 119, 1831, New Orleans Notarial Archives.

300-06 Magazine, bound by Gravier, Natchez, Tchoupitoulas. Three, four-story brick stores. Corner store was designed by well-known New Orleans architect Henry Howard and erected in 1851 after a fire destroyed a portion of the Banks Arcade, which formerly occupied the entire square. John Freeland, who had purchased the property in 1843 from Thomas Banks, commissioned John Sewell to build the store at a cost of $11,800.

Building contract specifications (T. Guyol, August 23, 1851) show that some material from the burned portion of Banks Arcade was used in construction. According to specifications, the front was faced with Baltimore pressed brick; Lake brick, and country brick were used elsewhere. Mortar of the facade was composed of marble dust. Other mortar was of Natchez or Horn Island sharp sand. Doors and windows fronting on the arcade were to have iron shutters. Other windows were to have blinds painted Paris green. Doors were four-folds with moulded paneled shutters, grained to imitate oak. Building had a wrought iron balcony with scroll border and scroll braces. In 1855 this and the adjacent store were occupied by Munroe's Clothing and Furnishing Depot.

Second and third stores from corner, also built in 1851 after this portion of Banks Arcade burned, were erected for Mark Davis of Petersburg, Virginia, at a cost of $11,000 by John Mitchell and Joseph M. Howell, builders, more or less following Henry Howard's scheme of the adjacent structure. Building contract specifications (A. Barnett, April 4, 1851) show that these fronts were also to be of Baltimore brick, with all other parts built of country brick. Quincy granite was used for windows, lintels and sills. Ground floor was to have cast-iron pillars and to be "finished like the fronts of #59 Camp Street belonging to Mr. Slocomb." In this way buildings were sometimes designed by analogy. This is a commendable example of careful maintenance.

301-07 Magazine, corner Gravier, bound by Camp, Natchez Alley. A three-story granite building, erected by the New Orleans Canal and Banking Company at a cost of $33,000 to house five stores and a bank. A noteworthy design by architect James H. Dakin, it was built in 1843 by Robert Seaton. The old Canal Bank located on this site and built in 1832 by architects J. Reynolds and J. M. Zacherie, was demolished to erect this structure. Similarities will be noted between the decorative features of the existing building and the original design for the old bank. The columns and entablature of the entrance appear to have been used in the present building, as well as the frame of the center window of the second story, the hood mould above it and central parapet.

Building contract specifications (J. Mossy, December 2, 1843) state that granite from the old bank was to be used in the construction of this building. Quincy granite was procured for the pillars and surmounting belt course of the first level, but the ashlar of the upper floors was to be from the old building. The "super incumbent" walls were to be of country brick. The specifications state: "The loose and careless manner of laying bricks as generally practiced in New Orleans shall not be taken as the guide or standard of laying the bricks in the walls of these buildings." Store doors were to have four folds each, with moulded panel shutters, glazed sashed and brass recessed shutter lifts and screws, and were to be grained in imitation of oak. However, the bank door was to be painted in imitation of bronze. Bank entrance, at center of first floor facade, is embellished with fluted Doric columns and a frieze of triglyphs and metopes in the belt course. Center window on the second story is framed by pilasters supporting a lintel architrave band. There is a cornice over the center third-floor window. On the roof are blocky parapet forms with recessed panels.

In 1858 architects Gallier and Esterbrook erected a new house (since demolished) for this Banking Company across the street, and the old bank was converted to stores (see 512 Gravier for illustrations of the side stores).

Board of Trade Building. Detail.

316 Magazine, bound by Natchez, Gravier, Tchoupitoulas. The present Board of Trade Plaza is an adaptation of a segment of the St. James Hotel. The St. James occupied the site of one segment of the former Banks Arcade, which had burned in 1851. A little-damaged section was reopened between 1852 and 1857 as the Arcade Hotel, and architect Lewis E. Reynolds replaced the old structure. The new building opened as the St. James Hotel in 1859. It was a notable example of extensive use of cast-iron. In 1883 the property was purchased by the Produce Exchange and renovated, at which time the old St. James Hotel (Reynold's Building) was leased as the Vonderbank Hotel.

James Freret was the architect for the 1883 building of the Produce Exchange (behind the hotel), with O'Neill and Carvey the builders. Cost was $29,040. By 1889 the Board of Trade had acquired the property, and in 1967 the hotel section, in bad structural condition, was demolished. Freret's Produce Exchange of 1883 is now visible from Magazine. It is typical of the weighty, fantastic and original adaptation of classical motifs, loosely based on late Renaissance and Baroque influences. The oak doors are particularly handsome, and the glass rotunda, which lets light into the business rooms, was retained. The facade features paired pilasters flanking shouldered arch fenestration. Cast-iron portions of Reynold's St. James Hotel facade were incorporated into the present plaza in 1967, with Koch and Wilson architects.

The open court and fountain enhance the street scene here. The renovations on this side of the street suggest that similar treatment could be given the fine stores opposite, producing a major area of the Central Business District.

336 Magazine, corner Natchez, bound by Gravier, Tchoupitoulas. Remaining sections of a block-long group of three-story stores designed by architect Charles F. Zimpel for Thomas Banks. As built in 1833, the red brick structure was a unified building, with granite pillars at the first level and a parapet with central pediment. It was intended to be a gathering place for merchants and to serve the community above Canal in the same manner as Maspero's Exchange did below Canal. The Magazine front was occupied by stores, behind which the glass pedestrian arcade extended through the block. There was a restaurant operated by the celebrated John Hewlett and a coffee room where 500 people might assemble at one time. The office of the Commercial Bulletin was at the Gravier corner of the building. By June, 1843, Banks was bankrupt because of his support of the Texas Revolution and financial speculations in New Orleans, and the arcade was acquired by Joseph Danforth Weaver.

J. Aron & Company, Inc., has restored and modernized a part of the old building seen here. The restoration was based on the appearance of the segments of the Banks Arcade at Magazine and Natchez after the Civil War when a double-level cast-iron gallery had been added to the corner unit and the balustrade at roof level removed. The restoration was arranged by Emilio Levy. Thomas Banks resided in his arcade at No. 19 Natchez.

Banks Arcade. (Courtesy Louisiana State Museum.)

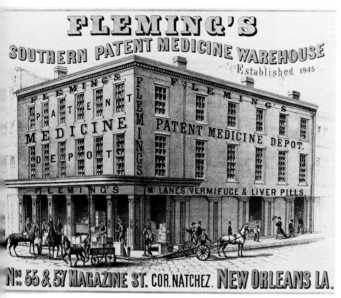

401 Magazine. B. Simon lithograph. (Courtesy Historic New Orleans Collection.)

401 Magazine, corner Natchez Alley, bound by Poydras, Camp. This fine example of a mid-nineteenth century brick, classic style commercial structure of six bays was commendably restored in 1971. At ground level of the Magazine facade are cast-iron pillars from the Julia Street Foundry. They have anthemion decoration and foliated capitals. On the Natchez Alley facade are brick piers with paired brick pilasters. Only the Magazine front has granite lintel course. An 1871 lithograph shows the building, plastered at the time, as Fleming's Patent Medicine Depot. John Fleming had purchased the property in 1867. Extending through Natchez Alley at the rear of building (see 500 block Natchez) are similar stores, which, along with this building, complete almost an entire block and present an uninterrupted view of a mid-nineteenth century commercial row.

309, 311, 317, 319, 321, 323 Magazine, bound by Natchez, Gravier, Camp. A fine row of seven, four-story brick stores designed by architect Louis Reynolds and erected in 1854. First in the row (from right) was erected for Henry Buckner. Second and third were built for A. B. James as wholesale dry goods stores. Fourth and sixth stores were built for H. Albin Michel d'Grilleau of Paris, with Little and Middlemiss as builders. Fifth was owned by J. L. Dulan in 1869. The last store was erected for Diego E. Morphy and Nevins, auctioneers.

Building contracts (T. O. Stark, notary, May 23, 1854, Vol. 11, Folios 101 and 113; and T. Guyol, notary, June 22, 1854) specify that each store was to be built like the adjoining stores in the row. Fronts were to be cemented with black Rosendale cement and sharp sand, then colored and penciled. Doors, which were to have portable shutters on the outside, secured by thumb screws and sash on the inside, were to be painted in imitation of oak. Windows were English sheet glass; roofs were Welsh slate. Interior offices would have "neat pilaster pattern mantels" painted in imitation of marble. Paneled cast-iron pillars at first level with Corinthian capitals support a denticulated cast-iron lintel course. Windows at second level are arched. Windows were originally surmounted by cornices with consoles, such as remain on the end building at the right. The entablature has a course with dentils and a cornice with medallions which once extended along the entire roofline. Fragments of original doors remain on the buildings.

400, 406, 408 Magazine, bound by Natchez, Poydras, Tchoupitoulas (see frontispiece). These five, four-level stores were built to replace houses which had been part of a speculative development of Benjamin Laurent Millandon and Lizardi Brothers. The three buildings to the left of the row in 1865 were called the "marble store," the edifice being constructed of marble blocks, a rarity in New Orleans. The other two have scored plaster fronts, giving a unified appearance to the row. Entire front at first level is composed of granite pillars with a granite lintel course. The marble stores have a cornice over the lintel course, decorated with guttae. Granite pillars of the marble stores have beak capitals, a type that was not used until after 1840.

The two end stores at right have ovolo caps, dating from 1830s. By 1866 each store, with values ranging from $12,000 to $24,000, had been sold to separate owners (left to right respectively): H. H. Slotter, Sam A. Shemway, E. A. Conery, Alfred Kearney and the minor children of Gustave Soniat-Dufossat. The awning at the first level, a late 19th century addition, is supported by especially fine cast-iron brackets.

501 Magazine. Part of William Brand Building. (Courtesy Historic New Orleans Collection.)

501 Magazine, corner Poydras, bound by Camp, Lafayette. Among the earliest surviving buildings in the business district, the fine buildings on this corner were built as warehouses in 1830 by architect William Brand for James Maxwell Reynolds. They are also among the few existing buildings by Brand. In the style of buildings in the Vieux Carre, the structures originally had arched openings on the ground floor. A remnant of the top of one is visible on the Poydras facade.

Building contract specifications (H. Pedesclaux, March 22, 1830) show that "country bricks" were to be used in construction. The building was then plastered, as was the custom when soft bricks were used. The plaster has been stripped from the corner buildings. Iron lintels were to be placed over the windows. These cast-iron lintels have three decorative divisions containing floral motifs, with the center one a pineapple. Identical lintels appear on two other buildings in the business district, at 448 Julia and 748 Camp.

The buildings were to have a wood cornice "like Capt. McCutcheon's," and lower front doors "like Mr. Carleton's corner Customhouse and Chartres," of cypress with "circular sashheads and irons." The roof is of English slate, and the bricks are laid in American bond. Cost was $14,500. Cast-iron pillars have been added to the ground floors of three of the warehouses. A former occupant of one of these buildings was photographer T. Lilienthal, who had his shop at old No. 102 Poydras, the last unit to the right in the photograph.

501, 509, 515, 517, 519, 521, 523, 525, 535, 537, 539, 545 Magazine, bound by Lafayette, Poydras, Camp. A block-long row of surviving mid-nineteenth century stores, one of the few remaining virtually intact. Samuel Stewart, of the building firm Sidle and Stewart, owned the corner lot on which he built the brick store at the left side of the photograph as an investment. The store features granite piers with beak capitals, splayed brick lintels on the front facade windows and a brick cornice with dentils. The second store from the right was standing in 1853 and was rented by the firm of S. S. and E. S. Levy, who commissioned Samuel Stewart to build a new store for them next door (to the right) to their old store. Only two floors of this building remain.

The 1853 building contract specifies that it was to be "of the same size and finish as the store [to its left] which was rented by S. S. and E. S. Levy." The cost was $6,250. The two hard red brick, four-story stores (fourth and fifth from the right) are, in proportion and present condition, particularly fine examples of mid-nineteenth century commercial buildings. These and the Levy stores correspond in first-floor treatment to Stewart's corner store. The repetition of identical pillars gives a unified street-level appearance. There are four similar four-bay, three-story stores with cast-iron pillars on the ground level completing the block. They have street-level canopies with ornate brackets added in the late 19th century. The last two buildings in the row are discussed separately (see 501 and 509 Magazine).

512-14-16 Magazine. Drawing by C. A. Hedin, 1853, Book 95, Folio 28, New Orleans Notarial Archives.

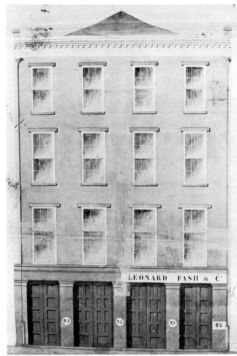

509 Magazine. Drawing by A. Castaing (1859), Book 85, Folio 31, New Orleans Notarial Archives.

512, 514-16 Magazine, bound by Poydras, Lafayette, Constance. Two, four-story stores, part of a row of six, four of which remain, built in 1838 by Sidel and Stewart, builders, for James Huie at a cost of $36,750. The other two surviving stores stand at 500 Magazine and at the corner of Poydras (see Poydras Street for illustration).

According to building contract specifications (William Christy, notary, June 21, 1838), all the stores were to front on Magazine, but the Poydras front was "to be finished in the same manner" as the Magazine Street front. Fronts were to be constructed of Baltimore brick, and the rest of the buildings were to be built of "country brick." Huie was to furnish the brick, as well as the granite for the window lintels and sills, ground-floor pillars and lintel course. Granite pillars exhibit the ovolo capitals used in the 1830s. Cornice was to be similar to stores of Erwin and Denton on Magazine Street opposite the arcade (since demolished). Window glass was to be from Baltimore. Doors were to have sash, glass and shifting shutters, painted in imitation of oak. Windows were fitted with inside shutters, paneled and folding into jambs. Corner store has a depth of about 66 feet, the next three stores a depth of about 57 feet, the fifth store a depth of about 66 feet and the sixth store a depth of about 100 feet. The sixth store (pictured here on the right) runs through the block and also faces on Foucher. At the rear, the other stores had courtyards paved with flagstones, with privy and cistern.

The two buildings pictured here were auctioned three times in the 1850s—in 1851, 1853 and 1858 (New Orleans Notarial Archives, Book 10, Folio 10: Book 95, Folio 28; Book 42, Folio 33). The auction drawings show that in the 1850s the doors were painted green instead of in simulated wood graining (*faux bois*) as specified in the building contract. The 1851 drawing shows that the doors were two-tone green, two-fold, with six panels each. These were perhaps the original doors. By 1853 the stores had two-fold doors paneled below and glazed above. These doors remain on the stores at 500 Magazine. The doors originally had removable wooden panels that could be placed over the glass for protection when the store was not in use. No. 512 Magazine has a late 19th century canopy supported by cast-iron brackets.

The present owner and business occupant, John Geiser, has carefully restored the building and has removed exterior silver and red paint.

509 Magazine, bound by Poydras, Lafayette, Camp. This four-story, four-bay brick store with granite pillars is documented by a notarial drawing dated 1859. Note that the tie rods with star circle anchors were added after the drawing was made. Originally the front was plastered, as was the custom when the bricks used were soft lake or country bricks which had to be covered to avoid deterioriation. Cornice and frieze were given emphasis by contrast in paint color. A canopy, without the iron scroll brackets seen in the adjoining building, has been added. It should be lowered to the height of the lintel course. Doors at far right are original. The glazing, however, has been altered. Four-fold doors with recessed panels seen in the photograph are dissimilar to those in the drawing but are certainly of mid-nineteenth century vintage. Caps on the granite pillars are of the beak variety, dating the store after 1840.

500 block Magazine. From *Martin Behrman Administration Biography, 1904-16.* (Courtesy Historic New Orleans Collection.)

701 Magazine, corner Girod, bound by Julia, Camp. A large two-story brick warehouse in the Italianate style, with segmental arched windows and paired brackets in a heavy cornice. On the ground floor are cast-iron pillars with chamfered corners. This was possibly the warehouse of the Maginnis Cotton Mills (incorporated in 1881), a large concern. Members of the Maginnis family have owned the property since 1862 and, according to the Robinson Map of 1883, C. B. and W. D. Maginnis owned the warehouse. The building probably was erected about 1860. A good example of adaptive use, with adequate maintenance. Interesting, reasonably restrained signs could be more cleverly arranged.

530-534 Magazine, corner Lafayette, bound by Constance, Poydras. Complex of three, three-story brick stores and a four-story store, which was occupied by the Elmer Candy Company, as illustrated in a 1916 advertisement. The three-story stores are plastered and scored and have iron pillars at ground level and a dentiled cornice. The four-story store has granite pillars. These buildings, which need a minimal amount of rehabilitation, visually contribute to a block with numerous mid-nineteenth century stores on both sides of the street.

520-528 Magazine, bound by Poydras, Lafayette, Constance. Four-story, three-bay brick commercial buildings, typical of the 1830s and 1840s, with lintel courses, granite lintels and sills. Once part of an entire row on the River-side of Magazine.

540 Magazine, bound by Poydras, Lafayette, Constance. Four-bay, four-story brick commercial building, part of the Elmer Candy Company complex. Built later than the row of similar buildings which existed before demolition broke the street's unity.

643 Magazine, bound by Capdevielle, Girod, Camp. Four-story commercial building, with rounded brick corners and paneled cast-iron pillars with decorated capitals. Arched openings at upper levels and deep-decorated brick cornice add to the progression of types and styles along the street. The side elevations feature the hexagonal silhouetted pillars of cast-iron as seen across the street at 701 Magazine. They pre-date the building's front facade, which is late 19th century.

755 Magazine. La Belle Creole Tobacco Co. letterhead. (Courtesy New Orleans Public Library.)

913, 917-923 Magazine, bound by St. Joseph, Howard, Camp. Two once-identical brick houses, with wooden cornices with dentils. Both houses have had Greek Key entrances altered. Lower windows have been cut into doors. The two should remain as attractive reminders of another era, along with the adjacent two-story brick house barely visible at the extreme left of the photograph. Greek Revival features indicate that the cornice fringe, a jigsaw wood design, was a later addition. No. 923, presently Triangle Machine Works, is one of the few remaining residences set back from the street, indicating a larger lot with side yard.

755 Magazine, corner Julia, bound by Camp, Girod. This large factory was erected in 1882 by S. Hernsheim Brothers and Company for La Belle Creole Cigar Factory. Simon Hernsheim had purchased the property from Timothy Foley in 1881. La Belle Creole was a large industry, employing more than 1,000 people and in 1882 was the largest manufacturer of cigars in the United States. The concern was later taken over by Liggett and Myers Tobacco Company. The building, with a front-age of 130 by 120 feet, was constructed of white sandstone. The walls are pierced with semicircular arched windows. A tower form emphasizes the corner of the building. The vertical members are decorated with geometric tie rod anchors. The same anchor design was later used in the I. L. Lyons Building at 224-28 Camp. The upper part of the tower has been removed. The walls were plastered at a later date.

900 Magazine, corner St. Joseph, bound by Howard, Tchoupitoulas. A small corner neighborhood store, a rare example of a frame structure remaining in Faubourg St. Mary. Similar to those built from the 1820s onward with hipped roof. This small frame building is a whimsical picture from the past.

902-910 Magazine, bound by St. Joseph, Howard, Constance. Three brick two-story stores which were originally a row of four stores.

945 Magazine, bound by St. Joseph, Howard, Camp. Gallagher's Transfer and Storage. Four-story commercial building built by Henry Howard, architect. It housed the Louisiana Brewery in 1887.

415, 419, 421, 423, 425 Natchez, bound by Magazine, Tchoupitoulas, Gravier. A row of commercial buildings, plastered brick with granite pillars on the ground levels. Recessed panels under the windows of the second floor and a cornice without dentils add variation to this otherwise typical row of stores. A. Bonnabel, who owned the adjacent building backing this row on the right, built a two-story warehouse in 1856 on the site of these stores, which therefore were constructed after that date.

510, 512, 516, 520, 524, 526 Natchez Alley, bound by Magazine, Camp, Poydras. A fine row of three-story brick stores having granite pillars at ground level, granite trim and cornices with dentils. The four stores at the end of the row to the right (starting with the white building) were erected in 1851 by Joshua Peebles, builder, for William Silliman at a cost of $12,500 (W. L. Poole, notary, May 17, 1851). In 1852 the four stores were evaluated at $45,000. The *Merchant's Directory* of 1854 shows that the stores in this row were occupied by a wine importer, commission merchants, tobacco merchant, coffee broker, tobacco brokers, produce broker and ship broker.

Penn, corner Poydras, bound by Baronne, Perdido. This three-story masonry combination store-residence was built for Samuel J. Peters, Jr., by the architectural firm of Gallier, Turpin and Company in 1850. One remaining of three identical structures fronting both on Penn and Poydras, the building has cast-iron pilasters and fluted Ionic columns *in antis* on the first floor and a wrought iron balcony at the second level. Original plan for this building is in the Labrot collection, Tulane University Library, Special Collections Division.

523 Natchez, corner Picayune Place, bound by Magazine, Gravier. Three-story brick store with two-bays, each with triple window treatment popular during the 1880s. Corners have rounded bricks; Picayune elevation has arched openings. *Clarion Herald* newspaper is housed in this building.

802, 804, 806, 814, 822 Perdido, corner Carondelet, bound by Poydras, Baronne. Factors Building. Row of six masonry four-story commercial buildings, among the finest surviving examples with cast-iron decoration. Designed in 1858 by Lewis Reynolds, architect; built by Samuel Jamison and James McIntosh, builders, who also owned the two corner buildings. Intended for use by cotton buyers and sellers. Each floor of windows has a different treatment in cast-iron Italianate ornamentation. The parapet above an elaborate cast-iron cornice bears the name "Factors Row" in relief on the Carondelet Street fronts.

Note the central grouping of windows on the Carondelet front. Cast-iron pillars with Corinthian capitals on the ground level support an iron lintel course with arches over the bays. The building originally had a cast-iron gallery and was painted white with gilded decorative trim. This was an important center for cotton trade in the South and is an important building, both architecturally and historically. Except for a few changes, such as the insertion of glass bricks, the entire exterior design is exceptionally well-maintained almost in its original state.

Michel Musson, uncle of artist Edgar Degas, had an office in Factors Row, and it was here in 1873 that Degas painted the famous scene of a cotton office interior, now in the Municipal Museum in Pau, as well as a sketch of the same subject in the Fogg Museum of Art at Cambridge, Massachusetts.

826, 828, 830 Perdido, corner Carroll, bound by Carondelet, Poydras. Three-story commercial building designed by architect Henry R. Thiberge and erected in 1869. High Victorian Italianate in style, the building has arched fenestration, a heavy, broken and bracketed cornice, quoins, keystones, string courses, bifurcated windows—all features of the style. Built as the New Orleans Real Estate Board and Auction Exchange, it also was formerly Spencer's Business College.

Spencer College was founded in 1891 by Lucius Clay Spencer, educator, author, and penman, who for forty-five years served as president of the institution which bears his name. The college first occupied the building, which became known as the Young Men's Christian Association, but by 1903 had moved into the Spencer Building on Canal Street, the site now occupied by Godchaux's. In 1924 the school moved again, to the corner of Carondelet and Gravier. The building is now known as the Hibernia Homestead. In 1963 the college moved into the (renamed) Spencer College Building at the corner of Perdido and Canal. It is presently located on St. Charles.

Factors Row and Spencer Business College.

500-08, 510 S. Peters, bound by Poydras, Lafayette, Fulton. Two, three-story brick stores, with granite pillars, built after 1840, as indicated by the beak capitals on pillars. These are fine examples of the typical New Orleans commercial buildings which were originally, and still could be, stores-apartments combined. The two-story brick store with cast-iron paneled pillars on ground level has altered window lights, but interior shutters remain. Paneled doors and windows have been removed between the pillars. Civic improvement information of 1856 indicates that Joshua Peebles built three, two-story stores on N. Levee for J. B. Oliver at a cost of $6,000.

528 S. Peters, bound by Poydras, Lafayette, Fulton. This three-story, three-bay brick store with granite pillars and lintel course follows proportions of the typical commercial structures of Faubourg St. Mary from the 1830s to 1870s. The iron exterior shutters are seen often on buildings near the riverfront. Bricks are in American Bond pattern. A building contract, recorded Nov. 29, 1853 by G. Rareshide, notary, shows that a two-story brick warehouse on lots 14 and 15 was built by Crozier and Wing, builder for Benjamin Rodriguez. The buildings partially visible in this photograph may be the Rodriguez buildings, which are greatly altered from the 1853 style.

537 S. Peters, bound by Poydras, Lafayette, Commerce. Three-story, four-bay brick store, with paneled cast-iron columns beneath brick lintel course retaining fine original four-fold paneled doors. This is an Italianate version of the typical New Orleans commercial building, featuring segmental arched openings and a tall parapet. Note the splayed brick lintels at the windows, with the voussoir pattern continuing down the sides of the window frames. Original muntin arrangement remains.

600 block S. Peters, bound by Fulton, Lafayette, Girod. A block of commercial houses with fronts on Fulton and S. Peters, having a variety of window treatment, lending interest to the street scene. Beak-type capitals on plastered brick pillars suggest a date after 1840. Valuable as part of the 19th century scene, with granite brick and cobblestone streets. Of sturdy masonry with large open spaces within, these buildings should be retained as a contrast and complement to future modern development.

701 S. Peters, corner Girod, bound by Notre Dame, Tchoupitoulas. Outstanding three-story, multi-bay brick commercial building, listed in Robinson in 1883 as "Old Commercial House." The flat-head cast-iron lintels with center decoration are notable and were used as early as 1830. The exterior is of scored plaster, and the windows have granite sills. Adjacent is a three-level commercial warehouse built in the 20th century, but comforming to the street scene.

900 block S. Peters, bound by Fulton, St. Joseph, N. Diamond. Three-level, multi-bay brick commercial complex with granite drip stones and louvered shutters with heavy iron strap hinges. The location of these stores at the foot of the park where St. Mary's Market stood lends importance to these pleasant 19th century buildings.

901 S. Peters, corner St. Joseph, bound by N. Diamond, Tchoupitoulas. Two-bay, three-story brick building. Once part of a row, this altered building is one of the older in the St. Mary's Market area. Presently occupied by P. L. Hilbert and Co., the structure is in poor condition, but should be retained as a valuable part of New Orleans' heritage.

200 block Poydras, bound by S. Peters, Fulton, Lafayette. Four, three-story commercial buildings with granite pillars and brick cornice articulated with courses of bricks. Excellent contrast to modern structures being erected on Poydras.

422, 424 Poydras, corner Magazine, bound by Constance, Lafayette. The two corner buildings (at right) which face Magazine were part of a row of six stores which included 512 and 514-16 Magazine, built in 1838 by Sidel and Stewart, builders, for James Huie at a cost of $36,750. Some of the store doors, while not original, appear in an 1853 archival drawing of stores in this row. They are paneled below and glazed above, and originally had removable wooden panels that could be placed over the glass. Some of the folding inside shutters remain on the upper floor (see 512, 514-16 Magazine). Fronting on Poydras and Constance are two more stores of similar design.

510 Poydras. Letterhead, 1888. (Courtesy Historic New Orleans Collection.)

510 Poydras, bound by Camp, Magazine, Lafayette. A three-story brick store in the Italianate style, with cast-iron moulded lintels over segmental arched windows, paired brackets and modillions at the cornice and a parapet. An 1888 letterhead pictures this store as Smith Brothers and Co., grocers. The store ran through the block, and the rear, facing on Lafayette, also pictured on the letterhead, still stands. This facade has brick voussoirs over segmental arched windows and a heavy cornice.

520-22 Poydras, bound by Camp, Magazine, Lafayette. This four-bay, three-story, plastered brick commercial building could once again become part of a classical street scene if the ground floor entrances were restored.

525-530 Poydras, bound by Camp, Magazine, Lafayette. Two, three-story brick stores erected in 1843 by John Mitchell, Joseph Howell and Moses H. Coates for Benjamin Florance (acting for William Florance). Cost was $5,600. Building contract specifications (H. B. Cenas, notary, July 18, 1843) show that they were constructed of "country brick" and the facades faced with Lake brick, which was then painted and penciled. Windows were to have granite lintels, with roof slated with "countesses or dutchesses" and doors oak-grained. The cast-iron pillars of the ground level have acanthus leaf capitals, and the iron lintel course has a dentiled cornice, corresponding to the dentiled cornice at the roofline. An 1875 advertisement shows that these stores were occupied by the Pelican Steam Book and Job Printing Office.

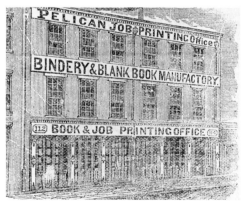

525-530 Poydras. J. C. Waldo's *Visitors Guide to New Orleans* (1875). (Courtesy Louisiana Collection, Special Collections Division, Tulane University Library.)

728-30, 732, 734, 738 Poydras, corner Carondelet; **500 Carondelet** bound by Lafayette, St. Charles. A row of stores dating from the mid-nineteenth century, with the exception of the second from right (built in 1925). The store at the far left is part of a row of five, three-story brick stores with two-story back buildings built by Ernest Goudchaux in 1849 for A. Zenon Trudeau for $25,850. They were designed by noted architect J. N. de Pouilly, who was responsible for the design of the St. Louis Cathedral. Building contract specifications (T. Guyol, notary, June 25, 1849), with attached plans and elevations, show that the buildings had granite pillars on the ground floor. These and the window lintels and sills were to be blue Quincy granite. The facades were to be constructed of Lake brick and others walls of "country brick." Windows, which were double-hung, were of Jersey glass. Cypress entrance doors were to be either grained or bronzed. The corner building probably was erected in the late 1850s (see 500 Carondelet).

900, 902, 906, 908, 910, 912, 914, 916, 918 Poydras, corner Baronne, Lafayette, O'Keefe. Alexander Baggett, builder, constructed these seven, three-story brick stores for Samuel D. Fagot in 1840 at a cost of $24,000. Ground levels of the stores have been totally altered, but building contract specifications (L. T. Caire, notary, October 7, 1840) show that each store was to have "3 square headed doors 9 feet hight by 4 feet wide...with glazed sash." Fronts were built of Lake brick and were painted and penciled. Stores were to be built "like those Alexander Baggett built for Mr. Amery" on Canal. In 1854 Fagot hired Auguste Roy and Louis Clairain to build seven kitchens for these stores at a cost of $21,000. A kitchen wing is visible on Baronne.

Site of Poydras Market. A photograph of Poydras Street, taken in the 1920s, shows the two buildings of Maylie's Restaurant, which was established in 1876 when Bernard Maylie and Hypolite Esparbe moved their coffee shop to the corner building. It was previously located in a stall of the Poydras Market, which stood on Poydras between Baronne and S. Rampart until 1932. For many years this restaurant was popular with market people. The corner building was demolished in 1959 when O'Keefe was widened. Maylie's now occupies the building at the left.

930-932 Poydras, bound by Baronne, O'Keefe, Lafayette. Three-and-one-half story, brick double-house retaining one dormer and service wings. This is a good example of a Greek Revival house. The lower levels should be restored.

Poydras Market. Drawn by John Durkin, *Harper's Bazaar*, February 7, 1885. It was described as having been handed down to posterity in honor of Julien Poydras. It was behind the site of the house of "Doctor" Gravier, the childless, wifeless, companionless old man whose kindness to Negroes won him his professional title, and whom another New Orleanian, author George Washington Cable, mentions as one of a "strange group of men who in the last century led lonely lives and left large fortunes."

Near this dilapidated house once ran the Poydras Canal, long since filled in and built upon. At the same time, between Poydras and Girod, was a campo de Negroes, a slave camp of Guinea or Congo slaves. Later, a gas works rose beyond the spot where the ruined Gravier House raised its high pillars.

The markets of New Orleans were not visited for their artistic beauty, but for their local associations. The attraction of the scene was in the throngs who frequented them. Here was a picturesque confusion of nationalities—Italian fruit vendors, Indians with herbs and Irish and Germans with vegetables. (Courtesy Louisiana Collection, Special Collections Division, Tulane University Library.)

1009 Poydras, bound by O'Keefe, S. Rampart, Perdido.

501 S. Rampart, corner Poydras, bound by Lafayette, Basin. This once-handsome store is pictured in an 1888 letterhead as the grocery of Charles Feahney. The windows of the second level are tied together by a continuous archivolt moulding. At the roofline is a large cornice and parapet, portions of which are now missing. The corners of the building are rounded. The illustration shows a balcony at the second level, overhanging the sidewalk and supported by posts. Some of the pillars have been replaced by windows. A canopy added to the building below the pillar termination spoils the facade effect. With minimal attention the store could be returned to its original handsome appearance.

129 Royal, bound by Bourbon, Iberville, Canal. Cosmopolitan Hotel. Designed by Thomas Sully in 1892, this new and elegant hotel opened its doors with 125 rooms and two entrances: one, on Royal, had triple bay-windows ornamented with cast-iron; the other, on Bourbon, maintained the more traditional facade, with rustication at first level and heavy bracketed cornice deeply denticulated. The Royal entrance was for transient visitors, while the Bourbon was for family and permanent guests. The Royal side remains between buildings of earlier architectural design. The Bourbon side was demolished when the Woolworth store was built in the 1950s. With a minimum of sign control and first-level refurbishment, the side on Royal could be improved, even with the 20th century motel across the street. Photograph from George Engelhardt's *City of New Orleans.* Chamber of Commerce, 1903. (Courtesy New Orleans Public Library.)

501 S. Rampart. Letterhead, 1888. (Courtesy Historic New Orleans Collection.)

115 St. Charles, Corner Canal, bound by Carondelet, Common. Pickwick Club. The first building on this site was erected in 1826 for Cornelius Paulding, purchased in 1858 by Mrs. Cora Slocomb and remodeled into the Merchant's Hotel, then converted in 1865 into the Crescent Billiard Hall by Colonel A. Walker Merriam. This three-level plastered brick building was again remodeled to its present design by architect Henry Howard and builder Frederick Wing in 1875. *Cohen's* 1853 illustration shows the building used for stores before Mrs. Slocomb's purchase. In 1866 a sheet music illustration furthers its progression to Merriam's Crescent Billiard Hall.

The Italian flavor is determined by cornice and pediment brackets and small pilaster rustication. Heavily framed fenestrations have stilted arches, round-headed and segmental, wide and narrow, in a liberally varied scheme. The bifurcated design of sash windows recalls the early Renaissance style of Florence and Venice. There are many individualized details, including the exaggerated verticality of keystone motifs and arched paneling flanking the windows on the St. Charles facade, the highly condensed "tondo" panels in the spandrels and the frieze-like repeat pattern of the pilaster capitals. Only the cast-iron railings and Corinthian capitals are familiar details. The simplified forms of the parapet have survived from the earlier design of 1865.

Thomas Sully designed extensive interior improvements in 1886, with Dressel and May of New Orleans furnishing woodwork. In 1888 the building was bought by Joseph A. Walker. It is presently leased from his heirs by the Pickwick Club. In 1950 interior remodeling was

executed by architect Theodore Perrier and contractor Gordon Lee, along with murals by Vera Du Vernay and Charles Reinike. The Pickwick Club, begun in 1857 as a social club, is one of the few private clubs of continuous existence. The founders began the Mystic Krewe of Comus, from which the club became disassociated in 1888.

The club has had nine other locations: 309½ St. Charles (Judah Touro Buildings); 6 Exchange Alley, 1865-1885; Mercer Mansion (present Boston Club), 824 Canal, 1881-1883; old No. 180 Canal, 1883-1884; Canal and Carondelet (present Gus Mayer & Co.), 1884-1894; No. 2 and No. 4 Carondelet, 1894-1896; 1028 Canal, 1896-1934; and 19th and 20th floor of Hibernia Bank Building, 1934-1950. The Pickwick leased the property on Canal and Carondelet from Armand and Michel Heine of Paris and selected architects Hinsdal and Barble of St. Louis to design the red pressed brick structure which cost $132,000. The ground was appraised at $10,000.

This four-story Queen Anne style structure, with elaborate varied textures, became the Pickwick Hotel after the club moved to 1028 Canal. The stained glass, designed by J. & R. Lamb of New York, was moved to the new location and has been preserved in the present Pickwick Club. In 1896 the Club purchased No. 1028 from Gus Seiger and hired Shepley, Rutan and Coolidge of St. Louis and Toledano and Reusch of New Orleans to design their eighth home, which they occupied for 38 years (see 1028 Canal). The club has been located in the old Crescent Billiard Hall for the past 22 years.

115 St. Charles. Crescent Hall. Sheet music illustration, 1866. (Courtesy Historic New Orleans Collection.)

Pickwick Club. Detail of upper level.

115 St. Charles. Henry Clay Monument. Merchant's Hotel. (Courtesy Historic New Orleans Collection.)

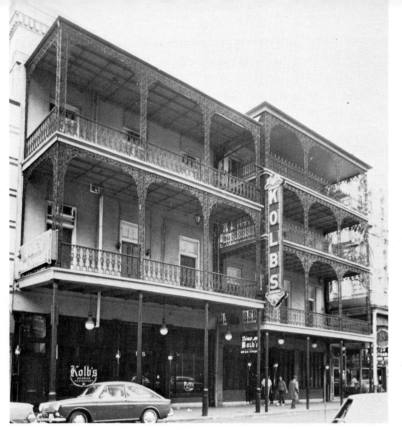

119, 125 St. Charles bound by Canal, Common, Carondelet. Two, three-story, three-bay plastered brick buildings (formerly Nos. 11 and 13). Each has a deep cast-iron gallery at the second and third levels supported by reeded cast-iron columns below. These galleries were possibly added after the construction of the buildings. Galleries were on both buildings between 1858-65 when Merchant's Hotel was on the corner, as they appear in an old illustration.

No. 125 has a deep entablature and cornice with dentils above the gallery and paneled pillars at the first level. No. 119 has granite pillars at the first level. The dimensions of the two lots are 30 feet by 115 feet and 32 feet by 153 feet. The former lot (No. 119, at right) was acquired March 23, 1842, by John and Thomas Hagan in a suit against Mrs. E. Lefevre. The building was erected before May 25, 1853, when Hagan sold the lot with buildings to John Egerton. The building on the left (No. 125) probably was built before 1844, when a museum housing the art collections of James Robb, R. D. Shepherd, Glendy Burke, H. R. W. Hill, Joseph M. Kennedy and others opened at this location. The gallery was short-lived, and the Louisiana Jockey Club had quarters here in 1845.

In 1899 Conrad Kolb, a German from Landau, opened his restaurant in the building closest to Canal. He shared it with another small restaurant run by Valentine Merz and a hat store at the front ground floor. The restaurant has flourished and occupies the two buildings.

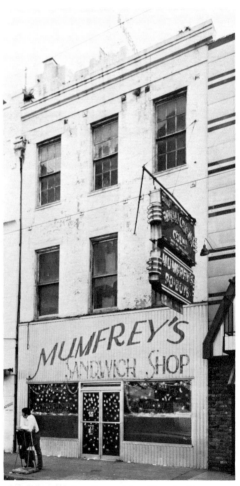

135 St. Charles, bound by Canal, Common, Carondelet. A simple three-story brick store. James Gallier, Sr., built three "stores or tenements" on the north corner of St. Charles and Common for the City Bank of New Orleans in 1844. Cost was $16,400.

The specifications indicate that this may be the only remaining store of this group (H. B. Cenas, notary, June 26, 1844): "The buildings shall be three stories high, the lower floor 8 in. above the pavement, first story 13 ft., second story 11 ft., third 10 ft. Bricks of the fronts on both streets shall be of the best Lake manufacture and all others well burnt country brick to be painted two coats red and pencilled white. A brick cornice and blocking course as per elevation shall be built around building on both streets, returned back from the front at the end on Common. A base course of granite 16" by 8". The lintel course all round to be 22" deep by 14" thick. The cornice or belt course will be 8 inches deep moulded on top; granite sills and lintels and granite steps. Banquette, yard and entrance hall of square Yorkshire flagstone. Store doors 11' high by 6' 3". Three inch thick paneled shutters outside hung in four-folds, grained oak. Entrance doorways from street to second stories shall be 2" thick with transom and fanlight over each door hung in bored and moulded frames trimmed with architraves on both sides [this part of the complex has been torn down]. Front windows of second story to have 12 lights with paneled shutters and moulded architraves inside, third story 12 lights."

An auction drawing, dated January 24, 1855, shows the standard floor plan of such stores, and the elevation shows that the store in 1855 held the offices of notaries W. Christy and H. B. Cenas. The doors that appear here are two-fold, and the windows have more muntins than specified in the contract. The facade is a brownish tone of exposed brick. At this location in 1864 was Lamothe's Restaurant and Oyster Salon, reported to be the "oldest restaurant in town," according to *Englehardt's* (1903), referring perhaps to the Faubourg St. Mary. In 1864 Armstrong and O'Neill, builders for owner August Pino, installed two oyster counters with marble tops 104 feet long for $2,682 and refurbished the store as an oyster bar, according to a contract recorded with William Shannon, notary, October 24, 1864.

135 St. Charles. Drawing by C. A. Hedin, 1855, Book 27A, Folio 41, New Orleans Notarial Archives.

130-138 St. Charles. From Jewell's *Crescent City.* (Courtesy New Orleans Public Library.)

130-138 St. Charles, corner Common, bound by Canal, Camp. Gallier and Turpin designed this group of six stores in 1855 for J. W. Zacharie, president of the Chamber of Commerce and a prominent entrepreneur. The *Times-Picayune* (September 4, 1855) cites these stores as promising "to form the handsomest block in town" and to built by Little and Middlemiss, builders. The lower floor has been altered, but could be restored according to plans in the Labrot Collection, Special Collections Division, Tulane University Library. According to an 1872 illustration in *Jewell's,* there was a gallery at the second level, with a crested cornice and cast-iron posts at the first level, creating a deep, covered walkway. The decorative cast-iron hood moulds, with brackets in the Italianate style, surmount the segmental arch openings at the second and third levels, contrasting with the bracketed block lintels above. At the roofline is a simple frieze with denticulated cornice above.

The Zacherie building was occupied by mercantile firms: in 1859 by L. W. Lyons and Company Clothing Emporium and Furniture Store, and in 1872 by H. B. Stevens and Company, a clothing and furniture store. It became the Imperial Building, owned by D. A. Chaffraix and Mrs. S. W. Miller who lived in Europe, with P. A. Lelong, agent. The lot was site of the famous old Verandah Hotel built by Dakin and Dakin in 1836-38.

100 block St. Charles, corner Canal, bound by Common, Camp. In 1820 architect William Brand purchased the property on which these buildings are located and in 1833 erected the corner building at left (see Canal, corner St. Charles) and four adjoining buildings on Canal (now demolished). These structures had courtyards at the rear and service wings extending lengthwise behind the buildings. An 1840 plan in the Notarial Archives (Plan Book 61, Folio 31) shows that the courtyard of the corner building, which was screened from the street by a curtain wall, occupied the site of the stores with denticulated cornice. These stores therefore were built after that date.

At the right of the photograph is a three-story townhouse with fine anthemion-scroll and cast-iron grills in the attic frieze. This house also was built after 1840, as the notarial drawing shows a store, which William Brand sold, occupying the lot at that date. The lower floors of all the buildings have been completely altered, and the iron balconies are additions. The buildings now form part of the complex of Rubenstein's Clothing Store.

Original St. Charles Hotel, completed in 1837. (Courtesy Louisiana State Museum.)

Second St. Charles Hotel. From *Harper's,* August 18, 1866. (Courtesy Historic New Orleans Collection.)

211 St. Charles, bound by Common, Gravier, Carondelet. Sheraton Charles Hotel—St. Charles Hotel. Built by Thomas Sully, architect, following a fire in 1894 and reopened in 1896.

For generations, until recent times, this building and its two predecessors formed the major center of social, political and commercial life of the central core and the community-at-large. They were the settings for eventful scenes in a varied history of clashes and celebrations, as well as for the conduction of normal business. Here, President Jefferson Davis met with Southern leaders, and later General Butler's presence led to stormy wartime confrontations. Charles Dickens, usually hypercritical of everything American, wrote of the "excellent dinners at the magnificent St. Charles Hotel."

The first St. Charles or Exchange Hotel, begun on this site by architect James Gallier in 1835 and completed in 1837, was built at a cost of $600,000, including $100,000 for the land. With its rival counterpart, the St. Louis in the French sector, it stood as a symbol of the divided Franco-American population, as well as the new grand style of hotel-keeping, in contrast to hostelries of earlier times. Gallier's building followed closely in date, plan and mode of operation the pace-setting Tremont House in Boston, built by Isaiah Rogers, who shortly afterwards produced the Astor House in New York.

The St. Charles, with its dome, cupola, and flagstaff aloft at 203 feet, far surpassed these Northern types in imposing eminence and formed a commanding landmark on the skyline of New Orleans. Under the rotonda, as at the St. Louis in the French Quarter, slave auctions were among the customary public transactions. After a fire of 1851, the hotel was rebuilt on the old foundations almost as a replica of the original, except for the dome, which, "though beautiful, was costly," as Gallier said in his autobiography, "and added little to the value of the building as a hotel." The work of rebuilding has been variously attributed to the younger Gallier or Isaiah Rogers, although contract records reveal that architect George Purvis was at least partially involved (H. B. Cenas, notary, Vol. 50, pp. 553, 601, 621). The granite work was by Newton Richards, who had performed that work on the original building.

The present building has provided accommodations for Presidents McKinley, Roosevelt and Taft, heads of state, royalty and famous personalities of the stage (Bernhardt, Caruso, Galli-Curci). Its original character is fairly intact, although somewhat modified over the years by various renovations or additions (Sam Stone, architect, ca. 1901-1912), and a covering of paint (February, 1961) more in keeping with current taste. At the time of its initiation, it was described as a "handsome, steel-frame fireproof structure...completed in red brick with terra cotta trimmings, in the imposing Italian Renaissance style." The second-floor loggia once opened onto a roof terrace "with palms and bananas waving amid its columned promenades." Although not one of Sully's most appealing designs, it is among his largest. This is a most notable work and a creditable accomplishment for its time, still viable after almost 80 years. (Illustration from *The Picayune's Guide to New Orleans* (1897), courtesy Historic New Orleans Collection.)

Ruins of St. Charles Hotel, one day after being gutted by fire. (Courtesy Historic New Orleans Collection.)

211 St. Charles. Sheraton Charles Hotel.

301-311-317 St. Charles. Drawing by Hedin and Schlarbaum, 1854, Book 62, Folio 16, New Orleans Notarial Archives.

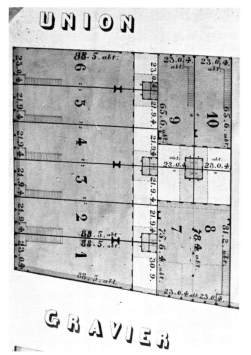

301-311-317 St. Charles. Plot plan drawing by Hedin and Schlarbaum, 1854, Book 62, Folio 16, New Orleans Notarial Archives.

Union Street. Side elevation of Judah Touro buildings.

301-311-317 St. Charles, corner Gravier, bound by Carondelet, Union. A row of six stores which Judah Touro had Thomas Murray build in this square in 1851 for $60,000. The two stores at 317 St. Charles were covered with a turn-of-the-century tile front. Although marring the unity of the row, this is one of the better examples of tile facade in the city. At the rear, two, three-story stores face Union, and two, three-story stores formerly faced Gravier. These were part of the complex. The specifications (Thomas Layton, notary, September 1, 1851) describe the buildings as follows:

The heights of the stories from ground level were to be thirteen feet, twelve feet, ten feet and nine feet, respectively. The fronts of the stores were to be of iron and "in pattern and in all other respects like that of Crescent Insurance office, corner Commercial Alley and Camp [see No. 401 Camp] and to be filled in with fire bricks."

There was to be an "iron balcony or gallery in front of all stores on St. Charles, Gravier and Union supported on iron beams similar in style and construction to front of Montgomery's dwelling on corner Canal and Burgundy. The front cornice to be like that of the row of stores now building for H. C. Cammack and Company, corner of Carondelet and Common [see Notarial Archives drawing of Cammack's stores]. Front sash on outside to be painted imitation of black walnut; store doors grained like oak or any imitation the owner may desire, Waterford glass in rear windows. Glass in first story to be like that in Pontalba Buildings with French glass, base to be painted a dark brown. Entire front and flanks of stores to be plastered with best Rosendale cement and colored to suit owner; Countess or Dutchess slate roof. Front lintels and window sills of openings to be of granite or Connecticut brown stone as owner may desire.

An auction drawing of 1854 shows the original appearance of the stores. The cast-iron pillars at the ground level had Corinthian capitals and applied decoration. Between the pillars were paneled four-fold doors. A cast-iron balcony and canopy ran the length of the building. Windows had cap-moulded lintels (pedimented lintels, as well as quoins, have been added to the store at the corner of Gravier). A side elevation on Union shows two, three-story stores of the same design at the rear of the St. Charles stores, connected by a passage containing service buildings. This Union store remains and has retained the original cast-iron pillars.

An identical store facing on Gravier has been demolished. This lot was the site of the First Congregational Church, built in 1819 by William Brand in the Gothic style. No. 309½ was the first home of the Pickwick Club between 1857-1865.

317 St. Charles. B. Simon lithograph. (Courtesy Historic New Orleans Collection.)

317 St. Charles. Part of Judah Touro row facing St. Charles with Union elevation. Simon lithograph illustrates this building in its original state. Terra cotta front is a fine example. However, the unity and symmetry of the original row has been destroyed by this 20th century facade. The Louisiana Club, founded in 1877, is presently housed in this building. The original home was at old No. 24 Baronne (demolished); second location was on corner Baronne and Canal. By 1884 the club house was located at old No. 144 Canal (demolished), between the Pickwick and Boston Clubs. Club quarters were recently moved from a commercial building designed by James Gallier at the uptown river corner of St. Charles and Gravier.

545 St. Charles, at Lafayette Square. City Hall (Gallier Hall). Architect James Gallier, Sr., and builder Robert Seaton designed and constructed this landmark between 1845 and 1850 for a projected cost of $120,000, which eventually totalled $342,000 (*Picayune,* March 25, 1851). It was dedicated on May 10, 1853.

The best surviving example of Greek Revival architecture in a city that once had more monumental Grecian specimens than ancient Athens in its prime, and an outstanding example nationally. It was to be built of marble on a granite basement, but actually was constructed predominantly in brick, plastered over, colored and scored to resemble stone. The marble portico and finely detailed portal are modeled after the North porch of the famed Erechtheum on the Acropolis. The hexastyle front has a total of ten columns, however, instead of the Erechtheum's six, in a tetrastyle arrangement. The bases of the columns have plinths and the frieze is unornamented but surmounted by dentils.

Very pure Greek detail by this follower and former associate of Minard Lefever can be seen in the acroteria topping the pediment, the anthemion (honeysuckle) ornament on the raking cornice, the plain moulded capitals of the pilasters and the angled volutes at the corner capitals, with oddly intersecting scrolls at the inner corner (as in the Erechtheum porch). Exceptions to the Greek tradition are the Roman podium and broad stairs, the tomb-like parapet motives above the Lafayette Street facade—so like the Regency designs of Sir John Soane—and the American figures in high

relief in the tympanum, with Liberty supporting Justice and Commerce, by Robert A. Launitz of New York.

The decor of the spacious mayor's parlor is intact, and the broad central hall, extending the length of the building, could be an impressive space if divested of the expensive, garish chandeliers recently hung there. The stairway to one side of the central hall originally rose to a third-story Lecture Hall or Lyceum, the most spacious and beautiful apartment in the building," as Gallier noted in his autobiography. "The ceiling is arched, elaborately ornamented and furnished with large ventilators very tastefully designed," he wrote. This impressive room, "of sufficient capacity to contain three or four hundred persons," was destroyed to make offices after the Civil War. Its details and

high arched ceiling, as well as the unusual construction, with a span of eighty-six feet, according to Gallier, "partly of wood and partly of iron," may be seen in the surviving drawings. Only seven sheets were required, for which the architect received a fee of 2½ percent of cost, plus $1,000 paid in advance.

This headquarters of the Second Municipality was built toward the end of a seventeen-year period of internal strife, when the entirely separate government of the First Municipality remained housed in the Cabildo on Jackson Square. In 1852 the three divisions of the City were reunited, and Gallier's monument became the City Hall of New Orleans. (Lithograph by T. K. Wharton, 1848. Courtesy Historic New Orleans Collection.)

304 St. Charles, corner Gravier, bound by Camp, Commercial Alley. Two, four-story masonry stores with cast-iron hood moulds, brackets and cornice in Italian Renaissance design, a fine example of that style in commercial buildings. Designed and built in 1855 by Gallier, Turpin and Company for Charles Mason, agent of Robert Heath in England, for $14,000. Drawing of original elevation shows buildings painted in pastel shades, with covered cast-iron gallery supported on iron slender columns (Labrot Collection, Tulane University Library). Gallier and Turpin built for Robert Heath on this block several other identical stores which are no longer standing.

Across the street in the 200 block of St. Charles, Gallier and Turpin built two more four-story stores in 1855 for Charles Mason for his own investment. These structures were later demolished. The building at 304 St. Charles replaces an earlier one designed possibly by J. H. Dakin in 1845. It was destroyed by fire in 1845. In 1855 the *Picayune* reported that the 1845 building was occupied by ice cream saloons and Vannuchi's Wax Works.

500 block St. Charles, bound by North, Poydras, Camp. (Old Nos. 110, 112, 114.) Row of large three-and-one-half story plastered brick houses and stores designed by James Gallier for Amaron Ledoux to house the firm Ledoux and Hall and built in 1841 on property that Ledoux bought from James H. Caldwell in 1836. This important building appears in the 1852 skyline view of New Orleans from St. Patrick's Church by B. F. Smith and J. W. Hill (see cover).

The corner part of this complex is heavily rusticated at the ground level and has galleries at the second and third levels across the front and sides. These features were added after 1852 as the galleries do not appear in the Smith and Hill view. A stepped gable end and cap-moulded, slightly arched window cornices enhance the appearance of the complex. The continuing facade is unified by denticulated cornice and a deep frieze, which once served as an architrave to an entablature which included the attic windows. The attic windows have been enlarged, cutting the architrave. The facade is scored plaster; alterations appear at the first level; windows have been changed and wrought iron balcony at second level removed.

This outstanding block of buildings, designed by the city's most renowned architect and still intact, should receive recognition. The property, however, has received poor treatment by owners subsequent to Ledoux, who died in 1875. The corner section was sold separately to Smithson Davis in 1877 for $4,500. Mrs. Mary Robinson Miles sold it to People's Homestead May 5, 1892, for $8,650, and Andrew McDermott received title the same year for $6,800. Adam Wirth acquired it February 28, 1907, for $17,500 and his heirs own the property now.

208 St. Charles, bound by Common, Gravier, Camp. Four-story, plastered brick, six-bay building in the style of the late 1880s, with emphasis on Italianate arches, rustication and variety of pilasters and decorated spandrels.

308-10, 314 St. Charles, bound by Gravier, Commercial Alley, Camp. These two simple, brick, four-story Greek Revival stores are an interesting contrast to the adjoining Italianate structure. They were built in 1850 for Charles Pride, builder for Charles Mason, as the St. Charles fronts of 317 Camp. They probably had cast-iron pillars similar to those at 317 Camp.

401 St. Charles, corner Commercial Place, bound by Poydras, Camp. The St. Charles facade of the Balter Building at the corner of Commercial Place on the Riverside of the street is discussed in a Camp Street listing.

316-18 St. Charles, bound by Gravier, Poydras, Magazine. In *Englehardt's* (1903), this was the New Orleans home of John Deere Plow Company, "manufacturers of Deere Vehicles, John Deere Plows, Cultivators, etc. St. Louis, Mo., Dallas, Texas to New Orleans, La." Based on a description from a picture in *Englehardt*, the building had a semicircular parapet in the center of the roofline, which has been removed. The bottom floor had iron columns fronting masonry piers, four-fold doors, paneled at the bottom and glazed at the top, arches between the columns under the lintel course. The building was red brick. It is possible that this store was designed by Henry Howard and was erected in 1872.

603 St. Charles. Soule College Building, 1870. (Courtesy Historic New Orleans Collection.)

603 St. Charles, corner Lafayette, bound by Carondelet, Girod. Soule College. Four-story red brick building erected in 1902 for George Soule to house the Soule Commercial College and Literary Institute which Soule had founded in 1856. In 1874 Soule bought the first Second Municipality Hall on this site, remodeled it and used it for the school until he had it demolished to build the present structure. The building remains intact, with the exception of the clock tower, which is missing. This building and many on the uptown side are reported to be owned by the Stringer family who, if willing, could restore a sizeable link of 19th century New Orleans architecture facing Lafayette Square. (Photograph from George W. Engelhardt's *City of New Orleans,* Chamber of Commerce, 1903. Courtesy New Orleans Public Library.)

603 St. Charles. Old Second Municipal Hall watercolor, c. 1840. (Courtesy Confederate Memorial Museum.)

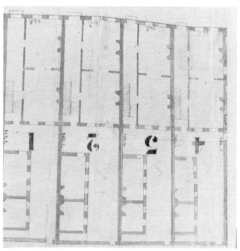

629, 631-33, 635-37, 639-41 St. Charles. Drawing and floor plan by Isaac L. McCoy, 1837, Book 23, Folio 55, New Orleans Notarial Archives.

629, 631-33, 635-37, 639-41 St. Charles, bound by Girod, Lafayette, Carondelet. Lots each have 24 feet, 6 inch front on St. Charles, by 101 feet. The first and fourth buildings from the left, in extremely mutilated condition, are two remaining of four brick houses built by James Gallier in 1836 for speculator Samuel Moore for $32,000.

As seen in the 1837 archival drawing, each house had two-and-one-half stories with a simple entrance, all openings having marble sills and cap-moulded lintels. There was a wrought iron balcony of simple design at the second level and an entablature with a deep architrave, attic windows in a frieze and a narrow cornice. Such an entablature with architrave was a favorite Gallier hallmark. The plans show the simple and typical three-bay design, with stairhall to one side and double parlors with sliding doors having two windows across the front. Note that the service wing here was detached from the rear of the house (signifying the early date of the building in Faubourg St. Mary).

The building contract gives these details (Hilary Breton Cenas, notary, January 28, 1836): "The foundations are to be dug two feet below the banquette." The fronts on both streets were to be "Baltimore or Philadelphia pressed bricks…the front walls to be two bricks thick from the banquette to the height of three and one-half feet, and one and a half bricks thick from thence to the tops. The first story…thirteen feet in height, the second story…twelve feet and the attic story… five feet five inches." There were to be "two oval cast-iron and framed gratings at the front; the roofs to be covered with zinc with the roof of the corner house to be hipped. The front entrance doors to have tongued and moulded casings and large composition rosettes fixed in the face of the architrave round the door in the recess. The upper panels of the door to have glass set in them to light the hall and inside shutters fitted against the lights. The parlour doors to be framed in four panels hung in proper rebatted casings with architraves and door caps. The sliding doors to have casings trimmed with pilasters fixed on each side." There was to be a "small upper cornice with dentils underneath…The blinds, iron railings and lattice work to be painted green."

Samuel Moore apparently suffered financial reverses while the buildings were being erected and sold them to Thomas Barrett at an auction in 1837 for $20,100. Their disposition did not improve and successive sheriff's sales ensued, one for only $12,000 in 1867. No. 641, the corner building, was the home and dentists' office of Drs. George J. and Andrew G. Freidrichs in the late 19th century. The property had been used as sugar land by Jean Gravier in 1803 before its sale to Jean Joseph Jourdan. The heirs of Jourdan sold it in 1832 to Samuel Moore.

The two, three-story, party wall townhouses standing between the remaining Gallier houses and the three-story brick townhouse to the right in the photograph show vestiges of fine construction and decorative detail beneath their present mutilation. The facade of the third house from the left was altered in the 1880s. The proportions and floor plan of the earlier house remain illustrating the popularity of the old classic forms and floor plans in New Orleans.

629-41 St. Charles, corner Girod, bound by Lafayette, Carondelet. Drawing by Isaac L. McCoy, Plan Book 23, Folio 55, New Orleans Notarial Archives.

609 St. Charles, bound by Lafayette, Girod, Carondelet. Three-story, plastered brick Greek Revival house with cast-iron gallery on two levels. Door with sidelight and transom with brackets behind a classic entrance with wood pilasters and denticulated entablature. First-floor windows have been removed. Information in the books of J. B. Walton, auctioneer, and a building contract dated October 25, 1853, indicate that Mrs. Cuthbert Bullit had this house rebuilt in 1853 by Edward Gotthiel, builder, for $10,000. One of the two remaining of the many residences that once faced Lafayette Square.

628 St. Charles, bound by South, Girod, Camp. Lafayette Hotel. Built in 1908 for Adam Wirth, the hotel replaced a "two and a half [story] brick slated residence," according to Williams and Patton's description of property, May 6, 1887. In 1852 the lot, measuring 149 feet front on St. Charles and 25 feet depth on South and Girod, was owned by W. H. Avery and J. B. Winston and valued at $16,000. This yellow brick, five-story hotel has clean, subtle lines, quoins and terra cotta architraves around casement transom doors on second level. The monogrammed wrought iron balcony is supported with paired "S" scroll brackets. The rusticated first level has rounded arched sections and a handsome art nouveau-type marquee.

711, 713, 715 St. Charles, bound by Girod, Lafayette, Carondelet. Two, three-story Italianate stores. Remaining entrance at No. 715 gives a glimpse of the former elegance here. The cornice has paired brackets and dentils.

727 St. Charles, bound by Girod, Lafayette, Carondelet. Mutilated three-story, brick, three-bay townhouse, part of a former row probably built in the 1840s. Cast-iron gallery at second and third levels. All galleries are covered. Formerly had a wood Greek Key entrance. Lintels are marble, brick cornice has deep dentils and windows have original lights. The house was owned by John Larkin Strong in 1862 and valued by J. B. Walton, auctioneer, at $10,000. Adjacent to the left was the Davidson mansion, set back in a large lot. It was one of the important mansions of Faubourg St. Mary. Next to Davidson's residence the Exposition Building for the Washington Artillery, running through to Carondelet, was built.

St. Charles, corner Julia, bound by Carondelet. Remnant of carriage house, once part of the complex of the famous Campbell Mansion, perhaps the most resplendent of Faubourg St. Mary's mansions.

Lafayette Square, from St. Charles Street, as depicted in *Ballou's Pictorial Drawing Room Companion,* April 30, 1859. (Courtesy Louisiana Collection, Special Collections Division, Tulane University Library.)

822 St. Charles, bound by Julia, Camp, St. Joseph. (Old No. 218 in 1866; No. 850 in 1899). Four-story, detached masonry townhouse with scored facade. Even with the false entrance to the left and 20th century neo-Italianizing, there is evidence of the one-time grandeur of this home. This property, 50 feet front by 172 feet depth, was purchased by John Davidson, along with No. 826 (38 feet by 172 feet). The plan and elevation of a house which formerly occupied this lot and of which this may be a rebuilding are illustrated, along with that of the adjacent house, in an 1857 auction drawing. The two houses were identical, simple three-story Greek Revival structures (see drawing for 826 St. Charles).

The house was standing on the lot in 1857 when it was to be sold at public auction with the adjoining house. The Davidson family avoided the sale at the last minute and apparently sold it on April 2, 1866, to Humphrey Woodhouse for $26,000 after the property had been transferred the same year from John to James Davidson. Misfortune followed Civil War inflationary real estate values, and Woodhouse lost his home to Joseph Herwig at public auction for $9,000. Since then, it has been a portion of large real estate holdings of various investors and realty companies. What had been a lovely residence inhabited by the owners became an impersonal piece of low-rent property, changing hands frequently. By the time Ralph Katz acquired it in 1942 the front footage had been cut to 34 feet.

826 St. Charles, bound by Julia, St. Joseph, Carondelet. (Old No. 206.) The successive stages in the history of this once-fine Greek Revival house are both visually and historically documented. When John Davidson partitioned his 85-foot front lots in 1844, Needler Robinson Jennings acquired this lot. It changed hands rapidly from Jennings to Maunsell White, who sold to Mrs. Maria Davis Taylor. There had been buildings on the property when Mrs. Taylor acquired it on May 18, 1846, for $4,560, but they did not include this three-story house.

On November 16, 1848, Joseph Saul purchased the property from Mrs. Taylor for $5,000. He had this house built as a three-story, detached brick townhouse before 1851, since a building contract of that date for 822 Camp specifies a feature of Saul's house was to be copied. This house, as it appeared then, is seen in the Notarial Archives drawing.

The new building was sold at public auction in 1857, and a group of men, including Dr. William Newton Mercer and Samuel Smith, purchased it for $15,700. The house had a grained paneled door with transom and sidelights recessed behind pilasters *as antae* supporting an entablature. The facade had neither balcony nor gallery, and the bricks were exposed in Eastern seaboard fashion. A simple denticulated cornice complimented the denticulated cornice of the entrance entablature. The windows had green louvered shutters. Fronting the house was a fine iron fence which, according to building contract specifications, was duplicated on the house at 822 Camp. The floor plan shows the house to have been three rooms deep, with the two front parlors sided by a stair hall. A service wing extended at the rear.

Samuel Smith acquired the house from his associates, living there until 1866 when on November 21 of that year he sold it to Joseph Henry Oglesby. Oglesby was a prominent commission merchant from 1850 and was wealthy at the time of his death in 1888. He left an estate valued at $200,997, including $25,000 in New Orleans property and the

Blue Bay Plantation in St. Mary Parish. The Oglesby residence, as pictured in *Jewell's* (1873), shows that fine galleries with cresting on the second level, front and side, had been added to the house. The facade had been plastered. After Oglesby died, Joseph Herwig bought the house from his widow, Margaret Hendricks Oglesby, in 1888.

By 1936 the house had become rental property of the St. Charles Realty Company, and the facade had been covered, an attic story added and an annex built between the former carriage-way and the house. An interested owner could restore the entrance and remove recent additions, thus restoring a lovely facade to its former appearance. The attic story might remain, since it was a tasteful addition to enlarge interior space.

826 St. Charles. From Jewell's *Crescent City* (1873). Residence of Jos. H. Oglesby, Esq. (Old No. 206 St. Charles.) (Courtesy New Orleans Public Library.)

826 St. Charles. Drawing, Plan Book 43, Folio 46, May 4, 1857, New Orleans Notarial Archives.

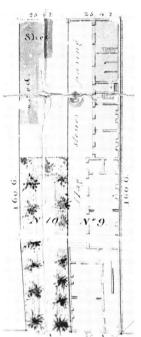

827 St. Charles. Drawing and floor plan by Charles A. de Armas, 1866, Book 43, Folio 68, New Orleans Notarial Archives.

863-865-67 St. Charles, corner St. Joseph, Carondelet, Howard. Two detached four-bay, two-story storehouses. Cap moulded lintels, formerly cast iron galleries on both structures. These structures exemplify an early type of which few remain in the old Faubourg St. Mary

827 St. Charles, bound by St. Joseph, Julia. This three-story, brick Greek Revival townhouse resembled two others (now demolished) built in this block between 1856 and 1860. Built in 1856 by J. H. Murphy, builder for John P. Cody, at cost of $12,250, according to building contract specifications (W. H. Peters, notary, May 2, 1856). The house has a 25-foot, four-inch front and an iron verandah at the second-floor level. The house was "to resemble in style and structure that of Mr. Behan. To be built of hard well burned country or lake bricks set in river sand and fresh Thomaston lime mortar.... Yard and banquet to be of North-river Blue flagstone...Welsh slate roof, French glass in window lights [except] the parlor windows to have best English glass."

There were specifications for a wine and china closet in the passage leading from the dining room to the kitchen and two wardrobes in the passage on the third story lined with cedar. There were stipulations for a wood and coal shed at the end of the yard opposite the carriage house, stables, chicken coop and an 18-inch-high brick wall to form a flower bed, cast-iron hitching post and cast-iron hydrant. The interior specifications included a cornice in the parlours, hall, sitting rooms and dining rooms and a three-foot center in the hall. "Doors and sashes of first and second story sitting room and the dining room...to be grained imitation of oak....Base to be painted imitation of marble."

The openings in the hall and parlours were to receive four coats "of gloss white; blinds to be Paris green.... Gas pipes to be laid to parlour, hall, sitting room and dining room [with pipes for two fittings] in nursery and in each other room....Ten bells to be installed in different rooms. Parlours to have instead of sliding doors one elliptic arch with smaller ones at each side supported with fluted columns and caps after the Corinthian order of architecture. There will be inside shutters in front windows in parlour."

This outstanding home has most of its interior features preserved and is in excellent condition because of the care of Mrs. Maria de Molina. This block, so desirable for development in the 1850s, had been donated in 1817 by Julien Poydras to the Female Orphan Society, which retained ownership of half the block in 1852, according to J. B. Walton, auctioneer-surveyor. In March, 1856, this lot and four others were leased to R. W. Montgomery for a long term lasting into the 20th century. The lessee was obliged to improve the property, but he "shall not erect... any foundry blacksmith or other workshops, livery stables or slate lumber brick depots or grog shops." The adjacent house to the right (now demolished) was built by Samuel Stewart, builder, for Mrs. Joseph E. Walter, at a cost of $9,400 in 1860, according to an act of W. J. Castell, notary, January 17, 1860.

735-37 St. Joseph, bound by St. Charles, Carondelet, Julia. This two-story, Greek Revival plastered brick residence with cast-iron gallery at second level has a heavy segmented parapet, gabled ends with chimneys and deep dentils. After the original subdivision by the Delord family, Nicholas Franklin bought the square and in 1830 sold to Maunsell White this lot and four others to the corner of Carondelet. White sold two of the five lots to Mrs. A. White Franklin, Nicholas' widow, for $5,000. She built a row of houses, two of which remain. She sold the house pictured here for $5,000. This once-attractive house is located on a cobblestone street in an area that again could be desirable. It has been sold ten times since its erection for sums ranging from $3,000 to a high of $8,500 in the earlier part of this century. Among the residents of this home were Thomas Parker, sheriff of Orleans Parish in 1869, who rented the building, and John Finney, associate in the law firm of Judah P. Benjamin.

810 St. Joseph, bound by Baronne, Carondelet, Howard. This three-story brick house, with cast-iron gallery at the second and third levels, has a fine Greek Key entrance capped by a denticulated cornice. Granite steps lead to a recessed paneled door, which may be original. The two windows of the lower facade have been removed. The window lintels of the upper levels are cap-moulded, and the window muntin arrangement remains intact. The balconies have been removed from the adjacent house, and the first level has been considerably altered.

Lots in this block were acquired by prominent cotton exporter Richard Terrell, who lived in the Lower Garden District on Magazine. When Terrell owned the land, a two-story house, kitchen and stable were erected, but he lost the property to the Citizen's Bank of Louisiana in 1843. The bank sold the lot and buildings at a sheriff's sale in 1846 to Mrs. Adelaide T. Morgan Eastman for $4,000. Soon after, she had the present house built. She also had an identical house (partially visible at right in photograph) built on the adjacent lot. Each had a 25-foot front. By 1866 they were valued at $14,000 each by J. B. Walton, auctioneer. Mrs. Eastman lost this house in an 1874 sheriff's sale for $4,700, and at eight subsequent sales through 1939 the property did not increase in value beyond the 1917 value of $5,000.

468 St. Joseph, bound by Magazine, Howard, Constance. B. F. Nichols, architect, designed this three-story brick townhouse, built in 1846 by John Mitchell, Joseph Howell and Moses H. Coats, architects and builders, for John B. B. Voisin. Joseph and J. B. B. Voisin owned all the property along St. Joseph in this block and probably had similar houses built. This once-fine residence has a Greek Key frame entrance, a simple wrought iron balcony at the second level, a brick denticulated cornice, frieze and parapet and granite lintels above on the original multi-light windows. At present a refacing of the ground floor and fire escape and absence of the original door alters the otherwise fine facade. The lot has a 22-foot, 6-inch front on St. Joseph and is 84 feet, one inch deep.

Riverfront of Faubourg St. Mary. Detail from an old engraving, drawn on stone by D. W. Moody, courtesy Historic New Orleans Collection.

Fourteen-year-old John Rowlands, later known as Sir Henry Morton Stanley, the celebrated African explorer, arrived in New Orleans in the winter of 1855 by ship, having worked his way from Liverpool as a cabin boy. The young and destitute orphan observed New Orleans carefully and found a great deal about it to admire, although he certainly was exposed to the city's worst elements and lived a hand-to-mouth existence.

Included here are excerpts from his autobiography, published by the Riverside Press [Cambridge: 1909], in which he describes the New Orleans Central Business District: "We reached the top of Tchapitoulas Street [sic.], the main commercial artery of the city. The people were thronging home from the business quarters, to the more residential part.... The soft, balmy air, with its strange scents of fermenting molasses, semi-baked sugar, green coffee, pitch, Stockholm tar, brine of mess-beef, rum and whiskey drippings, contributed a great deal towards imparting the charm of romance to everything I saw. In the vicinity of Poydras Street, we halted before a boarding house where we sat down to okra soup, grits, sweet potatoes, brinjalls, corn scones, mush-pudding, and 'fixings'—every article but the bread was strange and toothsome. [The next day], hastening across the levee, I entered the great commercial street of the city, at a point not far from St. Thomas Street, and after a little inward debate, continued down Tchapitoulas Street, along the sidewalk....

"The store-owners' names were mostly foreign, and suggestive of Teutonic and Hibernian origin; but the larger buildings were of undeniable Anglo Saxon. At the outset, lager-beer saloons were frequent; then followed more shanties, with rusty tin roofs; but beyond these, the stores were more massive and uniform, and over the doors were the inscriptions, 'Produce and Commission Merchants' etc. I obtained a view of the interior.... Negroes commenced to sweep the long alleys be-tween the good piles and to propel the dust and rubbish of the previous day's traffic towards the open gutter. Then flour, whiskey, and rum barrels, marked and branded, were rolled out, and arranged near the kerbstone. Hogsheads and tierces were set on end, cases were built, sacks were laid out in orderly layers, awaiting removal by drays, which, at a later hour, would convey them to the river-steamers....Soon after seven, I had arrived near the end of the long street; and I could see the colossal Custom-House, and its immense scaffolding....

"I was permanently engaged at twenty-five dollars a month [at Speake and McCreary, commission merchants, 109 Tchoupitoulas]. Such a sum left me with fifteen dollars a month, net, after payment of board and lodging, and was quite a fortune in my eyes....I shared in the citizens' pride in their splendid port, the length and stability of their levee, their unparalleled lines of shipping, their magnificent array of steamers, and their majestic river. I believed with them, that their Custom-House, when completed, would be a matchless edifice, that Canal Street was unequalled for its breadth, that Tchapitoulas Street, was, beyond compare, the busiest street in the world, that no markets equalled those of New Orleans for their variety of produce, and that no city, not even Liverpool, could exhibit such mercantile enterprise or such a smart go-ahead spirit, as old and young manifested in the chief city of the South....

"Mrs. Stanley [who later adopted him] resided on St. Charles Street....I went to St. Charles Street, a quarter greatly superior to St. Thomas Street. The houses were aristocratic, being of classic design, with pillared porticoes, and wide, cool verandahs, looking out upon garden-shrubbery and flowering magnolias....The summer of 1859 was extremely unhealthy. Yellow fever and dysentery were raging. What a sickly season meant I could not guess; for, in those days I never read a newspaper, and the city traffic to all appearance was much as usual. On Mr. Speake's face, however, I noticed lines of suffering. Three or four days later he was dead."

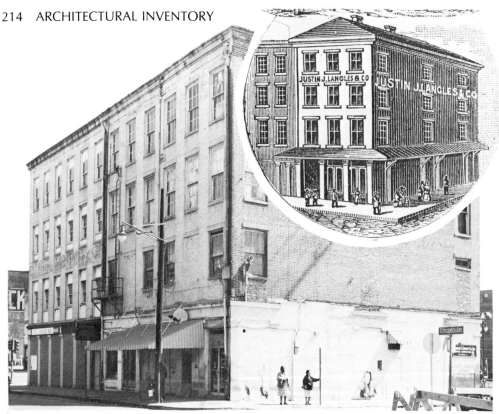

300 block Canal, the same building which fronts on 106-110 Tchoupitoulas.

106-108-110 Tchoupitoulas, corner Common, bound by S. Peters, Canal. Four-story masonry commercial building filling a triangle plot. The portion fronting Canal was built in 1842 by Ambrose C. Fulton for Jacob Florance. It was recorded as a house to stand on "New Levee," corner Canal and Tchoupitoulas, with similarities to the adjoining buildings owned by Paul Tulane and Woolfolk.

The building contract recorded by Wm. Cristy (Vol. 44, Folio 87) specifies: "Walls facing streets…one and a half brick faced with first quality Lake brick laid in Flemish bond with mortar of sharp sand; rear wall two bricks thick…country brick with mortar of Thomaston lime…cornice of Lake brick of same style and pattern as the buildings of Peter and Millard on Tchoupitoulas next to the buildings of the Orphan Girls Asylum….Doors of basement to be grained imitation of oak, color of brick front to resemble J. S. Florence block of buildings in Magazine between Gravier and Common….four double folded sash doors with movable shutters. Shutters in second story to be paneled like Tulane's and cut across so as to open to lower or upper sash but those of third and fourth stories to be same as Woolfolk's adjoining Paul Tulane's store…granite sills and lintels."

Cost was $5,000. In *Soards* (1882), the store at 110 Tchoupitoulas was illustrated as Langles and Co., producers of biscuits, crackers, cakes, vermicelli and macaroni. Ground floor at that time had a canopy. (Courtesy New Orleans Public Library.)

300 Tchoupitoulas, corner Gravier, bound by Natchez, S. Peters. There remains on this square a fine group of commercial buildings, two small three-story, four-bay stores of the mid-nineteenth century on Gravier, a four-story store at the corner of Tchoupitoulas and Gravier, dating from the 1840s, and a late Italianate store at the right of the photograph. The four-story group of stores has granite pillars and a lintel course. The masonry facades are scored with a crisp frieze and denticulated cornice. The complex retains most of the original window muntins and the paneled windows at the first level. The property was owned in 1862 by M. A. Montgomery and Mary Noonan. An 1881-82 advertisement indicates the four-story corner building was occupied by W. R. Irby and Brother, wholesale tobacconists.

109 Tchoupitoulas, bound by Common, Canal, Magazine. The store on the right of the photograph was built by Sidle and Stewart for Julien Colvis and Joseph Dumas in 1840. It was one of a group. The other two, on Common, between Magazine and Tchoupitoulas,

are no longer standing. Cost of the three stores was $24,500. In 1854 this was the wholesale grocery firm of Speake and McCreary (old No. 3). Sir Henry Morton Stanley, the renowned explorer, came to New Orleans from Liverpool in 1854 as an orphan named John Rowlands and worked in this store. The young boy was befriended by an acquaintance of McCreary and Henry Hope Stanley adopted the boy, giving him his name.

Sir Henry's autobiography describes his daily activities in this store and his impressions of New Orleans in 1854. According to J. B. Walton, Paul Tulane owned the brick store in the middle of the group, built in the 1840s. The corner store at Common, with granite pillars below, has iron scroll brackets supporting a sidewalk canopy which was added in the late 19th century. The building probably dates after 1840, as indicated by beak capitals on granite pillars. By 1852 James H. Dudley owned the property, selling it to Miss Ida Slocomb and George W. Munson by 1866.

300 Tchoupitoulas. From Land's *Pen Illustrations of New Orleans, 1881-82.* (Courtesy Historic New Orleans Collection.)

300 Block Tchoupitoulas, Natchez, Gravier, Magazine. At the corner of Tchoupitoulas and Natchez is the four-story brick store Henry Howard designed for Mrs. Henry Bonnabel (Julia Macartney) in 1856. He also designed for her a two-story warehouse (now demolished) around the corner fronting on Natchez. John Collins built the complex for $9,600. The site had previously housed Bonnabel's house and pharmacy, built in 1832 for $30,000. Mrs. Bonnabel arranged for the old buildings and works to be carefully dismantled and the material reused.

The building contract (S. Magner, notary, June 14, 1856) specifies that the first story front on Tchoupitoulas would have cast-iron posts and lintels, moulded cornice and plain blocking on top. The posts were to be 18 inches on the face and 15 inches deep, paneled on the side and front. The roof was to be of English tile. Some old walls of the previous building were left standing and the earlier granite sills and lintels reused. The doors were four-fold, 2¾-inch-thick cypress, framed in moulded panels hung on solid timber jambs secured to iron posts. The upper panels were glazed with double-thickness French cylinder glass and grained to resemble oak. The facade was painted light-brown stone-color and properly sanded, jointed and painted to imitate masonry. The interior stairs were cypress, and the mantels of the second story of the store were to be of a wood "with a neat pilaster pattern, painted black and varnished." Four-fold interior shutters covered the windows.

Five adjacent buildings in the block may have been built in 1842 when James H. Dakin made a plan of the block (December 15, 1842). Mrs. Cora Ann Cox, widow of Samuel B. Slocomb, bought six stores from the Union Bank of Louisiana for $112,500 on December 7, 1846. The four stores to the right have a continuous cornice with dentils. Some original, or early, doors remain on the stores.

301-05 Tchoupitoulas, corner Gravier, bound by Natchez, Magazine. This late Italianate, three-story commercial building has large keystones in the segmental arches on the second level and in the full arches above featuring moulded architraves. It was built for Edward Conery, Sr., after he acquired the property at a sheriff's sale on September 5, 1866. The Conery family retained the property until 1898 when it was acquired by the Hibernia National Bank.

308 Tchoupitoulas, bound by Gravier, Natchez, S. Peters. Four-story commercial building erected at the turn of the century and divided by pilasters into three-bays, the center one wider, with paneled spandrels and decorative mouldings. The central emphasis of the facade is continued by a large curved parapet. The cornice is of pressed metal, with garlands and ribbons decorating the frieze. The wide overhang is supported by paired brackets. The tri-fold doors at the first level are protected by decorative iron grills. A canopy supported by ornate brackets shades the entrance.

401, 411 Tchoupitoulas, corner Poydras, bound by Natchez, Magazine. Two, three-story commercial buildings, one larger in scale. The store on the right was erected after 1840, as the granite pillars have beak capitals. In 1871 this store was occupied by Mayer Brothers, dealers in chewing, smoking and leaf tobacco, a firm established in 1849. The *City Directory* (1871) and a Simon lithograph of the same year illustrate that the windows had louvered shutters. The building on the left is an Italianate version of the same type, with hood moulds over the windows, segmental arches in the upper windows, a cornice with paired brackets and a parapet. The entire building was formerly plastered as the cornice, but the plaster has been stripped away and the bottom floor enclosed.

510 Tchoupitoulas, Corner Poydras, bound by Commerce, Lafayette. A row of six stores, built as a unit, with Italianate cast-iron hood moulds over segmental arched windows, modillions at the cornice and a parapet in the center of the roofline. The roof projection at right is a modern addition. The ground floor has cast-iron pillars supporting an iron lintel course, with shouldered arches between the pillars. These stores probably were built before 1869 when Nicholas Burke, owner of the last store to the right, had a three-story brick building erected at the rear of his store (W. J. Castell, notary, July 27, 1869). At the turn of the century the structures were occupied by the large concern of H. T. Cottam & Co., wholesale grocers, as indicated in the *Englehardt* (1903) illustration.

510 Tchoupitoulas. From George Engelhardt's *City of New Orleans,* Chamber of Commerce, 1904. Courtesy New Orleans Public Library.)

400-410 Tchoupitoulas, corner Natchez, bound by Poydras, S. Peters. Three, three-story commercial buildings, the center one of smaller scale. The taller buildings have cast-iron pillars on the ground floor. The center building has brick pillars and a parapet. The store at the left has retained original four-fold doors and a shop window.

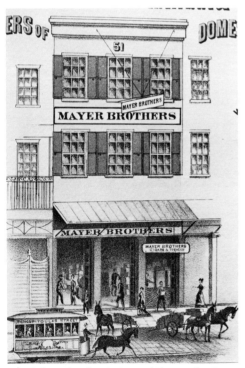

411 Tchoupitoulas. B. Simon lithograph. (Courtesy Historic New Orleans Collection.)

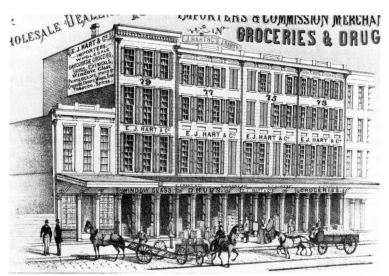

517, 529, 531, 533 Tchoupitoulas. B. Simon lithograph. (Courtesy Historic New Orleans Collection.)

517, 521, 525, 527, 529, 531, 533 Tchoupitoulas, bound by Lafayette, Poydras, Constance. Several of the stores in this block are well-documented. No. 529, the second store from the corner of Lafayette (from the left in the photograph), was erected by William Belly, builder, for Julien Clovis in 1854 at a cost of $6,350. It appears in an 1870 lithograph by Simon when it and the adjoining buildings comprised E. J. Hart and Company, importers and commission merchants. At ground level are cast-iron pillars with acanthus leaf capitals. The store has granite lintels over the windows and dentils at the cornice.

In 1854 Aldophe D'Aquin had Samuel Jamison and James McIntosh, builders, erect a store for him on the third lot from the corner, now occupied by a modern building (old No. 77 in Simon lithograph). Jamison and McIntosh also completed a store in 1854 for Samuel J. Peters and the late Charles Millard next to D'Aquin's store at old No. 75 (fourth building in row from left). Presumably, the fifth building in the row (old No. 73), which is identical, was built at the same time for Peters and Millard.

No specifications accompany the building contract for the Peters and Millard store (T. Guyol, October 26, 1854), but the contract stipulated that the store was to be built like the adjoining D'Aquin store (now demolished, old no. 77). Therefore, the specifications for the D'Aquin store (T. Guyol, August 22, 1854) can be used to describe the three identical buildings in the row. The best quality, well burnt, "country bricks" were used. The fronts were to be plastered with hydraulic cement and sharp sand, then "colored and blocked off to represent sand stone of such a shade as the owner may select." Windows were to have granite sills and lintels and the ground-level store iron pillars. These iron pillars, which remain on one store, are identical to those on the Clovis store (old no. 79). The interior also was to have "iron columns." Doors were to be paneled, four-fold, with glass in the upper panels and removable shutters, and were to be painted two-tone green. The window shutters, which appear in the Simon lithograph, were iron and painted chrome green. The iron pillars and lintel course were to be "painted two heavy coats and sanded" to resemble stone.

The lithograph shows the stores with a sidewalk canopy supported by scroll brackets. Part of it remains. The stores have recessed panels between the upper-floor windows and panels and paired corbels at the cornice and parapets, all of which add interest to the facades. The eighth building in the row, no. 517 (at the right in the photograph), is identical to these stores, except that the ground floor contains granite pillars with beak capitals.

Millard also owned this property, and the store probably was erected by him. The simpler brick stores at 521-525 have massive granite piers with beak capitals. Peters and Millard also owned this property. These stores at the right of the photograph have a sidewalk canopy with ornate cast-iron brackets. All these stores run through the block.

517-533 Tchoupitoulas. View from Poydras to end of block.

534, 538-40 Tchoupitoulas, bound by Poydras, Lafayette, Commerce. The building on the left is a three-story, masonry commercial structure with cast-iron pillars at the ground level (two have been removed) and cornice with paired brackets surmounted by a parapet. The windows have iron shutters; an awning with ornate cast-iron brackets has been added at the first level. At right is a two-story Italianate store with segmental arched windows, corbel table and parapet and cast-iron supports at the first level. The cast-iron balcony, overhanging the sidewalk and supported by cast-iron posts, is probably a late 19th century addition.

600, 606, 608, 610, 614 Tchoupitoulas, bound by Lafayette, Girod, Commerce. Six, three-level brick stores, five in the classic style and one with segmental arched windows, cast-iron pillars and two sets of original doors. This classic style row was built in 1843 by John R. Pike, builder, who owned the second store from the left. The fourth and fifth stores from the left were erected by Pike for J. R. Geddes in 1843 at a cost of $4,300 (J. B. Marks, notary, June 1, 1843). The facades were to be built of Lake brick, painted and penciled, and other brick was to be "country brick." The first levels were to be of granite, and the buildings were to conform to the others in the row.

T. Nash owned the first and third stores from the left. In 1852 Geddes also owned a store on the site of the building, first from right in photograph, as well as other properties in the block. The building contract also lists Newton Richards as a builder. His large granite yard probably supplied the granite. In 1835 Richards' advertisement stated that his business was at 147 Customhouse (Iberville), between Dauphin and Burgundy. A note includes the information that the lower part of brick buildings could be removed and granite inserted with no risk and little inconvenience to the occupants.

633 Tchoupitoulas, bound by Lafayette, Girod, Constance. In 1849 Samuel Stewart built four, four-story brick stores at this location for Samuel Packwood. They were designed by noted architect Henry Howard. A fire in 1860 destroyed these buildings and much of the rest of the block. The walls of some of the buildings, which according to a newspaper report of that date were "a brick and a half thick and very poorly and scantily mortared," collapsed, and thirty or forty people were buried in the flaming rubble, with many being killed. The two stores standing at 633 Tchoupitoulas were built after the 1860 fire. They are of three stories with denticulated cornice, cap-moulded window lintels and cast-iron pillars at the first level.

701-703 Tchoupitoulas, corner Girod, bound by Notre Dame, Magazine. Two, two-story buildings, built in the Vieux Carre tradition of combining a store with a dwelling. Stores were located on the lower floors, with semi-circular arched openings, while the upper floors were devoted to living quarters. The buildings were standing in 1846 when Harvey North purchased the "stores with dwellings" from Logan Hunter for $15,600. They probably were built about 1830, which would make them among the earliest buildings in the business district area. The arched openings, small-scale fenestration and lack of Greek detailing point to this early date.

640, 648 Tchoupitoulas, corner Girod, bound by Common, Lafayette. Two, three-story masonry stores and one four-story. The three-story buildings have segmental arches over the windows and cast-iron pillars on the lower floors. The first floors of all three buildings have been altered.

923 Tchoupitoulas, Opposite N. Diamond, bound by Howard, St. Joseph. Gallier, Turpin and Company, architects and builders, constructed this store and warehouse in 1852 for the Leeds Iron Foundry, a firm established in New Orleans in 1825. The building is a rare example of the Gothic style in a commercial structure. The clustered columns and hood moulds are of cast-iron. The pointed windows at the second level have cast-iron tracery in a trefoil motif and the hood moulds are squared. Cap-moulding extend almost half-way down the window, terminating in bosses. The hood moulds at the third level conform to the outline of the pointed arches.

The original drawing for this building is in the Labrot Collection, Special Collections Division, Tulane University Library. Original doors between the clustered columns had glass panes two-thirds of the length, and the top pane was pointed in a Gothic arch. The lower one-third of the doors was paneled with inset quatrefoil motifs. By 1861 Leeds, which had specialized in the manufacture of agricultural equipment, began to divert its resources to the manufacture of war materials. Leeds manufactured the Saunders rifled cannon and other guns and cannon. The nearby Shakespeare Ironworks and John Armstrong's Foundry also were converted to war uses. The Leeds Foundry was built on the site of the E. E. Parker Iron Foundry, housed in thirteen three-story buildings which burned in 1835. In the late 19th century Schwartz Foundry took over Leeds' establishment. The location of this fine building works attractively in the park area opposite site of St. Mary's Market.

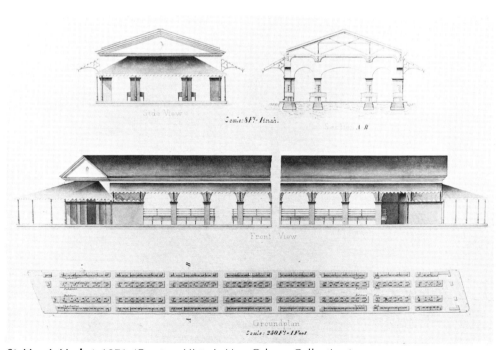

St. Mary's Market, 1871. (Courtesy Historic New Orleans Collection.)

323 S. Diamond, bound by Tchoupitoulas, S. Peters, St. Joseph. This two-story, plastered brick, four-bay commercial building faces the neutral ground which was the site of famous St. Mary's Market. The street is named for a prominent citizen and entrepreneur of the 1840s, Charles Diamond, for whom James Gallier built a number of buildings nearby on Tchoupitoulas. Fine Greek Revival residences, house-stores and commercial buildings lined the street on both sides. Many of these fine buildings, cannibalized by modern facades, remain intact at the third level and within. This structure, although altered, represents a commendable effort to recapture the original environment in an historic area. The original granite piers and remnants of the cast-iron gallery, now a balcony, remain.

University Place. Hotel Grunewald (Roosevelt Hotel). From *Architectural Art and Its Allies* (1908). (Courtesy New Orleans Public Library.)

University Place, bound by Canal, Common, Baronne. The thirteen-story Roosevelt Hotel was built as the Hotel Grunewald in 1908, with Toledano and Wogan architects. Typical of other hotels erected in New Orleans in the early 20th century, it had a rusticated and ornamented base, rows of bay windows and a heavy cornice. A 1908 drawing of the building shows that except for the removal of the original marquee over the entrance, the building has not been altered. When erected, the interior provided every luxury of the period, including hot and cold water, long distance telephones in every room, public baths on every floor, porcelain lavatories and tubs and carpeted corridors. This structure stands on the site of Grunewald Concert Hall, which was destroyed by fire in 1892. While the Roosevelt Hotel has enlarged the complex pictured here, with main entrances on Baronne, the University Place facade is the most commendable.

712 Union, bound by St. Charles, Carondelet, Perdido. Three-bay, three-story, brick commercial building with granite pillars in the style of the 1840s. The facade is plastered and scored.

718 Union, bound by St. Charles, Carondelet, Perdido. Three-bay, three-story, brick commercial building with altered lower level. This store probably was identical to the one next to it, No. 712.

736 Union, bound by St. Charles, Carondelet, Perdido. Dalton Steamship Company. The stores facing Union in this block and the one between Carondelet and Baronne were built in 1856. That year Jamison and McIntosh built a three-story store for G. M. Pinckard and Company. Jamison and McIntosh also built a four-story store in the block for a Dr. Gustine for $8,000 in 1856. The buildings are probably those listed here.

830-840 Union, bound by Carondelet, Baronne, Perdido. A row of four-bay, four-story commercial buildings with cast-iron pillars below. According to title research, this row was part of the sale by the Freret brothers to the businessmen who bought 826 Union in 1856. These stores may have been built by William Freret for his relatives, replacing their cotton press.

826 Union, bound by Carondelet, Baronne, Perdido. Three-bay, three-story brick store with cast-iron pillars. Windows have splayed brick lintels and brick sills. The lot on which the building stands was part of a purchase by James Freret, Sr., from Jean Gravier for a cotton press. William Freret, architect, may have built the store in 1856 for his family, selling it later to a group of investors that included Octave Saulay, George M. Pinckard, W. G. Robinson and Payne & Harrison Company.

129 University Place, bound by Common, Canal, S. Rampart. The Orpheum Circuit Co. built this theatre in 1918, spending approximately a half-million dollars, including $85,000 for the site. The company was represented in the transaction by Col. C. E. Bray, who introduced high-class vaudeville to New Orleans. The owners, Meyer Feld, Jr., and Martin Beck, announced that the vaudeville center which had been on St. Charles since 1901, would continue the 1917-18 season, as well as hold performances in the Palace on Iberville and Dauphine (presently a parking building). The Palace was also known as the Greenwall and Triangle. The theatre facade is typical of a national trend in the first quarter of the 20th century toward terra cotta buildings. The front elevation had applied forms and decorations emanating from various periods. The lower level features paired segmental arched openings and a wide string course with three pedimented windows. The central tier here has large panels with decorative relief carving and paired pilasters with ornamental composite capitals between panels for vertical emphasis. The entablature terminates the top section of the tripartite facade and has a cornice carved with floral motifs and a paneled parapet. Few of these many details can be seen at the present time without judicious scrutiny, because a modern marquee and signs deface the structure. (Illustration from *Martin Behrman Administration Biography, 1906-16.* Courtesy Historic New Orleans Collection.)

NEW ORPHEUM THEATRE.

127 Elk Place, bound by Canal, Common. Built by the Benevolent and Protective Order of Elks in 1917, at a cost of $500,000, Toledano, Wogan, and Bernard, architects, with John Thatcher and Sons of Brooklyn, New York, contractors. Local sub-contractors included Weiblen Marble, which supplied marble and stone. The building stands on the site of an earlier structure occupied by the Masonic Order, which came to Louisiana in 1884. The group was domiciled in the first building from 1897 to 1916, renovating once for $75,000 in 1907 before demolishing it to build the present structure. Previous residences of Lodge No. 30 in New Orleans were at old No. 193 Gravier and old No. 4 Carondelet. In 1922 the building was partially restored and rebuilt after sustaining damages totaling $250,000.

Purchased by Samuel Zemurray for $150,000 in 1940, the building was to be demolished and replaced by a Child Guidance Center. These plans were not realized and Gulf Oil Company presently occupies the building. Designed in the Italian Renaissance manner, this two-story masonry structure is only slightly altered on the exterior. A third section has been added above the ornate cornice.

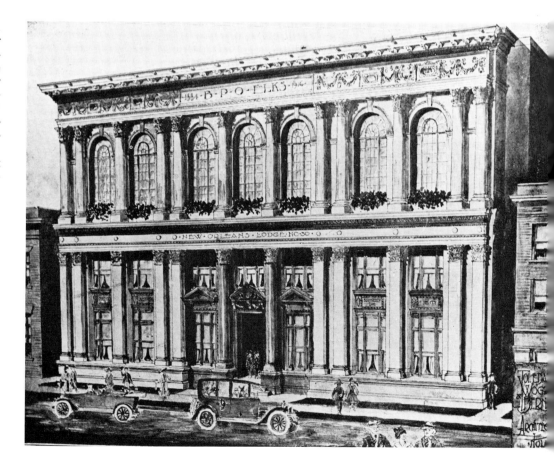

INVENTORY OF ARCHITECTS

Presented below is a listing of the architects and builders whose names appear on building contracts of structures, both extant and demolished, in the New Orleans Central Business District. The reader may recognize well-known architects whose works have been documented in the past by exhibitions and publications of the American Institute of Architects, Louisiana Landmarks, the Friends of the Cabildo and others.

Many names appear in print for the first time, including numerous full-fledged architects of major buildings and builders, carpenters, journeymen, joiners, and bricklayers—all workers who contracted to erect or rebuild structures. Some listed here may emerge in time as major architects. Hopefully, this list will provide a base of information for future scholarship and documentation.

Dates following the names indicate the year or years that an individual architect's name appeared on a building contract of a structure in the Central Business District.

John Allison, 1829. Associated with the firm Allison and Roa in 1828.

Jonathan Alston, 1831. The 1842 City Directory lists "Alston, J., Race between Magazine and Constance."

Paul Andry, born 1868, died 1946. A descendant of Louis Andry, engineer and surveyor sent to Louisiana by the King of Spain. Born and educated in New Orleans at the University of Louisiana, Andry studied his profession in the offices of James Ferris and B. M. Harrod and established his own office in 1889. Credited with building the Morris Public Baths, St. John Berchman's Asylum, he was the official architect for the New Orleans School Board. Married to Marie Louis Ricau. The 1893 directory lists "Andry, Paul, architect, 41 Kenner Block, residence 295 Marais." But according to the 1893 City Directory he was associated with "Harrod and Andry, architects, 85 St. Charles, room 19."

Charles A. de Armas, 1849, 1859, 1861. Born 1830, died 1905.

C. Arthur de Armas, born 1823, died 1889. The 1855 City Directory lists "De Armas, C. Arthur, architect, 178 Royal, domicile 12 Pontalba, St. Ann."

Michele de Armas, 1818. Born ?, died 1882.

William Arms, 1871. The 1871 City Directory lists "Arms, Wm., builder, residence Thalia.

Armstrong & O'Neill, 1864. The 1866 City Directory lists "Armstrong, Wm., builder 164 Baronne, domicile 288 Calliope; and O'Neill, Thomas, builder, 119 Bolivar." In the 1855 City Directory William Armstrong is listed as a member of the firm of Harrington & Armstrong, 199 Baronne.

Atkinson, W. L., 1840, 1841, 1841. The City Bank, situated on Camp near Canal, was begun in 1837 from a design of Atkinson and erected under the supervision of James Gallier at a cost of $50,000. The 1842 City Directory lists "Atkinson, W. L., architect, 45 Camp."

Maurice Aulif, 1850.

Alexander Baggett, 1834, 1836, 1838, 1840, 1840, 1840, 1840, 1863. Born 1805, died 1865. A native of Alexandria, Virginia, Baggett married a New Orleans girl, Miss Harriet Love, in 1832. In the 1842 City Directory he is listed as "Baggett, Alexander, architect, 208 Baronne." At his death he resided at 171 St. Claude.

Joseph D. Baldwin, 1837.

John Barnett, 1853. Born 1804, died 1871. This prominent architect designed the First Congregational Unitarian Church (Church of the Messiah) on St. Charles at Julia. Built 1853-1855 by Giraud and Lewis, it is now destroyed. He was also responsible for the plans for Clapp's residence (demolished), St. Paul's Church and the Baptist Church on Camp. Barnett's plans were adopted for the New Varieties Building in 1855. At his death, Barnett resided at 76 Coliseum. According to the 1855 City Directory, his office was at 31 Commercial.

Baumiller & Goodwyn, 1854. The 1853 City Directory lists "Baumiller & Goodwyn, manufacturers of iron railings, etc., 7 Carroll, First District. Baumiller, Jacob, above firm, residence Austerlitz corner Live Oak, Jefferson City, Goodwyn, H. H., residence 88½ Bacchus." Baumiller was born 1808 and died 1887. This firm was known to have designed the iron verandahs for the residence of J. C. Morris, corner of First and Coliseum.

William Beard, 1830.

William Belly, 1854. The 1853 City Directory lists "Belly, William, bricklayer, Villere, between St. Phillip and Ursulines."

Albert Bendernagle. Designed the old Stock Exchange Building on Gravier. A partner in the firm of Burton and Bendernagle, and later, Andry and Bendernagle. With Burton he designed some of the academic buildings at Tulane University.

Bickel & Hamblet, 1824. Tobias Bickel, born 1785, died 1834.

Archibald Boulware, 1871. The 1871 City Directory lists "Boulware, Archibald, builder, residence 41 Constance."

_____ **Bourcicault,** 1855. Sketched the plan of the New Varieties Building, which was drawn by John Barnett.

A. Bourgerol, 1833. The 1842 City Directory lists "Bourgerol, A., architect, 358 Royal."

William Brand, 1826, 1830, 1833, 1835. Born 1778, died 1849. One of New Orleans' early prominent architects, Brand built the old Orleans Theater about 1810 and later rebuilt the Ballroom in 1817. He is also credited with building the First Congregational Church, built in 1819 and the Christian Women's Exchange, 823 St. Louis. He was married to Hettie H. Reed. In 1812 he was elected Alderman for the 5th District. His offices were located on Magazine. He died in Louisville, Kentucky, but was buried in the Girod Street Cemetery in New Orleans.

Francois Briou, 1866. The 1871 City Directory lists "Briou, F., 292 Rampart, second district."

Auguste C. Brunet & Pierre Pinson

James E. Campbell, 1856, 1859. The 1855 City Directory lists "Campbell, J. E., builder, 221 Hercules, domicile 116 Nayades."

Thomas W. Carter, 1881. The 1881 City Directory lists "Carter, T. W., architect, residence 378 St. Andrew."

A. Castaing, 1865. In 1881 Castaing supervised the repairing of the St. Louis Cathedral.

Bernard Charpien, 1828.

John Christie, 1858. The 1858 City Directory lists "Christie, J., carpenter, Jackson, near Apollo, domicile, Felicity, near Magazine." Also listed is "Christie, J., Christie & Cornwell, iron railing manufactory, 323 Rampart."

Louis Clairin, 1853. Born 1800, died 1875. The 1849 City Directory lists "Clairin, L., carpenter, 5 Craps, domicile 7 Craps."

Joseph P. Clohecy, 1842. Born 1800, died 1853. Clohecy died in a fall while working on St. Patrick's Church. He is listed in the City Directory of 1842 as "a builder, Liberty, between Calliope and Clio."

Nathaniel Codd, 1835.

Michael Collins. Associated with James Gallier, Sr., for a short period before 1838.

Collins & Sayre, 1853. J. K. Collins and T. I. Sayre. The 1855 City Directory lists "Collins, J. K., builder, 18 Apollo." Collins practiced alone in 1854, 1856, 1857.

Isaac H. Conde and Thomas Mercer, 1839.

Cook & Morehouse, 1849, 1851, 1853, 1855. The 1849 City Directory lists "Cook, W. B., builder St. Peter, between Gravier and Common." The 1855 Directory lists "Morehouse, Joseph, firm Cooke and Morehouse, residence St. Paul near Perdido."

Francois Correjolles, 1853. In the 1860 Census of the Sixth Ward, F. Correjolles is listed as "63-year-old, personal estate of $3,500, originally from Maryland." He was married to Julie Meunier, who died at the age of 80 in 1904. The 1842 City Directory listed "Correjolles, F., builder, 110 St. Phillip St." Published in the _Courier_ in 1835 was this notice: "Dissolution of partnership — Francois Correjolles and Jean Chaignehu. Home Builders, by mutual consent, dissolved the partnership known as Correjolles & Chaignehu. Mr. Correjolles will undertake all buildings and other jobs." The Correjolles family was prominent in building and architectural work. Francois built the Le Carpentier house (the Beauregard House) on Chartres.

Francois Coulon, Laurent Tabony and Charles Durand, 1833. The 1842 City Directory lists "Coulon, Francois, 49 Conde."

Paulin and Romain Coumes, 1844.

Etienne Courcelle. The 1853 City Directory contains this listing: "Architect and Keeper of Old Catholic Cemetery, No. 1 Office at the Cemetery, Old Basin, between St. Louis and Conti, respectfully informs his friends and public that he still continues construction of tombs and vaults in granite or marble, inscriptions and railings at the lowest price and shortest notice."

Joachim Courcelle, 1818. The 1842 City Directory lists "Courcelle, J., builder, Ursuline between St. Claude and Treme." A. B. Courcelle is listed as a builder at the same address.

Elijah Cox, 1857, 1857, 1858, 1859, 1860. Born 1817, died 1864. A builder of several public schools, Cox is known to have built one on the site of the old St. Phillipe Ballroom in 1861. In 1859 this notice appeared in the _Daily Picayune:_ "Messrs. E. Cox & Co., efficient architects, inaugurated a stately public school on Barracks during the week with a cold snack." In the 1858 City Directory Cox is listed as a carpenter at 271 Baronne. In 1860 he is listed as a builder, 244 Baronne, residence 444 Rampart.

Charles Crampon, 1866. The 1866 City Directory lists "Crampon, Charles, lumber merchant, 225 Common, domicile 64 Prieur."

John Williamson Crary, 1853. The 1853 City Directory lists "Crary, J. W., and J. A., bricklayers and builders, Dryades, corner Triton, domicile Dryades, corner Euterpe."

John Croft, 1858. The 1858 City Directory lists "Croft, John, carpenter, Roman, corner of Poydras."

Crozier and Wing, 1852, 1858, 1858. Robert Crozier, born 1806, died 1867. Frederick Wing, born 1814, died 1895. The 1850 City Directory lists "Crozier and Wing, carpenters, Triton Walk, corner Bacchus." (See also Frederick Wing).

Dakin and Dakin, 1838, 1839, 1840. C. H. Dakin and James H. Dakin. Listed in 1842 City

Directory as "Dakin, James H., architect, 48 Canal Street, residence 8 Erato," and "Dakin, C. H., architect, Erato Street, between Prytania and Nayades." James Dakin came to New Orleans with James Gallier. He had been a pupil and associate of Alexander Jackson Davis in New York.

George Daniels, 1837.

Henry DeMahy, 1869. Born 1830, died 1877. "DeMahy, Henry" is listed in the City Directory of 1869 as residing at 89 Rampart, second district.

James Denny and Thomas Martin, 1842.

Jacques N. De Pouilly, 1849. Born 1805, died 1875. The 1842 City Directory lists "De Pouilly, Jacques, architect, 121 Conti Street." In 1842 DePouilly and E. Goudchaux were associates.

William Desmond and Laurence O'Conner, 1838. The 1842 City Directory lists "O'Connor, Lawrence, Villere near corner Conti.

John Diamond, 1851.

Collins Cerre Diboll, Sr. Born 1868, died 1936. When orphaned at the age of nine, Diboll became the ward of Frederick Wing, prominent New Orleans architect who later greatly influenced his career in architecture. Diboll was born in New Orleans and received his education at Tulane and in New York City. He was an apprentice of Muir and Fromerz and an associate of Torgeson, architect of the Harmony Club at St. Charles and Jackson, which later became the headquarters for Standard Oil Co. He married Mary Jesse Blocker of Marshall, Texas. In 1895 he met Gen. Allison Owen and soon after formed a partnership. Among the buildings credited to Diboll's firm are the old Metairie Bank and the Prytania Street Presbyterian Church. He resided at 1907 Octavia.

Diboll, Owen & Goldstein. The 1910 City Directory lists their offices at 305 Baronne. This firm was composed of Collins Cere Diboll, Sr., residence 1907 Octavia; Allison Owen, Major General, retired, residence 1237 State; and Moise Goldstein, residence 1631 Octavia. Diboll and Owen were associated in 1905 before Goldstein was admitted to the firm.

Albert Diettel. Diettel was architect of the Church of St. John the Baptist, Dryades Street near Clio. It was built from 1869-1872 by Thomas Mulligan. Diettel also built the Southwestern Exposition Building, St. Charles and Carondelet, between Julia and Girod, in 1872. Under the firm of Mr. Albert and Messrs. Diettel & Son, No. 28-30 Camp, replacing the building at one time occupied by F. F. Hansell & Bros., was built for Charles E. Alter in 1890. It was a five-story building.

Jean Louis Dolliole, 1831. The 1842 City Directory lists "Dolliole, Jean Louis, corner Bayou Road and Villere."

Andrew Downey, 1873. The 1871 City Directory lists "Downey, Andrew, builder, 304 Terpsichore first district, residence, same." In 1869 Downey was associated with John Swords, sheriff of Assumption Parish, residing at 12 Louisa.

William Drews, 1855. The 1855 City Directory lists "Drew, Wm., firm of Drew & Hillger, builders, Josephine, corner Magazine."

Nicholas Dunn, 1853.

John K. Eichelberger, 1851, 1851, 1854. The 1853 City Directory lists Eichelberger, John, Perdido, between Baronne and Carondelet.

Diedrich Einseidel, 1888. The 1888 City Directory lists "Einsiedel, D., and John Henry, architects, Rooms 18, 33 and 35 Carondelet, residence 277 Royal."

Jesse Ellis, 1840, 1840, 1847.

Owen Evens, 1832.

Faehnle & Kuntz, 1869.

Charles Ferguson, 1851. The 1851 City Directory lists "Ferguson, Charles, architect, corner Magazine and Washington, Lafayette."

J. M. Fernandez, 1838. The 1842 City Directory lists "Fernandez, J. M., builder, corner Caliborne and Bienville."

O. Fister, 1850.

William Fitzner, 1881. The 1880 City Directory lists "Fitzner, William, architect, 31 Carondelet, residence 28 Philip."

Casper Morris Fogg, 1851. The 1851 City Directory lists "Fogg, C. M. builder, 250 Magazine."

Louis Folliet, 1857. The 1857 City Directory lists "Folliet, Louis, carpenter, domicile Liberty near Calliope."

Benjamin Fox, 1833, 1835. With Latrobe, Fox built in 1822 the Louisiana State Bank, corner of Royal and Conti. This was Latrobe's design. The old mortgage office on Royal and Conti (now the New Orleans Tourist Commission) was erected in 1826 by Bickle, Hamlet and Fox.

L. M. Francois, 1837, 1838, 1842. The City Directory lists "Francois, L. M., carpenter, 44 Orleans."

James Freret, 1866, 1866. Born 1838, died 1897, age 60. A younger brother of William A. Freret, James began work in 1856 as architect in the sash factory of George Purves, who was then erecting the First Presbyterian Church. From 1857-1860 he worked in his brother's office, drawing plans for Touro Alms House, the Moresque Building, corner of Camp and Poydras, and three iron buildings on Canal. Beginning in 1860 Freret studied at *L'Ecole des Beaux Arts* in Paris and traveled over Europe. In 1862 he returned home through the Union Navy blockade and entered the engineering service of the Confederacy. When the war ended, Freret again returned to architecture, completing the Moresque Building and designing the first Fair Buildings, the Louisiana Savings Bank, a four-story building on the corner of Common and Magazine, the New Orleans Gas Light Co., Spring Hill College, the extension of the Convent of Visitation and a new front for the cathedral in Mobile. He also served briefly as sheriff of Orleans Parish. The City Directory of 1866 lists "Freret, James, architect, 25 Commercial Place, residence Louisiana Avenue near Prytania."

William Alfred Freret, 1859, 1860, 1861. Born 1804, died 1864. Freret was the son of a distinguished family of southern Louisiana. His maternal ancestor, the Chevalier D'Arensbourg of Sweden, was made governor of the German Coast in 1721. His paternal grandfather, an Englishman, emigrated in 1790 and started the first cotton press in New Orleans. He studied engineering and the mechanical arts in England, and although he continued to manage the family firm, the cotton press, he also maintained his active interest in architecture. In 1840 he was elected mayor as a member of the Native American Party, which was strongly opposed by the Creoles. He was elected again in 1844. Due to his background he devoted much of his time as mayor to problems of engineering—surveying, drainage, road construction. During his administration the first free public school was established in New Orleans in 1841. In 1850 he was appointed a collector of customs by the President of the United States. Freret designed the New Orleans Savings Institution and was one of the designers of the Henry Clay Monument on Canal, between Royal and St. Charles, in 1851. The 1869 City Directory lists "William Alfred Freret, architect, 33 Carondelet, residence Second Street near Carondelet."

Hiram D. Fuller, 1837.

Ambrose C. Fulton, 1842.

Gallier and Esterbrook, 1858. From 1858 until his death in 1868, James Gallier, Jr., and Richard Esterbrook, construction foreman, formed this firm. Both Turpin and Esterbrook had worked for James Gallier, Sr.

James Gallier, Sr. 1835, 1835, 1835, 1836, 1838, 1838, 1839, 1839, 1840, 1842, 1844, 1844, 1844, 1845, 1845, 1845. Born 1798, died 1866. One of the best known of New Orleans' architects, Gallier, Sr., was a native of Ravensdale, Ireland, and the son of a builder and engineer. He was educated in Dublin and Dundalk. In 1823 he married an English girl, Elizabeth Tyler. While in London he received much of his practical knowledge of building under Sir William Wilkins, designer of the National Gallery and London University. Gallier came to New York in 1833 and worked for Charles Dakin; one year later he moved his family to New Orleans, where he had heard prospects for a builder were ex-

cellent. Gallier's works were in the Greek Revival manner so popular in those years. He designed both private and public buildings. Among the best-known and admired were the following:

The St. Charles Exchange Hotel (later called the St. Charles Hotel., which he built for $700,000.

Gallier Hall, 545 St. Charles.

The Merchant's Exchange on Royal.

The Bank of New Orleans (currently the recently remodeled and restored New Orleans Tourist and Convention Commission Center, Royal Street), a remodeling of the old mortgage office, 1826.

First and Second Christ Church, Canal Street.

The alteration and reconstruction of St. Patrick's Church.

The Boston Club on Canal, built in 1844 as a residence for a prominent physician.

In 1849 Gallier retired, leaving his firm in the hands of his only son, James Gallier, Jr. At this time he married his second wife, Catherine Robinson, his first wife having died some years earlier. Gallier and his wife died in 1866 in the wreck of the ship *Evening Star* returning to the United States after a tour of Europe.

James Gallier, Jr. Born 1827, died 1868. James Gallier, Jr., was born when Gallier, Sr., was working in Huntington, England. He was five years old when the family moved to the United States. He was educated by the Rev. Mr. Hawks on Long Island and in Mississippi and continued his studies at the University of North Carolina. At the age of 25 he married Josephine Aglae Villavaso, a Creole of St. Bernard Parish. They had four girls. From 1849 to 1858 his firm was known as Gallier, Turpin and Co., and from 1858 to 1868 he worked as Gallier and Esterbrook. Gallier, Jr., designed the following buildings and residences:

The French Opera House, on the corner of Toulouse and Bourbon, perhaps his best-known and most admired work, built in 1859 for a cost of $118,000. It burned in 1919.

The Bank of America, 111 Exchange Place, built in 1866.

Leeds Iron Foundry, 923 Tchoupitoulas, built in 1852.

The Fair Grounds gates and gatehouses.

The Bank of New Orleans, 312 St. Charles (now demolished).

The residence built for Lavinia Dabney, now the Episcopal Diocesan House, 2265 St. Charles.

The Florence A. Luling House, 1436 Leda Street, built in 1865. It later became the Jockey Club.

His own residence at 1132 Royal, recently restored and opened as a museum.

Gallier, Turpin and Company, 1850, 1850, 1851, 1851, 1851, 1851, 1851, 1851, 1851,

1853, 1855, 1855, 1855, 1855, 1856, 1857, 1857. Between 1849 and 1858, James Gallier, Jr., and John Turpin, bookkeeper, worked under this firm name as architects and builders. The 1855 City Directory lists "Gallier, Turpin and Co., 11 Carondelet."

Theodore Giraud and Thomas Lewis, 1853. Builders of the First Congregational Unitarian Church, St. Charles at Julia, in 1853-1855. Now destroyed, it was designed by John Barnett.

Ed Gotthiel, 1853. The 1853 City Directory lists "Gotthiel, Edward, architect, Nayades, corner Felicity."

F. D. Gotts, 1840, 1840, 1841, 1841, 1845, 1849, 1853, 1856. The 1858 City Directory lists "Gott, F. D., carpenter, Rampart near Canal, first district." In 1842 Gott was associated with Jamison and McIntosh and John R. Pike. Pike resided at 212 Carondelet.

F. E. Goudchaux, 1850. The 1850 City Directory lists "Goudchaux, Franklin E., builder, Franklin, between Bienville and Conti.

Andrew Gregory, 1831.

Francois Groment and Victor Guyard, 1844. The 1842 City Directory has a listing for Guyard, Victor at 366 Bourbon.

P. Gualdi, 1855. Artist and architect P. Gualdi is listed in the 1855 City Directory as an architect at 34 Marais. He was the artist for the First Presbyterian Church on Lafayette Square. He also drew many of the plans in the Notarial Archives.

S. B. Haggart, 1873. An architect and builder, Haggart was well known in many phases of New Orleans life. He converted 35 Camp into the Cosmopolitan Bank in 1871. He is also thought to have designed and constructed the New Orleans National Bank, 54 Camp, the monument for Chalmette Cemetery (at a cost of $1,000) and the railroad lamp at the corner of Camp and Common, a well-known landmark in the city. This lamp also served as a sign to the Jackson Railroad Office. Haggart's address was No. 5 Commercial Place in 1873.

Albert Hanemann, 1872. The 1870 City Directory lists "Hanemann, Albert, painter, 58 Frenchmen" but in 1872 he resided "at 9 Marigny, house and sign painter."

Harrington & Armstrong, 1855, 1855, 1856. The firm was located at 199 Baronne, according to the 1855 City Directory.

Benjamin Morgan Harrod, 1866. Born 1837, died 1912. Graduating from Harvard College in 1856, Harrod returned to Louisiana and was appointed assistant United States engineer for the district extending from the Mississippi River to the Rio Grande. From 1859 through 1877 Harrod maintained his private architectural offices in New Orleans, interrupted only by the Civil War, when he was a division engineer and captain of the engineering corps for the

Confederacy. In 1865 he married a native New Orleanian, Miss Harriet S. Uhlhorn. He became state engineer of Louisiana in 1877, but resigned in 1879 to become a member of the Mississippi River Commission and a member of the drainage commission, which prepared plans for the drainage of New Orleans. Credited with building many of the fire engine houses in the city, such as the one at 1043-45 Magazine, Harrod also rebuilt the Varieties Theater in 1871 at a cost of $150,000.

Carl Axel Hedin, 1852, 1852, 1854, 1854, 1856. Born 1810, died 1858. Hedin signed maps in the plan book of the Notarial Archives as "C. A. Hedin, civil engineer, office Banks Arcade Alley, No. 8 upstairs" in 1852. He was a surveyor and architect and in 1853 worked with Schlarbaum.

Nicholas Herron, 1869.

James Hill, 1849.

Charles Lewis Hillger, 1868. Architect of the Temple Sinai, Carondelet and Tivoli Square (Lee Circle), Hillger is also credited with: the German Protestant Church, Jackson and Chippewa, in 1872; the Zion Evangelical Lutheran Church, at St. Charles, corner St. Andrews, built in 1871 at a cost of $13,000 for the ground and $18,000 for the building; and the Lafayette Fire Insurance Co., 2123 Magazine, built in 1869. The 1870 City Directory lists "Hillger, Charles Lewis, architect, 28 Carondelet, residence Tchoupitoulas corner of Nashville."

John Hoey, 1848. The 1849 City Directory lists "Hoey & Byington, brickmakers, yard at Hoeyville, Carrollton, Hoey, John, above firm, saddlery, etc. 134 Poydras, residence at Hoeyville." In 1865 Hoey was granted the right-of-way to construct a double-track street railway in Carrollton.

Benjamin Howard, 1851. The 1851 City Directory lists "Howard, Benjamin, Jr., Gravier near Circus."

Henry Howard, 1851, 1866, 1867, 1874. Born 1818. Henry Howard was born in Cork, Ireland, the son of a noted Cork builder. He studied at the Mechanics Institute in Cork before emigrating to New York City in 1836. While working as a carpenter and joiner in 1837, he moved to New Orleans. He gained practical experience as a stair builder, at which he worked for five years until promoted by builder E. W. Sewell to foreman. He married a Miss Richards of New Orleans in 1839 and they had 11 children. In 1849 Howard studied architecture with James Dakin. He also studied under Henry Moellhausen, a surveyor and civil engineer of New Orleans. A year earlier he had opened his own architectural office in Exchange Place. During the Civil War, Howard served as principal draughtsman in the Confederate States Naval Iron Works at

Columbus, Georgia. The following public buildings are attributed to Howard:

First Presbyterian Church, Lafayette Square.

Second Presbyterian Church, Washington Square.

St. Peter's Roman Catholic Church, Third District.

Importer's Bonded Warehouse, Second District.

Hale's Warehouse, First District.

Buildings for the Louisiana Fair Grounds.

Engine house and engine foundations for the Commercial Water Works.

Zoilly's Brewery, Magazine and Delord.

Home Mutual Insurance Buildings, First District.

Crescent Mutual Insurance Buildings, First District.

Conery's Stores, corner Common and Water.

Avendano Stores, corner Delta and Common.

St. Elizabeth's Asylum, Magazine Street, Fourth District.

Protestant Boys Asylum, Third District.

Charity Hospital Extension, Common.

He also constructed and designed many private buildings:

Pontalba Building, Jackson Square.

Kate's five dwellings, Camp.

Conery's dwelling, Prytania.

Burthes residence, St. Charles.

Palacios residence, St. Charles.

Miltenberger residence, St. Charles.

Grinnan and Short's Villa, Prytania, Fourth District.

Buildings Nos. 8, 9, 13, Commercial Place.

He built many plantation homes and courthouse buildings in the bayou country. As an associate in the firm of Henry T. Longsdale, George O. Sweet and Henry Howard, he built the Nelson McStea house on Prytania between Jackson and Louisiana in 1855.

Abraham Howell, 1859. The 1851 City Directory lists "Howell, A., builder, 12 Bacchus." In 1837 and 1838 Howell was associated with Edward Johnson.

Joseph Howell, 1850, 1867. The 1851 City Directory lists "Howell, Jos., carpenter, Jackson near Villere."

Joseph M. Howell and John Kirwin, 1866. The 1866 City Directory lists "Kirwin, John, laborer, 70 Laurel.

Robert Huyghe, 1853. Born 1814, died 1877. Born in Baltimore, Huyghe was a resident of New Orleans for 40 years. He built the Jefferson City market house, Magazine at Berlin. The 1850 City Directory lists "Huyghe, R., builder, Josephine, b. Tchoupitoulas." At his death he resided at 56 First Street.

Francois Illig, 1861. In the 1861 City Directory the following advertisement was inserted in bold type: "Illig, Francois, carpenter,

(menusier), 217 late 251 Dauphine, between Main and St. Philip. Jobbing done with dispatch and neatness at the lowest rates."

Ivens and Broas, 1866, 1867. The 1869 City Directory listed "Ivens, Edward, builder, 73 Liberty."

James W. Jackson and Francis Jackson, 1861.

John R. Jacobs, 1851. The 1851 City Directory lists "Jacobs, John R., carpenter, Philip, between Rousseau and Fulton, Lafayette."

Samuel Jamison, 1846. Born 1808, died 1880. First as a bricklayer and then as a builder and architect, Jamison was prominent in New Orleans construction. Associated with James McIntosh from the 1840s through the 1850s, he was known mainly for his brickwork. In the 1859 City Directory he is listed at 273 Baronne. Jamison did the brickwork for the Moresque Building, for the sum of $17,000, about 1866; he designed and built the residence of J. C. Morris, corner of First and Coliseum. The ornamental iron verandahs were made by Jacob Baumiller. He built the octagonal wing to the residence of John T. Hardie, corner Philip and Chestnut, in 1869, and the Lewis-Richardson House, 2405 Prytania, circa 1860 (demolished in the 1950s). In 1865 the following advertisement appeared: "Samuel Jamison, Thomas Murray—JAMISON & MURRAY, Architects and Builders, Works—Corner Hercules and Erato Street. Office 46 Carondelet St. Having formed a partnership and resumed the building business in all its branches."

Jamison and McIntosh, 1843, 1848, 1851, 1852, 1853, 1853, 1853, 1854, 1854, 1854, 1857, 1859. Samuel Jamison and James McIntosh, according to the 1859 City Directory, were partners in the firm "Jamison & McIntosh, bricklayers, 250 Baronne, domicile 248 Baronne." They were builders of the Fourth Presbyterian Church (later the Central Congregational Church), S. Liberty, corner Gasquet. It was built in 1860 and demolished in 1935. They also built a five-story store on Canal between St. Charles and Carondelet for Giquel & Jamison Dry Goods.

Joel W. Jewell, 1857. Born 1801, died 1885. He is listed in the 1857 City Directory as "Jewell, J. W., builder, domicile 275 Tchoupitoulas."

James Johnson, 1855, 1857, 1858, 1858, 1859, 1861. The 1858 City Directory lists "Johnson, James, carpenter, Common near Howard."

J. P. Kernan, 1844, 1845.

Bartholemy Lafon, 1807. Born ?, died 1820. Engineer, geographer, and architect, Lafon is most widely known for his work in subdividing the four large plantations upriver from the older Faubourg St. Mary, between St. Joseph and Howard up to Felicity, and the Faubourgs Delord, Soulet, La Course and Annunciation, or what comprised the Second Municipality.

Appointed by the City Council in 1805, Lafon laid out this section, giving mythological names to many of the streets along what is now St. Charles. Today, only along Prytania can one find the streets named for the Muses. Governor Claiborne in 1804 authorized Lafon to re-survey and make plans of lands legally granted to individuals by the French and Spanish governments within the provinces of Louisiana. In 1809 he was hired by Daniel Clark to survey and subdivide Clark's large plantation at the end of Bayou Road. This area was to be called Faubourg St. John.

Isaac Lambert, 1829.

Henry Lathrop, 1844.

Pierre Laurent and Charles Durand, 1831.

Alexander Law, 1832.

Charles Ledig, 1861.

Louis A. Lemoyne, 1834.

Christian Lindauer, 1844.

Christian Lindauer and Henry Wegel, 1843.

James Lindsey, 1847.

Little & Middlemiss, 1851, 1856, 1857, 1857, 1859. Peter R. Middlemiss and Robert Little formed the contracting firm of Little and Middlemiss. They built six stores on St. Charles and one on Common for J. W. Zacharie, store for Ward & Jonals on Gravier, and, in 1858, for Charles Kock, Esq., on Rampart between Canal and Common, a three-storied building with a pure white marble front which ran entirely through to Basin, with a front of 56 feet on Rampart and 125 feet on Basin.

George P. McConnell, 1859.

William McElvain, 1860.

Michael McIntosh, 1849.

Duncan B. McKennon, 1843, 1843, 1844, 1844.

David McLeod, 1840, 1842.

James McPherson, 1838.

John McVittie, 1857. Born 1813, died 1887. In the 1842 City Directory McVittie is listed as a carpenter residing at 866 Rampart. In 1857 he is listed as "McVittie, John, carpenter, residence Toulouse and Claiborne." He resided 1432 Magazine in a home he built around 1867 for himself.

Louis Amant Marin, 1848, 1851.

Sebastien Pizarro Martinez, 1865. The City Directory of 1866 lists "Martinez, S. P., 208 Esplanade."

Jose Marty and Louis St. Amant, 1830.

Francois Mazerat, 1839.

John Michel and David Gouldwere, 1831.

Peter R. Middlemiss, 1866, 1867. Born 1826, died 1887. Born in Montreal, Canada, Middlemiss came to New Orleans at the age of 21. He entered into partnership with Robert Little until 1860 when Little retired. Temple Sinai and nearly all the synagogues and a number of churches were built under his supervision. One of the first buildings on which he worked

was the second St. Charles Hotel. He was also architect for the home of Capt. W. Whamn, Esplanade at Bourbon, and the store of Piaggio & Viosca, 62-64 Old Levee, in 1861. "Middlemiss, Peter R., builder and contractor, 462 Baronne" is listed in the 1866 City Directory. By 1871 he had moved to 215-217 Erato.

Henry Millhausen, 1844.

John Mitchell, 1833. The 1849 City Directory lists "Mitchell, John, builder, Notre Dame, between Magazine and Tchoupitoulas." Mitchell was associated at various times with the following: Mitchell and D. G. Wire, 1830, 1827; Mitchell, L. A. Lemoine and James Lambert, 1822; Mitchell and Joseph M. Howell, 1850, 1851, 1852, 1852, 1853; and Mitchell, Howell and Coates, 1843, 1844, 1844, 1845, 1845, 1846, 1846.

Henry Mollhausen. The 1842 City Directory lists "Mollhausen, H., architect and surveyor, Exchange Alley."

Mondelli and Reynolds, 1836, 1837. The 1838 Gibson's Guide and Directory lists "Mondelli & Reynolds, architects, 53 Magazine." The 1842 City Directory lists "Mondelli, A., Camp between St. Joseph and Delord." As a firm, Mondelli and Reynolds designed the U.S. Marine Hospital at McDonogh, opposite New Orleans. It was built in the Gothic style in 1834, but because of inadequate appropriations by the government, the work was suspended. In 1845 James H. Caldwell contracted to complete the work. Mondelli and Reynolds also prepared plans for the State Capitol in Baton Rouge in 1847. They designed 1458 Constance and the St. Charles Theater. An advertisement in the *Daily Delta,* August 29, 1848, read: "Mondelli & Reynolds. Painting— House, Sign and Ornamental Painters. No. 76 Gravier St. Flags, banners, Transparencies, etc., done with dispatch at reasonable rates." Antoine Mondelli was born in Italy and was active in New Orleans 1821-1856. He painted many scenes in the French Opera House and assisted Pomerade, his father-in-law, on the ceiling paintings at St. Patrick's. Pomerade and Mondelli also painted together in St. Louis.

David Moores, 1840, 1841.

Thomas Morrow, 1841.

Thomas Mulligan, 1874. Born 1823, died 1877. A native of Raphoe County, Donegal, North Ireland, Mulligan emigrated to Mobile in 1836 and in June, 1847, came to New Orleans. He is said to have drawn the plans for St. Alphonso's Parochial School, St. Andrew Street; Academy of Holy Cross, Third District, corner of Love and Congress; St. Vincent's Infant Orphan Asylum, corner Magazine and Race; St. Elizabeth's Orphan Asylum, Napoleon Avenue; St. Mary's Dominican Convent; and two parochial schools in St. Theresa

Parish, Erato. He also built the church of St. John the Baptist from plans drawn by Albert Diettel and St. Vincent DePaul Church on Greatmen, between Montegut and Clouet, in 1866. The 1874 City Directory lists "Mulligan, Thomas, builder, residence 466 S. Basin."

John Henry Munday, 1856, 1857.

Thomas Murray, 1851, 1853, 1853. The City Directory of 1855 lists "Murray, Thomas, Hercules, corner Erato."

Theophilus Nash, 1842.

B. F. Nichols, 1852, 1852, 1853, 1853, 1853.

Peter Ogier, 1834, 1835. Associated in 1826 with the firm Ogier, Williams, Horton and Tuthill. In 1827 and 1829 he performed work as Ogier and Williams.

Francois Muray Pierre T. Oliver, 1841.

L. N. Olivier. Builder of the New Orleans Savings Institute, Canal, designed by W. A. Freret.

Thomas O'Neill, 1866, 1866, 1866, 1868.

General Allison Owen. Born 1869, died ?. An 1885 graduate of Tulane and a New Orleans native, Owen attended the Massachusetts Institute of Technology, 1892-94. He served in the U. S. Army and retired as a major general. Associated with Diboll and Owen, Ltd., after 1895, he married Blanche Plothier in 1924. He is believed to have been the architect of the $4 million White Slum Clearance, the New Orleans Public Library, the Municipal Office Building, the Louisiana Bank Building, the Metairie Bank Building, the United Fruit Company Building, the Notre Dame Seminary, the American Sugar Refining Offices, in association with Sully and Toledano. The Pythian Temple Office Building, the Mergenthaler Building, the New Orleans Athletic Club, the Criminal Court and Jail Building. He also was president of the City Planning and Zoning Commission.

Paul Pandely, 1834.

Joshua Peebles, 1838, 1838, 1848, 1849, 1851, 1853, 1853, 1854, 1855, 1856, 1858. The 1861 City Directory lists "Peebles, Joshua, 186 and 188 Carondelet."

Marie Adrian Persac, 1862. Born about 1823, died 1873. Best known as an artist, Persac was also an architect and civil engineer. Born in France and married to Odile Daigre. At one time he was a partner of a Mr. Legras in making "artistic photographs, Ambrotypes, Melanotypes." In 1869 he established an Academy of Drawing and Painting, 75 Camp Street, where he taught portraiture and landscapes in oil and watercolor. Persac won several gold medals and first prizes for watercolors and drawings in the mechanical and architectural fairs of the 1860s. Many of the architectural drawings in the Notarial Archives are his works. His best known work, however, was the original survey drawing for "Norman's Chart of the Mississippi River from Natchez to New Orleans," published in 1858. In 1860 Persac was associated with E. Surgi.

John Randolph Pikes, 1843, 1844.

Joseph Pilie, 1827. Born ?, died 1846. The 1842 City Directory lists "Pilie, Joseph, surveyor 2nd municipality, r. 266 Royal." He also resided at 910 Royal. In *Old New Orleans*, Stanley Arthur writes of Pilie: "He was a talented engineer and surveyor and his carefully executed maps are relied upon today by surveyors in determining ownership of various properties in the Vieux Carre. Gil Joseph Pilie, a native of Mirbalis, Santo Domingo, was a son of Louis Pilie and Marguerite Elizabeth Deschamps. He came to New Orleans when the Dominguois were expelled from that West Indies island by the uprising of the black slaves. In 1813 Joseph married Therese Anne Deyant, daughter of Louis Christophe Deyant and Marie Therese Valade, a native of Dondon, Santo Domingo. J. Pilie's son, Louis, succeeded his father as city surveyor and many descendants bearing this name have been prominent in the engineering life of N.O." Civil engineer and architect by profession. City Surveyor, beginning April 18, 1818, and renominated for many years. Employed by U.S. government to survey lakes near New Orleans and to establish forts from Bayou St. John to Mobile. Salary as surveyor was $100 a month. Pilie designed the following:

Vegetable market, fronting on Old Levee, St. Philip, Ursuline, and the river. Completed in 1830, at a cost of $25,800.

Cenotaph for Thomas Jefferson and John Adams, 1826.

Triumphal arch to honor General Lafayette during his visit to New Orleans in 1825. His fee was $400.

Obelisk, built in 1832, to commemorate battle of 1814.

Mausoleum in memory of Napoleon, 1834.

Scenery for the Orleans Theatre, 1816.

He opened a school of drawing with the following advertisement: "Notice. The Subscriber has just opened a School of Drawing in which he Teaches Drawing, Portraits, Landscape, Artificial Flowers, as also Architecture and its principles, in the manner of copying, reducing and colouring Plans and Charts. He will copy, and reduce to any scale, charts and plans which may be entrusted to him. The Whole will be executed with punctuality."

Louis H. Pilie, 1860, 1861. Born 1820, died April 23, 1884, at age 64. Resided at 216 Royal. Educated at Janin's College in St. Louis, he served as deputy surveyor of the First Municipal District (1846-1852) and later City Surveyor. In 1862, he was ousted by General Butler and imprisoned in the Customhouse. In 1867 he was elected surveyor again. In August of that year Sheridan deposed him because of his opposition to the Nicholson pavement. He had four sons and five daughters. With Jules Allan d'Hemecourt, Pilie was employed by the City Council to make a plan of city property at a cost of $30,000 and sent to Paris for engraving. It became the basis of all maps since drawn of New Orleans. He designed the following:

Facade of the St. Louis Cathedral, with tall central spire and twin lateral spires, after 1855.

Decorated the St. Philip Street Theatre, 1816.

Designed the iron door of City Hall, executed by Pelane Brothers, blacksmiths of the Municipality, 1851.

As Deputy Surveyor of the First Municipality, was author of plan for erection of iron fence around Jackson Square, 1845.

Remodelling and improvements of St. Louis Hotel by A. Surari, architect, under the supervision of Crescent City.

Theatrical sets.

Decorating of theaters.

An advertisement in the New Orleans *Republican* (October 31, 1869) read: "Pilie and Murray (Thomas) Architects, Surveyors, and Builders. Office Room No. 12 Auctioneers' Exchange, Royal St. Workshops and Yards, Corner Erato and Rampart St. Plans, Surveys, Jobbing, Fitting Up, Repairing and other work in their line promptly and satisfactorily attended to."

Pierre Pinson and Pisetta, 1821, 1825. Best known for their work in the French Quarter, they designed and built the Musson Building, 633-37 Canal, and the once-fine Creole house at 507 Canal.

Charles Pride. Born ?, died 1862, in Marietta, Georgia. The City Directory lists "Pride, Charles, architect and builder, 301 Magazine, residence corner Camp and Bartholomew."

George Purves, 1855, 1856. Born ?, died 1883. A native of Scotland, Purves first emigrated to New York, where he married, and then came to New Orleans in 1847. His first work in New Orleans was on the City Hall. He competed with six architects for a first prize of $300 in the designing of the Odd Fellows Hall. Plans for the second St. Charles Hotel were the idea and plan of a committee and Purves, who revised and adopted many portions of those submitted by Isaiah Rogers.

Rand and Spoon, 1844, 1845.

James M. Reid, 1836.

Reid and Harrod, 1867. In the 1867 City Directory the firm is listed at 26 Natchez, over the City Bank.

L. Reizenstein, 1867.

Ferdinand Reusch, 1881, 1881.

John Reynolds, 1825, 1825. The 1850 City Directory lists "Reynolds, John, architect, corner Natches and Arcade Passage."

L. E. Reynolds, 1854, 1854, 1861, 1867, 1868. Born 1816, died ?. Born in Norwich, Chenango County, New York, Reynolds moved to Cincinnati at an early age and worked as a carpenter and studied architecture. He also worked and studied in Louisville, Kentucky, and New York City for 10-15 years before becoming a public lecturer, teacher and active architect. He invented five original methods of handrailing and published a treatise on the subject. He was well known for his professional library and authored "Mysteries of Masonry" and "The Science and Philosophy of Creation." After coming to New Orleans in the course of his lecturing, he decided to reside there permanently in 1843. Among the more outstanding buildings he claimed to have built are:

Mr. Lafayette Folger's, corner St. Charles and First.

Dr. Campbell's, corner St. Charles and Julia.

Mr. Hale's, corner Delord and Camp.

The Canal Bank, Camp.

The Story Buildings, corner of Camp and Common.

Mr. W. M. Perkins, corner Jackson and Coliseum.

The St. James Hotel, on Magazine Street.

Crescent Mutual Insurance Building, Camp.

Mr. H. S. Buckner, Coliseum and Jackson.

Factors Row, Carondelet.

The row of stores opposite the St. James Hotel on Magazine Street.

S. H. Kennedy's, corner First and Camp.

Andrew Smith, corner St. Charles Avenue and Tivoli (now Lee Circle).

The Jackson and Manson stores on New Levee.

When the Banks Arcade was demolished in 1859, Reynolds designed the five-story hotel that replaced it. The 1860 City Directory lists "Reynolds, L. E., architect, 31 Camp Street, residence 109 Gaienne."

R. P. Rice, 1845. The 1861 City Directory lists "Rice, Richard P., builder and architect, 368 Baronne." In 1838 Rice was associated with C. J. Tibbets.

Newton Richards, 1833, 1835, 1835, 1843, 1843, 1851.

Henry Hobson Richardson. Born 1838, died 1886. Although Richardson designed only one building for his native New Orleans—the Howard Memorial Library on Lee Circle—he is perhaps one of its best known architects. Richardson was born at Priestly Plantation, St. James Parish, but he studied in New Orleans at George Blackman's private school and, after one year at LSU, attended Harvard. For five years he studied in Paris at the *Ecole des Beaux Arts* with the French architect Henri Labrouste.

At the time of the Civil War he returned to the U. S., but remained in the Northeast.

Isaac Rodrigiez, 1868.

Peter Ross, 1859. In bold type in the 1871 City Directory is the listing: "Ross, Peter, shop and office corner Prytania and Washington, Box 1, Mechanic's Exchange, and P. O. Box 488, Particular attention given to the alterations and repairs of stores and dwellings."

F. G. Rothass, 1836. The 1861 City Directory lists "Rothass, F. G., builder and architect, 487 Dryades."

Auguste Roy and Louis Clairain, 1854.

John Rust and Jeremiah Fox, 1822.

Pierre Sabatier, 1832.

William Saunders, 1840. The 1850 City Directory lists "Saunder, W. P., 215 Camp."

E. Schlarbaum, 1854. The 1855 City Directory lists "Schlarbaum, E., 7 Commercial, builder and architect."

Robert Seaton, 1843, 1845, 1845. The 1842 City Directory lists "Seaton, Robert, builder, 181 St. Joseph." In 1861 his address was 216 Carondelet.

E. W. Sewell, 1835, 1838, 1838, 1838, 1838, 1839, 1839, 1841, 1846, 1846. Born 1805, died 1864. Edward William Sewell is listed in the 1861 City Directory as a builder and architect at Clio near St. Charles. He was the scene painter for the Camp Street Theater in 1838. Henry Howard worked and studied with Sewell at one time.

John Sewell, 1850, 1851, 1852. Born 1817, died 1860. The 1855 City Directory lists "Sewell, John, builder, Thalia near Bacchus."

S. S. Seymour, 1859.

Charles H. Shaw and Frederick H. Robinson, 1849.

Philip W. Sherwood, 1888.

Isaac Shubert, 1856, 1857, 1859, 1861. The 1861 City Directory lists "Shubert, Isaac H., builder and architect, 219 Girod."

Dedward Sidel. As chief assistant architect to G. M. Torgeson, Sidel assisted in designing the Cotton Exposition Building. He was a graduate of the School of Arts of Paris. A native of New Orleans, he resided at 235 Chartres.

Sidle and Stewart, 1833, 1833, 1833, 1834, 1834, 1837, 1838, 1839, 1839, 1840, 1841, 1841, 1841, 1841, 1842, 1842, 1844, 1845, 1845. The 1842 City Directory lists "Sidle and Stewart, builders, 257 Camp." The Gas Bank, St. Charles between Canal and Common, was erected in 1839 under the direction of Sidle and Stewart at a cost of $50,000.

Duncan Sinclair, 1850.

Samuel Slack and Samuel Smelledge, 1836.

Small and McGill, 1844.

Solyman Brown, 1849.

Thomas Stackhouse, 1832. The 1849 City Directory lists "Stackhouse, Thomas, 250 Camp."

Frederick Staudt, 1849.

James Stewart, 1850.

James and Charles Stewart, 1855.

James and William Stewart, 1851.

Samuel Stewart, 1846, 1847, 1851, 1851, 1853, 1860, 1860. Born 1832, died 1890. The 1860 City Directory lists "Stewart, Samuel, builder, Magazine, corner Calliope, residence 209 Camp."

Joseph Stinson, 1849.

Stone Brothers. Samuel Stone, born 1869, died 1933, and his brother, Guy, were architects for the Maison Blanche Building in 1905. They were listed in the City Directory of that year at 818 Common.

Sullivan & Company, 1856.

Thomas Sully. Born 1855, died ?. Thomas Sully, the senior member of the firm, was born in Mississippi City, Mississippi, son of a cotton merchant. He was educated at Dr. Sanders' School in New Orleans. First working in Austin, Texas, Sully later worked with J. M. Slade in New York. He returned to New Orleans in 1882 and married Miss Jennie Rocchi. Sully resided at 998 St. Charles.

Eugene Surgi, 1848. Born 1826, died after 1900. A civil engineer and architect, Surgi was born in Paris, France, son of an officer in the French army under Napoleon. Graduating from school in France in 1843, he pursued his profession there. He came to New Orleans in 1845. In 1846 he was an assistant for a survey of Mobile, Alabama, and the bay of Mobile. From 1851-1861 he was deputy surveyor-general of the state of Louisiana. According to the 1855 City Directory, Surgi was deputy surveyor of the State and proprietor of California Planing and Saw Mills, Lee, near Congress, Third District. During the War Surgi was superintendent of a company whose purpose was to build bridges and fortifications. Although continuing in the building and architecture line, Surgi also engaged in sugar planting, operated several sawmills and made porcelain. In 1849 Surgi married Miss Aimee Materre, and they had six children. In 1888 Surgi became a partner of Ed Topp, in the firm of Surgi & Topp. Topp served as superintendent of the work. They are credited with constructing the Quarantine Sugar Station, the Experiment Station, Grand Island Railroad Depot and the Ocean Club Hotel.

Louis Surgi, 1847. Born 1815, died 1869. The 1842 City Directory lists "Surgi, Louis, surveyor and architect, corner St. Peter and Chartres Streets, residence Robertson Street near Ursuline." He was City Surveyor at his death. He was also associated with De Pouilly, with offices in Exchange Alley, between Conti and Bienville, in 1844. The 1858 City Directory lists "Surgi, Louis, engineer and contractor of public works, 8 Carondelet, residence Bayou

Road, near Villere." He was associated then with Job Bennett, carpenter.

Jean Terrade, 1831.

Isaac Thayer, 1853. The 1861 City Directory lists "Thayer, Isaac, builder and architect, Jackson, near Baronne."

Henry R. Thiberge, 1868. Born 1837, died 1882. A native of New York, Thiberge was the architect of the August J. Tete House, Esplanade and Prieur. It was built in 1882 when Thiberge was associated with Henry Howard. The builder was Edward Murray. He designed the Real Estate Exchange, 828 Perdido, in 1869, and the Leathers House, 2027 Carondelet, in 1859.

W. Thornton Thompson, 1844. The 1842 City Directory lists "Thompson, W. T., corner Customhouse and Rampart Streets."

Sully & Toledano. Thomas Sully and Albert Toledano established a partnership in 1882. To this firm are credited the following buildings: the New Orleans National Bank Building, Whitney National Bank Building, Morris Building, A. Baldwin & Co. Building, the American Sugar Refining Co. Building, the Brooklyn Cooperage Building and five private homes for J. Newman, J. Hernshein, S. Hernshein, P. O. Fazende, Henry Abraham, Julian Pecard, John A. Walls, H. T. Howard. They also erected many fine buildings outside New Orleans.

Albert Toledano. Born 1858, died 1923. Albert Toledano was born in St. John the Baptist Parish, son of Jules Toledano. He was educated in New Orleans and learned his profession there. For several years he traveled and studied throughout the U. S. In 1886 he married Anna Wogan of New Orleans. About 1905 he is listed as an associate of Victor L. Wogan, residence 918 Orleans. The firm of Toledano and Wogan had its offices in rooms 710-724-726 Macheca Building, 830 Canal. In 1900 the firm of Toledano and Reusch is listed in the directory of that year at 121 Carondelet. Ferdinand Reusch, Jr., was councilman of the 19th Ward, residing at 1734 Josephine. Toledano resided at 305 Esplanade.

G. M. Torgeson, 1880s. Torgeson is said to have designed the Cotton Exposition building.

F. N. Tourne, 1857, 1859. The 1855 City Directory lists "Tourne, F. N., architect, 127 Exchange Place." He is known by many of his sketches in the notarial archives.

Stephen Trudeau, 1832.

Daniel H. Twogood, 1833, 1833, 1838. Built the Julia Street Row.

James M. Vandervort & William Hyde, 1860.

————**Voilquin,** 1843.

David Wells and Peter Agier, 1830, 1838.

James Williamson, 1841, 1841. The City Directory of 1855 lists "Williamson, John, builder, Terpsichore, near Coliseum."

Joseph C. Wills, 1846.

Frederick Wing, 1872. Born 1814, died 1895. Wing was born in Philadelphia, but in 1835, at the age of 21, he went to New York to work at his trade. After one year he came to New Orleans where he was associated with Robert Crozier and later Jacob Wing. Paul Tulane employed him. He is listed in the 1871 City Directory as "Wing, Frederick, builder, 315 Calliope, residence 231 Seventh, Fourth District." In association with Samuel Jamison he built the old Picayune Building, 326-328 Camp. The Moody Mansion, Canal between Treme and Marais, was built by Wing but designed by Howard and Diettel. In the 1850s Wing was listed under the firm of Crozier and Wing.

Alexander T. Wood, 1833, 1834. Born 1804, died 1854. The controversial Wood in 1848 was appointed the original architect of the new Custom House. This followed his serving in the penitentiary after being found guilty of murder. He journeyed to Washington to secure funds for the construction of the Custom House. In 1850 he was associated with C. Ritter, civil engineer, in the building of this prominent edifice. Wood also submitted plans for the State Capitol in 1847. The 1849 City Directory lists his office on the "Canal Street neutral ground, between Techoupitoulas and Magazine, residence corner Prytania and St. Mary."

SELECTED BIBLIOGRAPHY

(For additional bibliographical material, see *New Orleans Architecture*, Vol. I, *The Lower Garden District*.)

AIA and Louisiana Landmarks Society. *A Century of Architecture in New Orleans.* Catalogue of Exhibition sponsored by New Orleans Chapters at the Customhouse, Canal Street. New Orleans, December 4-31, 1957.

Architecture and Decorative Art. Vol. 13 in series. "Origins of Cast Iron Architecture in America." New York: Da Capo Press, 1970.

Art Work of New Orleans. New Orleans: W. H. Parish Publishing Co., 1895.

Badger, Daniel D. *Illustrations of Iron Architecture Made by the Architectural Iron Works of City of New York.* New York: 1865.

Basso, Etolia S. *The World from Jackson Square.* Farrar, Straus and Co., 1948.

Baudier, Roger. *The Catholic Church in Louisiana.* New Orleans: Hyatt Stationery Manufacturing Co., 1939.

Bayley, G. W. R., ed. by Prichard, Walter. "History of Railroads in Louisiana." *Louisiana Historical Quarterly.* Vol. 30, No. 4, October, 1947.

Bell, A. W. *The State Register: Statistical Account of Louisiana.* Baton Rouge: T.B.R. Hatch & Co., 1855.

Biographical and Historical Memoirs of Louisiana. 2 vols., Chicago: Goodspeed Publishing Co., 1892.

Boatner, Frank H. Photograph Collection. Special Collections Division, Tulane University Library, New Orleans.

Bogardus, James. *Cast Iron Buildings: Their Construction and Advantages.* New York: J. W. Harrison, 1856.

Bonham, Milledge L. "Financial and Economic Disturbance in New Orleans on the Eve of Secession." *Louisiana Historical Quarterly.* Vol. 13, No. 1, January, 1930.

Boyle, James E. *Cotton and the New Orleans Cotton Exchange.* New York: Country Life Press, 1934.

Bremer, Laville. *Guide to New Orleans and Environs.* New Orleans: 1936.

Bunn, A. and Richardson, H. *Reports of Commissary, Sixth Ward, 1835-1836.* City Archives Department, New Orleans Public Library.

Burns, Francis P. "The Graviers and Faubourg Ste. Marie," *Louisiana Historical Quarterly.* Vol. 22, No. 2, April, 1939.

Butler, Benjamin F. *Butler's Book.* Boston: Thayer, 1892.

Cable, George Washington. *Old Creole Days.* Charles Scribner's Sons, 1879.

Campbell, T. W. *Manual of the City of New Orleans.* [New Orleans]: 1903.

Carey, Rita Katherine. "Samuel Jarvis Peters," *Louisiana Historical Quarterly.* Vol. 30, No. 2, April, 1947.

Chambers, Henry E. *A History of Louisiana.* Chicago and New York: American Historical Society, Inc., 1925.

Chase, John. *Frenchmen, Desire, Good Children and Other Streets of New Orleans.* New Orleans: Robert L. Crager and Co., 1949.

The City of New Orleans: The Book of the Chamber of Commerce and Industry of Louisiana. New Orleans: George W. Engelhardt, 1894.

Clark, John G. *New Orleans 1718-1812: An Economic History.* Baton Rouge: Louisiana State University Press, 1970.

Confederate Memorial Hall. Painting Collection.

Craig, James P. *New Orleans Illustrated in Photo Etching.* New Orleans: F. F. Hansell & Bro., 1892.

Crescent City Business Directory. New Orleans: Office of the Price-Current. 1858-59.

Crescent City Directory. New Orleans: Graham Co., 1867.

Daily Crescent. [New Orleans], March, 1848-November, 1869.

Daily Picayune. [New Orleans], 1837-April, 1914.

Daily States. [New Orleans], January, 1880-March, 1918.

Didimus, H. *New Orleans As I Found It.* New York: Harper & Bros., 1845.

Dimitry, Charles Patton. *Helpful Branch Banks of Early Local Banks.* Miscellaneous Articles, Book No. 2.

Dunbar, Clarence P. *A Study of Bank Failures in Louisiana 1920-22.* [New Orleans]: 1934.

Evans, Harry Howard. "James Robb, Banker and Pioneer Railroad Builder of Antebellum Louisiana." *Louisiana Historical Quarterly.* Vol. 23, No. 1, January, 1940.

Federal Writers Project of the Works Progress Administration. *New Orleans City Guide.* Boston: Houghton, Mifflin Co., 1938.

———. *New Orleans City Guide.* Revised by Robert Tallant. Boston: Houghton, Mifflin Co., 1952.

Fleming, Walter L. *The Freedman's Saving Bank: A Chapter in the Economic History of the Negro Race.* Chapel Hill: University of North Carolina Press, 1927.

Fossier, Albert E. *New Orleans the Glamour Period, 1800-1840.* New Orleans: Pelican Publishing Co., 1957.

Franck, Charles. Photograph files.

Gallier, James. *Popular Lectures on Architecture.* Brooklyn, New York: (n.d.).

General Advertiser and Crescent City Directory. [New Orleans]: Gibson Co., 1838.

Giedion, Sigfried. *Space, Time and Architecture.* Cambridge, Mass.: Harvard University Press, 1963.

Green, Constance McLaughlin. *American Cities in the Growth of the Nation.* Harper and Row, 1953.

Green, Simon. *Reports on the State of the Ward, Fourth Ward.* [New Orleans]: City Archives Department, April 22, 1847-February 10, 1848.

Greer, James Kimmins. "Louisiana Politics, 1845-1861." *Louisiana Historical Quarterly.* Vol. 13, No. 1, January, 1930.

Guide and Directory of the State of Louisiana and the Cities of New Orleans and Lafayette. New Orleans: J. Gibson, 1838.

Hamilton, Thomas. *Men and Manners in America.* London: William Blackwood, 1833.

Hamlin, Talbot. *Greek Revival Architecture in America.* London: Oxford University Press, 1944.

Harris, Francis Byers. "Henry Clay Warmoth, Reconstruction Governor of Louisiana," *Louisiana Historical Quarterly.* Vol. 30, No. 2, April, 1947.

Hibernia Rabbit. May, 1926; October, 1928; June, 1921; January, 1929; September, 1930; October, 1930.

Historical Epitome of the State of Louisiana, with an Historical Notice of New Orleans, Views and Descriptions of Public Buildings. New Orleans: 1840.

Huber, Leonard V. *New Orleans, A Pictorial History.* New York: Crown Publishers, Inc., 1971.

Ingraham, J. H. *The South West, 1835.* [n.p.].

————, ed. *The Sunny South: Five Years' Experience of a Northern Governess.* Philadelphia: G. G. Evans, 1860.

Jackson, Joy J. *New Orleans in the Gilded Age; Politics and Urban Progress, 1880-1896.* Baton Rouge: Louisiana State University Press, 1969.

Jewel, Edwin L., ed. *Jewell's Crescent City, Illustrated.* New Orleans: 1873.

Kendall, John S. "Old New Orleans Houses and Some of the People Who Lived in Them." *Louisiana Historical Quarterly.* Vol. 20, No. 3, July, 1937.

————. "Paul Tulane." *Louisiana Historical Quarterly.* Vol. 20, No. 4, October, 1937.

Koch, Richard. Photograph Collection. New Orleans.

Korn, Bertram Wallace. *The Early Jews of New Orleans.* Waltham, Mass.: American Jewish Historical Society, 1969.

Labrot, Sylvester. Sylvester Labrot Collection. Special Collections Division, Tulane University Library, New Orleans.

Lafever, Minard. *The Modern Builder's Guide.* Reprint of 1833 edition. Introduction by Jacob Landry. New York: Dover Publications, Inc., 1969.

Land, Ino. E. *Pen Illustrations of New Orleans—1881-1882.* New Orleans: 1882.

Lawyers Title Insurance Corporation. Unpublished Plan Books, by D. M. Brosman, city surveyor, ca. 1886.

————. Unpublished Plan Book, by D'Hemecourt, city surveyor.

————. Unpublished New Orleans Savings Institute Plan Book, by D'Hemecourt, deputy city surveyor, 1875-1876.

————. Unpublished Sketch Book, 1832, by Louis Pilie, city surveyor.

Lemann, Bernard. *Historic Sites Inventory.* New Orleans: Rader and Associates, for Regional Planning Commission, 1969.

Louisiana Architectural Association. *Architectural Art and Its Allies.*

Louisiana Landmarks Society. Photograph Collection. Special Collections Division, Tulane University Library, New Orleans.

Louisiana State Museum. Photograph files.

Lowenstern, M. Isadore. *Les Etats Unis et La Havre.* Leipsick: 1842.

MacKay, Alex. *The Western World, Or Travels in the United States in 1846-47.* Philadelphia: Lea and Blanchard, 1849.

MacKay, Charles. *Life and Liberty in America.* New York: Harper and Bros., 1859.

Martin Behrman Administration Biography, 1904-1916.

Massey, Mary Elizabeth. "Free Market of New Orleans, 1861-1862." *Louisiana History.* Vol. III, No. 3.

Menn, Joseph Karl. *The Large Slaveholders of Louisiana, 1860.* New Orleans: Pelican Publishing Co., 1964.

Neu, Irene D. "J. B. Moussier and the Property Banks of Louisiana." Reprinted from *Business History Review,* Vol. 35, No. 4, Winter, 1961. Boston: Harvard School of Business Administration.

New Orleans Annual and Commercial Directory for 1843. [New Orleans]: Michel Co., 1843.

New Orleans and Southern Directory. [New Orleans]: Cohen Co., 1849-56.

New Orleans Board of Trade, Ltd., 316 Magazine Street, 1968.

New Orleans City Directory. [New Orleans]: R. L. Polk Co., 1874-1900.

New Orleans City Engineers Records. City Hall, New Orleans.

New Orleans, The Crescent City. "New Orleans Picayune," 1903-04.

New Orleans Directory. [New Orleans]: Edwards Co., 1870-73.

New Orleans Directory. [New Orleans]: Gardner Co., 1850-69.

New Orleans Directory. [New Orleans]: Mygatt Co., 1857.

New Orleans Directory 1832. [New Orleans]: Perey Co., 1832.

New Orleans Directory for 1842. [New Orleans]: Pitts and Clarke, 1842.

New Orleans, Louisiana. New York: Sanborn Map and Publishing Co., 1885.

New Orleans Public Library. Dakin Collection.

_____. Photograph files.

New Orleans States, March, 1918-September, 1958.

New Orleans Times, September, 1863-December, 1881.

New Orleans Times-Democrat, December, 1881-May, 1914.

New Orleans Times Picayune, May, 1914-1956.

Nolte, Vincent Otto. *Fifty Years in Both Hemispheres, Or Reminiscences of a Merchant's Life.* London: Trubner Co., 1854.

Norman, Benjamin Moore. *Chart of the Lower Mississippi.* New Orleans: 1858.

_____. *Norman's New Orleans and Environs.* New Orleans, 1845.

Nuhrah, Arthur G. "John McDonogh: Man of Many Facets." *Louisiana Historical Quarterly.* Vol. 33, No. 1, January, 1950.

Orleans Parish. Conveyance Office Books.

Orleans Parish. Mortgage Office Records.

Orleans Parish. Notarial Archives Records.

Peters, Martha Ann. "St. Charles Hotel: New Orleans Social Center, 1837-1860." *Louisiana History.* Vol. I, No. 3, Summer, 1960.

The Picayune's Guide to New Orleans. New Orleans: The Picayune Publishing Co., 1892-1900, 1905.

Record of Building Permits, 1883-1887. City Archives Department, New Orleans Public Library.

Register of Merchants, 1854. First District Vol., City Archives Department, New Orleans Public Library.

Reinders, Robert C. *End of an Era: New Orleans 1850-1860.* New Orleans: Pelican Publishing Co., 1964.

Rightor, Henry, ed. *Standard History of New Orleans.* Chicago: Lewis Publishing Co., 1900.

Ripley, Eliza. *Social Life in Old New Orleans.* New York and London: D. Appleton and Co., 1912.

Robinson, Elisha. *Atlas of the City of New Orleans, Louisiana.* New York: E. Robinson, 1883.

Roussel, Willis J. *Jottings of Louisiana: Illustrated Historical Sketch of the Most Illustrious Landmarks of New Orleans and the Only Remaining Buildings of Colonial Days.* New Orleans: Mendola, 1905.

Simon, Benedict. *The Southern Index.* No. 1. New Orleans: B. Simon, 1870.

Sitterson, J. Carlyle. *Sugar Country.* University of Kentucky Press, 1953.

Smith, B. F. *New Orleans from St. Patrick's Church.* New Orleans: Smith Bros. and Co., 1852.

Soard's Elite Book of New Orleans. New Orleans: Soard's Directory Co., (n.d.).

Soards, L. *Soard's New Orleans City Directory.* Soard's Directory Co., 1870-1890.

Sparks, W. H. *The Memories of Fifty Years.* Philadelphia: Claxton, Remsen and Haffelfinger, (n.d.); Macon, Ga.: Burke and Co., 1870.

Surveyors Department Estimates, 1852-1865. City Archives Department, New Orleans Public Library.

Surveyors Office Plan of Second Municipality, 1852, Third, Fourth and Fifth Wards. City Archives Department, New Orleans Public Library.

Surveyors Office Measurement Book—Second Municipality, 1836-1838. City Archives Department, New Orleans Public Library.

Tannesse, J. *Map of the City of New Orleans in 1807.* New Orleans: 1908.

Waldo, J. Curtis. *Illustrated Visitors' Guide to New Orleans.* New Orleans: L. Graham, Printer, 1876, 1879.

Walton, J. B. *Plans of First District.* Vols. 2-7, 1860-1862. City Archives Department, New Orleans Public Library.

Whiffen, Marcus. *American Architecture Since 1780.* Cambridge, Mass.: The M. I. T. Press, 1969.

Wiggins, Richard H. "Louisiana Press and the Lottery." *Louisiana Historical Quarterly,* Vol. 31, No. 3, July, 1948.

Wilson, Samuel, Jr. "Collection of Building Contracts and Excerpts, 1800-1900." Special Collections Division, Tulane University Library, New Orleans.

_____. *A Guide to Architecture of New Orleans, 1699-1959.* New York: Reinhold Publishing Corp., 1959.

_____. *A Guide to the Early Architecture of New Orleans.* New Orleans, 1967.

_____, comp. *James Gallier, Architect: An Exhibition of His Work Presented in Commemoration of the Centennial of City Hall.* New Orleans: Louisiana Landmarks Society, 1950.

_____, ed. *Henry Howard, Architect: An Exhibition of Photographs of His Work by Clarence John Laughlin.* New Orleans: Louisiana Landmarks Society and the Newcomb Art School, 1952.

Woodman, Harold D. *King Cotton and His Retainers.* Lexington: University of Kentucky Press, 1968.

Young Men's Business League. *Progressive New Orleans.* New Orleans: 1895.

Zacharie, James S. *New Orleans Guide.* New Orleans: The New Orleans News Co., 1885.

INDEX

Designed by J. Barney McKee
Color plates by Colortek
Composed in Optima by Southwestern Typographics
Printed by Moran Industries, Inc., Baton Rouge, La.
Bound by Kingsport Press, Kingsport, Tenn.